Famous Fables of Economics

*To Ronald H. Coase*

# FAMOUS FABLES OF ECONOMICS

*Myths of Market Failures*

EDITED BY DANIEL F. SPULBER
*Northwestern University*

Copyright © Blackwell Publishers Ltd 2002; editorial organization and introduction
copyright © Daniel F. Spulber 2002

First published 2002

2 4 6 8 10 9 7 5 3 1

Blackwell Publishers Inc.
350 Main Street
Malden, Massachusetts 02148
USA

Blackwell Publishers Ltd
108 Cowley Road
Oxford OX4 1JF
UK

*Library of Congress Cataloging-in-Publication Data*

Famous fables of economics : myths of market failures / edited by Daniel F. Spulber.
p.    cm.
Includes bibliographical references and index.
ISBN 0–631–22674–5 (alk. paper) — ISBN 0–631–22675–3 (pb. : alk. paper)
1. Business failures—History.  2. Economic policy—History.  I. Spulber, Daniel F.

HG3761 .F36 2001
338—dc21

2001025583

*British Library Cataloguing in Publication Data*

A CIP catalogue record for this book is available from the British Library.

Typeset in 10 on 12pt Book Antiqua
by Ace Filmsetting Ltd, Frome, Somerset
Printed in Great Britain by T.J. International, Padstow, Cornwall

This book is printed on acid-free paper.

# Contents

# Acknowledgments

I would like to thank Dean Donald P. Jacobs of the Kellogg Graduate School of Management, Northwestern University, for his great encouragement and support for my research. I would also like to thank Academic Dean Dipak Jain for his understanding and consideration for my work, and Dean David E. Van Zandt of the Northwestern University Law School for his encouragement and highly helpful comments on the subject of this work.

I gratefully acknowledge the support of a research grant from the Searle Foundation. I am responsible for any opinions expressed in my work.

6.   Va Nee L. van Vleck, "Delivering Coal by Road and Rail in Britain: The Efficiency of the 'Silly Little Bobtailed' Wagons," *Journal of Economic History*, 57 (1997), pp. 139–60. Published by Cambridge University Press.

7.   Ronald H. Coase, "The Acquisition of Fisher Body by General Motors," *Journal of Law and Economics*, 43 (April 2000), pp. 15–31. Published by University of Chicago Press. © copyright 2000 by the University of Chicago. All rights reserved.

8.   Ramon Casadesus-Masanell and Daniel F. Spulber, "The Fable of Fisher Body," *Journal of Law and Economics*, 43 (April 2000), pp. 67–104. Published by University of Chicago Press. © copyright 2000 by the University of Chicago. All rights reserved.

9.   Steven N. S. Cheung, excerpt from Chapter 3, "Traditional Views of Sharecropping and Tests of Alternative Hypotheses," *The Theory of Share Tenancy: With Special Application to Asian Agriculture and the First Phase of Taiwan Land Reform* (Chicago: University of Chicago Press, 1969), pp. 30–61 (excerpts) and pp. 165–73 (appendices). © copyright 1969 by the University of Chicago. All rights reserved.

10.   John S. McGee, "Predatory Price Cutting: The Standard Oil (N.J.) Case," *Journal of Law and Economics* (October 1958). Published by University of Chicago Press. © copyright 1974 by the University of Chicago. All rights reserved.

11.   John E. Lopatka and Paul E. Godek, "Another Look at *Alcoa*: Raising Rivals' Costs Does Not Improve the View," *Journal of Law and Economics*, 35 (1992), pp. 311–30. Published by University of Chicago Press. © copyright 2001 by the University of Chicago. All rights reserved.

12.   Peter Thompson, "How Much Did the Liberty Shipbuilders Learn? New Evidence for an Old Case Study," *Journal of Political Economy*, (2001). Published by University of Chicago Press. © copyright 2001 by the University of Chicago. All rights reserved.

13.   "Financial Legends," *The Economist* (June 15, 1996), pp. 79–80. © copyright 1996 The Economist Newspaper Group, Inc.

# Introduction: Economic Fables and Public Policy

## Daniel F. Spulber

> The ideas of economists and political philosophers, both when they are right and when they are wrong, are more powerful than is commonly understood. Indeed, the world is ruled by little else. Practical men, who believe themselves to be quite exempt from any intellectual influences, are usually the slaves of some defunct economist. Madmen in authority, who hear voices in the air, are distilling their frenzy from some academic scribbler of a few years back. . . . Soon or late, it is ideas, not vested interests, which are dangerous for good or evil.
>
> **John Maynard Keynes,** *The General Theory of Employment,*
> *Interest and Money* **(1935), p. 383**

Economic discourse is replete with picturesque moral tales meant to illustrate or even support fundamental economic theory. Although some of these fables are factually inaccurate, their appeal to economists continues undiminished, being recited in countless classrooms, textbooks, and academic seminars. Because the oral and written traditions of economists eventually affect public policy, it is imperative to set the record straight. As John Maynard Keynes observed, the ideas of economists have a lasting and powerful influence. Accordingly, it is troubling that many economists often are themselves the slaves of some well-known fable. This book contains a number of articles that shed light on some of the most cherished stories of economists.

Everyone loves a good story. Besides providing entertainment, telling stories conveys information, creates social bonds and passes along moral values. Storytelling formed the oral tradition of the earliest civilizations, explaining the creation in Genesis and depicting history in Homer's *Iliad*. Yet myths are forward looking as well. The anthropologist Claude Lévi-Strauss (1963, p. 202) observes that "On the one hand, a myth always refers to events alleged to have taken place long ago. But what gives the myth an operational value is that the specific pattern described is timeless; it explains the present and the past as well as the future."

The anecdotes told by economists are entertaining, instructive, and undoubtedly create social and intellectual bonds within the profession. Many of these anecdotes have a common purpose. They attempt to show the existence of some type of *market failure*. These anecdotes also have operational value: government intervention in the economy may be needed to set matters right.

The articles in this volume have a common purpose as well: they demonstrate that these alleged market failures are mythical. The specific examples of market failure reviewed here contain errors of both fact and interpretation. By correcting the account of events, the articles demonstrate that economic analysis of market efficiency should rely on systematic analysis of market institutions rather than casual anecdotes. Moreover, many of the articles suggest that public policy prescriptions should have a stronger foundation than popular fables.

Of course, market economies can be inefficient. Transaction costs, imperfect information, social customs, legal deficiencies, and government regulatory shortcomings adversely affect the functioning of market institutions. The articles in this volume address specific situations and therefore they do not intend to show that markets always work perfectly. Rather, they seek to illustrate the complexity of market institutions and the creative ways that consumers and firms address difficult economic problems and handle transaction costs.

In this introduction, I try to place the articles in context within the economics literature. There is not enough space in this volume to include the original version of the fables, although the articles correcting the fables generally provide detailed references as to their origin. Moreover, this volume does not contain the occasional replies that the articles have engendered. The introduction takes note of some of the disagreements and opposing viewpoints. It is hoped that the collection will stimulate further discussion among students and scholars in economics and additional empirical investigation.

This book is dedicated to Ronald H. Coase because of his principled insistence that economists check their facts. Much of the work in this volume was directly motivated by his approach to economic analysis. In his proposal for a large-scale systematic study of the organization of industry in the United States, Coase (1988, p. 71) states that

> An inspired theoretician might do as well without such empirical work, but my own feeling is that the inspiration is most likely to come through the stimulus provided by the patterns, puzzles, and anomalies revealed by the systematic gathering of data, particularly when the principal need is to break our existing habits of thought.

As I worked on this book, I had the great pleasure of meeting with Ronald Coase. We discussed the lighthouse and Fisher Body at some length, the subject of Coase's two essays in this volume. These essays show his balanced perspective and careful attention to detail. They provide examples of his deep and nuanced understanding of market institutions. Coase's path-breaking work continues to inspire economic theorists and empiricists alike.

## THE FABLES

Examining the accuracy of economic fables is important because of their potential impact on future public policy recommendations. Even if an example of market failure is shown to be false, the validity of the theory based on the example is not necessarily in question. Moreover, the correction of a myth does not in itself serve as an argument against public policies that may derive from economic theory. However, by causing economists and public policy makers to examine the foundations of their beliefs, correcting myths can provoke better theoretical debates and encourage more precise empirical testing. The plethora of market failure myths suggests that such a reexamination is worthwhile.

Because economists are great champions of efficient markets, it seems paradoxical that the economics profession would be so taken with examples of market inefficiency. Like physicians searching for cures for various pathologies, economists seek public policy remedies for market problems. Stories of market failure often are sufficient to inspire government intervention in the economy. Such influential ideas form the danger that Keynes foresaw. The historical clarifications or corrections presented in this volume serve to provide a caution against public policies that are founded on unsupported anecdotes.

The fables tend to juxtapose a description of a market failure with a theoretical ideal case. Thus, these anecdotes illustrate what Harold Demsetz (1969) characterized as the "nirvana" approach to public policy, in which an imperfect institutional arrangement is contrasted with an ideal norm. The proper comparison should be in the realm of the possible, that is, the choice should be between transactions that are feasible in practice. It is necessary to evaluate transaction costs, market institutions, social customs, legal systems, and government regulations to examine the range of feasible transactions.

In some cases the problem may be more serious that the nirvana approach. Some of the accounts are simply not true. The fables compare a theoretical ideal with an apocryphal version of events. The authors of articles in this volume carefully examine the facts behind the fables. It often turns out that supposedly imperfect institutional arrangements perform more efficiently than was previously imagined.

Each of the fables discussed here corresponds to one or more of the major fields in economics. The fables have been advanced in support of some of the most fundamental concepts in economic analysis. The list of fables, their related fields and the alleged market failures are presented in table I.1. I briefly review the fables and how they have been applied in economics.

These fables have spread beyond economics, exerting great influence in the fields of law and management. Of course, mythical accounts are by no means unique to economics. Textbooks in psychology and in management have long recounted the "Hawthorne effect," allegedly based on a study from 1927 to 1933 of factory workers at Western Electric's Hawthorne Plant in Illinois. The study purported to show that any change in working conditions resulted in increased productivity, but was based loosely on the experiences of five workers, two of whom were replaced for low productivity and insubordination.[1] Professor Richard Nisbet called the Hawthorne effect "a glorified anecdote" and observed that some researchers apparently believed that "Once you have the anecdote, you can throw away the data."[2]

---

[1] Gina Kolata, "Scientific Myths That are Too Good to Die," *New York Times*, December 6, 1998, Week in Review Section, p. 2.
[2] Quoted in ibid.

**Table I.1**   The economic fables in this volume, the fields of economics in which they are commonly cited, and the market failures that they illustrate

| Fable | Field of economics | Market failure |
|---|---|---|
| The lighthouse<br>The turnpike | Public finance | Public goods,<br>Free rider problem |
| The bees | Welfare economics | Externalities |
| The keys<br>The video cassette<br>The coal wagon | Technological change<br>Industrial organization | Technology lock-in,<br>Path dependence,<br>Network externalities |
| Fisher Body | Contract theory,<br>Theory of the firm | Contract hold-up |
| Sharecropping | Agency theory,<br>Development | Moral hazard |
| Standard Oil (N.J.)<br>Alcoa | Industrial organization,<br>Antitrust | Predation,<br>Foreclosure |
| Liberty ships | Industrial organization,<br>Learning by doing | Barriers to entry |
| Tulip mania | Finance | Speculative bubbles |

Just as economics has well-known myths of market failure, the law profession has stories of the failure of the legal system. Professor Marc Galanter (1998) uncovers many "legal legends" that reflect what he terms the "jaundiced view" of American civil justice.[3] These popular legends reflect beliefs that the legal system is "arbitrary, unpredictable, berserk, demented; it has spun out of control." For example, Galanter examines an often-repeated horror story of a Philadelphia psychic who received a $1 million award for medical malpractice after she claimed a CAT scan led to a loss of her psychic powers. Contrary to popular belief and repetition by official sources, he finds that the trial judge reversed the verdict and no damages were awarded.[4]

Many of the fables reexamined in this volume have become divorced from their original context.[5] As in the child's game of telephone, economists have distorted and magnified the original version to enhance its impact on students and colleagues so that the stories are stylized and simplified in the retelling. Often the standard version of the fable departs substantially from its original source. Thus, the Fisher Body story becomes an example of contract failure that is completely disconnected from the historical background of the U.S. auto industry in the early 1920s.

[3] See also William Glaberson, "When the Verdict is Just a Fantasy," *New York Times*, June 6, 1999, Section 4, p. 1.

[4] The legend of the psychic was repeated by the President's Council on Competitiveness in its Agenda for Civil Justice Reform in America, August 5, 1991. The alleged outcome of the case was put forward in the report as an example of junk science in the courtroom (see Galanter, 1998).

[5] Marc Galanter (1998, p. 731) notes that as they circulate, the legal legends are "further simplified and decontextualized. They are placed in a timeless narrative present."

The stories are idealized examples that illustrate a particular point of economic theory or a public policy prescription without having to use more complicated jargon. The fables provide a convenient shorthand for illustrating the basic message. Rather than describing parks or national defense as public goods, economists can say simply that they are "like the lighthouse." Rather than mentioning hold-up and asset specificity, contracts can be said to cause problems "as in Fisher Body." The fables provide a self-evident reference point that has greater impact on the audience than the application of a more technical economic model. Moreover, economists can demonstrate that they are cognoscenti by wisely reciting a familiar fable.

By grounding the fable in its original setting, the articles in this volume reintroduce the complexity of historical events. The application of theory to the situation requires a verification that the conditions of specific assumptions are met. Public policy prescriptions must be tempered by recognizing the market context. The alleged market failure must confront the diversity of market institutions and the intricacy of voluntary agreements between economic actors.

## PUBLIC GOODS AND THE FREE RIDER PROBLEM: THE FABLE OF THE LIGHTHOUSE AND THE FABLE OF THE TURNPIKE

Much of the critical reexamination of market failure stories originates with Professor Ronald H. Coase's classic article "The Lighthouse in Economics," which appeared in the *Journal of Law and Economics* in 1974 and is reprinted in this volume (chapter 1). The story of the lighthouse appears in the work of such renowned economists as John Stuart Mill (1848), Henry Sidgwick (1883), A. C. Pigou (1938) and Paul A. Samuelson in his text *Economics: An Introductory Analysis,* as well as in countless public finance textbooks.

Governments around the world undertake a diverse set of activities including education, health care, scientific research, postal and telecommunications services, electric power generation, water and sewer services, and product quality certification and testing. Government provision of these types of services is the result of historical circumstances and political decisions. However, in the debate over the role of government, the argument that governments should provide public goods due to potential market failure has been persuasive to students and public policy markers. The stories of the lighthouse and the turnpike suggest the need for careful scrutiny of the applicability of the public goods argument to specific industries on a case-by-case basis.

In the field of public finance, the lighthouse and the road are often held up as examples of public goods that cannot be provided by the market. A pure public good is defined as a good with two characteristics. First, once the good is provided to one consumer, it is difficult for the provider of the good to exclude other consumers from access to the good. Second, consumption of the good by one person does not prevent consumption of the good by another person, so that consumption of the good does not exhaust its supply.

It is evident that lighthouses have these two properties since the services of the lighthouse are available to all ships and consumption of lighthouse services does not affect their supply. Roads are more problematic since access can be excluded by the establishment of toll booths and excessive consumption of turnpike services leads to congestion and wear and tear on the roadway. However, roads are used to illustrate public goods because restricting access is difficult for some types of roads and because motorists can use the services of a road up to its carrying capacity without impeding the supply of those services.

A public good generally is desirable if the total benefits of consumers exceed the total costs of providing the good. Yet, how should the money to pay for the good be collected? If access cannot be restricted, can people be trusted to make voluntary contributions? The standard assertion is if access cannot be restricted, the government must collect taxes to pay for a public good because otherwise there would be no lighthouses, roads or other necessary infrastructure.

Even if access to a good can be restricted, such as by toll booths on a turnpike, what should be the price of the types of services provided by a public good? Everyone using the good is likely to have a different willingness to pay for the services of the public good. It is possible to design a reporting system in which consumers report what they are willing to pay and the good is supplied only if total payments exceed total costs. However, these mechanisms generally run a surplus or a deficit.

Charging everyone the same price also runs into problems because this might exclude some potential customers. If the common price is set too high, there may not be enough usage to pay for the public good. On the other hand, if the price is set too low, there may not be enough revenue to pay for the public good. Then, a public good such as a lighthouse or the road would not be constructed even though public benefits exceeded the cost of the providing the public good. For example, suppose that it costs $80 to provide the public good. There are only two consumers, one who values the good at $30 and one who values the good at $70. A price of $40 per person would pay for the public good but the first consumer would not be willing to pay. A price of $80 charged to one customer would also be sufficient but neither customer would agree. There is no uniform price that would attract both customers and still pay for the public good.

One solution to the problem of uniform pricing is to ask for voluntary contributions from consumers in which everyone would pay based on their benefit from the public good. Can people be trusted to reveal voluntarily their different levels of willingness to pay? Economic theory and beliefs about human nature suggest that customers would understate their willingness to pay to reduce their burden. Hence, a free rider problem would ensue in which each consumer would try to shift the burden of payment to others. Again, the public good would not be provided even though total benefits exceeded the costs of provision. Thus, it is argued, the government would enhance social welfare by providing such a public good from general taxation.

The lighthouse is a staple of discussions of public goods and courses on public finance. The fable of the lighthouse asserts that the service of guiding ships cannot be privately financed since ship owners cannot be relied upon to support the service voluntarily. The lighthouse example is used to illustrate the failure of markets to provide public goods and the necessity of government provision of various services.

Coase traces the history and evolution of the British lighthouse system that should have been familiar to the early writers on the topic. He observes that private individuals began building lighthouses and collecting tolls in the seventeenth century and notes that by 1820, over three-quarters of the lighthouses had been built by private individuals. Trinity House, what Coase terms "a private organization with public duties," eventually took over the provision of lighthouses, but continued to finance the service by tolls levied on ships. The lighthouses were privately financed through user fees rather than publicly financed through general tax revenues. Coase observes that "[t]he lighthouses were built, operated, financed, and owned by private individuals, who could sell a lighthouse or dispose of it by bequest." Thus, the British lighthouse provides an example of a public good provided by private enterprise.

David E. Van Zandt (1993) agrees with Coase that private provision of lighthouse services "dominated the British system until the early 1800s" but differs with Coase's interpretation. An entrepreneur petitioned the King's Privy Council or Parliament for a patent or grant to build and maintain a lighthouse. After 1679, the Privy Council or Parliament issued patents directly to Trinity House, which would employ the patent or lease it to an individual. Van Zandt points out that a patent granted the entrepreneur an exclusive right, fixed the dues and charges that the entrepreneur could collect, and entitled the holder to invoke the power of the Crown to enforce payment. He argues that these features of the patent system involved the government beyond simple property protection and contract enforcement and thus blur the line between public and private provision of lighthouse services. Van Zandt concludes that the institutional features of lighthouse provision reflect a combination of public and private involvement. These additional institutional features qualify standard economic justifications for government provision of lighthouse services. As Van Zandt suggests, motivations for public provision of lighthouse services from general revenues in France, Spain, Germany, Russia and the United States included promoting international trade and fostering good international relations.

Daniel B. Klein, in "The Voluntary Provision of Public Goods? The Turnpike Companies of Early America" reprinted in this volume (chapter 2), examines the role of the government in providing social services. He examines the turnpike companies in America in the period between 1795 and 1840. The turnpikes did not exclude access and people could use the road without paying tolls. Moreover, there were many indirect beneficiaries of the turnpikes since travel and transportation on the turnpikes increased social interaction and commerce. The turnpikes were financed through stock subscription. State legislatures stipulated powers of eminent domain and sometimes granted monopolies over routes, while imposing regulation on toll rates and collection. Klein demonstrates that since unprofitability of turnpikes was clearly foreseen by stock subscribers, the purchase of stock became a means of making voluntary contributions to the construction of roads. Klein demonstrates that despite the fact that conditions were ripe for the free rider problem, private turnpike provision was an apparent success. The voluntary contributions to the hundreds of private turnpike companies reflected the benefits they generated for the towns along their routes.

A related historical fable about the provision of a particular public good is worth noting. For at least a century, historians have maintained that the end of volunteer fire fighting was due to violence by fire fighters competing for insurance company rewards. Fred S. McChesney (1986) points out that city governments justified their entry into the provision of fire fighting in the mid-nineteenth century by alleging failure in the market for private fire fighting. Fire fighting in the United States generally is provided by local governments although it was provided by volunteers for over two hundred years. Volunteers fought fires to prevent their spread from house to house as occurred in the great Chicago fire. McChesney corrects the market failure story by showing that public control was motivated by patronage positions and the shifting of costs of fire fighting from insurance companies to taxpayers, and that moreover, public authorities achieved control by tolerating and even encouraging the violence by not defining and enforcing property rights. Ultimately, larger municipalities instituted prohibitions on volunteer fire fighting. The history of fire fighting sheds light on the provision of a host of public services by municipalities, including water, electricity, transportation, police, and health care.

## EXTERNALITIES: THE FABLE OF THE BEES

Environmental regulation has become one of the most important areas of government regulation, with controls over the pollution of air and water and the disposal of industrial and municipal waste. Environmental concerns such as global warming extend beyond national borders and are playing an increasing role in international relations. Environmental pollution remains a significant problem with far-reaching implications for environmental quality and human health and well-being.

The economic analysis of environmental pollution has a long history. A. C. Pigou (1920) highlighted the discrepancy between private net product and social net product, altering Marshall's concept of external economies as the difference between economies at the firm and industry level. The notion of externalities is that economic agents sometimes impose costs, or perhaps benefits, on innocent bystanders. Because these costs or benefits are outside market transactions, there is no basis for economic incentives. Economic agents will engage excessively in activities such as pollution that impose costs on others and will engage insufficiently in activities such as neighborhood beautification that create benefits for others.

The market is said to fail when externalities are present (see for example Mishan, 1971). If pollution imposes costs on others, the social benefits resulting from the activity generating the pollution will be less than the private benefits, because of the harm to bystanders. In the market, manufacturers causing the pollution care only about their costs of manufacturing a good and consumers purchasing the good care only about their private benefit from the good. The transactions between the manufacturer and the consumer reflect their private costs and benefits, not the harm to a third party. Society will produce too much of the good since the market does not take into account the full costs. Conversely, if neighborhood beautification provides benefits to others, the social benefits resulting from the activity will be greater than the private benefits, because of the benefits received by third parties. Society will produce too little of the good since the market does not take into account the full benefits.

Ronald Coase (1960) in "The Problem of Social Cost" emphasizes that if there were no transaction costs, private bargaining would alleviate the problem of external damages from pollution. Those generating pollution or neighborhood beautification, and the affected bystanders could get together and reach an efficient bargain. The outcome of the bargain would be less pollution or more neighborhood beautification. Coase concludes that the problem of social cost stems from the presence of transaction costs.

Coase further shows the importance of allocating property rights as a basis for private bargaining over external effects. Without an initial assignment of liability or establishment of rights, "there can be no market transactions to transfer and recombine them" (p. 8). The main assertion, which has come to be known as the Coase theorem, is that "the ultimate result (which maximizes the value of production) is independent of the legal position if the pricing system is assumed to work without cost" (ibid.). With low transaction costs, the assignment of property rights affects the transfers between the parties in the negotiation but does not interfere with the efficiency of the outcome, see Spulber (1989, chapters 12 and 13) for further discussion.

Coase's insight about the way that bargaining adjusts to legal institutions to achieve an efficient outcome has proven to be fundamental to the economic analysis of law. Consumers and firms adjust the terms of their transactions and contracts in response to the particular form of legal rules. When transaction costs are low, alternative legal rules often have neutral effects on economic agreements as long as the law provides a clear assignment of rights. Moreover, when transaction costs are low, private bargaining can resolve problems of social costs without government intervention in the direct regulation of external effects. Certainly, common and statutory law and the judiciary are aspects of government. However, laws that apply general rules tend to be less intrusive in economic activities than detailed regulation by administrative agencies.

It was Ronald Coase who inspired Professor Steven N. S. Cheung to undertake his investigation of "The Fable of Bees," which is reprinted in this volume (chapter 3). In the original fable, bees pollinate an orchard providing benefits to the orchard owner and make nectar, thus benefiting the beekeeper. The beekeepers and orchard owners each receive uncompensated benefits so that society has less orchard farming and beekeeping than it should. Cheung's article provides a compelling illustration of Coase's insight that private bargaining internalizes social benefits and costs.

The story of the bees and the orchard describes positive externalities and also by implication negative externalities such as pollution. The fable of the bees was introduced by J. E. Meade (1952) and was used by Francis M. Bator (1958) to illustrate market failure (see also E. J. Mishan 1965). The fable of the bees is frequently recounted in courses on public finance and environmental economics. It is important as a justification for public regulation of pollution. Cheung finds the credence given to the fable of the bees surprising because "in the United States, at least, contractual arrangements between farmers and beekeepers have long been routine." Cheung studies the beekeeping industry in Washington state and details the private contractual arrangements that set prices and allocate services between beekeepers and farmers.

The fable of the bees illustrates economists' concern about the market's failure to take account of certain types of benefits or costs, which might lead to excessive production of negative externalities and insufficient production of positive externalities. The correction of the fable of the bees shows that in practice, private bargaining and contractual agreements can reduce or eliminate such inefficiencies. In this case, beekeepers and farmers enter into voluntary agreements that capture the benefits of pollination provided by the bees and if applicable, the benefits to honey production from the orchard. The story that beekeepers and orchard owners cannot enter into transactions is a myth. There is no market failure that calls out for action by a government agency.

The correction of the fable of the bees implies that one should not derive public policy prescriptions favoring environmental regulation from this anecdote. Neither should one recommend against environmental regulation based on the existence of contracts between beekeepers and orchard owners. The bees and the orchard are, of course, a very special situation. External benefits are involved rather than damages. Moreover, the story fits with Coase's suggestion that small numbers of agents keep down transaction costs. Market institutions in beekeeping would appear to have limited value in understanding markets with diffuse environmental damages, particularly when there are many polluters and many victims of pollution.

What the correction of the fable of the bees does imply is the need to pay attention to existing market institutions rather than abstract predictions in making general policy recommendations. There may be market institutions capable of addressing the harm of pollution or the benefits of beautification efforts. The absence of such institutions might indicate the need for legal reform to devise an assignment of rights that would allow private bargaining to take place or reliance on legal action to resolve disputes over damages. Even if rights are carefully specified, transaction costs may be too high for private parties to negotiate effectively. Public policy responses that reduce private transaction costs might be more effective than regulatory action.

Closely related to the problem of externalities is the exhaustion of a natural resource due to competing usage is known as the tragedy of the commons. The expression is due to Garrett Hardin (1968) who cites a pamphlet written in 1833 by a mathematical amateur named William Forster Lloyd (1794–1852). Hardin discusses overpopulation, pollution and resource depletion using a hypothetical story about overgrazing in the common area of medieval villages:

> Picture a pasture open to all. It is to be expected that each herdsman will try to keep as many cattle as possible on the commons. Such an arrangement may work reasonably satisfactorily for centuries because tribal wars, poaching, and disease keep the numbers of both man and beast well below the carrying capacity of the land. Finally, however, comes the day of reckoning, that is, the day when the long-desired goal of social

stability becomes a reality. At this point, the inherent logic of the commons remorse-
lessly generates tragedy.

If the common grazing area belongs to everyone it belongs to no one, the argument
goes; villagers will have no incentive to preserve the resource and will put more
farm animals to graze on it until the grass is depleted. The problem of overgrazing
also appears in historical accounts such as Gonner (1966), Slater (1932), and Coleman
(1977). For example, Gonner (1966, p. 25) states that "As many beasts are put on the
common as possible . . . with the result that the common is overstocked."

The story of the feudal and medieval commons has been often repeated in public
policy discussions of natural resources and environmental pollution and bears further examination. The notion that the Enclosure Acts were intended to replace an
inefficient institution and that enclosure enhanced efficiency has been challenged.
As Ostrom (1990, p. 224) notes, economic historians have provided a different picture of English land tenure before and after the Enclosure Acts (see Thirsk, 1967;
McClosky, 1976; Dahlman, 1980; Yelling, 1977; Allen, 1982; Fanoaltea, 1988).

Economists have written widely on the exhaustion of rents from common property resources (see for example Gordon, 1954; Cheung, 1970; Spulber, 1982). If property rights to a natural resource are not properly specified, individuals will compete
to deplete the resource, whether it is a fishery, forest, or pool of crude oil under-
ground. Even if the costs of extracting the resource prevent its depletion, competition without property rights will result in the dissipation of economic returns to
the resource. If the resource were owned by one individual, then it would presumably be managed so as to maximize the economic returns from the resource. As
with environmental pollution, which takes advantage of common ownership of air
and water resources, the use of exhaustible resources is likely to depend on property rights.

How then to resolve the property rights problem? Rousseau's *Social Contract* and
Hobbes' *Leviathan* address the origins of property rights and the social agreements.
One approach is to assign property rights to the government, which can exploit the
resource itself, regulate access, or license private parties to use the resource in a
controlled fashion. An important question is whether rent dissipation is inevitable
in the absence of law or government assignment of property rights.

John Umbeck (1977) examines the private establishment of property rights in the
context of the California gold rush of 1848 and 1849. There were no property rights
since California had just become a territory of the United States and the Governor,
Colonel Mason, abolished Mexican laws pertaining to acquisition of mining rights
on public lands without offering an alternative (Umbeck, 1977, p. 203). The gains to
establishing property rights are likely to increase the more valuable is the resource.
However, Umbeck suggests that the transaction costs of establishing property rights
also will increase the more valuable is the resource. If the gains outweigh the costs
for valuable resources, private parties may then establish property rights themselves without government intervention. In the case of the gold rush, the miners
formed explicit contracts that allowed them to exploit their claims exclusively, to
enforce their claims, and even to buy and sell those claims, thus creating a system
of private property rights.

Ostrom (1990) identifies cooperative agreements as means of governing the commons, in contrast with the extremes of unified private ownership or government control. She distinguishes between open access resources and common property when managed by a clearly defined social group. Ostrom provides evidence that cooperative-choice arrangements for managing common property functioned well in some cases for centuries in Swiss alpine meadows, Japanese mountain commons, irrigation institutions, the Spanish *huertas* or the Philippine *zanjeras* (see also Feeny, Hanna, and McEvoy, 1996). Ostrom also identifies problems that may arise by examining Turkish fisheries and groundwater allocation in California basins when access is not restricted and there are high transaction costs of cooperative agreements. These studies highlight the critical effects of transaction costs.


## TECHNOLOGY LOCK-IN AND NETWORK EXTERNALITIES: THE FABLE OF THE KEYS, THE FABLE OF THE VIDEO CASSETTE AND THE FABLE OF THE COAL WAGON

Thomas Schelling (1978) identified the effects of *critical mass* on many types of economic and social behavior. Neighborhoods improve or deteriorate due to self-confirming expectations, social conventions become self-enforcing, and prophecies become self-fulfilling. The notion of critical mass also appears in discussions of *network externalities* (see Katz and Shapiro, 1985). Do critical mass effects imply that consumer choices collectively create market inefficiencies? Are market outcomes subject to the phenomenon of *tipping* in which inferior products are purchased by all due to problems of coordination. If coordination problems cannot be remedied by market coordination mechanisms, the potential inefficiencies caused by the phenomenon of critical mass are daunting. The result, say advocates of network externalities, is a market failure known as *technology lock-in*: markets select inefficient technologies as an almost inescapable standard.

The notion of technology lock-in is similar to the broader concept of *path dependence* in economic history advanced by Brian Arthur (1989, 1994), Paul David (1985, 1992) and others. The term path dependence comes to economics by analogy from physics and biology, where it denotes the effects of initial conditions on physical systems of biological processes. Arthur (1990) claims that recognizing positive feedbacks creates an entirely new economics. The idea is more than the uncontroversial assertion that "history matters." Advocates of path dependence seemingly argue that economies are necessarily captives of historical accidents. (See Liebowitz and Margolis, 1994, 1995, for a critical evaluation of path dependence.)

The public policy implications are disturbing. If markets cannot choose the right technology, efficiency would require government industrial policy aimed at picking winners. The notion that markets get locked-in to inferior technologies would suggest that the government should replace clear winners in the marketplace with what government planners think would be superior technology. As a consequence, governments may feel justified in subsidizing specific technologies or protecting domestic industries against international competition from companies using distinct technologies. Government planners would be expected to solve the impossible problem of predicting technological change, as opposed to multiple competing technologies offered by markets. Moreover, government planners are unlikely to accurately reflect the diversity of customer preferences about new products.

The notion of lock-in has another dangerous implication. It would imply that successful companies such as Intel in microprocessors, Cisco Systems in routers, or eBay in online auctions may be imposing inefficient technology standards on their customers who are harmed because they could have benefited from less successful or even hypothetical technologies. If markets are consistently locked-in to inefficient choices, then antitrust policy should target successful high-tech companies who presumably suppressed technologies offered by competitors.

The Justice Department and attorneys general for nineteen states made similar assertions in their Microsoft antitrust suit. The government's case turned on a new theory of monopoly as a constraint on technological change.[6] Among other allegations, the government charged that Microsoft suppressed Netscape's browser despite the fact that the browser continued to be readily available to consumers, even after the acquisition of Netscape by America Online for a substantial sum. Consumers might have been even better off with hypothetical technological alternatives had the market not been locked-in, the popularity of Microsoft's Windows operating system or its Internet Explorer browser notwithstanding. Judge Jackson wrote that "The ultimate result is that some innovations that would truly benefit consumers never occur for the sole reason that they do not coincide with Microsoft's self-interest."[7] Liebowitz and Margolis (1999) review these arguments and demonstrate that Microsoft's products competed and prevailed because consumers preferred them to market alternatives.

The main example given to show that markets fail due to technology lock-in is the design of the typewriter keyboard. The standard design, known as the QWERTY design after the arrangement of letters in the upper left hand of the keyboard, was patented by Christopher Sholes in 1868 and purchased by Remington in 1873. The fable states that the supposedly inefficient QWERTY maintained its market dominance despite the later advent of a more efficient arrangement known as the Dvorak keyboard. The fable of the keys was introduced into the literature by economic historian Paul David (1985) and continues to be widely cited in the literature on standard setting and network externalities. Carl Shapiro and Hal Varian (1999) ask, "Why, then, are we all still using QWERTY keyboards?" They suggest that the costs to individuals of switching to the allegedly superior Dvorak layout are simply too high or that the costs of coordination make collective switching costs prohibitive.

Stan J. Liebowitz and Stephen E. Margolis, in their article in this volume titled "The Fable of the Keys" (chapter 4), debunk the QWERTY story. There is no evidence that the arrangement of keys on a typewriter or computer keyboard is inefficient. As it turns out, the tests showing the superiority of the Dvorak machine conducted by the U.S. Navy were managed by Lieutenant-Commander August Dvorak, the inventor and patent owner. Alternative keyboards competed with each other in the market.

---

[6] See Steve Lohr, "The New Math of Monopoly," *New York Times*, April 9, 2000, Section 4, p. 1.
[7] Ibid.

As other evidence that markets tend to choose the wrong technology and then get locked-in, economists usually point to the success of VHS over Beta in the market for videocassette recorders. Supposedly, the market standard VHS was inferior to the failed Beta technology but VHS was more established. However, there is substantial evidence that this example of technology lock-in is also historically and technically inaccurate. In their article in this volume titled "Beta, Macintosh, and Other Fabulous Tales" (chapter 5), Liebowitz and Margolis show that VHS won over Beta due to advantages of longer playing time, allowing VHS to come from behind and win the market. They also show that other examples of alleged lock-in, such as the dominance of IBM-compatible computers over Apple's Macintosh computer, do not hold up to close scrutiny.

The notion of path dependence in history is deftly addressed by Va Nee L. Van Vleck's article in this volume titled "Delivering Coal by Road and by Rail in Great Britain: The Efficiency of the 'Silly Little Bobtailed' Wagons" (chapter 6). Historians have lamented the inefficiency of small rail cars used to carry coal in Great Britain. It is clear that larger cars would realize economies of scale due to the volume–surface relationship of containers. Larger rail cars are in use in the United States and in Europe. However, Van Vleck observes that the coal cars were part of a larger system that included local delivery by horse cart and later by truck. Large rail cars would have been likely to raise total costs of delivery and so were efficient as part of the transportation system. Van Vleck's history of the coal car shows that technological efficiency cannot be evaluated in isolation. Rather, customer preferences and complementary services play an important role.

The fables of the keys, the videocassette, and the coal car are meant to imply that markets make incorrect choices and that they cannot switch easily to a new technology once a standard has been established. The repeated use of these somewhat arcane examples suggests that few, if any, examples of technology lock-in can be discovered in contemporary markets. The high rate of technological change and rapidly shifting technology standards in computer hardware and software, the Internet, consumer electronics, telecommunications, biotechnology and other industries belie the notion that technologies are frozen once they are established.

These corrections of myths of technology lock-in are valuable because they remove critical examples of market failure in technological change. It is important to carefully investigate how new technologies diffuse and how product standards are established. There are transaction costs associated with switching to new technologies or adopting product standards. However, the market institutions for changing technologies are complex involving consumer choice and competition between companies introducing innovative technologies. Companies that offer new products employ introductory prices, marketing and promotion efforts to induce consumers to switch from existing products. Companies that supply complementary goods and services write contracts to share the benefits of providing compatible products. Industry trade associations establish and disseminate new technology standards. There are many other mechanisms for technology diffusion including educational institutions, scientific and technical publications, and industry imitation. The challenge for historians of technology is to fully explore the complex effects of consumer choice and producer competition on technology standards.

## CONTRACT HOLD-UP: THE FABLE OF FISHER BODY

*Contract hold-up* is another type of alleged market failure. The contract hold-up story is as follows. It is costly to enforce contracts and infeasible to write complete contingent contracts. Some types of performance may be unobservable or unenforceable. Parties to contracts, particularly companies, make irreversible investments that are specific to the contractual relationship. Suppose that one party to a contract has made such an investment, say a seller, and that they are subject to hold-up by the other party, say a buyer. The buyer takes advantage of the investment commitment by the seller by renegotiating the contract to pay less to the seller. Because the two parties to the contract foresee this unfortunate turn of events they will enter into contracts that entail less-than-optimal investment, thus reducing gains from trade and creating contractual inefficiency. Alternatively, the parties may be motivated to use costly governance mechanisms for the contract to overcome hold-up, including vertical integration.

The idea that private contracts are generally inefficient underpins the vast economic literature on contracts. Benjamin Klein, Robert Crawford, and Armen Alchian (1978) state their crucial assumption: "as assets become more specific and more appropriable quasi rents are created (and therefore the possible gains from opportunistic behavior increases), the costs of contracting will generally increase more than the cost of vertical integration" (1978, p. 298). They conclude that vertical integration between firms provides a solution to the problem of contractual hold-up.

Oliver Williamson (1985) refers to contractual hold-up as "opportunism" which he defines a "self-interest seeking with guile." Williamson (1985, p. 95) suggests that investments may be specific to a relationship in several different ways; if they are confined to a specific location, embodied in capital equipment, involve dedicated assets or are in the form of human capital. According to Williamson, hold-up causes firms to vertically integrate so as to substitute organizational governance for market contracts. Oliver Hart (1995) explains the formation of firms based on the need to alleviate contractual problems related to hold-up by owning physical assets.

The public policy implications of the contract hold-up story are uncertain. Klein, Crawford, and Alchian (1978, p. 325) suggest that the search for better contractual relationships and ownership rights will require "using market and governmental (regulatory, legislative, and judicial) processes." While contract hold-up is portrayed as a market failure, vertical integration is a market solution. Accordingly, the theory would appear to imply greater antitrust tolerance of vertical mergers and acquisitions as a means of reducing the impacts of inefficient contracts. Williamson (1985, p. 99) however suggests that antitrust policy should take into account that "vertical integration by dominant firms can place smaller rivals at a disadvantage," and notes that "such anticompetitive effects also have transaction cost origins." The hold-up notion has been applied in antitrust analysis of post-contract market power in vertical relationships. Klein (1999) argues that the Kodak decision requires a showing that a franchiser held-up its franchisees by making a post-contract change in the franchise contract.

Yoshiro Miwa and Mark Ramseyer (2000) survey the empirical evidence on relationship-specific investments in various industries. They suggest that the evidence on occasional location specificity may be the strongest, such as a generating plant locating near a coal mine. The evidence outside of the aerospace, defense, and public utilities industries has been mixed. Miwa and Ramseyer examine relationship-specific investment in contracts between suppliers and assemblers in the Japanese auto industry. They find that such investments tend to be low and equity cross-ownership is low as well.

Economists who study contracts and the theory of the firm are fond of citing General Motors' (GM) acquisition of Fisher Body as an example of the failure of market contracts and the replacement of an unworkable contract by vertical integration. The Fisher Body acquisition is used to illustrate contractual hold-up by Klein, Crawford, and Alchian (1978), who introduce the story of the merger in the economics literature. Williamson (1985) in his work on transaction-cost economics also discusses the acquisition to illustrate asset specificity and the substitution of corporate governance for private contracts. Hart (1995) draws upon the Fisher Body story to illustrate the property-rights theory of the firm and the advantages to firms of consolidating ownership of physical assets.

The notion that contract hold-up motivated GM to acquire Fisher Body in 1926 is a fable. GM acquired a controlling interest in Fisher Body in 1919 and completed the acquisition in 1926. According to the popular version, the contract between Fisher Body and GM allowed the body maker to take advantage of GM. Not only did Fisher Body price opportunistically, or so the story goes, but also it refused to locate its plants next to those of GM. The auto maker had to acquire Fisher Body when the situation became intolerable. This version of events is not supported by the historical record. Relations between the two companies were highly amicable and the aftermath of the merger shows that the alleged contract failures had little to do with the merger.

Ronald H. Coase in "The Acquisition of Fisher Body by General Motors", reprinted in this volume (chapter 7), brings a truly unique perspective to the study of these events. Not only was Coase a supremely qualified observer, being the founder of transaction cost economics, but also he had the good fortune to discuss the acquisition with an executive at General Motors shortly after it had occurred, during Coase's visit to the United States on a scholarship in the year 1931–2. Coase concludes that the problem of asset specificity is best handled by a long-term contract rather than by vertical integration.

Ramon Casadesus-Masanell and Daniel F. Spulber, whose article in this volume is titled "The Fable of Fisher Body" (chapter 8), are in broad agreement with Coase's analysis of events surrounding the acquisition. They extend the analysis by placing the fable in the context of its application in economic theory and by examining specific aspects of the story that have been highlighted in the economics literature. They show that the two companies sought to merge to coordinate their operations more closely. By the 1920s, GM had acquired a large number of its parts suppliers and sought to be fully integrated into parts manufacturing. In addition, the merger was driven by personnel considerations, since GM valued the manufacturing and management talents of the Fisher brothers.

Robert Freeland's (2000) important study analyzes the merger between GM and Fisher Body.[8] Freeland extends the analysis to examine the relationship between the two companies after the merger takes place. He suggests that the Fisher brothers took advantage of GM after the merger, essentially behaving in an opportunistic fashion within the GM organization. This interpretation of the influence of the Fishers within the organization extends the notion of contractual hold-up to behavior within the organization. Freeland's work contributes to an understanding of how organizations can change after mergers take place.

Klein (2000) replies to Coase, Freeland, and Casadesus-Masanell and Spulber and responds to criticisms of his version of the GM–Fisher Body merger. Klein (2000) acknowledges that the main economic force behind the merger was the need for coordination:

> As body design became more important and more interrelated with chassis design and production, the amount of coordination required between a body supplier and its automobile manufacturer customer increased substantially . . . These economic forces connected with annual model changes ultimately led all automobile manufacturers to adopt vertical integration.

Klein creates a new fable: the Flint plant problem. He alleges that Fisher Body refused GM's request to build a plant in Flint, Michigan to supply bodies to GM's Buick division. According to the new story, GM's merger with Fisher Body in 1926 stemmed from a disagreement over whether or not to relocate a single plant from Detroit to Flint 57 miles away. Klein contends that the 1925 breakdown of the Fisher–General Motors manufacturing contract was triggered by a dramatic rise in demand in 1925–6 that pushed the contract out of its "self-enforcing" range.

Further review of the evidence shows that GM and Fisher Body could not have merged based on such a minor matter. The two companies operated a large number of plants. GM's Buick division itself operated three assembly plants and two large body manufacturing plants in Flint before 1924 and Fisher Body already built Buick bodies in its Flint plant that was established in 1923. Buick does not appear to be constrained since it expanded production in 1925 and 1926 with sales in those two years among the largest of all of Buick's history. The notion that GM sought a merger to avoid a fictional legal action against Fisher is another unverifiable proposition. The so-called Flint plant problem alleges instead that Fisher held up GM by *not* making such an investment, something that is impossible to verify since it depends on something having not occurred (see Casadesus-Masanell and Spulber, 2000).

---

[8] The paper by Robert Freeland (2000) appears in the same issue of the *Journal of Law and Economics* as the papers by Coase and by Casadesus-Masanell and Spulber reprinted in this volume. His historical analysis is in agreement with those of Coase and of Casadesus-Masanell and Spulber where they overlap. Freeland's paper makes a very important contribution to the discussion of the history of Fisher Body and I regret that space limitations prevented its inclusion in this volume. Readers interested in GM's acquisition of Fisher Body are urged to read Freeland's highly interesting paper.

## MORAL HAZARD IN THE PRINCIPAL–AGENT
## RELATIONSHIP: THE FABLE OF SHARECROPPING

The principal–agent relationship refers to a contract in which one party, the principal, delegates responsibility to carry out a task to the other party, the agent. The area of law that deals with these types of contracts, known as agency law, examines the responsibilities of the principal and agent to each other and to third parties. In economics, the principal–agent relationship is one of the most widely studied theoretical frameworks. The fable of sharecropping plays a fundamental role in the economic theory of agency.

In the economic model of agency, the principal pays the agent to carry out the designated task and the agent makes decisions about how much effort to devote to the task. The economic model of agency studies the design of incentives for the agent to perform the task. The model has been applied to the analysis of a wide variety of relationships including firm–employee, company–subcontractor, patient–doctor, client–attorney, shareholder–corporate director, and regulator–firm.

In the economic model of agency, it is generally assumed that the principal has less information than the agent. There are two variations of the model: either the agent's action cannot be observed or the agent's characteristics cannot be observed. The economic analysis of the agency model generally demonstrates how these information problems complicate the design of incentives. I will focus only on the case of unobservable effort.

Because the principal delegates authority to the agent, and monitoring is costly, the agent's efforts are not directly observable. The agent's actions cannot be inferred from outcomes since outcomes are assumed to be uncertain. For example, the agent devotes effort to agricultural production, and agricultural output is uncertain because it is subject to random effects such as weather, so the agent's farming effort cannot be inferred from agricultural production. As a result, the contract cannot explicitly specify effort levels and must reward the agent's performance.

Effort is costly for the agent. If the principal were to give the agent a fixed wage, the model therefore presumes that the agent would *shirk*, that is, the agent would not devote any effort to the task at hand. The principal must rely on performance-based rewards such as bonuses or commissions to induce the agent to devote greater effort to the task.

However, performance-based reward systems have a drawback in that they shift the risk to the agent. If the agent is averse to risk, too great a reliance on performance incentives will impose the cost of risk on the agent. The principal will then have to compensate the agent for the cost of risk to be able to employ the agent. Accordingly, the model predicts that the principal gives the agent both a fixed payment and some performance-based rewards. This means that contract between the principal and agent involves some shirking because the agent's rewards are not entirely based on performance.

The problem of agent shirking is known as *moral hazard*. This term comes to economics from the insurance industry. Because insurance contracts by their very nature absorb some of the risk of loss, an insurance customer has reduced incentive to take care in avoiding accidents. Features of insurance contracts such as deductibles are designed to reduce the moral hazard problem by sharing the risk of loss.

The principal–agent model in economics has an important ancestor: the model of sharecropping. There are a number of alternative contractual arrangements between a landowner and a tenant farmer. The landowner can hire the farmer at a fixed wage, the farmer can pay a fixed rent to the landowner, or the farmer can pay the landowner a share of the agricultural production. The system of sharing output between a landowner and a tenant farmer is known as sharecropping or share tenancy. The output share is commonly set at 50/50, the literal meaning of *metayage*, the French term for sharecropping.

Adam Smith (1776) and John Stuart Mill (1848) emphasized the advantages of fixed-rent tenancy, which was common in England, as compared with the inefficiencies of sharecropping, which was common in France. Adam Smith condemned sharecropping because he claimed that the tenant would be reluctant to employ his own capital on the farm, and recommended that taxes be used to encourage landlords to use other contractual arrangements: "such rents are always more hurtful to the tenant than beneficial to the landlord" (see D. Gale Johnson, 1950, p. 112, for additional discussion).

Many economists have repeated the story that sharecropping leads to inefficient incentives in agriculture. Keijiro Otsuka, Hiroyuki Chuma, and Yujiro Hayami (1992) present a comprehensive overview of the literature that tries to sort through the theory and facts of agrarian contracts. Based on the 1970 World Census of Agriculture of the United Nations Food and Agriculture Organization, owner cultivation is the most common form of farming. Although there is greater use of share tenancy in Europe and North America, Asia has the highest percentage of share tenancy in tenanted land.

Alfred Marshall (1890) presented a theoretical model of sharecropping demonstrating that such an arrangement results in an inefficient reduction in the effort of the farmer, since the farmer does not receive the full marginal product of his labor. Marshall's analysis effectively framed the modern economic literature on contracts. The prediction that sharing output results in inefficient effort is essentially the theme of moral hazard that pervades the economic theory of principal and agent. Marshall's insight that the farmer's effort is lowered by not receiving the full marginal product of effort is essentially the same as shirking in principal–agent models and underinvestment in models of contracts with transaction-specific investment.

Steven N. S. Cheung, in his book *The Theory of Share Tenancy*, an excerpt of which is reprinted in this volume with the title "Sharecropping" (chapter 9), examines the early discussion of the subject and suggests that the story of inefficiency of sharecropping is a myth. Marshall (1890), as well as Johnson (1950), suggested that share tenancy need not be inefficient if the landowner could observe the farmer's effort. Cheung observes that the basic economic theory of share tenancy ignores the fact that the landowner can vary the allocation of land to tenants, giving the landowner another instrument to enhance incentives for performance. The landowner and tenants also build trust due to long-term relationships since they have the choice of whether or not to renew their relationship each year. The notion that the landowner can observe the farmer's effort and that contract terms are enforceable has generated considerable controversy in the literature on sharecropping (see Otsuka et al., 1992).

In their survey, Otsuka et al. (1992, p. 2013) conclude that fixed wage contracts tend to dominate when share tenancy is illegal, but that share tenancy dominates in the absence of such regulatory constraints. They further find that the "empirical evidence is largely consistent with the general hypothesis that, when choices are available to them, rural people in developing economies make efficient choices from a wide spectrum of agrarian contracts." However, they also find that the results of many studies are difficult to interpret because they tend to test the Marshallian hypothesis by comparing share tenancy and owner cultivation, or leasehold tenancy, without examining broader issues such as institutional constraints and the labor management ability of landowners.

Cheung's work is significant because it suggests that need for a reexamination of the view that despite their widespread usage, share contracts in agriculture were inefficient. This bears on public policy recommendations dating back to Adam Smith that governments should intervene in the agricultural sector to alleviate inefficiency due to the sharecropping system.

The writings of Adam Smith and Alfred Marshall on sharecropping underpin the modern principal–agent model (see Stiglitz, 1974; Otsuka et al., 1992). Cheung's analysis implies that long-term contracts and other instruments of control such as varying the tasks assigned to agents may be ways in which markets alleviate or avoid the moral hazard problem. Cheung's work is important because its observations about incentives in sharecropping should motivate economists to reexamine the foundations of the principal–agent model.

## PREDATION: THE FABLE OF *STANDARD OIL (N.J.)* AND THE FABLE OF *ALCOA*

Companies are said to engage in *predation* if they unfairly exclude their competitors from the market. If companies can somehow discourage rivals through excessive competition, the market would fail to be efficient. Economists and antitrust advocates have identified many types of predation including price predation, nonprice predation, raising rivals' costs, and dumping in international trade. However, defining predation is a problem since it is difficult in practice to distinguish vigorous competition from unfair exclusion of rivals from the market. Companies facing tough competition are likely to bring complaints against predation. Antitrust policy is intended to protect competition not to help unsuccessful competitors. The market system is driven not only by the freedom to succeed but also by the freedom to fail. Prosecuting companies for predation runs the risk of protecting inefficiency and discouraging competition.

The definition of predation must meet several requirements. The incumbent firm's competitive actions must be profitable to show that the firm is pursuing a rational strategy. The predatory actions must potentially exclude rivals. Finally, the actions must be shown to reduce economic efficiency, so that predation is a form of market failure. Upon closer examination, the evidence for predation turns out to be mythical. The cases often cited as evidence of predation, *Standard Oil (N.J.)* and *Alcoa*, do not stand up to close scrutiny.

Predatory pricing is said to occur if a company prices sufficiently low, perhaps below costs, to drive out rivals and then more than recoups its losses by monopoly pricing after its rivals have quit the market. The problem is that there is no clear way to tell the difference between low competitive prices and predatory prices. Companies make losses all the time, whether they are first establishing a business or seeking to expand. Some losses result from errors of business judgement in the face of declining demand or rising costs. Regulating pricing to prevent losses would inevitably restrict the growth of business and prevent risk taking. Consumers certainly benefit from vigorous competition and lower prices. If the low-price leader benefits from scale economies, cost efficiencies, or superior products, this simply means that competitors should commit capital to efficient production facilities or expend resources to build brand recognition.

Companies are unlikely to pursue predatory strategies. A willingness to incur greater losses than one's rivals is neither a means to success nor a credible threat. Recoupment is unlikely to occur. Rivals can ride out price cuts or retaliate by making price cuts of their own if they can be supported by cost efficiencies and the returns from attracting customers. Easterbrook (1981) details the range of predatory counter-strategies. Even if vigorous competition drives out some companies, new competitors always arise to take their place, even more so if the incumbent firm is setting prices far above costs. The greater the mark-up over costs, the better the incentives for new companies to enter the industry. The incumbent threats will not be credible to existing rivals or potential entrants unless the incumbent's strategy is profitable, as McGee (1980) demonstrated.

Often, the incumbent is alleged to have cash reserves, known as a long purse, or it is alleged that the incumbent uses revenues from other endeavors to subsidize losses in a price war. Such an explanation does not address the question of whether such losses can ever be recovered. Alternatively, it is alleged that the predator has better access to capital markets than its rivals, an explanation that relies on imperfections in other markets. If the returns to remaining in the market are significant, competitors should be able to obtain financial backing as well, as noted by Stigler (1967).

The Chicago school of antitrust criticized early theories of predation as being unprofitable and therefore irrational (see Posner, 1976; Bork, 1978). Beginning in the 1980s, a voluminous theoretical literature attempted to show that predation may be an equilibrium strategy (for overviews see Ordover and Saloner, 1989; Spulber, 1989; Klevorick, 1993; Lott, 1999; Church and Ware, 2000). Yet, according to Joskow (1991), "the assumptions embedded in these models do not fit real markets very well" (p. 58). The theoretical literature has increasingly focused on asymmetric information as a possible explanation for why predatory pricing strategies might be observed in a market equilibrium. Lott (1999) presents a detailed empirical refutation of the assumptions that underlie the asymmetric information models of predatory pricing.

Observed instances of predation are decidedly rare despite numerous court cases. For example, Koller (1971) reviews the over 120 federal court cases from 1890 onwards that alleged predatory pricing and finds its practice to be a myth. Burns (1986) presents evidence of predation by American Tobacco between 1891 and 1906 but notes that the results are consistent with perfectly competitive behavior. Lott (1999) critically evaluates the empirical evidence on predation and suggests that much of it is anecdotal.

Perhaps the best known antitrust case involving allegations of predation is *Standard Oil (N.J.)*. Standard Oil is said to have engaged in a form of predatory pricing that used local price cutting to force competitors out of the market. The moral of the story is that the company's predatory behavior resulted in its eventual breakup. The predatory pricing story was popularized by journalist Ida Tarbell (1950) in a book chapter critical of John D. Rockefeller titled "Cutting to Kill." Evaluating the accuracy of the 1911 *Standard Oil (N.J.)* example is critical because, as McGee (1980, p. 292) observes, "I still believe that attempts at predation have been rare, and that successful attempts will be found to be rarer still."

*Standard Oil (N.J.)* turns out to be another fable. In his article reprinted in this volume "Predatory Price Cutting: The Standard Oil (N.J.) Case" (chapter 10), John S. McGee notes that Standard Oil serves as the "archetype of predatory monopoly."[9] McGee finds little evidence that such predatory price discrimination occurred. McGee further points out that acquisition would have been a less costly and more effective means of increasing market share than price wars at a time when mergers were permitted by antitrust policy. Armentano's (1982) history of the case supports McGee's analysis: "No economic analysis of Standard Oil's conduct and performance in the period under consideration was made by the Court to determine whether its business activities were reasonable" (p. 71).[10]

The *Alcoa* antitrust case has been cited as an example of the predatory behavior known as "raising rivals' costs."[11] A company that is able to increase the costs of its rivals allegedly creates an umbrella that allows it to increase prices without losing sales to rivals or even drive competitors out of the market and price monopolistically. If a company can deliberately raise the costs of its rivals it would potentially violate antitrust rules forbidding monopolization.[12] Thomas Krattenmaker and Steven Salop (1986) and others allege that Alcoa attempted to control access to electricity and bauxite, inputs that are critical in the manufacture of aluminum.

John E. Lopatka and Paul E. Godek, in their article reprinted in this volume titled "Another Look at Alcoa: Raising Rivals' Costs Does Not Improve the View" (chapter 11), show that Alcoa had limited control over inputs and that exclusionary agreements were ancillary to its purchasing agreements. Alcoa purchased a very small fraction of electric power production and the company's purchases of bauxite had little effect on its price or availability. Correcting the myth that Alcoa raised rivals'

[9] John McGee wrote to me that just before receiving my request for permission to republish his article he spoke with Aaron Director, the first editor of the *Journal of Law and Economics*, who originally published the Standard Oil article in 1958.

[10] Randall Mariger (1978) performed a simulation analysis based on data from the Standard Oil case and found support for pricing by a dominant firm in response for declining market share rather than alleged predatory price discrimination.

[11] *United States v. Aluminum Co. of America*, 148 F. 2d 416 (2d Cir. 1945).

[12] See Salop and Scheffman (1983), Spulber (1989), and Church and Ware (2000) for additional discussion of raising rivals' costs.

costs is particularly worthwhile because it is one of the few examples of such behavior given by proponents of the theory.

There are theoretical problems associated with establishing the feasibility of raising rivals' costs. Moreover, even if a firm could successfully raise its rivals' cost, would it have an incentive to do so? The feasibility of raising rivals' costs depends on whether a firm could successfully control access to a critical supplier or critical inputs without rivals discovering alternative suppliers or substitute inputs. Even if a firm can increase the price of critical inputs by bidding competitively for those inputs, its increased costs would be likely to outweigh any competitive benefits. As with predatory behavior generally, the returns to raising rivals' costs after rivals are driven from the market must be greater than the costs of driving them out. Moreover, once rivals are driven out, the incumbent firm must be able to defend the market against future entrants to secure returns to predation.

In addition to predation, economists have alleged that other types of activities cause market foreclosure. Reviewing the most important antitrust cases of the twentieth century, Lopatka and Kleit (1995) conclude that "the quest for foreclosure among these cases has been fruitless." Cases that are frequently cited as examples of market foreclosure are *Terminal Railroad*, *United Shoe*, *Klor's*, and *Lorain Journal*.[13] Closer analysis of these cases fails to support foreclosure.

*Terminal Railroad* is the classic example of foreclosure of access to an essential facility, generally a capital investment that cannot be duplicated profitably by entrants. In that case a group of railroads were accused of controlling access to bridges over the Mississippi River to St. Louis. Reiffen and Kleit (1990) find little support for the essential facilities doctrine; instead the railroads charged themselves the same price that they charged competitors and did not exclude anyone. They show that the case does not support a vertical theory of antitrust harm: "Consistently misinterpreted, it has served as a source for misbeliefs about the economics of vertical integration" (1990, p. 437).

In the *United Shoe* case, Masten and Snyder (1993) suggest that the company did not use equipment leases to exclude rivals but rather designed the contracts to reduce transaction costs. Regarding *Klor's*, Coate and Kleit (1994) show that the San Francisco department store Broadway-Hale signed exclusive agreements with appliance manufacturers to prevent Klor's, a discount store next door, from free-riding on Broadway-Hale's sales and promotion efforts. *Lorain Journal* concerns a newspaper by that name that refused to take advertising from local merchants who simultaneously advertised on a radio station. Lopatka and Kleit (1995) demonstrate that the *Lorain Journal's* actions posed no threat to the profitability of the radio station and yielded little if any benefit to the *Lorain Journal* itself.

The proponents of predatory pricing have public policy agendas that at times resemble price regulation. As Spulber (1989) demonstrates, many of the antitrust approaches to predatory pricing advocated by economists and legal scholars can be interpreted as a form of price regulation. For example, the widely applied

---

[13]  *United States v. Terminal Railroad Association* 224 U.S. 383 (1912), *United States v. United Shoe Machine Corp.* 110 F. Supp. 295 (D. Mass. 1953) aff'd per curiam, 374 U.S. 521 (1954), *Klor's Inc. v. Broadway-Hale* 359 U.S. 207 (1959), and *Lorain Journal Co. v. United States* 342 U.S. 143 (1951).

Areeda-Turner test checks whether alleged predators are pricing below average variable cost.

Advocates of market foreclosure scenarios seek antitrust action to protect competition from alleged predators. Such antitrust actions may have the opposite effect. The Supreme Court in the 1986 *Matsushita* decision found accusations of predation unwarranted and chilling to competition and the 1993 *Brown & Williamson* decision further rejected predation arguments.[14]

The government's case against Microsoft, which is likely to reach the Supreme Court, renews the predatory pricing debate. The case combines accusations of predation with arguments based on technology lock-in and network externalities. It should not be surprising that press accounts frequently compare Microsoft's founder Bill Gates to John D. Rockefeller, usually based on inaccurate portraits of both men and of their companies. McGee's correction of the fable of *Standard Oil (N.J.)* is of great interest in understanding the many flaws in such historical comparisons.

## LEARNING BY DOING: THE FABLE OF THE LIBERTY SHIPS

Learning-by-doing potentially leads to first-mover advantages and economies of experience that are alleged to create market power for early entrants. Returns to learning in manufacturing is an influential idea in the economics of industrial organization, see the empirical studies of Lieberman (1984) and Dick (1991). Learning-by-doing is an important concept in management strategy as a means of obtaining a cost advantage (see for example Barney, 1997, pp. 192–8). The concept has been popularized through the efforts of the Boston Consulting Group (1972).

Peter Thompson's article reprinted in this volume titled "How Much Did the Liberty Shipbuilders Learn? New Evidence for an Old Case Study" (chapter 12) examines a classic story used to buttress the theory of learning-by-doing. Thompson uses an extensive but previously unavailable database showing information on individual ships and capital investments in the shipyard. As Thompson points out, previous research was based on Fischer (1949), which was devoid of data on capital investment expenditures.

Labor productivity under the Emergency Shipbuilding Program during World War II increased rapidly and significantly. The fable of the Liberty ships attributes the growth in labor productivity to learning as a function of the cumulative output produced. Leonard Rapping (1965) first identified learning as a source of productivity improvements in the Liberty shipbuilding program. Robert Lucas (1993) terms the Liberty ships learning process a "miracle." In contrast, Thompson shows that productivity increases were due in large part to capital investment and reductions in product quality.

Learning-by-doing dates back at least to Adam Smith's pin factory. The learning curve in the Liberty ships program and other studies of learning-by-doing underlie the notion that firms are learning organizations. Although it seems apparent that

---

[14] *Matsushita Electric Industrial Co. v. Zenith Radio* (475 U.S. 574) and *Brooke Group Ltd. v. Brown & Williamson Tobacco Corp.* (113 S. Ct. 2578)

organizations learn over time, the question is whether learning is simply a function of cumulative output (see also Sinclair et al., 1999). Some of the productivity gains can be due to capital investment or product quality changes as in the Liberty ships program. Other productivity gains might be the result of investment in human capital, research and development expenditures, information gathering, and organizational reforms that are independent of cumulative output. Mishina (1999) revisits the World War II building program for the B-17 heavy bomber, known as the Flying Fortress, and finds that at Boeing's No. 2 Plant in Seattle, Washington, productivity changes were associated with improvements in the production system associated with greater scale and increased coordination by the production control department.

In the industrial organization literature, the learning curve has been associated with first-mover advantages and market power (see Gilbert and Harris, 1981; Ross, 1986; Dasgupta and Stiglitz, 1988). Lee (1975) and Spence (1981) consider entry barriers associated with learning. Cabral and Riordan (1994) cite learning-by-doing studies in a wide variety of industries and obtain conditions under which the first mover's market dominance increases. Cabral and Riordan also examine incentives for predatory pricing with learning-by-doing in production. Fudenberg and Tirole (1983) show that a monopolist learns too slowly by producing less than is socially optimal. They show further that learning increases welfare when there is duopoly competition and suggest that governments should tax output in the early period when firms have a greater incentive to produce and subsidize output in the mature period when competitive outputs decline.

Thompson's results suggest the need to reexamine empirical results on the learning-by-doing hypothesis by carefully considering competing explanations. Such a reexamination would be particularly useful in management discussion of the determinants of the learning organization. The story of the Liberty ships raises doubts about public policy designed to enhance learning-by-doing or to counter alleged anticompetitive effects of the learning curve.

## SPECULATIVE BUBBLES: THE FABLE OF TULIP MANIA AND OTHER FINANCIAL LEGENDS

Worries about market failure extend to financial markets, where economists are deeply concerned about the possibility of speculative bubbles followed by panics and market crashes. In his well-known history, Charles P. Kindleberger (1996) details financial bubbles and argues that "Speculative excess, referred to concisely as a mania, and revulsion from such excess in the form of a crisis, crash, or panic can be shown to be, if not inevitable, at least historically common" (p. 2). The identification of speculative bubbles has great contemporary significance. Alan Greenspan, the chairman of the Federal Reserve Bank, mused that the U.S. securities markets in the late 1990s seemed to exhibit irrational exuberance. Taking his cue from Alan Greenspan, Robert Schiller (2000) analyses investor perceptions and other cultural factors that he believes have led to irrational exuberance in the United States and argues that the entire U.S. stock market is inflated by a speculative bubble.

As might be expected when the wealth of so many is tied to financial market conditions, rumors and apocryphal stories abound. The *Economist* article "Financial Legends" reprinted in this volume (chapter 13) recites some of these stories. The best known of these is certainly the Dutch tulip speculation of 1634–7. Standard discussions in the economics literature generally cite Charles Mackay's anecdotal account *Memoirs of Extraordinary Popular Delusions and the Madness of Crowds* (written 1852). Burton Malkiel (1999) recites the history of tulip mania without any source other than Mackay and states that panic reigned "as happens in all speculative crazes." Malkiel's argument is circular: a speculative craze is exemplified by tulip mania which in turn is a speculative craze because it is like all the others. Without any evidence of causality, Malkiel concludes that the shock generated by the boom and collapse sent the Netherlands into a prolonged depression: "No one was spared." Garber (1989) critically examines the tulip mania history and concludes that the high prices for rare bulbs reflected high prices for unique new varieties while later price declines were due to expanding supplies.

The tulip mania story has inspired work on coordination known as "sunspots" in financial markets (see for example Azariadis, 1981; Azariadis and Guesnerie, 1986). The efficiency of financial markets is the subject of intense debate and sophisticated empirical analysis (see for example Lo and MacKinlay, 1999). The debate is likely to continue since, as Flood and Garber (1980) observe, data analysis cannot distinguish empirically between a hypothesized speculative bubble and a misspecified model of market behavior. Garber (1989) observes that the tulip mania story "predisposes economists to advance bubble theories of asset pricing."

The story of tulip mania is joined by other fables that surround speculative bubbles including the South Sea Bubble and the Mississippi Bubble, both of 1720 (see also Garber, 1990). Other apocryphal tales pertain to the Great Crash of October 1929 on Wall Street. These legends are meant to illustrate panic and irrationality among investors, not only as moral tales but also as precursors to regulation of financial markets or money market intervention by central banks. As might be expected, the question of whether investors behave rationally and whether financial markets operate efficiently has significant public policy implications. If the existence of speculative bubbles and subsequent market crashes can be established, then financial markets fail to operate with full efficiency.

Many of those who seek to identify speculative bubbles have public policy prescriptions in mind. Kindleberger (1996, p. 190) makes the case that a lender of last resort such as the Federal Reserve Bank or the International Monetary Fund should alleviate "the business depression that follows financial crises" both in national and international economies. Shiller (2000) argues against the privatization of the social security system based on his concerns about financial markets. Correcting financial legends is useful for a reasoned discussion about the efficiency of financial markets and the role of financial regulation.

## CONCLUSION

The articles in this volume demonstrate that many cherished stories of market failures pervading the economics literature are mythical. While anecdotal evidence is a valuable device for illustrating key points about economics, it is incumbent on researchers to carefully check the details of historical accounts. Anecdotes that fit theories too neatly should raise caution flags. The examples presented in this book illustrate the great need for empirical investigation in economics.

The problem with many of these fables is not only their historical inaccuracies. Rather, it is that many of the stories share a common moral – markets fail and the government should intervene in the economy to solve the problem. Economics students and researchers should examine familiar fables with a critical eye to determine whether the interpretation of a historical event is accurate or whether it is designed to serve a particular public policy agenda.

Markets do not always function perfectly – market institutions are often more complex than is commonly supposed. Consumers and firms often find innovative ways to resolve market imperfections and mitigate transaction costs. These essays highlight Ronald H. Coase's great understanding about the critical role of transaction costs in the economy.

## REFERENCES

Allen, R. C. (1982) "The Efficiency and Distributional Implications of *18th* Century Enclosures," *Economic Journal*, 92, pp. 937–53.

Armentano, Dominick (1982) *Antitrust and Monopoly* (New York: Wiley).

Arthur, Brian (1989) "Competing Technologies, Increasing Returns, and Lock-In by Historical Events," *Economic Journal*, 97, pp. 642–65.

Arthur, Brian (1990) "Positive Feedbacks in the Economy," *Scientific American*, 262, February, pp. 92–9.

Arthur, Brian (1994) *Increasing Returns and Path Dependence in the Economy* (Ann Arbor, Mich.: University of Michigan Press).

Azariadis, Costas (1981) "Self-Fulfilling Prophecies," *Journal of Economic Theory*, 25, December, pp. 380–96.

Azariadis, Costas and Roger Guesnerie (1986) "Sunspots and Cycles," *Review of Economic Studies*, 53, October, pp. 725–37.

Barney, Jay B. (1997) *Gaining and Sustaining Competitive Advantage* (Reading, Mass.: Addison-Wesley).

Bator, Francis M. (1958) "The Anatomy of Market Failure," *Quarterly Journal of Economics*, 72 (August) pp. 351–79.

Bork, Robert (1978) *The Antitrust Parodox: A Policy at War with Itself* (New York: Basic Books).

Boston Consulting Group (1972) *Perspectives on Experience*, (Boston, Mass.: Boston Consulting Group).

Burns, Malcolm R. (1986) "Predatory Pricing and the Acquisition Cost of Competitors," *Journal of Political Economy*, 94, April, pp. 266–96.

Cabral, Luis M. B. and Michael H. Riordan (1994) "The Learning Curve, Market Dominance and Predatory Pricing," *Econometrica*, 62, September, pp. 1115–140.

Casadesus-Masanell, Ramon and Daniel F. Spulber (2000) "The Fable of Fisher Body Revisited," Working paper, Northwestern University.

Cheung, Steven N. S. (1970) "The Structure of a Contract and the Theory of a Non-Exclusive Resource." *Journal of Law and Economics*, 13, April, pp. 49–70.

Church, Jeffrey and Roger Ware (2000) *Industrial Organization: A Strategic Approach* (Homewood, Ill.: McGraw-Hill).

Coase, Ronald H. (1960) "The Problem of Social Cost," *Journal of Law and Economics*, 3 (October), pp. 1–44.

Coase, Ronald H. (1988) *The Firm, the Market and the Law* (Chicago: University of Chicago Press).

Coate, Malcolm B. and Andrew N. Kleit (1994) "Exclusion, Collusion, or Confusion: The Underpinnings of Raising Rivals' Costs," *Research in Law and Economics*, 16, pp. 73–93.

Coleman, D. C. (1977) *The Economy of England, 1450–1750* (Oxford: Oxford University Press).

Dahlman, C. (1980) *The Open Field System and Beyond: A Property Rights Analysis of an Economic Institution* (Cambridge: Cambridge University Press).

Dasgupta, Partha and Joseph Stiglitz (1988) "Learning-by-Doing, Market Structure, and Industrial and Trade Policies," *Oxford Economic Papers*, 40, pp. 246–68.

David, Paul (1985) "Clio and the Economics of QWERTY," *American Economic Review*, 75, pp. 332–7.

David, Paul (1992) "Heroes, Herds and Hysteresis in Technological History: 'The Battle of the Systems' Reconsidered," *Industrial and Corporate Change*, 1, pp. 129–80.

Demsetz, Harold (1969) "Information and Efficiency: Another Viewpoint," *Journal of Law and Economics*, 12, April, pp. 1–22.

Dick, A. R. (1991) "Learning by Doing and Dumping in the Semiconductor Industry," *Journal of Law and Economics*, 34, pp. 133–59.

Easterbrook, Frank (1981) "Predatory Strategies and Counterstrategies," *University of Chicago Law Review*, 48, Spring, pp. 263–337.

Fanoaltea, S. (1988) "Transaction Costs, Whig History, and the Common Fields," *Politics and Society*, 16, pp. 171–240.

Feeny, David, Susan Hanna, and Arthur F. McEvoy (1996) "Questioning the Assumptions of the 'Tragedy of the Commons' Model of Fisheries," *Land-Economics*, 72, May, pp. 187–205.

Fischer, Gerald J. (1949) *A Statistical Summary of Shipbuilding Under the U.S. Maritime Commission During World War II* (Washington, D.C.: Historical Reports of the War Administration, United States Maritime Commission).

Flood, Robert P. and Peter M. Garber (1980) "Market Fundamentals versus Price-Level Bubbles: The First Tests," *Journal of Political Economy*, 88, August, pp. 745–70.

Freeland, Robert (2000) "Creating Hold-up Through Vertical Integration," *Journal of Law and Economics*, 43, April, pp. 33–66.

Fudenberg, Drew and Jean Tirole (1983) "Learning by Doing and Market Performance," *Bell Journal of Economics*, 14, Autumn, pp. 522–30.

Galanter, Marc (1998) "An Oil Strike in Hell: Contemporary Legends about the Civil Justice System," *Arizona Law Review*, 40, Fall, pp. 717–52.

Garber, Peter M. (1989) "Tulipmania," *Journal of Political Economy*, 97, pp. 535–60.

Garber, Peter M. (1989) "Famous First Bubbles," *Journal of Economic Perspectives*, 4, Spring, pp. 35–54.

Gilbert, Richard J. and Robert G. Harris (1981) "Investment Decisions with Economies of Scale and Learning," *American Economic Review: Papers and Proceedings*, 71, pp. 172–7.

Gonner, E. C. K. (1966) *Common Land and Inclosure* (1912) (reprinted, New York: Kelly).

Gordon, H. Scott (1954) "The Economic Theory of the Common-Property Resource: The Fishery," *Journal of Political Economy*, 62, April, pp. 124–42.

Hardin, Garrett (1968) "The Tragedy of the Commons," *Science*, 162, December 13, pp. 1243–8.

Hart, Oliver (1995) *Firms. Contracts, and Financial Structure* (Oxford: Clarendon Press).

Hobbes, Thomas (1991) *Leviathan*, ed. Richard Tuck (New York: Cambridge University Press).

Johnson, D. Gale (1950) "Resource Allocation under Share Contracts," *Journal of Political Economy*, 58, April, pp. 111–23.

Joskow, Paul L. (1991) "The Role of Transaction Cost Economics in Antitrust and Public Utility Regulatory Policies," *Journal of Law, Economics and Organization*, 7, special issue.

Katz, Michael L. and Carl Shapiro (1985) "Network Externalities, Competition, and Compatibility," *American Economic Review*, 75, June, pp. 424–40.

Keynes, John Maynard (1964) *The General Theory of Employment Interest and Money* (1935) (New York: Harcourt Brace).

Kindleberger, Charles P. (1996) *Manias, Panics and Crashes: A History of Financial Crises*, 3rd edn (New York: Wiley).

Klein, Benjamin (1999) "Market Power in Franchise Cases in the Wake of Kodak: Applying Postcontract Holdup Analysis to Vertical Relationships," *Antitrust Law Journal*, 67, pp. 283–326.

Klein, Benjamin (2000) "Fisher–General Motors and the Nature of the Firm," *Journal of Law and Economics*, 43, April, pp. 105–41.

Klein, Benjamin, Robert G. Crawford, and Armen A. Alchian (1978) "Vertical Integration, Appropriable Rents, and the Competitive Contracting Process," *Journal of Law and Economics*, 21, pp. 297–326.

Klevorick, Alvin K. (1993) "The Current State of the Law and Economics of Predatory Pricing," *American Economic Review*, Papers and Proceedings, 83, May, pp. 162–7.

Koller, Ronald H. (1971) "The Myth of Predatory Pricing: An Empirical Study," *Antitrust Law and Economics Review*, 4, Summer, pp. 105–23.

Krattenmaker, Thomas G. and Steven C. Salop (1986) "Anticompetitive Exclusion: Raising Rivals' Costs to Achieve Power over Price," *Yale Law Journal*, 96, pp. 297–326.

Lee, W. Y. (1975) "Oligopoly and Entry," *Journal of Economic Theory*, 11, pp. 35–54.

Lévi-Strauss, Claude (1963) *Structural Anthropology* (New York: Basic Books).

Lieberman, M. B. (1984) "The Learning Curve and Pricing in the Chemical Processing Industries," *Rand Journal of Economics*, 15, pp. 213–28.

Liebowitz, Stanley J. and Stephen E. Margolis (1994) "Network Externality: An Uncommon Tragedy," *Journal of Economic Perspectives*, 8, pp. 133–50.

Liebowitz, Stanley J. and Stephen E. Margolis (1995) "Path Dependence, Lock-In and History," *Journal of Law, Economics, and Organization*, 11, pp. 205–26.

Liebowitz, Stanley J. and Stephen E. Margolis (1999) *Winners, Losers and Microsoft: Competition and Antitrust in High Technology* (Oakland, Calif.: The Independent Institute).

Lloyd, William Foster (1883) *Two Lectures on the Checks to Population* (Oxford: Oxford University Press).

Lo, Andrew W. and A. Craig MacKinlay (1999) *A Nonrandom Walk Down Wall Street* (Princeton, N.J.: Princeton University Press).

Lopatka, John E. and Andrew N. Kleit (1995) "The Mystery of Lorain Journal and the Quest for Foreclosure in Antitrust," *Texas Law Review*, 73, May, pp. 1255–306.

Lott, John R. (1999) *Are Predatory Commitments Credible? Who Should the Courts Believe?* (Chicago: University of Chicago Press).

Lucas, Robert E. (1993) "Making a Miracle," *Econometrica*, 61, March, pp. 251–72.

McChesney, Fred S. (1986) "Government Prohibitions on Volunteer Fire Fighting in Nineteenth-Century America: A Property Rights Perspective," *Journal of Legal Studies*, 15, January, pp. 69–92.

McClosky, D. N. (1976) "English Open Fields as Behavior Toward Risk," in P. Uselding (ed.) *Research in Economic History: An Annual Compilation*, vol. 1 (Greenwich, Conn.: JAI Press).

McGee, John S. (1980) "Predatory Pricing Revisited," *Journal of Law and Economics*, 23, October, pp. 289–330.

Mackay, Charles (1852) *Memoirs of Extraordinary Popular Delusions and the Madness of Crowds*, reprint edition, 1932 (Boston, Mass.: L. C. Page).

Malkiel, Burton G. (1999) *A Random Walk Down Wall Street* (New York: Norton).

Mariger, Randall (1978) "Predatory Price Cutting: The Standard Oil of New Jersey Case Revisited," *Explorations in Economic History*, 15, pp. 341–67.

Marshall, Alfred (1890) *Principles of Economics*, 8th edn (London: Macmillan).

Masten, Scott E. and Edward A. Snyder (1993) "United States Versus United Shoe Machinery Corporation: On the Merits," *Journal of Law and Economics*, 36, pp. 33–70.

Meade, J. E. (1952) "External Economies and Diseconomies in a Competitive Situation," *Economic Journal*, 62, pp. 54–67.

Mill, John Stuart (1848) *Principles of Political Economy* 1926, (London: Ashley Edition.)

Mishan, E. J. (1965) "Reflections on Recent Developments in the Concept of External Effects," *Canadian Journal of Political Economy*, 31, February, pp. 3–34.

Mishan, E. J. (1971) "The Postwar Literature on Externalities: An Interpretive Essay," *Journal of Economic Literature*, 9, March, pp. 1–28.

Mishina, Kazuhiro (1999) "Learning by New Experiences: Revisiting the Flying Fortress Learning Curve," in Naomi Lamoreaux, Daniel M. G. Raff, and Peter Temin (eds), *Learning by Doing in Markets, Firms, and Countries* (Chicago: University of Chicago Press).

Miwa, Yoshiro and J. Mark Ramseyer (2000) "Rethinking Relationship-Specific Investments: Subcontracting in the Japanese Automobile Industry," *Michigan Law Review*, 98, August.

Ordover, Janusz and Garth Saloner (1989) "Predation, Monopolization, and Antitrust," in Richard Schmalensee and Robert D. Willing (eds) *The Handbook of Industrial Organization* (Amsterdam: North Holland).

Ostrom, Elinor (1990) *Governing the Commons: The Evolution of Institutions for Collective Action* (Cambridge: Cambridge University Press).

Otsuka, Keijiro, Hiroyuki Chuma and Yujiro Hayami (1992) "Land and Labor Contracts in Agrarian Economies: Theories and Facts," *Journal of Economic Literature*, 30, December, pp. 1965–2018.

Pigou, A. C. (1920) *The Economics of Welfare* (London: Macmillan).

Pigou, A. C. (1938) *The Economics of Welfare* 4th edn (London: Macmillan).

Posner, Richard A. (1976) *Antitrust Law: An Economic Perspective* (Chicago: University of Chicago Press).

Rapping, Leonard (1965) "Learning and World War II Production Functions," *Review of Economic Statistics*, 47, pp. 81–6.

Reiffen, David and Andrew N. Kleit (1990) "Terminal Railroad Revisited: Foreclosure of an Essential Facility or Simple Horizontal Monopoly," *Journal of Law and Economics*, 33, pp. 419–38.

Ross, D. R. (1986) "Learning to Dominate," *Journal of Industrial Economics*, 34, pp. 337–53.

Rousseau, Jean-Jacques (1948) *The Social Contract, or Principles of Political Right*, translated with intro. and notes by Henry J. Tozer, 3rd edn (London: George Allen & Unwin).

Salop, Steven C. and David T. Scheffman (1983) "Raising Rivals' Costs," *American Economic Review Papers and Proceedings*, 73 (May), pp. 270–1.

Schelling, Thomas C. (1978) *Micromotives and Macrobehavior* (New York: Norton).

Shapiro, Carl and Hal Varian (1999) *Information Rules* (New York: Free Press).

Shiller, Robert J. (2000) *Irrational Exuberance* (Princeton, N.J.: Princeton University Press).

Sidgwick, Henry (1883) *Principles of Political Economy*, 1st edn, 3rd edn published 1901 (London).

Sinclair, Gavin, Steven Klepper, and Wesley Cohen (1999) "What's Experience Got to Do with It? Sources of Cost Reduction in a Large Specialty Chemical Producer," Working paper, Carnegie-Mellon University.

Slater, G. (1932) *The Growth of Modern England* (Boston, Mass.: Houghton Mifflin).

Smith, Adam (1776) *The Wealth of Nations* (1937, New York: Modern Library Edition).

Spence, Michael A. (1981) "The Learning Curve and Competition," *Bell Journal of Economics*, 12, pp. 49–70.

Spulber, Daniel F. (1982) "A Selective Survey," in Leonard J. Mirman and Daniel F. Spulber (eds) *Essays in the Economics of Renewable Resources* (Amsterdam: Elsevier-North Holland).

Spulber, Daniel F. (1989) *Regulation and Markets* (Cambridge, Mass.: MIT Press).

Stigler, George (1967) "Imperfections in the Capital Market," *Journal of Political Economy*, 75 June, pp. 287–92.

Stiglitz, Joseph E. (1974) "Incentives and Risk Sharing in Sharecropping," *Review of Economic Studies*, 41, April, pp. 219–55.

Tarbell, Ida (1950) *The History of the Standard Oil Company* (New York: Peter Smith).

Thirsk, J. (1967) *The Agrarian History of England and Wales* (Cambridge: Cambridge University Press).

Umbeck, John (1977) "The California Gold Rush: A Study of Emerging Property Rights," *Explorations in Economic History*, 14, pp. 197–226.

Van Zandt, David E. (1993) "The Lessons of the Lighthouse: 'Government' or 'Private' Provision of Goods," *Journal of Legal Studies*, 23, January, pp. 47–72.

Williamson, Oliver E. (1985) *The Economic Institutions of Capitalism* (Englewood Cliffs, N.J.: Prentice-Hall).

Yelling, J. A. (1977) *Common Field and Enclosure in England 1450–1850* (Hamden, Conn.: Archon).

# 1

# The Lighthouse in Economics

## Ronald H. Coase*

## I  INTRODUCTION

The lighthouse appears in the writings of economists because of the light it is supposed to throw on the question of the economic functions of government. It is often used as an example of something which has to be provided by government rather than by private enterprise. What economists usually seem to have in mind is that the impossibility of securing payment from the owners of the ships that benefit from the existence of the lighthouse makes it unprofitable for any private individual or firm to build and maintain a lighthouse.

John Stuart Mill in his *Principles of Political Economy*, in the chapter "Of the Grounds and Limits of the Laissez-Faire or Non-Interference Principle," said:

> it is a proper office of government to build and maintain lighthouses, establish buoys, etc. for the security of navigation: for since it is impossible that the ships at sea which are benefited by a lighthouse, should be made to pay a toll on the occasion of its use, no one would build lighthouses from motives of personal interest, unless indemnified and rewarded from a compulsory levy made by the state.[1]

Henry Sidgwick in his *Principles of Political Economy*, in the chapter, "The System of Natural Liberty Considered in Relation to Production," had this to say:

> there is a large and varied class of cases in which the supposition [that an individual can always obtain through free exchange adequate remuneration for the services he renders] would be manifestly erroneous. In the first place there are some utilities which, from their nature, are practically incapable of being appropriated by those who pro-

\* It is with great pleasure that I acknowledge the helpfulness of members of Trinity House and of officials in the Department of Trade and of the Chamber of Shipping in providing me with information on the British lighthouse system. They are not, however, in any way responsible for the use I have made of this information and should not be presumed to share the conclusions I draw.

[1] John Stuart Mill, Principles of Political Economy, vol. 3 of *The Collected Works of John Stuart Mill*, ed. J. M. Robson (1965), p. 968.

duce them or would otherwise be willing to purchase them. For instance, it may easily happen that the benefits of a well-placed lighthouse must be largely enjoyed by ships on which no toll could be conveniently imposed.[2]

Pigou in the *Economics of Welfare* used Sidgwick's lighthouse example as an instance of uncompensated services, in which "marginal net product falls short of marginal social net product, because incidental services are performed to third parties from whom it is technically difficult to exact payment."[3]

Paul A. Samuelson, in his *Economics*, is more forthright than these earlier writers. In the section on the "Economic Role of Government," he says that "government provides certain indispensable *public* services without which community life would be unthinkable and which by their nature cannot appropriately be left to private enterprise." He gives as "obvious examples," the maintenance of national defense, of internal law and order, and the administration of justice and of contracts and he adds in a footnote:

> Here is a later example of government service: lighthouses. These save lives and cargoes; but lighthouse keepers cannot reach out to collect fees from skippers. "So," says the advanced treatise, "we have here a divergence between *private* advantage and money cost [as seen by a man odd enough to try to make his fortune running a lighthouse business] and true *social* advantage and cost [as measured by lives and cargoes saved in comparison with (1) total costs of the lighthouse and (2) extra costs that result from letting one more ship look at the warning light]." Philosophers and statesmen have always recognized the necessary role of government in such cases of "external-economy divergence between private and social advantage."[4]

Later Samuelson again refers to the lighthouse as a "government activit[y] justifiable because of external effects." He says:

> Take our earlier case of a lighthouse to warn against rocks. Its beam helps everyone in sight. A businessman could not build it for a profit, since he cannot claim a price from each user. This certainly is the kind of activity that governments would naturally undertake.[5]

Samuelson does not leave the matter here. He also uses the lighthouse to make another point (one not found in the earlier writers). He says:

> in the lighthouse example one thing should be noticed: The fact that the lighthouse operators cannot appropriate in the form of a purchase price a fee from those it benefits certainly helps to make it a suitable social or public good. But even if the operators were able – say, by radar reconnaisance – to claim a toll from every nearby user,

---

[2] Henry Sidgwick, *The Principles of Political Economy*, 3rd edn, (1901), p. 406. In the first edition (1883), the sentence relating to lighthouses is the same but the rest of the wording (but not the sense) is somewhat changed.

[3] A. C. Pigou, *Economics of Welfare* 4th edn, (1938); pp. 183–4.

[4] Paul A. Samuelson, *Economics: An Introductory Analysis*, 6th edn (1964), p. 45. All references to Samuelson's *Economics* will be to the 6th edition.

[5] Ibid., p. 159.

that fact would not necessarily make it socially optimal for this service to be provided like a private good at a market-determined individual price. Why not? Because it costs society *zero extra cost* to let one extra ship use the service; hence any ships discouraged from those waters by the requirement to pay a positive price will represent a social economic loss – even if the price charged to all is no more than enough to pay the long-run expenses of the lighthouse. If the lighthouse is socially worth building and operating – and it need not be – a more advanced treatise can show how this social good is worth being made optimally available to all.[6]

There is an element of paradox in Samuelson's position. The government has to provide lighthouses because private firms could not charge for their services. But if it were possible for private firms to make such a charge they should not be allowed to do so (which also presumably calls for government action). Samuelson's position is quite different from that of Mill, Sidgwick or Pigou. As I read these writers, the difficulty of charging for the use of a lighthouse is a serious point with important consequences for lighthouse policy. They had no objection to charging as such and therefore, if this were possible, to the private operation of lighthouses. Mill's argument is not, however, free from ambiguity. He argues that the government should build and maintain lighthouses because, since ships benefitted cannot be made to pay a toll, private enterprise would not provide a lighthouse service. But he then adds a qualifying phrase "unless indemnified and rewarded from a compulsory levy made by the state." I take a "compulsory levy" to be one imposed on ships benefitted by the lighthouse (the levy would be, in effect, a toll). The element of ambiguity in Mill's exposition is whether he meant that the "compulsory levy" would make it possible for people to "build lighthouses from motives of personal interest" and therefore for government operation to be avoided or whether he meant that it was not possible (or desirable) for private firms to be "indemnified and rewarded from a compulsory levy" and that therefore government operation was required. My own opinion is that Mill had in mind the first of these alternative interpretations and, if this is right, it represents an important qualification to his view that building and maintaining lighthouses is "a proper office of the government." In any case, it seems clear that Mill had no objection in principle to the imposition of tolls.[7] Sidgwick's point (to which Pigou refers) raises no problems of interpretation. It is, however, very restricted in character. He says that "it may easily happen that the benefits of a well-placed lighthouse must be largely enjoyed by ships on which no toll could be conveniently imposed." This does not say that charging is impossible: indeed, it implies the contrary. What it says is that there may be circumstances in which most of those who benefit from the lighthouse can avoid paying the toll. It does not say that there may not be circumstances in which the benefits of the lighthouse are largely enjoyed by ships on which a toll could be conveniently laid and it implies that, in these circumstances, it would be desirable to impose a toll – which would make private operation of lighthouses possible.

It is, I think, difficult to understand exactly what Mill, Sidgwick and Pigou meant without some knowledge of the British lighthouse system since, although these

---

[6] Ibid., p. 151.
[7] Compare what Mill has to say on tolls in note 1 (above) at pp. 862–3.

writers were probably unfamiliar with how the British system operated in detail, they were doubtless aware of its general character and this must have been in the back of their minds when they wrote about lighthouses. However, knowledge of the British lighthouse system not only enables one to have a greater understanding of Mill, Sidgwick and Pigou; it also provides a context within which to appraise Samuelson's statements about lighthouses.

## II   THE BRITISH LIGHTHOUSE SYSTEM

The authorities in Britain which build and maintain lighthouses are Trinity House (for England and Wales), the Commissioners of Northern Lighthouses (for Scotland) and the Commissioners of Irish Lights (for Ireland). The expenses of these authorities are met out of the General Lighthouse Fund. The income of this Fund is derived from light dues, which are paid by shipowners. The responsibility for making the arrangements for the payment of the light dues and for maintaining the accounts is placed on Trinity House (whether the payments are made in England, Wales, Scotland or Ireland) although the actual collection is made by the customs authorities at the ports. The money obtained from the light dues is paid into the General Lighthouse Fund, which is under the control of the Department of Trade. The lighthouse authorities draw on the General Lighthouse Fund to meet their expenditures.

The relation of the Department of Trade to the various lighthouse authorities is somewhat similar to that of the Treasury to a British Government Department. The budgets of the authorities have to be approved by the Department. The proposed budgets of the three authorities are submitted about Christmastime and are discussed at a Lighthouse Conference held annually in London. In addition to the three lighthouse authorities and the Department, there are also present at the conference members of the Lights Advisory Committee, a committee of the Chamber of Shipping (a trade association) representing shipowners, underwriters and shippers. The Lights Advisory Committee, although without statutory authority, plays an important part in the review procedure and the opinions it expresses are taken into account both by the lighthouse authorities in drawing up their budgets and by the Department in deciding on whether to approve the budgets. The light dues are set by the Department at a level which will yield, over a period of years, an amount of money sufficient to meet the likely expenditures. But in deciding on the program of works and changes in existing arrangements the participants in the conference, and particularly the members of the Lights Advisory Committee, have regard to the effect which new works or changes in existing arrangements would have on the level of light dues.

The basis on which light dues are levied was set out in the Second Schedule to the Merchant Shipping (Mercantile Marine Fund) Act of 1898.[8] Modifications to the level of the dues and in certain other respects have been made since then by Order in Council but the present method of charging is essentially that established in

---

[8]  61 & 62 Vic., c. 44, sch. 2.

1898. The dues are so much per net ton payable per voyage for all vessels arriving at, or departing from, ports in Britain. In the case of "Home Trade" ships, there is no further liability for light dues after the first ten voyages in a year and in the case of "Foreign-going" ships, there is no further liability after six voyages. The light dues are different for these two categories of ship and are such that, for a ship of given size, ten voyages for a "Home Trade" ship yield approximately the same sum as six voyages for a "Foreign-going" ship. Some categories of ship pay at a lower rate per net ton: sailing vessels of more than 100 tons and cruise ships. Tugs and pleasure yachts make an annual payment rather than a payment per voyage. In addition, some ships are exempt from light dues: ships belonging to the British or Foreign Governments (unless carrying cargo or passengers for remuneration), fishing vessels, hoppers and dredges, sailing vessels (except pleasure yachts) of less than 100 tons, all ships (including pleasure yachts) of less than 20 tons, vessels (other than tugs or pleasure yachts) in ballast, or putting in for bunker fuel or stores or because of the hazards of the sea. All these statements are subject to qualification. But they make clear the general nature of the scheme.

The present position is that the expenses of the British lighthouse service are met out of the General Lighthouse Fund, the income of which comes from light dues. In addition to expenditures on lighthouses in Great Britain and Ireland, the Fund is also used to pay for the maintenance of some colonial lighthouses and to meet the cost of marking and clearing wrecks (to the extent that these are not reimbursed by a salvaging firm), although these payments amount to only a very small proportion of total expenditures. There are also expenditures on lighthouses which are not met out of the Fund. The expenses of building and maintaining "local lights," those which are only of benefit to ships using particular ports, are not paid for out of the Fund, which is restricted to the finance of lighthouses which are useful for "general navigation." The expenditures for "local lights" are normally made by harbour authorities, and are recovered out of port dues.

## III   THE EVOLUTION OF THE BRITISH LIGHTHOUSE SYSTEM

Mill, writing in 1848, and Sidgwick, in 1883, to the extent that they had in mind the actual British lighthouse system, would obviously be thinking of earlier arrangements. To understand Mill and Sidgwick, we need to know something of the lighthouse system in the nineteenth century and of the way in which it had evolved. But a study of the history of the British lighthouse system is not only useful because it helps us to understand Mill and Sidgwick but also because it serves to enlarge our vision of the range of alternative institutional arrangements available for operating a lighthouse service. In discussing the history of the British lighthouse service, I will confine myself to England and Wales, which is, presumably, the part of the system with which Mill and Sidgwick would have been most familiar.

The principal lighthouse authority in England and Wales is Trinity House. It is also the principal pilotage authority for the United Kingdom. It maintains Homes and administers charitable trusts for mariners, their wives, widows, and orphans.

It has also many miscellaneous responsibilities, for example, the inspection and regulation of "local lights" and the provision of Nautical Assessors or Trinity Masters at the hearing of marine cases in the Law Courts. It is represented on a number of harbour boards, including the Port of London Authority, and members of Trinity House serve on many committees (including government committees) dealing with maritime matters.

Trinity House is an ancient institution. It seems to have evolved out of a medieval seamen's guild. A petition asking for incorporation was presented to Henry VIII in 1513 and letters patent were granted in 1514.[9] The charter gave Trinity House the right to regulate pilotage, and this, together with its charitable work, represented its main activity for many years. It did not concern itself with lighthouses until much later.

There seem to have been few lighthouses in Britain before the seventeenth century and not many until the eighteenth century. There were, however, seamarks of various kinds. Most of these were on land and were not designed as aids to mariners, consisting of church steeples, houses, clumps of trees, etc. Buoys and beacons were also used as aids to navigation. Harris explains that these beacons were not lighthouses but "poles set in the seabed, or on the seashore, with perhaps an old lantern affixed to the top."[10] The regulation of seamarks and the provision of buoys and beacons in the early sixteenth century was the responsibility of the Lord High Admiral. To provide buoys and beacons, he appointed deputies, who collected dues from ships presumed to have benefitted from the marks. In 1566 Trinity House was given the right to provide and also to regulate seamarks. They had the responsibility of seeing that privately owned seamarks were maintained. As an example, a merchant who had cut down, without permission, a clump of trees which had served as a seamark, was upbraided for "preferring a tryfle of private benefitt to your selfe before a great and generall good to the publique."[11] He could have been fined £100 (with the proceeds divided equally between the Crown and Trinity House). There seems to have been some doubt as to whether the Act of 1566 gave Trinity House the right to place seamarks in the water. This doubt was removed in 1594, when the rights of beaconage and buoyage were surrendered by the Lord High Admiral and were granted to Trinity House. How things worked out in practice is not clear since the Lord High Admiral continued to regulate buoyage and beaconage after 1594 but gradually the authority of Trinity House in this area seems to have been acknowledged.

Early in the seventeenth century, Trinity House established lighthouses at Caister and Lowestoft.[12] But it was not until late in the century that it built another lighthouse. In the meantime the building of lighthouses had been taken over by private individuals. As Harris says: "A characteristic element in Elizabethan society were the promoters of projects advanced ostensibly for the public benefit but in reality

---

[9] G. G. Harris, *Trinity House of Deptford 1515–1660* (1969), pp. 19–20. My sketch of the early history of Trinity House is largely based on this work, particularly ch. 7: "Beacons, Markes and Signes for the Sea," and ch. 8: "An Vncertaine Light."

[10] Ibid., p. 153.

[11] Ibid., p. 161.

[12] Ibid., pp. 183–7.

intended for private gain. Lighthouses did not escape their attention."[13] Later he says: "With the completion of the lighthouse at Lowestoft, the Brethren rested content and did no more . . . when in February 1614 they were asked to do something positive, and erect lighthouses at Winterton in response to a petition by some three hundred shipmasters, owners and fishermen, they seem to have done nothing. Failure to respond to demands of this sort not only shook confidence in the Corporation; since there was a prospect of profit, it was tantamount to inviting private speculators to intervene. They soon did so."[14] In the period 1610–75, no lighthouses were erected by Trinity House. At least ten were built by private individuals.[15] Of course, the desire of private individuals to erect lighthouses put Trinity House in a quandary. On the one hand it wanted to be recognized as the only body with authority to construct lighthouses; on the other, it was reluctant to invest its own funds in lighthouses. It therefore opposed the efforts of private individuals to construct lighthouses but, as we have seen, without success. Harris comments:

> The lighthouse projectors were typical of the speculators of the period: they were not primarily motivated by considerations of public service . . . There was a strong foundation of truth in what Sir Edward Coke told Parliament in 1621 "Proiectours like wattermen looke one waye and rowe another: they pretend publique profit, intende private."[16]

The difficulty was that those who were motivated by a sense of public service did not build the lighthouses. As Harris says later: "Admittedly the primary motive of the lighthouse projectors was personal gain, but at least they got things done."[17]

The method used by private individuals to avoid infringing Trinity House's statutory authority was to obtain a patent from the Crown which empowered them to build a lighthouse and to levy tolls on ships presumed to have benefitted from it. The way this was done was to present a petition from shipowners and shippers in which they said that they would greatly benefit from the lighthouse and were willing to pay the toll. Signatures were, I assume, obtained in the way signatures to petitions are normally obtained but no doubt they often represented a genuine expression of opinion. The King presumably used these grants of patents on occasion as a means of rewarding those who had served him. Later, the right to operate a lighthouse and to levy tolls was granted to individuals by Acts of Parliament.

The tolls were collected at the ports by agents (who might act for several lighthouses), who might be private individuals but were commonly customs officials. The toll varied with the lighthouse and ships paid a toll, varying with the size of the vessel, for each lighthouse passed. It was normally a rate per ton (say ¼d or ½d) for each voyage. Later, books were published setting out the lighthouses passed on different voyages and the charges that would be made.

In the meantime, Trinity House came to adopt a policy which maintained its

---

[13] Ibid., pp. 180–1.
[14] Ibid., p. 187.
[15] D. Alan Stevenson, *The World's Lighthouses before 1820* (1959), p. 259.
[16] Harris, op. cit., p. 214.
[17] Ibid., p. 264.

rights while preserving its money (and even increasing it). Trinity House would apply for a patent to operate a lighthouse and would then grant a lease, for a rental, to a private individual who would then build the lighthouse with his own money. The advantage to a private individual of such a procedure would be that he would secure the cooperation rather than the opposition of Trinity House.

An example of this is afforded by the building, and rebuilding, of what is probably the most celebrated British lighthouse, the Eddystone, on a reef of rocks some 14 miles offshore from Plymouth. D. Alan Stevenson comments: "The construction of four lighthouses in succession on the Eddystone Rocks by 1759 provides the most dramatic chapter in lighthouse history: in striving to withstand the force of the waves, their builders showed enterprise, ingenuity and courage of a high order."[18] In 1665, a petition for a lighthouse on the Eddystone Rocks was received by the British Admiralty. Trinity House commented that, though desirable, it "could hardly be accomplished."[19] As Samuel Smiles, that chronicler of private enterprise, says, "it was long before any private adventurer was found ready to undertake so daring an enterprise as the erection of a lighthouse on the Eddystone, where only a little crest of rock was visible at high water, scarcely capable of affording foothold for a structure of the very narrowest basis."[20] In 1692, a proposal was put forward by Walter Whitfield, and Trinity House made an agreement with him under which he was to build the lighthouse and Trinity House was to share equally in whatever profits were made. Whitfield did not, however, undertake the work. His rights were transferred to Henry Winstanley, who, after negotiating with Trinity House, made an agreement in 1696 under which he was to receive the profits for the first five years, after which Trinity House was to share equally in whatever profits were earned for 50 years. Winstanley built one tower and then replaced it with another, the lighthouse being completed in 1699. However, in a great storm in 1703, the lighthouse was swept away, and Winstanley, the lighthousekeepers, and some of his workmen, lost their lives. The total cost up to this time had been £8,000 (all of which had been borne by Winstanley) and the receipts had been £4,000. The government gave Winstanley's widow £200 and a pension of £100 per annum. If the construction of lighthouses had been left solely to men with the public interest at heart, the Eddystone would have remained for a long time without a lighthouse. But the prospect of private gain once more reared its ugly head. Two men, Lovett and Rudyerd, decided to build another lighthouse. Trinity House agreed to apply for an Act of Parliament authorizing the rebuilding and the imposition of tolls and to lease their rights to the new builders. The terms were better than had been granted to Winstanley – a 99 year lease at an annual rent of £100 with 100 percent of the profits going to the builders. The lighthouse was completed in 1709 and remained in operation until 1755 when it was destroyed by fire. The lease still had some 50 years to run and the interest in the lighthouse had passed into other hands. The new owners decided to rebuild and engaged one of the great engineers of the time, John Smeaton. He determined to build the lighthouse entirely of stone, the previous

---

[18] Stevenson, op. cit., p. 113.
[19] Ibid.
[20] Samuel Smiles, *Lives of the Engineers*, vol. 2 (1861), p. 16.

structure having been made of wood. The lighthouse was completed by 1759. It continued in operation until 1882, when it was replaced by a new structure built by Trinity House.[21]

We may understand the significance of the part played by private individuals and organizations in the provision of lighthouses in Britain if we consider the position at the beginning of the nineteenth century. The 1834 Committee on Lighthouses stated in their report that at that time there were in England and Wales (excluding floating lights) 42 lighthouses belonging to Trinity House, 3 lighthouses leased by Trinity House and in charge of individuals; 7 lighthouses leased by the Crown to individuals; 4 lighthouses in the hands of proprietors, held originally under patents and subsequently sanctioned by Acts of Parliament; or 56 in total, of which 14 were run by private individuals and organizations.[22] Between 1820 and 1834, Trinity House had built 9 new lighthouses, had purchased 5 lighthouses leased to individuals (in the case of Burnham, replacing the one purchased by building two lighthouses not counted in the 9 new built lighthouses) and had purchased 3 lighthouses owned by Greenwich Hospital (which acquired the lighthouses by bequest in 1719, they having been built by Sir John Meldrum about 1634). The position in 1820 was that there were 24 lighthouses operated by Trinity House and 22 by private individuals or organizations.[23] But many of the Trinity House lighthouses had not been built originally by them but had been acquired by purchase or as the result of the expiration of a lease (of which the Eddystone Lighthouse is an example, the lease having expired in 1804). Of the 24 lighthouses operated by Trinity House in 1820, 12 had been acquired as a result of the falling in of the lease while one had been taken over from the Chester Council in 1816, so that only 11 out of the 46 lighthouses in existence in 1820 had been originally built by Trinity House while 34 had been built by private individuals.[24]

Since the main building activity of Trinity House started at the end of the eighteenth century, the dominance of private lighthouses was even more marked in earlier periods. Writing of the position in 1786, D. A. Stevenson says:

> It is difficult to assess the attitude of Trinity House towards the English coastal lighthouses at this time. Judging by its actions and not by its protestations, the determination of the Corporation to erect lighthouses had never been strong: before 1806, whenever possible it had passed on to lessees the duty of erecting them. In 1786 it controlled lighthouses at 4 places: at Caister and Lowestoft (both managed in virtue of its local buoyage dues), and at Winterton and Scilly (both erected by the Corporation to thwart individuals keen to profit from dues under Crown patents).[25]

[21] This account of the building and rebuilding of the Eddystone lighthouse is based on Stevenson, op. cit., pp. 113–26.

[22] See Report from the Select Committee on Lighthouses, in Parl. Papers Sess. 1834, vol. 12, p. vi (Reports from Committees, vol. 8) [hereinafter cited as "1834 Report"].

[23] Ibid. p. vii.

[24] Of the 24 lighthouses operated by Trinity House in 1820, Foulness (1), Portland (2), Caskets (3), Eddystone (1), Lizard (2), St. Bees (1) and Milford (2), appear to have been acquired by the falling in of the leases and to have been built, as well as operated, by private individuals. This is based on information contained in D. Alan Stevenson, op. cit. I have assumed, when a patent for a lighthouse was obtained by Trinity House and was then leased to a private individual, that the construction was undertaken and paid for by that individual which appears to have been the case. See Stevenson, pp. 253, 261.

[25] Ibid., p. 65.

However, by 1834, as we have seen, there were 56 lighthouses in total and Trinity House operated 42 of them. And there was strong support in Parliament for the proposal that Trinity House purchase the remaining lighthouses in private hands. This had been suggested by a Select Committee of the House of Commons in 1822, and Trinity House began shortly afterwards to buy out certain of the private interests in lighthouses. In 1836, an Act of Parliament vested all lighthouses in England in Trinity House, which was empowered to purchase the remaining lighthouses in private hands.[26] This was accomplished by 1842, after which date there were no longer any privately owned lighthouses, apart from "local lights," in England.

The purchase by Trinity House between 1823 and 1832 of the remainder of the leases that it had granted for Flatholm, Ferns, Burnham and North and South Forelands cost about £74,000.[27] The rest of the private lighthouses were purchased following the 1836 Act for just under £1,200,000, the largest sums being paid for the Smalls lighthouse, for which the lease had 41 years to run and for three lighthouses, Tynemouth, Spurn, and Skerries, for which the grant had been made in perpetuity by Act of Parliament. The sums paid for these four lighthouses were: Smalls, £170,000; Tynemouth, £125,000; Spurn, £330,000; Skerries, £445,000.[28] These are large sums, the £445,000 paid for Skerries being equivalent (according to a high authority) to $7–10 million today, which would probably have produced (owing to the lower level of taxation) a considerably higher income than today. Thus we find examples of men who were not only, in Samuelson's words, "odd enough to try to make a fortune running a lighthouse business," but actually succeeded in doing so.

The reasons why there was such strong support for this consolidation of lighthouses in the hands of Trinity House can be learned from the Report of the Select Committee of the House of Commons of 1834:

> Your committee have learned with some surprise that the Lighthouse Establishments have been conducted in the several parts of the United Kingdom under entirely different systems; different as regards the constitution of the Boards of Management, different as regards the Rates or Amount of the Light Dues, and different in the principle on which they are levied. They have found that these Establishments, of such importance to the extensive Naval and Commercial Interests of the Kingdom, instead of being conducted under the immediate superintendence of the Government, upon one uniform system, and under responsible Public Servants, with proper foresight to provide for the safety of the Shipping in the most efficient manner, and on the most economical plans, have been left to spring up, as it were by slow degrees, as the local wants required, often after disastrous losses at sea; and it may, perhaps, be considered as matter of reproach to this great country, that for ages past, as well as at the present time, a considerable portion of the establishments of Lighthouses have been made the means of heavily taxing the Trade of the country, for the benefit of a few private individuals, who have been favoured with that advantage by the Ministers and the Sovereign of the day.

[26] An Act for vesting Lighthouses, Lights, and Sea Marks on the Coasts of England in the Corporation of Trinity House of Deptford Strond, 6 & 7 Will 4, c.79 (1836).

[27] 1834 Report, p. vii.

[28] Report from the Select Committee on Lighthouses, in Parl. Papers Sess. 1845, vol. 9, p. vi [hereinafter cited as "1845 Report"].

Your Committee cannot consider it warrantable in Government, at any time, unnecessarily to tax any branch of the Industry of the Country; and particularly unwarrantable to tax the Shipping, which lies under many disadvantages, in being obliged to support unequal competition with the Shipping of other countries. Your Committee are of opinion that the Shipping ought, on very special grounds, to be relieved from every local and unequal tax not absolutely necessary for the services for which it is ostensibly levied.

Your Committee, therefore, strongly recommend that the Light Dues should in every case be reduced to the smallest sums requisite to maintain the existing Lighthouses and Floating Lights, or to establish and maintain such new Establishments as shall be required for the benefit of the Commerce and Shipping of the country.

Your Committee have, further to express their regret that so little attention should have been paid by the competent authorities to the continued exaction, contrary to the principle just expressed, of very large sums which have been annually levied, avowedly, as Light Dues, to defray the expenses of Lighthouses but, in reality, to be applied to the use of a few favoured individuals, and for other purposes not contemplated at the time of the establishment of the Lighthouses. It further appears particularly objectionable to have continued these abuses by the renewal of the Leases of several Lighthouses, after a Select Committee of this House had called the particular attention of Parliament, 12 years ago, to the subject.[29]

Although there was emphasis in this report on the untidiness of the then existing arrangements and suggestions (here and elsewhere) that some of the private lighthouses were not run efficiently, there can be little doubt that the main reason why the consolidation of lighthouses under Trinity House received such strong support was that it was thought that it would lead to lower light dues. The suggestion was, of course, made that lighthouses should be paid for out of the public treasury,[30] which would lead to the abolition of light dues, but this was not done and we need not discuss it here.

It is not apparent why it was thought that the consolidation of lighthouses under Trinity House would lower light dues. There is some basis for this view in the theory of complementary monopolies, but Cournot did not publish his analysis until 1838 and it could not have affected the views of those concerned with British lighthouses even if they were quicker to appreciate the significance of Cournot's analysis than the economics profession itself.[31] In any case, there were good reasons for thinking that little, if any, reduction in light dues would follow the consolidation. Since compensation was to be paid to the former owners of lighthouses, the same amount of money would need to be raised as before. And, as was pointed out by Trinity House, since "the Dues were mortgaged as security for the repayment of the money borrowed . . . the Dues cannot be taken off until the debt shall be discharged."[32] In

---

[29] 1834 Report, pp. iii–iv.

[30] For example, the Select Committee on Lighthouses of 1845 recommended. "That all expenses for the erection and maintenance of Lighthouses . . . be henceforth defrayed out of the public revenue." 1845 Report, p. xii.

[31] See Augustin Cournot, *Researches into the Mathematical Principles of the Theory of Wealth* (Nathaniel T. Bacon trans., 1897) pp. 99–104. See also Marshall's discussion of Cournot's analysis, *Principles of Economics* (9th Variorum) edn, 1961) vol. 1, pp. 493–5.

[32] 1845 Report, p. vii.

fact, the light dues were not reduced until after 1848, when the loans were paid off.[33]

Another way in which some reduction in light dues could have been achieved would have been for Trinity House not to earn a net income from the operation of its own lighthouses. This money was, of course, devoted to charitable purposes, mainly the support of retired seamen, their widows and orphans. Such a use of funds derived ultimately from the light dues had been found objectionable by Parliamentary Committees in 1822 and 1834. The 1834 Committee, noting that 142 persons were supported in almshouses and that 8,431 men, women and children received sums ranging from 36 shillings to £30 per annum, proposed that all pensions cease with the lives of those then receiving them and that no new pensioners be appointed, but this was not done.[34]

In 1853, the Government proposed that the proceeds of the light dues no longer be used for charitable purposes. Trinity House responded, in a representation to Her Majesty, claiming that this income was as much its property as it was for private proprietors of lighthouses (to whom compensation was paid):

The management of lighthouses has been entrusted to [Trinity House], from time to time, by special grants from the Crown or the Legislature. But the acceptance of such grants has in no respect changed the legal position of the Corporation as a private guild, except in so far as it has necessitated the maintenance of lights as a condition of retaining such grants. The legal position of the Corporation with regard to the Crown and the public has in no respect differed from that of individual grantees of light dues or other franchises, as markets, ports, fairs, etc. The argument that the Corporation was ever legally bound to reduce the light dues to the amount of the expenses of maintenance, inclusive or exclusive of interest on the cost of erection, and that they had no right to make any other appropriation, is altogether unfounded in reason or law . . . a grant is valid, if the dues granted are reasonable at the time of the grant, and continues so valid, notwithstanding that from a subsequent increase of shipping the dues may afford a profit. The Crown in these cases acts on behalf of the public; and if it makes a bargain, reasonable at the time, it cannot afterwards retract. . . . The title of the Corporation to the lighthouses erected by them is equally valid with the titles [of private proprietors], and the charitable purposes to which a portion of those revenues is applied, render the claims of the Corporation at least as deserving of favourable consideration as those of individuals . . . The lighthouses and light dues belong to [Trinity House], for the purposes of the Corporation, and are, in the strictest sense, their property for those purposes . . . The proposal of Her Majesty's Government appears to be that the use of the whole of this vast mass of property shall be given to the shipowners, without any charge beyond the expense of maintaining the lights. It is, as affecting the Corporation's charities, an alienation of property, devoted to the benefit of the decayed masters and seamen of the merchant's service, and their families, and a gift of that property to the shipowners.[35]

[33] T. Golding, *Trinity House from Within* (1929), p. 63.
[34] 1834 Report, p. xiii.
[35] Trinity House Charities: Representation from the Corporation of the Trinity House to Her Majesty in Council, on proposal of Government to prevent the Application of Light and Other Dues to Charitable Purposes, in Parl. Papers Sess. 1852–3, vol. 98, pp. 601, 602–3.

This representation was referred to the Board of Trade, which found the arguments of Trinity House without merit:

> The Lords of the Committee do not call in question the title of the Corporation of the Trinity House to the property so alleged to be vested in them; but there is . . . this distinction between the case of the Corporation and that of the individuals referred to, that the property so vested in the Corporation has been held and is held by them, so far at least as relates to the light dues in question, in trust for public purposes, and liable, therefore, to be dealt with upon considerations of public policy. Their Lordships cannot admit that is any violation of the principle of property in the reduction of a tax levied for public purposes, where no vested interests have been acquired in the proceeds of the tax; and where the tax in question is one levied upon a particular class of Your Majesty's subjects, without that class deriving any adequate advantage in return (and any excess of light dues beyond the amount necessary to maintain the lights is a tax of this character), the reduction of such a tax not only involves no violation of the principle of property, but is in the highest degree just and expedient. Their Lordships cannot recognise any vested interests in the expectants of the bounty dealt out to poor mariners and their families, at the pleasure of the Corporation, from the surplus revenues of the lights; since it is of the essence of a vested interest that the individuals to whom the privilege is secured are ascertained and known to the law; and while their Lordships would religiously abstain from interfering in the slightest degree with the pensions or other benefits already conferred upon any person whatsoever, they can acknowledge no injustice in resolving, upon grounds of public policy, to confer upon no new persons a right, to which at present no individual can advance any claim or title . . . Their Lordships consider that the lights should be maintained by the light dues; and that what the providence of former generations has done in applying dues levied upon ships to the erection of lights for the preservation of ships from shipwreck, is the natural and just inheritance of those who navigate the coasts of the United Kingdom at the present time, and ought to be freely enjoyed by them at the lowest possible charge which the circumstances of the case may permit, and that no other consideration whatever should on any account be suffered to enter into the question.[36]

The use of the proceeds of the light dues for charitable purposes ceased in 1853. As a result, some reduction in the light dues was made possible, price moved closer to marginal cost and numerous ancient mariners and their families, unknown to the law and to us, were worse provided for. But it will be observed that it was not necessary to have a consolidation of all lighthouses under Trinity House to bring about this result.

This change was part of the reorganization which, in 1853, established the Mercantile Marine Fund, into which the light dues (and certain other monies) were paid and out of which the expenses of running the lighthouse service and some other expenses incurred on behalf of shipping were met.[37] In 1898, the system was again changed. The Mercantile Marine Fund was abolished and the General Lighthouse Fund was set up. The light dues (and only the light dues) were paid into this fund, which was to be used solely for the maintenance of the lighthouse service. At

---

[36] Ibid., pp. 605–6.
[37] The Merchant Shipping Law Amendment Act 1853, 16 & 17 Vic., c.131 §§ 3–30.

the same time, the system for computing the light dues was simplified, the charge made on each voyage no longer depending, as it had before, on the number of lighthouses which a ship passed or from which it could be presumed to derive a benefit.[38] What was established in 1898 was essentially the present system of lighthouse finance and administration described in section II. There have, of course, been changes in detail but the general character of the system has remained the same since 1898.

## IV   CONCLUSION

The sketch of the British lighthouse system and its evolution in sections II and III shows how limited are the lessons to be drawn from the remarks of Mill, Sidgwick and Pigou. Mill seems to be saying that if something like the British system for the finance and administration of lighthouses is not instituted, private operation of lighthouses would be impossible (which is not how most modern readers would be likely to interpret him). Sidgwick and Pigou argue that if there are ships which benefit from the lighthouse but on which tolls cannot be levied, then government intervention may be called for. But the ships which benefit from British lighthouses but do not pay would presumably be, in the main, those operated by foreign shipowners which do not call at British ports. In which case, it is not clear what the character of the required government action is or what governments are supposed to act. Should, for example, the Russian, Norwegian, German and French governments compel their nationals to pay the toll even though their ships do not call at British ports or should these governments take action by paying a sum raised out of general taxation into the British General Lighthouse Fund? Or is the British government supposed to take action by raising revenue out of general taxation to be paid into the Lighthouse Fund to offset the failure of these foreign governments to compel their nationals to contribute to the Lighthouse Fund?

Now consider what would be likely to happen if support out of general taxation were substituted for the light dues (which seems to be what Samuelson would like). First of all, it would increase the extent to which the British Government and particularly the Treasury would feel obliged to supervise the operations of the lighthouse service, in order to keep under control the amount of the subsidy. This intervention of the Treasury would tend to reduce somewhat the efficiency with which the lighthouse service was administered. And it would have another effect. Because the revenue is now raised from the consumers of the service, a committee has been established, the Lights Advisory Committee, representing Shipowners,

---

[38] Merchant Shipping (Mercantile Marine Fund) Act 1898, 61 & 62 Vic., c44. See the Committee of Inquiry into the Mercantile Marine Fund, Report, Cd 8167 (1896), also found in Parl. Papers Sess. 1896, vol. 41, p. 113, for the reasons why this change was made in the way light dues were computed. The recommendations of this Committee were adopted by the Government and were incorporated in the 1898 Act. Objections to the old system arose because the list of lighthouses from which ships were presumed to benefit on a given voyage was based on the course of a sailing ship rather than that of a steamship, because the foreign rate was charged to the last port reached in the United Kingdom in the course of a voyage and not to the first, while much was made of the complexity of the old method of calculating the dues.

Underwriters and Shippers, which is consulted about the budget, the operations of the service and particularly about new works. In this way, the lighthouse service is made more responsive to those who make use of its service and because it is the shipping industry which actually pays for additional services, they will presumably support changes in the arrangements only when the value of the additional benefits received is greater than the cost. This administrative arrangement would presumably be discarded if the service were financed out of general taxation and the service would therefore become somewhat less efficient.[39] In general, it would seem to be a safe conclusion that the move to support the lighthouse service out of general taxation would result in a less appropriate administrative structure. And what is the gain which Samuelson sees as coming from this change in the way in which the lighthouse service is financed? It is that some ships which are now discouraged from making a voyage to Britain because of the light dues would in future do so. As it happens, the form of the toll and the exemptions mean that for most ships the number of voyages will not be affected by the fact that light dues are paid.[40] There may be some ships somewhere which are laid up or broken up because of the light dues, but the number cannot be great, if indeed there are any ships in this category.[41] It is difficult for me to resist the conclusion that the benefit

---

[39] The Chairman of the Committee of Inquiry into the Mercantile Marine Fund (see note 38 above), was Leonard Courtney, M.P. Mr. Courtney, who was an economist, made essentially the same point in the debate in the House of Commons. Replying to those who had suggested that the lighthouse service should be supported out of general taxation, Mr. Courtney commented: "there is one substantial argument in favour of our maintaining the service as it is, and that is that there is an impression among shipowners – and it is a very useful one – that they have to bear the burden, and they are extremely jealous of the expenditure, and they would claim hereafter, if not now, a share in the administration; that is to say, that they being the people called upon to pay in the first instance, scrutinise the expenditure in which they are interested, and jealously guard it. This is a great advantage, and I conceive that by it economy and efficiency in the coast light service are obtained, and I think that to change a system which secures a frugal and yet sufficient administration of the service would be most inexpedient. The shipowners are jealously watching the whole of the administration, and they claim, I think justly, to have a voice in the matter conceded them. If the cost of lighting the coasts were thrown directly upon the Votes every year, there would not be the same check as is now existing upon unbounded demands which might be made in those ebullitions of feeling to which the nation is always exposed after some great maritime calamity," 40 Parl. Deb. (4th ser.) 186–7 (1898). That is to say, Mr. Courtney was arguing that the method of finance meant that the shipowners were led to exercise at this early date the same influence over expenditures as is now exercised through the Lights Advisory Committee.

[40] There is no further liability for light dues after the first ten voyages in a year for "home-trade" ships and the first six voyages for "foreign-going" ships. It seems to be the opinion of those conversant with the shipping industry that the vast majority of ships will not need to pay light dues on their last voyages in the year. A cross-channel ferry could probably meet the requisite number of journeys in a few days. Ships trading with Europe or North America will normally not be required to pay light dues on their last voyages. However, the ships trading with Australia will usually not be able to complete the number of voyages necessary to avoid light dues.

[41] I have not been able to secure any precise figures but all indications are that light dues form a very small proportion of the costs of running a ship trading with the United Kingdom. Such statistics as exist support this view. Payments into the General Lighthouse Fund in 1971–2 were £8,900,000. General Lighthouse Fund 1971–2, H.C. Paper no. 301 (in cont. of H.C. Paper no. 211) at 2 (July 3, 1973). In 1971, the earnings of ships owned by U.K. operators and of ships on charter to them for carrying U.K. imports and exports, visitors to the U.K. and U.K. residents were about £700 million. In addition, about £50 million was earned in the U.K. coastal trade. Payments to foreign shipowners for carrying U.K. imports and exports were probably of the order of £600 million in 1971. This suggests that the annual costs of running ships trading with the U.K. must have been about £1,400 million. These estimates are based on figures kindly supplied to me by the Department of Trade. Some of the separate figures

which would come from the abandonment of the light dues would be very unimportant and that there would be some loss from the change in the administrative structure.

The question remains: how is it that these great men have, in their economic writings, been led to make statements about lighthouses which are misleading as to the facts, whose meaning, if thought about in a concrete fashion, is quite unclear, and which, to the extent that they imply a policy conclusion, are very likely wrong? The explanation is that these references by economists to lighthouses are not the result of their having made a study of lighthouses or having read a detailed study by some other economist. Despite the extensive use of the lighthouse example in the literature, no economist, to my knowledge, has ever made a comprehensive study of lighthouse finance and administration. The lighthouse is simply plucked out of the air to serve as an illustration. The purpose of the lighthouse example is to provide "corroborative detail, intended to give artistic verisimilitude to an otherwise bald and unconvincing narrative."[42]

This seems to me to be the wrong approach. I think we should try to develop generalizations which would give us guidance as to how various activities should best be organized and financed. But such generalizations are not likely to be helpful unless they are derived from studies of how such activities are actually carried out within different institutional frameworks. Such studies would enable us to discover which factors are important and which are not in determining the outcome and would lead to generalizations which have a solid base. They are also likely to serve another purpose, by showing us the richness of the social alternatives between which we can choose.

The account in this paper of the British lighthouse system does little more than reveal some of the possibilities. The early history shows that, contrary to the belief of many economists, a lighthouse service can be provided by private enterprise. In those days, shipowners and shippers could petition the Crown to allow a private individual to construct a lighthouse and to levy a (specified) toll on ships benefitting from it. The lighthouses were built, operated, financed and owned by private individuals, who could sell the lighthouse or dispose of it by bequest. The role of the government was limited to the establishment and enforcement of property rights in the lighthouse. The charges were collected at the ports by agents for the lighthouses. The problem of enforcement was no different for them than for other suppliers of goods and services to the shipowner. The property rights were unusual only in that they stipulated the price that could be charged.[43]

---

brought together to obtain these totals are very rough estimates but they give the order of magnitude and whatever error they contain would not affect the conclusion that payments into the General Lighthouse Fund form a very small proportion of the cost of running a ship trading with the U.K.

[42] William S. Gilbert, *The Mikado*.

[43] This arrangement avoided a problem raised by Arrow in discussing the lighthouse example. Arrow says: "In my view, the standard lighthouse example is best analysed as a problem of small numbers rather than of the difficulty of exclusion though both elements are present. To simplify matters, I will abstract from uncertainty so that the lighthousekeeper knows exactly when each ship will need its services, and also abstract from indivisibility (since the light is either on or off). Assume further that only one ship will be within range of the lighthouse at any moment. Then exclusion is perfectly possible; the lighthouse need only shut off its light when a nonpaying ship is coming into range. But there would be only one buyer and one seller and no competitive forces to drive the two into a competitive

Later, the provision of lighthouses in England and Wales was entrusted to Trinity House, a private organisation with public duties, but the service continued to be financed by tolls levied on ships. The system apparently favoured by Samuelson, finance by the government out of general taxation, has never been tried in Britain. Such a government-financed system does not necessarily exclude the participation of private enterprise in the building or operation of lighthouses but it would seem to preclude private ownership of lighthouses, except in a very attenuated form and would certainly be quite different from the system in Britain which came to an end in the 1830s. Of course, government finance would be very likely to involve both government operation and government ownership of lighthouses. How such governmental systems actually operate I do not know. Bierce's definition of an American lighthouse – "A tall building on the seashore in which the government maintains a lamp and the friend of a politician"[44] – presumably does not tell the whole story.

We may conclude that economists should not use the lighthouse as an example of a service which could only be provided by the government. But this paper is not intended to settle the question of how lighthouse service ought to be organized and financed. This must await more detailed studies. In the meantime, economists wishing to point to a service which is best provided by the government should use an example which has a more solid backing.

---

equilibrium. If in addition the costs of bargaining are high, then it may be most efficient to offer the service free." See Kenneth J. Arrow, "The Organization of Economic Activity: Issues Pertinent to the Choice of Market Versus Nonmarket Allocation," in U.S. Cong., Jt. Econ. Comm., Subcomm. on Economy in Government, 91st Cong., 1st Sess., *The Analysis and Evaluation of Public Expenditures: the PPB System*, vol. 1, pp. 47, 58 (*J. Comm. Print*, 1969). Arrow's surrealist picture of a lighthousekeeper shutting off the light as soon as it became useful while arguing with the captain about the charge to be made (assuming that the vessel has not run on the rocks in the meantime) bears no relation to the situation faced by those responsible for lighthouse policy. In Britain, no negotiation has been required to determine individual charges and no lighthousekeeper has ever turned off the light for this purpose. Arrow's conclusion that "it may be most efficient to offer the service free" is unexceptionable but also unhelpful since it is equally true that it may not.

[44] Ambrose Bierce, *The Devil's Dictionary* (1925), p. 193.

# 2

# The Voluntary Provision of Public Goods? The Turnpike Companies of Early America

*Daniel B. Klein**

## I

The heroic role of the agent called "government" in the simple public-goods model is clear enough, but the relevance of the model is still in dispute. A long history of doubters has challenged the premises that the government has the needed information, acts efficiently, and acts in the public interest. Also, doubters have contended that the free-rider problem of many social services is not as ineluctable as others often seem to suggest. Historical studies have shown the potency of voluntary association in such fields as lighthouse provision (Coase 1974), education (High and Ellig 1988), bee pollination (Cheung 1973), law and order (Anderson and Hill 1979; Benson 1989), neighborhood infrastructure (Beito 1990), agricultural research (Majewski 1989), among others (see Cowen 1988; Wooldridge 1970).

To help weigh the relevance of the simple public-goods model I discuss the American experience of private turnpike roads. The turnpike companies got started in the 1790s and were in sharp decline in the 1830s, though many turnpikes were operating at the turn of the twentieth century.[1] I treat turnpikes in New England, New York, Pennsylvania, New Jersey, and Maryland (the last four are called the "Middle Atlantic states"). Except in Pennsylvania,[2] the turnpikes were almost

* For constructive feedback, I thank Christopher Baer, Thomas Borcherding, Tyler Cowen, Walter Grinder, Bob Higgs, Jack High, Randy Kroszner, Timur Kuran, Don Lavoie, John Majewski, Janusz Ordover, Sheldon Richman, Ronald Seavoy, Jeremy Shearmur, David St. Clair, and Lawrence H. White. I also wish to thank those at historical societies, libraries, and archives who have helped me with this research. For financial assistance I thank the Institute for Humane Studies at George Mason University the Institute of Transportation Studies at UC-Irvine, the Austrian Economics program at New York University, and the C.V. Starr Center for Applied Economic Research at New York University.

[1] Especially in New Jersey, Maryland, and Pennsylvania. In later days turnpikes were numerous but shorter.

[2] In 1806 the Pennsylvania state government began subsidizing turnpikes by purchasing stock. In 1822 it held about 30 percent of the collective stock of the turnpike companies. See Durrenberger (1931: 55, 102).

entirely financed by private subscription to stock,[3] while those in most other states were mixed enterprises.[4]

Extreme publicness marked the turnpikes, both in jointness of consumption and in nonexcludability.[5] The excludability problem was partly the result of legal restrictions on toll collection. These restrictions were one cause of turnpike unprofitability, which was discovered quickly. The turnpikes afforded enormous indirect and external benefits, however, to the nearby farms, landholdings, and businesses. Since unprofitability was usually foreseen, stock subscription – necessary to construct the road – was essentially a means of paying for road benefits. There were two excludability problems: people could use the road without paying a toll, and people could indirectly benefit from the road without buying stock. Though related, the latter is the crux of the public-goods problem at hand.[6]

## II

## Turnpike creation and operation

The end of the eighteenth century saw a transition in road management. Until then, the roads were built and maintained, poorly, by towns and counties. As settlement expanded and the large Eastern centers sought improved trade routes, pressure for road improvement brought forth a radical alternative: turnpikes, a pay-as-you-go means of financing. A number of publicly operated turnpikes were organized, patterned after the British turnpike trusts of the day,[7] but even this method of road improvement demanded too much from the existing public administration. States turned to private initiative.[8]

The turnpike companies were legally organized like corporate businesses of the day. The first, connecting Philadelphia and Lancaster, was chartered in 1792, opened

---

[3] According to Durrenberger, there were four minor instances of state aid made in the states of New Jersey, New York, and Maryland, which combined amounted to $42,500, a minuscule sum relative to private investment (a small fraction of one percent) (1931: 98). The city of Albany subscribed to 100 shares of the (First) Great Western Turnpike Road, which accounted for no more than 7.5 percent of the company stock as of the middle of 1802; see Book I of Subscribers (BV Sec. Great Western), New York Historical Society. Parks (1966: 72–3) mentions a "few instances" of town aid in New England.

[4] G. Taylor (1951: 23–6) gives summary information on the turnpikes of Virginia, South Carolina, Ohio, Kentucky, and the lower South. The turnpike literature on the states outside New England, the Middle states, Maryland, and Virginia is minimal. Delaware seems to have had a few turnpikes which may well have been entirely privately financed. The best work on Virginia's substantial system of mixed enterprise is Hunter (1957).

[5] These two factors combined with an omniscient, omnipotent, and Paretian government and no further complications constitutes "the simple public goods model." The classic presentations are of the model in Samuelson (1954, 1955).

[6] For a discussion of the political decisions concerning the turnpikes, see Klein and Majewski (1988b).

[7] Like the American system, the British system of turnpike trusts was decentralized. However, the trusts were public bodies, borrowed to construct their roads, and performed better financially. See Pawson (1977).

[8] On road management prior to the turnpikes and the beginning of the turnpike era, see the two most important works on the turnpikes: Durrenberger (1931: 9–26) and Taylor (1934: 1–135); see also Ringwalt (1966 [1888]: 22–7). On the attempt at public turnpikes see Durrenberger (1931: 97); Taylor (1934: 122–5) and Hollifield (1978: 2–3).

in 1794, and proved a significant advantage in the competition for trade. Regional rivalries led state legislatures to take a favorable view toward petitions to establish turnpikes. By 1800, sixty-nine companies had been chartered in the states under investigation.[9]

While legislators readily sanctioned road provision by private associations, they wrote extensive regulation into company charters. Charters usually specified the company's total stock, but this merely reflected the company's recommendation and could be changed easily. Powers of eminent domain were stipulated, existing trails or public roadbeds were usually granted to the companies, and monopoly assurance against new parallel routes was sometimes granted. Details for construction were given, and, of course, toll rates and toll collection were tightly controlled. In most cases turnpikes were individually regulated, but on the major points all the states imposed similar regulations. Inspection and enforcement were assigned to state-appointed commissioners or county officials. While the companies abided strictly by the financial regulations, maintenance often did not live up to stipulations, and the local inspection machinery was known to be lenient.[10]

In some states the theory was that toll rates would be increased if dividends fell short of the low mark (usually 6, 8, or 10 percent of investment) or decreased if dividends surpassed the high mark (usually 10, 12 or 15 percent) (Durrenberger 1931: 111). In fact, in all states dividends persisted far short of the low mark; but, with rare exception, toll rates remained at their initial levels (P. Taylor 1934: 152). The legislature did not renege on its promise.[11] Rather, it was common for a company simply not to apply for toll increases.

There are two possible explanations for the absence of rate increases. The first is that the companies may have been responding to the unseemliness of making a profit from turnpike stock; this interpretation can be seen behind some of the discussion to follow.

Second, turnpikes could not have much enhanced returns by increasing toll rates because of the many concessions to local travelers. Charters required that toll gates be five or, more often, ten miles apart, permitting much traffic to go toll-free. Another means of free travel was the proliferation of informal routes bypassing the gate, known as shunpikes.[12] The location of a gate was set by the legislature and could be altered only by separate legislative enactment. Had turnpikes been free to multiply and relocate gates they could have better combatted shunpiking. Finally, there was the toll exemption. Typical exemptions included those traveling "on the common and ordinary business of family concerns," to or from public worship, a

[9] See Klein and Majewski (1988b) for a table of turnpike chartering from 1792 to 1845 in the states under consideration.

[10] On lax inspection see Durrenberger (1931: 94) and Taylor (1934: 112). For greater detail on the regulation of the turnpikes, see Klein and Majewski (1988b).

[11] New England states did not always set explicit profit margins, but the states were willing to change tolls for companies in financial distress. The Massachusetts General Turnpike Law, 1805, chap. 79, for example, makes no mention of legal profit margins. For an example of margins explicitly set in New England, see Wood (1919: 218). On the legislature not reneging see Durrenberger (1931: 155); Taylor (1934: 140, 152), Handlin and Handlin (1947: 120).

[12] Durrenberger (1931: 178) and Taylor (1934: 200–4) discuss the role of shunpikes. Turnpike president Fisher Ames reported that his company's revenues would be about 60 percent greater if not for shunpikes (Parks 1966: 154).

town meeting, a gristmill, a blacksmith's shop, and on military duty and those "residing within one mile of . . . [the] gate."[13] Gatekeepers found it troublesome to deny exemption and were forced to adopt a lenient attitude (Taylor 1934: 147). Under such conditions, higher tolls would not have increased revenue because travelers passing for free would not have paid higher tolls, and those inclined toward toll evasion would have done so more often. In addition, a small fraction of the through-traffic would have opted for public roads or other forms of transportation.

## Unprofitability

The first piece of our public-goods story is the nearly universal and well-documented poverty of the turnpikes.[14] Of the Middle Atlantic states, Durrenberger (1931: 112) says, "[c]onsidered from the standpoint of dividends, turnpike stocks were exceedingly poor investments," and of the many turnpikes of New England, Taylor (1934: 266) says, "it is doubtful whether more than five or six paid their proprietors even reasonably well." Though information from the period is fragmentary, Taylor (1934: 281) finds that turnpike dividends in New England were far below those of other enterprises:

> [I]t is quite obvious that no possible selection of turnpike companies could compare in earning power . . . Between the years 1825 and 1855, six of the largest textile factories in Massachusetts produced average yearly dividends ranging from 6.48% to 12.79%. The Massachusetts bank averaged 6.53% annual return on its capital investment from 1785 to 1855, while the Union bank produced an average of 6.91% between 1795 and 1855. Three Boston insurance companies doing fire and marine business produced annual dividends averaging 8.38%, 15.44%, and 20.34% during the period 1818–55.

In contrast, even the undiscounted total net payment of a turnpike was commonly negative. References to average yearly dividends usually put the figure barely above zero.[15] In Pennsylvania the state held a peak of $2 million in turnpike stocks, but

---

[13] The first quote comes from "General Powers of Turnpike Corporations," Law of Mass., 1805, chap. 79, 649; the second is from New York's general law, 1807, chap. 38, 56.

[14] A small number of turnpikes managed to consistently pay dividends above 3 percent (see Taylor 1934: 277; Durrenberger 1931: 113–15; Hollifield 1978: 4; Parks 1966: 127–32). Due to low initial expenditures, Connecticut turnpikes did much better than those elsewhere according to Taylor (1934: 190) and Parks (1966: 91–9).

[15] Tufts (1834: 867), a Massachusetts correspondent of Albert Gallatin (U.S. Secretary of Treasury, 1801–13), said in 1807 that aside from two turnpikes, "all the other turnpikes in the State will not, upon an average, yield more than 3 percent per annum, net income." In 1828, a report on Pennsylvania turnpikes said, "[n]one have yielded dividends sufficient to remunerate the proprietors. Most of them have yielded little more than expenditures for repairs" (quoted in Durrenberger 1931: 113–14). Bloodgood (1838: 97) remarks of the turnpikes of New York: "Generally they have never remunerated their proprietors, nor paid much more than the expense of actual repairs."

The fragmentary statistics in Taylor (1934: 270–1, 276–7) for fifteen companies show dividends for a combined 427 years of operation. All the companies are from Massachusetts, Connecticut, and Rhode Island; the figure for the Hingham & Quincy corporation is excluded because it operated a lucrative toll bridge in connection with a short piece of road. I calculated the average annual dividend to be 2.9 percent; Taylor evidently felt it was meaningless to calculate a summary figure, the reason surely being "annual dividends accruing from that investment invariably totalled less than $5,000" (one-fourth of 1 percent; see Hartz 1948: 92). Once we take into account assessments (occasional company demands on stockholders for additional payments), it is not clear whether yearly "earnings" for many turnpikes were even positive.[16] Moreover, the capital value of the stock was usually completely lost. The little trading that occurred was almost always on terms well below par. "Turnpike stock within a few years usually sold at far below its original cost."[17]

Turnpikes usually reverted to public control through abandonment. By that time the stock was usually worthless, and the owners were eager to relieve themselves of the responsibility of maintaining the road. Rarely was any compensation made to road investors. It appears that in all of New England only two turnpike companies recouped their original investments when they reverted to the public.[18] In fact, only 5 percent of the New England turnpikes received any compensation whatever when they surrendered their franchises.[19] It is quite safe to say that in the vast majority of cases turnpike stock was an abysmal investment.

## "Clear from the beginning"

[I]t seems to have been generally known long before the rush of construction subsided that turnpike stock was worthless (Wood 1919: 63).

[T]he turnpikes did not make money. As a whole this was true; as a rule it was clear from the beginning (Kirkland 1948: 45).

If we wish to show that the turnpikes were public goods and that stock subscription was, in essence, a voluntary contribution, it is incumbent to show not only that turnpike stock was a bad investment but also that investors expected as much.

---

that the sample is undoubtedly biased. It is much more likely that records would be preserved in a case where dividends were paid than where they were not. A strong indication of the bias is that for nine other companies in the tables no dividend figures are recorded, but in a separate column each one reports such comments as "$9660.35 net loss," "income . . . ceased to pay expenses," "have never been able to make but one dividend, and that at the rate of two percent," and "of but Little Profit to your Petitioners."

Thus, the fragmentary evidence and, more importantly, the impressions of contemporary observers, suggest that throughout the states under consideration turnpikes on average paid no more than two percent per year, *not counting the loss of capital value.*

[16] On assessments, see Taylor (1934: 159–60). Many companies simply issued no-par stock and demanded assessments as required. If assessment payments were delinquent, eventually the shares would be revoked and auctioned off. Long lists of delinquent shares can be found in *The Courier of New Hampshire* (Concord), June 11, 1804; October 23, 1808.

[17] Parks (1967: 19). Taylor (1934: 273) and Parks (1966: 119–20) detail rapidly falling stock prices. The great Pennsylvania auction of state-owned assets in 1843 gives a clear picture of the capital value of turnpike stock at that time. A total of 48,956 shares in scores of turnpike companies were put up for auction, and 32,224 of them were not sold because they could not command a price of one dollar. The 16,732 shares that were sold commanded an average price of $3.40. The state had paid $25, $50, or $100 for them ($50 was most common). See Hartz (1948: 104, 232–8) for details of the auction.

[18] There is ambiguity on this point in that Wood (1919: 181) refers to a company which was fully compensated which Taylor (1934: 324) does not list. Since Taylor uses Wood, perhaps he found an error in Wood's report, leaving only one company that recouped its investment.

[19] The calculation is based on Taylor's figures (1934: 324) using the figure of 238 for total operating turnpikes, as explained in note 29 below.

Investor expectations resist hard documentation, but a combination of factors strongly supports the two quotations above.

It is unlikely that investors knew from the very beginning that turnpike stock would be unremunerative. The first private toll-bridge company, the Charles-River Bridge, opened in 1786, was called "the greatest effect of private enterprise in the United States."[20] Its investors were rewarded with a return of 10.5 percent annually for its first six years. Davis says, "[i]ts clear promise of financial success, justified by the dividends of its early years drew attention to the profits awaiting claimants in similar fields" (1917, II: 189; see also 216). Through 1798, about fifty-nine bridge companies were chartered in the states under consideration, principally in New England. Many of them failed and some were unprofitable, but a considerable number, especially in the Boston area, had proven themselves lucrative by the end of the century. In contrast to the turnpikes, the bridges did not suffer from toll evasion and liberal exemptions, and when profits were low they commonly obtained toll increases (Davis 1917, II: 229). Investors may not have anticipated the special problems that would plague turnpikes, so perhaps the bridge companies were an encouraging example. Also, early turnpike investors could not foresee the competitors that were to be: the steamboat, the canal, and the railroad.

After the first decade of turnpike construction all save the most foolhardy realized what turnpikes held in store. As early as 1800 the president of the First Massachusetts Turnpike wrote a letter cautioning other investors not to expect remuneration from turnpike stock (Parks 1966: 73). Similarly, former Federalist Congressmen and turnpike president Fisher Ames wrote in 1802, "[t]urnpikes with fairest prospect of success have seldom proved profitable" (quoted in Parks 1966: 74). In Connecticut, where, viewed comparatively, turnpike dividends were enviable, a newspaper article in 1805 suggests that turnpikes receive "annually on their capital, little, if any, more than half the common and established interest on money."[21]

The examples of unprofitable companies were plain as day. The few moderately profitable companies were graced with a combination of advantages: low cost in land acquisition, good condition of the pre-existing roadbed, minimal bridge building, and substantial traffic volume.[22] Any moderately alert investor could easily discover whether his town's project had similar advantages. Almost invariably it did not.[23]

Perhaps the best reason for rejecting the claim that turnpike investors were searching primarily for direct remuneration is that an alternative hypothesis presents itself.

---

[20] *Massachusetts Centinel*, May 13, 1786 (quoted in Davis 1917, II: 188).

[21] *Connecticut Courant* (Hartford), June 19, 1805, 3.

[22] Compared to the others, the Derby Turnpike, running between Derby and New Haven, was outstanding in financial performance, averaging dividends of 5.1 percent annually from 1801 to 1896 and recouping its capital investment when reverting to the public in 1897. (Note that in comparison to other businesses this performance is mediocre at best; see the Taylor passage on p. 52). Taylor (1934: 279) ascribes its success to "a combination of factors – monopolistic situation in a productive area, no land damages, and therefore low capital investment, existence of a gate almost within the limits of a large city, careful control by a close corporation – [which] combined to make this a profitable enterprise."

## The quest for indirect benefits

Although dividends were meager, indirect and external benefits were copious. Improved roads lowered transportation costs, stimulated commerce, and increased land values. Henry Clay did not overstate the point when he said

> I think it very possible that the capitalist who should invest his money in these objects [turnpikes] might not be reimbursed three percent annually upon it; and yet society in various forms, might actually reap fifteen or twenty percent. The benefit resulting from a turnpike road made by private association is divided between the capitalist, who received his toll, the land through which it passes and which is augmented in its value, and the commodities whose value is enhanced by the diminished expense of transportation.   (Quoted in Durrenberger 1931: 125)

The quest for indirect benefits is abundantly evident in contemporary writings. An essay advocating turnpike roads in New York, appearing in 1795, says that such an improvement "lays open all the unexploited resources of a country to come forth to daylight, and to a market."[24] In 1797 we find a discussion in five installments of roads and turnpikes by "A Philanthropist." He expounds at great length on the social importance of good roads and argues that turnpikes are the best means of achieving them. Benjamin De Witt, writing in 1807 of New York's turnpikes, said that turnpikes "encourage settlements, open new channels for the transportation of produce and merchandise, increase the products of agriculture, and facilitate every species of internal commerce" (1972: 215). The 1811 tract by William J. Duane "Addressed to the People of Pennsylvania" challenged the notion that

> you are more benefited by having a paltry interest from the bank, than if your money was invested in stocks for roads and canals . . ., [M]oney invested in bank stock is waste in comparison with its employment in enabling you to carry your produce and manufactures to every market; and in raising the value of your woods as well as your cleared lands.   (1811: 5)

Likewise, Fisher Ames in New England said most turnpikes were built "to facilitate country produce on its way to market."[25]

---

[23] Philip Taylor, I should note, departs appreciably from all other turnpike historians on the question of investment motive. He agrees fully that turnpikes were unprofitable, and he says, "[i]n the smaller towns, the spirit of civic unity and progress played a part not unimportant," but his central claim is thus: "First and foremost, however, remains the fact that the prospect for respectable earnings on capital investment in tollroads was good, and most investment in turnpike stock was made with that in view" (1934: 102). Taylor's support for this claim is meager – he emphasizes a few hopeful remarks about early companies and says that investors underestimated upkeep cost (1934: 99–102, 267). There is no evidence that turnpikes suffered from rapid deterioration or that maintenance needs were systematically underestimated. Taylor's work, a Ph.D. thesis in economics, view the period almost exclusively in terms of speculative fanaticism; it shows no awareness of the fanaticism for community uplift. Notice that the quotations opening this section are written by scholars who, like Taylor, are treating only New England and who straddle Taylor chronologically.

[24] "Turnpike Roads," by A Friend to Turnpikes [Elkanah Watson], *Albany Gazette*, December 27, 1795; reprinted *Albany Register*, June 13, 1796, 2.

[25] Quoted in Parks (1966: 71). See also Reed (1964: 59–61, 125, 135–7).

Less explicit evidence for the "indirect benefits" interpretation is ample. Foremost is that "[s]hares in the various companies were almost invariably owned locally, that is, in the towns through which the road passed" (Taylor 1934: 165; see Durrenberger 1931: 102). Naturally, the people in the vicinity of the turnpike would reap the most benefits. In the few cases where a sizable portion of the stock was owned by outsiders, the quest for indirect benefits is still evident. Businessmen in larger commercial centers supported routes that would bring trade. For instance, "[m]erchants and traders in New York sponsored pikes leading across New Jersey in order to tap the Delaware Valley trade which would otherwise have gone entirely to Philadelphia" (Lane 1939: 156). It might be argued that local ownership was simply a consequence of marketing the shares locally, but the "indirect benefits" interpretation seems undeniable when we consider a second factor: those who contributed were generally those who most stood to gain from the project. "With but few exceptions, the vast majority of the stockholders in turnpike were either farmers, land speculators, merchants or individuals and firms interested in commerce."[26]

As Wood notes (1919: 63),

> The conclusion is forced upon us that the larger part of the turnpikes of New England were built in hopes of benefiting the towns and local business conducted in them, counting more upon collateral results than upon the direct returns in the matter of tolls.

Similarly, Durrenberger (1931: 104) says of the Middle Atlantic states,

> subscribers were usually more interested in the possible benefits the new lines of communication would bring than in the profitableness of the investment. In other words subscriptions were frequently looked upon as contributions to effect some public improvement that would pay its chief return in an indirect manner rather than in dividends.[27]

## A public goods problem?

To what extent can we expect private initiative to have been successful in providing roads? Despite the large social benefits of the roads, it would seem that the individual could find no advantage in supporting them. Since citizens knew that turnpike stock was a poor investment, purchasing stock was like paying for the road. Once stock subscriptions were sufficient to construct the road, there would be no way to withhold the benefits of the road from those who did not contribute. The input of a single individual would not make the difference, or so it would seem. For an arbitrary sample of fifty-four turnpike towns, the average population

---

[26] Durrenberger (1931: 104); see also Ringwalt (1966 [1888]: 31) and Lane (1939: 168).

[27] Legal historian James Hurst agrees: "these highways . . . principally served the need of local economies for low return, overhead capital beneficial much more to other activities dependent on the facilities than to the immediate gain of the providers" (1982: 103).

in 1810 was 2,153, 38 percent of which had reached twenty-seven years of age.[28] If, say, half of these people stood to gain significantly from a turnpike and a turnpike engendered benefits for two towns, then 818 people were the prospective beneficiaries of a turnpike (which typically had a construction cost of $1,000 to $2,000 per mile and a length of fifteen to forty miles).[29] This is hardly a small-group situation. On the basis of narrow self-interest it would have been foolish for any one person to make a voluntary sacrifice. Turnpike stock subscription appears to have been a free rider problem par excellence and we would expect to find the lamentable results of the simple public-goods model.

## Turnpike provision

In view of the apparent free rider problem, the success was striking. The movement built new roads at rates previously unheard of in America. Over $11 million was invested in turnpikes in New York, some $6.5 million in New England, and over $4.5 million (excluding state investment) in Pennsylvania (Durrenberger 1931: 61, 102; Taylor 1934: 211). Wood (1919: 63) informs us that, based on the population of 1830, per capita turnpike investment was approximately $3.90 in Massachusetts. Between 1794 and 1840, 238 private New England turnpike companies built and operated about 3,750 miles of road.[30] New York led all other states in turnpike mileage with over 4,000 as of 1821. Pennsylvania was second, reaching a peak of about 2,400 miles in 1832. New Jersey companies operated 550 miles by 1821; Maryland's operated 300 miles of private road in 1830 (Durrenberger 1931: 61, 56, 74, 70). Turnpikes also represented a great improvement in road quality (Taylor 1934: 334; Parks 1967: 23, 27).

The local turnpike was supported by the more prominent citizens, but it is not as though a handful of affluent landowners paid for the project. Stock subscription was broad-based. In most cases upwards of fifty people contributed, usually over 100 for a larger turnpike, no one with more than 15 percent of the stock.[31]

---

[28] For no particular reason, I listed proper nouns that appeared in the names of Massachusetts turnpike companies chartered from 1800 to 1810 which looked like the names of townships. I then searched for their populations in the 1810 census; those which I did not find presumably are not towns or are towns in other states. I excluded Boston (population 33,250) from the list; the largest in the list was Salem (12,613).

[29] There is great variance in construction costs. A key factor was whether the turnpike took over a preexisting road bed so construction would be reduced and land damages minimal. Also important was the extent to which bridges were necessary. Taylor (1934: 210) estimates the average cost per mile to have been $4,500 in Massachusetts, $1,065 in New Hampshire, $1,000 in Vermont, $700 in Rhode Island, and $640 in Connecticut. (See also Taylor 1934: 185–90, 348–40; Durrenberger 1931: 84–95).

[30] Taylor (1934: 208); note that Connecticut's two public turnpikes chartered in 1792, one of which was taken over by a private company, are excluded (see Taylor 1934: 122–5; Wood 1919: 334–6), and that Taylor made arithmetic errors (see note 32 overleaf for details).

[31] There were cases of concentrated holdings, particularly in New England. Unconcentrated stock holding was fostered in part by installment purchase with a very small down payment and, particularly in the Middle Atlantic states, restrictions on stock purchase and voting rights. (See discussions in Durrenberger 1931: 103–7; Taylor 1934: 101–2, 156, 158–65.)

Glazer (1972: 164, 166) finds that a relatively successful "minority of interested citizens dominated most voluntary associations" in Cincinnati in 1840 and concludes that such associations were as "pervasive and important, but probably not as popular, as Tocqueville observed." A disproportionate number of the activists in Glazer's sample, however, were settlers from New England, the focus of de Tocqueville's observations.

After the most traveled routes had been converted to turnpikes, it became more difficult to raise money for their construction,[32] nonetheless turnpikes continued to be built, even though, by 1810, hope of direct remuneration had disappeared. Yet between 1810 and 1845 over 400 turnpikes were chartered and built, each one representing a separate instance of public-good provision.[33] I make no claim that private association overcame the free-rider problem in every case, or that turnpike construction satisfied blackboard Paretian conditions. Rather, I claim that, even though the turnpikes offered enormous nonexcludable benefits, far outweighing the costs of the project, a straight application of the simple public-goods model would lead us to doubt that many turnpikes were built and that a single one was built after 1810. Why doesn't the model apply?

## III

The literature on turnpikes is old and primarily narrative. It is not surprising that, while emphasizing the inducement of indirect benefits in supporting turnpike construction, turnpike historians have failed to point out, much less address, the free rider problem involved. In taking up the matter, we must rely on more than narrow turnpike history.

## Towns, independent and vigorous

Towns of the early nineteenth century were independent and strong, characteristics that have since perished. Through the colonial period the town had become the organizing principle of society. In the first three decades of the republic, the township held almost all of the administrative power of government. The states had uncon-

[32] Of the 385 private New England turnpike companies chartered through 1842, 147 failed to build roads, or 38 percent. These numbers come from Taylor (1934: 208, 237–46) and Reed (1964: 75). Some errors in Taylor to account for: the sum of the incorporations listed on p. 208 is 241, not 230; Table VII, p. 208, disagrees with the individual listing (pp. 337–44) for 1796, 1800, 1801, 1804, and 1834. For incorporation of successful roads, I have used three for 1796, thirteen for 1800, ten for 1801, seventeen for 1804, and five for 1834; Appendix III, p. 346, lists one for Vermont for 1804; I have used zero. These alterations are all based on Taylor's own individual listings, which are corroborated by Wood. For total incorporation in Connecticut I have used Reed's figures, which differ from Taylor's for 1797, 1805, 1806, and 1818. I am assuming that the additional incorporations from Reed failed to build their road.

The figures given by Taylor (1934: 164, 337–41, 346) for Massachusetts, Rhode Island, and Connecticut show that of the companies chartered between 1794 and 1800 three of thirty-five failed to build roadway (9 percent stillborn); between 1801 and 1807, twenty-nine of 103 (28 percent) (the 1801 incorporation entry on page 164 should be twelve); between 1808 and 1814, thirteen of thirty-five (37 percent); between 1815 and 1842, thirty-one of eighty-five (36 percent). Of the Middle states and Maryland, Durrenberger (1931: 107) says, "it is safe to say that at least one-third of the turnpike corporations chartered never built a mile of road, due chiefly to their inability to raise necessary capital."

[33] Arriving at the lower bound of 400. Adding up individual listings in Taylor (1934: 337–44) we find 71 successful New England companies chartered between 1810 and 1845. For those years New York chartered 337 turnpike companies, Pennsylvania 305, New Jersey 28, and Maryland 69, but we do not know how many of these successfully built roads. Even if we suppose a 50 percent mortality rate for these incorporations, probably an overestimate, they would represent 370 turnpikes built after turnpike unprofitability was quite obvious.

tested lawmaking powers, and economies of scale dictated that the counties attend to a few services (courts, prisons, and road commissioners), but the towns governed their own affairs and executed the directives of the state. Alexis de Tocqueville, in his masterful opus *Democracy in America*, says the towns "are independent in all that concerns themselves alone; and among the inhabitants of New England I believe that not a man is to be found who would acknowledge that the state has any right to interfere in their town affairs." When carrying out state laws, "[s]trict as this obligation is, the government of the state imposes it in principle only, and in its performance the township resumes all its independent rights" (1945 [1835], I: 68). The participatory nature of town government in early America has been well noted. This feature often makes it pointless to draw lines separating private and public works.[34]

The unity and effectiveness of towns in part arose from their commercial and social isolation. Until the nineteenth century, people traveled rarely and traded little with those of other towns (Taylor 1934: 31–2). Self-sufficiency nurtured multitudinous social ties between the townspeople.

Certain historical currents may also have contributed to the spirit of participation. In Revolutionary times religious doctrine in the individual and religious organization in the community usually ran deep. After the Revolution religious fervor intensified in the movement known as the Second Great Awakening, which was probably helped along by the passage of general incorporation laws for religious congregations (such as New York's in 1784). Whether the "New Light" denominations or those of longer tradition, religious congregations often showed a penchant for making themselves busy in various improvement endeavors, such as schools, libraries, and poor relief. By generating the requisite social relations, or "social capital" (Coleman 1988), as well as human capital, as noted by Seavoy (1978: 60), the religious and benevolent activities not only incited but empowered the application of voluntary efforts to community goals (Matthews 1969; Brown 1973; 68). A related thesis, advanced by Elkins and McKitrick (1954), associates local activism with the pervasiveness of leadership roles in a young community.

## The cooperative citizenry

The strong cooperative spirit of Americans especially fascinated de Tocqueville.[35] In the 1830s, he wrote:

> In no country in the world do the citizens make such exertions for the common weal. I known of no people who have established schools so numerous, places of public worship better suited to the wants of the inhabitants, or roads kept in better repair. (1945 [1835], I: 95)

[34] Pisani (1987: 751) writes, "[r]ecent scholarship suggests that the line between public and private corporations has been overdrawn: that distinction was not as clear in the eighteenth and early nineteenth centuries as it became once the business corporation reached maturity. Virtually all corporations combined elements of both." See Kammen (1975) and Seavoy (1978) on the overlap of the public and private sectors.

[35] De Tocqueville's analytic contributions are nicely summarized in Wade (1985).

The citizens' cooperation with government efforts is noteworthy, but more significant is the willingness to forge public improvements by voluntary association.

> Americans . . . constantly form associations. They have not only commercial and manu-
> facturing companies, in which all take part, but associations of a thousand other kinds,
> religious, moral, serious, futile, general or restricted, enormous or diminutive. The
> Americans make associations to give entertainments, to found seminaries, to build
> inns, to construct churches, to diffuse books, to send missionaries to the antipodes; in
> this manner they found hospitals, prisons, and schools. If it is proposed to inculcate
> some truth or to foster some feeling by the encouragement of a great example, they
> form a society.   (1945 [1840], II: 114).

De Tocqueville speaks of another often-cited public good: crime prevention.
Although no state police existed, and local public forces were minimal, "in no
country does crime more rarely elude punishment. The reason is that everyone
conceives himself to be interested in furnishing evidence of the crime and in
seizing the delinquent . . . I witnessed the spontaneous formation of committees in
a country for the pursuit and prosecution of a man who had committed a great
crime" (1945 [1835], I: 99). Similar private, nonprofit institutions for fire fighting or
education in early American society have been studied by economists (McChesney
1986; High and Ellig 1988).[36]

The cooperative spirit expressed itself in enterprises much like the turnpikes. In
his comprehensive study of American business incorporations up to 1800, Davis
(1917, II: 284–5) points out that many enterprises were undertaken to make improvements, and debates whether to count them as business corporations. He readily
excludes the marine and agricultural societies, but then come corporations for land
improvement, lumber cultivation, and inland navigation. For example, a "case near
the line" is the River Machine Company, incorporated in 1790 to dredge the Providence River. "The merchants of Providence had agreed to raise $1,000 in forty 'equal
shares' " for the project. The company was to collect tolls from certain vessels, but
any surplus was to be used at the end of twenty years for other improvements.
"Thus no dividends were contemplated."

In financing, many turnpikes closely resembled this dredging company: numerous people contributed liberally for the large fixed costs and then just enough revenue was collected to sustain operation. Before it became standard practice to name
a turnpike company by the towns it connected, the first private turnpike company
chartered in New England (1794) was entitled "The Society for Establishing and
Supporting a Turnpike Road from Cepatchit Bridge, in Gloucester, to Connecticut
Line" (Taylor 1934: 125). Even after being given the standard business-sounding
titles, we occasionally find turnpike companies calling themselves a "society."[37]

---

[36] Pisani (1987: 744) argues that "federalism's tendency to disperse power to the local level reinforced
the dependence of Americans on quasigovernmental associations, such as commercial federations, civic
organizations, and booster clubs, that often served as better forums of collective action than did formal
institutions of government."
[37] Two examples are found in *Connecticut Courant*, July 17, 1801, pp. 2, 3.

## Selective incentives (social pressure, etc.)

Economic explanations of cooperation fall into two broad categories. One approach says that, for whatever reason, people have an irreducible demand to cooperate. Following Margolis (1982), we could say that people contributed to turnpikes due to strong group-interest utility functions, or following Sugden (1984, 1986), we could say that people felt they ought to contribute and they therefore behaved according to a system of moral obligations.

The second approach gets into the guts of cooperation by breaking down the situation and revealing hidden private advantages to cooperation. From de Tocqueville's searching discussion of the American devotion to "self-interest rightly understood" (1945 [1840], II: 129–35), we conclude that the gutsy approach to co-operation is especially fitting to our problem.[38] We could view turnpike communities as extended families and apply the Becker (1974) theory of social interaction. Perhaps the residents of a community practiced ongoing gift-giving sustained by the threat of withholding (as in Kurz 1977), or abided by social norms for fear of collective reprisal (as in Kandori 1989). While formal models could be loosely ap-plied to the turnpike case, instead I will depend on Mancur Olson's discussion (1971, 1982), which emphasizes the role of institutions.

In *The Logic of Collective Action* Olson develops the idea of selective incentives:

> [A] *"selective" incentive* will stimulate a rational individual in a latent group to act in a group-oriented way. In such circumstances group action can be obtained only through an incentive that operates, not indiscriminately, like the collective good, upon the group as a whole, but rather *selectively* toward the individuals in that group. The incentive must be "selective" so that those who do not join the organization working for the group's interest, or in other ways contribute to the attainment of the group's interest, can be treated differently from those who do.   (1971; 51)[39]

We are especially interested in negative selective incentives, which are punishments for failing to bear an appropriate share of the collective effort.[40] Selective incentives are particularly effective in closed, homogeneous groups. The failure of some to cooperate will attract attention. "Their friends might use 'social pressure' to en-courage them to do their part . . . and such steps might be effective, for . . . most people value the fellowship of their friends and associates, and value social status, personal prestige, and self-esteem" (Olson 1971: 60).[41] Such was the case for the

---

[38] In as much as one's demand or feeling of duty to cooperate is responsive to external prods and pressures – surely a great deal – the two approaches to understanding cooperation are not as distinct as I am making out.

[39] See also Olson (1982: 20–3, 32–9, 85–7).

[40] Using a standard of welfare, Olson views negative selective incentives as "coercive." I speak of "coercion" and "voluntarism" using a standard of property rights, with the social pressures presently discussed as *damnum absque injuria*. For a somewhat sanguine treatment of formal positive selective incentives, which Olson calls "tie-ins," see Klein (1987).

[41] In *Rise and Decline of Nations* (1982: 24), Olson adds to his discussion of selective incentives the notion that selective incentives are more effective the more homogeneous the group members are in taste, attitudes, and lifestyles. Turnpike communities would certainly be considered homogeneous by

turnpike communities of 1,000 or 5,000 people. For the average turnpike stock-holder "those in control [of the turnpike] were his neighbors and personally known to him" (Taylor 1934: 168). Of voluntary associations in Massachusetts in the turn-pike age, Brown (1973: 68) says, "[t]he feelings of personal recognition, self-im-provement, and mutual reinforcement that members derived from participation were sometimes as important as the more explicit purposes of the organization."

A number of social pressure tactics were employed in the turnpike case. Fore-most was the community gatherings called to make up a plan and sell stock in the company. The town meeting was a central institution in which all important resi-dents were expected to participate. Sly (1967 [1930]: 107) says that in the early 1800s "[t]he town meeting was . . . at the highest point of development." The turnpike meetings were well attended and stock pledges were made publicly. For example, Wood (1919: 69) says the Fifth Massachusetts Turnpike "was formally organized at a meeting held in the inn of Oliver Chapin, probably early in 1799, and 1,600 shares were issued with a par value of $100 each." Meetings with attendances of 50 and 100 people have been recorded.[42] Through introspection, if nothing else, we recog-nize one's susceptibility to the rousing speeches, pointed inquiries, and side-long glances operating at such fund-raisers.

Turnpike promoters relied of course on the most basic form of selective incen-tive, person-to-person solicitation. In an 1808 letter regarding the formation of the York and Conewago Canal Turnpike, the writer tells of those who "have with so liberal a hand contributed to the Turnpike feeling a considerable responsibility, having used every exertion with the people of this place to promote it."[43]

Bearing out de Tocqueville's claim that Americans formed associations no matter how "diminutive," we find cases of turnpike companies organizing solicitation forces. For the Hingham and Quincy Turnpike, "[s]everal committees were appointed to solicit subscriptions to the stock of the corporation, and one committee was intrusted with the single duty of so presenting the advantages of the enterprise to Reverend Henry Coleman of Hingham as to give his aid and influence to the undertaking" (Wood 1919: 178).[44] Similarly, we find in the minutes book of the Minisink and Montgomery Turnpike Company: "Resolved, That James Finch Jun. and David Mason be a Committee to apply to the People living west of the Shawangunk Mountain for subscriptions."[45]

---

today's standards. Landa (1981) discusses the importance of homogeneity in trading groups.

Regarding Olson's emphasis on face-to-face interaction, see Frank (1988) on how true feelings and intentions are reflected in physiological impulses. For an extended discussion of selective incentives and how traditional sociological questions can be addressed using the individualistic reasoning typical of economics, see Hechter (1987). On the study of community and cooperation, Higgs (1987) alerts economists to the achievements of sociologists and psychologists. For a brief survey touching on how communitarian factors in classroom experiments influence public good contributions, see Dawes and Thaler (1988: 193–5) and Isaac and Walker (1988). For evidence and discussion of honest preference revelation, see Bohm (1972) and Brubaker (1975).

[42] Kirk (1912: 22); *Connecticut Courant*, March 19, 1798,

[43] Letter from Henry Miller to Thomas Willing Francis, January 17, 1808, Conewago Canal Collec-tion, New York Public Library, Manuscripts. The turnpike was chartered and constructed in 1809.

[44] That so much energy was expended in securing the "aid and influence" of a clergyman suggests other forms of selective incentives.

Adam G. Mappa, president and chief organizer of the Utica Turnpike, needed no warrant to solicit his fellow townspeople. To win the support of the locals, he "set forth in forcible language and at great length the advantages that would accrue to Utica by completion of the road" (Durant 1878: 177). Some details of the campaign are provided in the following extract of an 1808 letter from Mappa to a Mr. Walton:

> I have begged with all my power & might pro bono publico. you my dear sir I hope will follow my example . . . [with] our friends Miller and Van Rensselear as soon [as] these gentlemen . . . return and can be taken hold of. Mr. Hogan informed me that he did not know the Turnpike Road was laid over his lands. How can it be possible that you, my dear Walton, did neglect to inform Mr. H. of this advantage and request (as you promised me) his assistance in subscribing generously towards our wants. O my friend, if you forget us, if you abandon the T. P. [turnpike] interest, all is over, we shall sink in the mud & that very dirty too. Retrieve therefore the opportunity lost on the return of friend Hogan, and do not forget any of all those whom you can reach. (Quoted in Jackson 1959: 22)

Mappa's letters are prime examples of what de Tocqueville (1945, [1840], II: 114) called "the extreme skill with which the inhabitants of the United States succeeded in proposing a common object for the exertions of a great many men and inducing them voluntarily to pursue it." Mappa's letters also show that generating selective incentives is itself a costly public good, but some people will eagerly take it upon themselves to provide them.[46] The Utica Turnpike never paid its stockholders reasonably well, but it lasted until 1848 when it was transformed into a plank road company.[47]

The struggle to gather support is shown in a letter to John Rutherford, a subscriber in several turnpikes, about a newly incorporated turnpike through Trenton: "We open the books on Thursday next – and shall try every means to get the company organized – you know how little spirit prevails with the citizens of this place for any public improvement – but intend pushing them hard." Further, the writer expresses his hope that Rutherford "may think so favorable of [the project] – as to give orders to some friend here to subscribe largely."[48]

De Tocqueville and Olson both speak of another organ of selective incentives used by turnpike communities. De Tocqueville (1945 [1840], II: 119) says, "nothing

---

[45] Minisink and Montgomery Turnpike Company Minute Book (BV. Sec.), entry July 8, 1811, New York Historical Society.

[46] See Kahneman, Knetsch, and Thaler (1986) for experimental evidence of people's demand to punish wrongdoers.

[47] Plank roads are turnpikes with plank surfacing. They came in an enormous wave in the late 1840s and 1850s. They constitute a separate chapter in private road management (see Klein and Majewski 1988a).

[48] Peter Gordon to John Rutherford, April 8, 1806, New York Historical Society, Rutherford Papers. Another letter to Rutherford regarding a different turnpike indicates that Rutherford promised to buy eight or ten shares provided that a certain route was settled on. Thus the writer concludes the letter. "The object is so important, that it makes us very solicitous to obtain funds, especially from those who have been so liberal as to offer their aid" (John Doughty to John Rutherford, June 28, 1810).

I have found other bits of evidence of conditional subscription – conditioned, that is, on the route of the road. I am confident that conditional subscription does not pose a challenge to the claim that participatory norms and social pressure account principally for turnpike financing. First, route selection was hardly an issue for most turnpikes, as most were constructed on preexisting road beds. Second, usually directness was an explicit requirement in turnpike laws, and in fact many turnpikes made a fetish of

but a newspaper can drop the same thought into a thousand minds at the same moment," and by means of a newspaper "you can persuade every man whose help you require that his private interest obliges him voluntarily to unite his exertions to the exertions of all the others." Similarly, Olson (1971: 63) says that through media propaganda "about the worthiness of the attempt to satisfy the common interest in question," members of a latent group may "develop social pressure not entirely unlike those that can be generated in a face-to-face group."[49]

Newspapers proliferated in America and people took a keen interest in reports on local affairs (de Tocqueville 1945 [1840], II: 114–22; Gunn 1988: 52). To spur feelings of duty, announcements of the formation of a turnpike company often spoke of the public worthiness of the road. Within a five month period the *Courier of New Hampshire* (Concord) carried communications of three different turnpike companies saying that their project "would be beneficial to the public in general," "would be of great public utility," and "would open extensive communication from West to East through the middle of New Hampshire . . . and would tend to increase the commerce of our own Metropolis."[50] In other announcements the element of moral suasion is more pronounced. After announcing that the books of the Great Northern Turnpike are open for subscription, a communication adds: "N.B. the object of the contemplated road is so obviously important to the public and to individuals, (as it will facilitate a direct intercourse between the cities of Montreal and Albany, without a single ferry, and generally over a level country,) that great hopes are entertained of its speedy execution."[51] A 1798 communication of the Hartford and New Haven Turnpike says, "And it being an object of great public utility, it is hoped the citizens of this state will manifest their public spirit on the occasion, and feel themselves disposed to promote it by an advance of the necessary sums of money, and will without hesitation fill up the subscription."[52]

Between Schenectady and Albany went to work the champion promoter, Elkanah Watson.[53] Using the names "A Friend to Turnpikes," "A.Z.," "A Republican," and "The Public Good," Watson appealed to public spirit, patriotism, and commercial interest in his campaigns for turnpikes. Rarely did he appeal to direct remuneration from the stock. In 1801, in one of his many pieces promoting the Albany and Schenectady Turnpike, Watson writes

> [A]s its importance is admitted on all hands, the adventurers are entitled from the public the most decisive and liberal encouragement to complete the road . . .

rectilinearity (Taylor 1934: 285; Durrenberger 1931: 85). Finally, it must be recognized that by any sensible geometry a turnpike route could be skewed in only a few places, and each possible skew will offer benefits to a sizeable group that would then face a free rider problem in bidding against other groups for their preferred route. But this is not to deny that conditional subscription may have played an occasional role in determining where a connecting stretch would be laid or how a corner would be cut.

[49] A classic study of social pressures exerted through the media is Merton (1946), which is entirely devoted to a marathon warbond broadcast by Kate Smith.

[50] April 11, August 1, March 14, 1804.

[51] *Albany Gazette*, June 6, 1805, 2.

[52] *Connecticut Courant* (Hartford), November 19, 1798, 2.

[53] Watson, an early exponent of a great canal through New York, made an avocation of promoting internal and agricultural improvements in the state. His promotionals show a supreme shrewdness, in marked contrast to the tracts by plank-road messiahs in later years (Klein and Majewski 1988a).

As respects the citizens of Albany, especially the mercantile interest, they must be asleep indeed if they can suffer another year to pass over without exerting all their efforts to bring about this important enterprise.    (p. 40)

In a later article Watson reports on the success of a preliminary meeting to found the turnpike and adds, "As our Citizens appear to be universally impressed with the importance of a Turnpike Road connecting the two cities of Albany and Schenectady, and as the same patriotic spirit prevails in the City of Schenectady, a doubt can no longer exist, but the SHARES will be all taken up in a few hours after the Books are opened" (p. 40). And, indeed, besides copies of these articles in his heavily annotated scrapbook, Watson scribbled, "the happy Moment was here – the foregoing publications paved the way + never anything more spiritedly received."

Watson labored hard for other turnpikes, including a connection between New York and Albany. In an article from 1800, he writes, "[t]he object is so truly important, so desirable, and so popular, that little doubt can be entertained, but that the legislature will grant a charter, and that the 3,000 shares . . . will be immediately taken up" (p. 36). Notice how Watson, by pretending confidence in imminent support, tries to mitigate the assurance problem in securing support and to incite the vigilant do-gooder to take up the call. In his scrapbook Watson penned, "unsuccessful attempts have been made to obtain a charter . . . It must eventually succeed." Later he adds, "1808 – the Road from N.Y. to Albany – has been executed this present year – who began it?" Besides testifying to Watson's self-satisfaction, these annotations testify to the social leverage of the newspaper.

Social pressure seems to have found its way into the assessment and payment of land damages. Right-of-way was commonly paid for in stock rather than money (Taylor 1934: 165). "A Philanthropist" (1797, no. III) says that those giving up land to a turnpike "will receive an equivalent to their damages, in the appreciate value of their farms and situations, and from other accommodations." Such benefits probably gave the turnpike a moral bargaining chip when coming to an agreement, as indicated in the 1798 announcement of the Hartford and New Haven Turnpike: "It is hoped that those persons through whose land said road is laid, will become subscribers to the amount at least of the sum assessed to them in damages."[54]

We could speculate on other forms of social pressure. In the few cases of turnpike-run lotteries it is easy to imagine a role for social pressure in the sale of tickets (Wood 1919: 293; Lane 1939: 161). The list of turnpike stockholders was public information and may have circulated to spur contribution.[55]

Even if selective incentives had been prevalent we could not expect them to have been well-recorded. Yet some tangible signs can be found. Supplemented by an understanding of the turnpikes and of the ethos of the day, it is fair to conclude that social pressures played a conspicuous role in the provision of hundreds of turnpikes.

---

[54] *Connecticut Courant* (Hartford), November 19, 1798, 2.
[55] Consider the fraternity magazines and neighborhood March of Dimes drives that reveal the names and contributions of donors.

## IV

Local freedom, . . . which leads a great number of citizens to value the affection of their neighbors and of their kindred, perpetually brings men together and forces them to help one another in spite of the propensities that sever them. (de Tocqueville 1945 [1840], II: 111)

Early American communities overcame an apparent free-rider problem in financing hundreds of turnpike companies. For companies organized after 1810, the hope of a small return surely oiled the willingness to invest turnpikes, but the central explanation for such investment lies elsewhere. Community isolation, citizen familiarity, and weak, decentralized government bred close social ties and an effective participatory ethic.

But does the quaint story of townspeople working together to build a highway have much bearing on modern problems? Hackensack has changed a lot since 1810. Neighbors are often strangers, so how can we expected social pressure and the like to curtail free riding? Two remarks follow.

First, despite the growing interest among economists in non-egoistic behavior, voluntary public-good provision still seems to be one of those areas in which the representative economist suffers from a trained incapacity. It has been shown experimentally that economists are comparatively insensitive to free riding (Marwell and Ames 1981); often they seem blind to its avoidance as well. Whether it be a block association or the American Cancer Society, suasion tactics often yield results, as reported regularly in *Nonprofit and Voluntary Sector Quarterly*. Such tactics, I am told, are operating for toll road projects underway in Virginia, California, and the Midwest, where groups of developers are donating land and volunteering to build some of the necessary secondary facilities (see Poole 1988: 511).

Second, if our voluntary forces are deemed ineffective in providing public goods, that in itself is a policy issue. The ability of voluntary association to provide infrastructure, education, security, and poor relief depends on the exercise and spontaneous development of certain institutions, activities, and sentiments. Since governmental bodies dominate these services it is no surprise that our faculties of sodality remain degenerate. When a problem arises, government is expected to deal with it. Participation does not become a personal responsibility and organizing leadership does not become a source of social esteem. Thus there is a lesson in the broader circumstances of early America which bred potent voluntary forces, as well as in the specific ways those forces established turnpikes.

## REFERENCES

Anderson, Terry and P. J. Hill, "An American Experiment in Anarcho-Capitalism: The *Not* so Wild, Wild West," *Journal of Libertarian Studies*, 1979, pp. 9–29.

Becker, Gary S., "A Theory of Social Interactions," *Journal of Political Economy*, December 1974, pp. 1063–93.

Beito, David, with Brace Smith, "The Formation of Urban Infrastructure through Non-Governmental Planning: The Private Places of St. Louis, 1869–1929," *Journal of Urban History*, May 1990, pp. 263–303.

Benson, Bruce, "The Evolution of Law: Custom versus Authority," Manuscript (Florida State University, 1989).

Bloodgood, S. De Witt, *A Treatise on Roads, their History, Character and Utility* (Albany, N.Y.: Oliver Steele, 1838).

Bohm, Peter, "Estimating Demand for Public Goods: An Experiment," *European Economic Review*, 3(2), 1972, pp. 111–30.

Brown, Richard D., "The Emergence of Voluntary Associations in Massachusetts, 1760–1830," *Journal of Voluntary Action Research*, Spring 1973, pp. 64–73.

Brubaker, Earl R., "Free Ride, Free Revelation, or Golden Rule?" *Journal of Law and Economics*, April 1975, pp. 147–61.

Cheung, Steven N. S., "The Fable of the Bees: An Economic Investigation," *Journal of Law and Economics*, April 1973, pp. 11–34.

Coase, R. H., "The Lighthouse in Economics," *Journal of Law and Economics*, October 1974, pp. 357–76.

Coleman, James, S., "Social Capital in the Creation of Human Capital," *American Journal of Sociology*, Supplement, 1988, pp. S95–S120.

Cowen, Tyler (ed.) *The Theory of Market Failure: A Critical Examination* (Fairfax, Va: George Mason University Press, 1988).

Davis, Joseph S., *Essays in the Earlier History of American Corporations* (Cambridge, Mass.: Harvard University Press, 1917).

Dawes, Robyn M. and Richard H. Thaler, "Anomalies: Cooperation," *Journal of Economic Perspectives*, Summer 1988, pp. 187–97.

DeWitt, Benjamin, "A Sketch of the Turnpike Roads in the State of New York," 1807. Reprinted in *The New American State Papers, Volume One* (Wilmington, Del.: Scholarly Resources, Inc., 1972, pp. 215–18).

Duane, William J., *Letters Addressed to the People of Pennsylvania Respecting the Internal Improvements of the Commonwealth by Means of Roads and Canals* (Philadelphia, Pa: Jane Aitken, 1811).

Durant, Samuel W., *History of Oneida County, New York* (Philadelphia, Pa: Everts & Ensign, 1878).

Durrenberger, Joseph A., *Turnpikes; a Study of the Toll Road Movement in the Middle Atlantic States and Maryland* (Valdosta, Ga.: Southern Stationery and Printing Co., 1931).

Elkins, Stanley and Eric McKitrick, "A Meaning for Turner's Frontier, Part I: Democracy in the Old Northwest," *Political Science Quarterly*, September 1954, pp. 321–53; "Part II: The Southwest Frontier and New England," December 1954, pp. 565–602.

Evans, Clinton J., "Private Turnpikes and Bridges," *American Law Review*, 1916, pp. 527–35.

Frank, Robert, *Passions Within Reason: Prisoner's Dilemmas and the Strategic Role of the Emotions* (New York: W. W. Norton, 1988).

Glazer, Walter S., "Participation and Power: Voluntary Associations and the Functional Organization of Cincinnati in 1840,"*Historical Methods Newsletter*, September 1972, pp. 151–68.

Gunn, L. Ray, *The Decline of Authority: Public Economic Policy and Political Development in New York, 1800–1860* (Ithaca N.Y.: Cornell University Press, 1988).

Handlin, Oscar and Mary Flug Handlin, *Commonwealth; A Study of the Role of Government in the American Economy: Massachusetts, 1774–1861* (New York: New York University Press, 1947).

Hartz, Louis, *Economic Policy and Democratic Thought: Pennsylvania, 1776–1860* (Cambridge, Mass.: Harvard University Press, 1948).

Hechter, Michael, *Principles of Group Solidarity* (Berkeley, Calif.: University of California Press, 1987).

Higgs, Robert, "Identity and Cooperation: A Comment on Sen's Alternative Program," *Journal of Law, Economics, and Organization*, spring 1987, pp. 140–2.

High, Jack and Jerome Ellig, "The Private Supply of Education: Some Historical Evidence," in *The Theory of Market Failure: A Critical Examination*, edited by Tyler Cowen (Fairfax, Va: George Mason University Press, 1988, pp. 361–82).

Hollifield, William, *Difficulties Made Easy: History of the Turnpikes of Baltimore City and County* (Cockeysville, Md: Baltimore County Historical Society, 1978).

Hunter, Robert-F., "The Turnpike Movement in Virginia, 1816–1860," Ph.D. dissertation (Columbia University, 1957).

Hurst, James W., *Law and Market in United States History: Different Modes of Bargaining Among Interests* (Madison, Wis.: University of Wisconsin Press, 1982).

Isaac, R. Mark and James M. Walker, "Communication and Free-Riding Behavior: The Voluntary Contribution Mechanism," *Economic Inquiry*, October 1988, pp. 585–608.

Jackson, Harry F., "The Utica Turnpike," *New York History*, January 1959, pp. 18–32.

Kahneman, Daniel, Jack L. Knetsch and Richard H. Thaler, "Fairness and the Assumptions of Economics," *Journal of Business*, Supplement, 1986, pp. S285–S300.

Kammen, Michael, "A Different 'Fable of the Bees': The Problem of Public and Private Sectors in Colonial America," in *The American Revolution: A Heritage of Change*, edited by J. Parker and C. Urness (Minneapolis, Minn.: Associates of the James Ford Bell Library, 1975, pp. 53–68).

Kandori, Michihiro, "Social Norms and Community Enforcement," photocopy (Stanford University, 1989).

Kirk, Edward R., "Turnpike Road from Buckingham to Newtown," *Bucks County Historical Society*, 1912, pp. 20–4.

Kirkland, Edward C., *Men, Cities and Transportation; A Study in New England History, 1920–1900* (Cambridge, Mass.: Harvard University Press, 1948).

Klein, Daniel, "Tie-ins and the Market Provision of Collective Goods," *Harvard Journal of Law and Public Policy*, spring 1987, pp. 451–74.

Klein, Daniel and John Majewski, "Private Profit, Public Good, and Engineering Failure: The Plank Roads of New York," Working Paper 88/3 (Institute for Humane Studies, George Mason University, 1988a).

—— "Privatization, Regulation, and Public Repossession: The Turnpike Companies of Early America," photocopy (University of California, Irvine, 1988b).

Kurz, Mordecai, "Altruistic Equilibrium," in *Economic Progress, Private Values, and Public Policy: Essays in Honor of William Fellner*, edited by Bela Balassa and Richard Nelson (New York: North Holland, 1977, pp. 177–200).

Landa, Janet T., "A Theory of the Ethnically Homogeneous Middleman Group: An Institutional Alternative to Contract Law," *Journal of Legal Studies*, June 1981, pp. 349–62.

Lane, Wheaton J., *From Indian Trail to Iron Horse: Travel and Transportation in New Jersey, 1620–1860* (Princeton, N.J.: Princeton University Press, 1939).

McChesney, Fred C., "Government Prohibitions on Volunteer Fire Fighting in Nineteenth Century America: A Property Rights Perspective," *Journal of Legal Studies*, January 1986, pp. 69–92.

Majewski, John, "Farming and the Public Good: Social Incentives and Agricultural Research in England, 1600–1850," photocopy (Department of History, University of California, Los Angeles, 1989).

Margolis, Howard, *Selfishness, Altruism, and Rationality* (New York: Cambridge University Press, 1982).

Marwell, Gerald and Ruth Ames, "Economists Free Ride, Does Anyone Else?" *Journal of Public Economics*, June 1981, pp. 295–310.

Matthews, Donald G., "The Second Great Awakening as an Organizing Process, 1780–1830: An Hypothesis," *American Quarterly*, spring 1969, pp. 23–43.

Merton, Robert, *Mass Persuasion: The Social Psychology of a War Bond Drive* (New York: Harper & Brothers, 1946).

Olson, Mancur, *The Logic of Collective Action: Public Goods and the Theory of Groups* (Cambridge, Mass.: Harvard University Press, 1971).

—— *The Rise and Decline of Nations* (New Haven, Conn: Yale University Press, 1982).

Parks, Roger N., "The Roads of New England, 1790–1840," Ph.D. dissertation (Michigan State University, 1966).

—— *Roads and Travel in New England, 1790–1840* (Sturbridge, Mass.: Old Sturbridge Inc., 1967).

Pawson, Eric, *Transport and Economy: The Turnpike Roads of Eighteenth Century Britain* (London: Academic Press, 1977).

Philanthropist, A., "Roads and Turnpikes." Five installments, *Connecticut Courant* (Hartford), "No. I," May 1, p. 3; "No. II," May 8, p. 2; "No. III," May 22, p. 1; "No. IV," May 29, p. 1; "No. V." June 26, p. 1. All 1797.

Pisani, Donald, J., "Promotion and Regulation: Constitutionalism and the American Economy," *Journal of American History*, December 1987, pp. 740–68.

Poole, Robert W., Jr. "Resolving Gridlock in Southern California," *Transportation Quarterly*, October 1988, pp. 499–527.

Reed, Nathaniel, "The Role of the Connecticut State Government in the Development and Operation of Inland Transportation Facilities from 1784 to 1821," Ph.D. dissertation (Yale University, 1964).

Ringwalt, John L., *Development of Transportation Systems in the United States*, 1888 (New York: Johnson Reprint Corp., 1966).

Samuelson, Paul A., "The Pure Theory of Public Expenditure," *Review of Economics and Statistics*, November 1954, pp. 387–9.

—— "Diagrammatic Exposition of a Theory of Public Expenditure," *Review of Economics and Statistics*, November 1955, pp. 550–6.

Seavoy, Ronald E., "The Public Service Origins of the American Business Corporation," *Business History Review*, spring 1978, pp. 30–60.

Sly, John F., *Town Government in Massachusetts, 1620–1930*, (Hamden, Conn.: Archon Books, 1967).

Sugden, Robert, "Reciprocity: The Supply of Public Goods through Voluntary Contributions," *Economics Journal*, December 1984, pp. 772–87.

—— *The Economics of Rights, Co-operation and Welfare* (New York: Basil Blackwell, 1986).

Taylor, George R., *The Transportation Revolution, 1815–1860* (New York: Rinehart, 1951).

Taylor, Philip E., "The Turnpike Era in New England," Ph.D. dissertation (Yale University, 1934).

Tocqueville, Alexis de, *Democracy in America*, 1835, 1840 (New York: Vintage, 1945).

Tufts, Cotton, Letter on Turnpike Roads of Massachusetts (1807), in Appendix to Gallatin's report on Roads and Canals, in *American State Papers, Miscellaneous*, vol. 1, pp. 866–7. (Washington, D.C.: Gales and Seaton, 1834).

Wade, L. L., "Tocqueville and Public Choice," *Public Choice*, 47(3), 1985, pp. 491–508.

Watson, Elkanah, "Commonplace Book, 1758–1842," Manuscript, in his papers, pkg. 1, v. 12 (New York State Library, Albany).

Wood, Frederick J., *The Turnpikes of New England and Evolution of the Same through England, Virginia, and Maryland* (Boston, Mass.: Marshall Jones, 1919).

Wooldridge, William C., *Uncle Sam, the Monopoly Man* (New Rochelle, N.Y.: Arlington House, 1970).

# 3

# The Fable of the Bees: An Economic Investigation

## Steven N. S. Cheung*

Economists possess their full share of the common ability to invent and commit errors . . .
Perhaps their most common error is to believe other economists.

**George J. Stigler**

Ever since A. C. Pigou wrote his books on "welfare," a divergence between private and social costs has provided the main argument for instituting government action to correct allegedly inefficient market activities.[1] The analysis in such cases has been designed less to aid our understanding of how the economic system operates than to find flaws in it to justify policy recommendations. Both to illustrate the argument and to demonstrate the nature of the actual situation, the quest has been for real-world examples of such defects.

Surprisingly enough, aside from Pigou's polluting factory and Sidgwick's light-house, convincing examples were hard to come by.[2] It was not until 1952, more than thirty years after Pigou's initial analysis, that J. E. Meade proposed further examples and revitalized the argument for corrective government actions.[3] Meade's prime example, which soon became classic, concerned the case of the apple farmer and the beekeeper. In his own words:

* Facts, like jade, are not only costly to obtain but also difficult to authenticate. I am therefore most grateful to the following beekeepers and farmers: Leonard Almquist, Nat Giacomini, Ancel Goolsbey, L. W. Groves, Rex Haueter, Harold Lange, Lavar Peterson, Elwood Sires, Clarence Smith, Ken Smith, John Steg, P. F. Thurber, and Mrs. Gerald Weddle. All of them provided me with valuable information; some of them made available to me their accounting records and contracts. R. H. Coase inspired the investigation, Yoram Barzel saw that it was conducted thoroughly, and Mrs. Lina Tong rendered her assistance. The investigation is part of a proposed research in the general area of contracts, financially supported by the National Science Foundation.
    [1] A. C. Pigou, *Wealth and Welfare* (1912); *The Economics of Welfare* (1920).
    [2] Pigou had offered other examples. The example of two roads was deleted from later editions of *The Economics of Welfare*, presumably in an attempt to avoid the criticism by F. H. Knight in, "Some Fallacies in the Interpretation of Social Cost," *Q. J. Econ*[38], (1924), p. 582. The railroad example has not enjoyed popularity. Most of Pigou's examples, however, were drawn from land tenure arrangements in agriculture, but an exhaustive check of his source references has revealed no hard evidence at all to support his claim of inefficient tenure arrangements.
    [3] See J. E. Meade, "External Economies and Diseconomies in a Competitive Situation," *Econ. J.* 52 (1952), p. 54.

Suppose that in a given region there is a certain amount of apple-growing and a certain amount of bee-keeping and that the bees feed on the apple blossom. If the apple-farmers apply 10% more labour, land and capital to apple-farming they will increase the output of apples by 10%; but they will also provide more food for the bees. On the other hand, the bee-keepers will not increase the output of honey by 10% by increasing the amount of land, labour and capital to bee-keeping by 10% unless at the same time the apple-farmers also increase their output and so the food of the bees by 10% ... We call this a case of an unpaid factor, because the situation is due simply and solely to the fact that the apple-farmer cannot charge the beekeeper for the bees' food.[4]

And Meade applied a similar argument to a reciprocal situation:

While the apples may provide the food of the bees, the bees may fertilize the apples ... By a process similar to that adopted in the previous case we can obtain formulae to show what subsidies and taxes must be imposed.[5]

In another well-known work, Francis M. Bator used Meade's example to infer "market failure":

It is easy to show that if apple blossoms have a positive effect on honey production ... any Pareto-efficient solution ... will associate with apple blossoms a positive Lagrangean shadow-price. If, then, apple producers are unable to protect their equity in apple-nectar and markets do not impute to apple blossoms their correct shadow value, profit-maximizing decisions will fail correctly to allocate resources ... at the margin. There will be failure "by enforcement." This is what I would call an *ownership* externality.[6]

It is easy to understand why the "apples and bees" example has enjoyed widespread popularity. It has freshness and charm: the pastoral scene, with its elfin image of bees collecting nectar from apple blossoms, has captured the imagination of economists and students alike. However, the universal credence given to the lighthearted fable is surprising; for in the United States, at least, contractual arrangements between farmers and beekeepers have long been routine. This paper investigates the pricing and contractual arrangements of the beekeeping industry in the state of Washington, the location having been selected because the Pacific Northwest is one of the largest apple-growing areas in the world.

Contrary to what most of us have thought, apple blossoms yield little or no honey.[7] But it is true that bees provide valuable pollination services for apples and other plants, and that many other plants do yield lucrative honey crops. In any event, it

---

[4]  Ibid., pp. 56–7.

[5]  Ibid., p. 58.

[6]  Francis M. Bator, "The Anatomy of Market Failure," *Q. J. Econ.* 72 (1958), pp. 351, 364.

[7]  The presence of apple honey in the market is therefore somewhat mysterious. While occasionally apple orchards in the Northwest do yield negligible amounts of nectar, beekeepers are frank to point out that the dandelion and other wild plants in the orchard are often the sources of "apple" honey, so called. Elsewhere, as in New York, it was reported that apple orchards yielded slightly more nectar. See, for example, A. I. and E. R. Root, *The ABC and XYZ of Bee Culture* (1923), p. 386. The explanation for this divergence of facts, to my mind, lies in the different lengths of time in which the hives are placed in the apple orchards: in Root's day the hives were probably left in the orchards for longer periods than today.

will be shown that the observed pricing and contractual arrangements governing nectar and pollination services are consistent with efficient allocation of resources.

## I  SOME RELEVANT FACTS OF BEEKEEPING

Although various types of bees pollinate plants, beekeeping is confined almost exclusively to honeybees.[8] The hive used by beekeepers in the state of Washington is of the Langstroth design which consists of one or two brood chambers, a queen excluder, and from zero to six supers. A brood chamber is a wooden box large enough to contain eight or ten movable frames, each measuring 9⅛ by 17⅝ by 1⅜ inches. Within each frame is a wax honeycomb built by the bees. In the hexagonal cells of this comb the queen lays her eggs and the young bees, or "brood," are raised. It is here also that the bees store the nectar and pollen which they use for food. Honey is not usually extracted from this chamber but from the frames of a shallower box, called a super, placed above the brood chamber. The queen excluder, placed between the super and the brood chamber, prevents the laying of eggs in the upper section.[9]

The bees, and consequently the beekeepers, work according to a yearly cycle. Around the beginning of March, a Washington beekeeper will decide whether he wants to prepare for the pollination season by ordering booster packages of bees from California to strengthen his colonies, depleted and weakened during the winter and early spring. Alternatively, he may decide to build up the colony by transporting the hives to farms or pastures in warmer areas, such as Oregon and California. The colony hatches continuously from spring to fall, and the growth rate is rapid. Reared on pollen, the infant bees remain in the brood stage for about three weeks before entering the productive life of the colony for five or six weeks. Active workers spend three weeks cleaning and repairing the brood cells and nursing the young, then live out the remainder of their short lives foraging for pollen and nectar.[10]

Because of the bees' quick growth, the working "strength" of a colony includes both brood and workers, and increases from about five frames in early spring to about twelve by late summer. Spring is the primary season for fruit pollination, and beekeepers usually market a standard colony strength of roughly four frames of bees and two to three frames of brood for pollination services. But since empty frames are needed to accommodate the expanding colony, two-story hives, with sixteen or twenty frames, are used. The swarming period, beginning in mid-summer and lasting until early fall, is the peak honey season, and the yield per

---

[8]  See George E. Bohart, "Management of Wild Bees," in U.S. Department of Agriculture, *Beekeeping in the United States* (Ag. Handbook no. 335, 1971), p. 109. (Hereinafter cited as *Beekeeping*) Leafcutters, for example, have recently been introduced for the pollination of alfalfa and clover seeds. But these bees yield no honey crop and are seldom kept.

[9]  For further details see Spencer M. Riedel, Jr., "Development of American Beehive," in *Beekeeping*, pp. 8–9; A. I. and E. R. Root, op. cit., pp. 440–58; Carl Johansen, *Beekeeping* (PNW Bulletin no. 79, rev. edn. March 1970).

[10]  For further details see Carl Johansen, op. cit., F. E. Moeller, "Managing Colonies for High Honey Yields," in *Beekeeping*, p. 23; E. Oertel, "Nectar and Pollen Plants," in *Beekeeping*, p. 10.

hive will vary positively with the colony strength. Because the maximization of honey yield requires that the colonies be of equal strength, they are usually reassorted in preparation for the major honey season, so that the number of colonies at the "peak" is generally larger than the number in spring.[11]

When pollen fails in late fall, the hives become broodless and the bee population begins to decline. During the idle winter months adult bees live considerably longer than in the active season, and they can survive the winter if about 60 pounds of nectar are left in the hive. But in the northern part of the state and in Canada, where cold weather makes the overwintering of bees more costly, the common practice is to eliminate the bees and extract the remaining honey. It should be noted here that bees can be captured, and that they can be easily eliminated by any of a large number of pesticide sprays.[12] The cost of enforcing property rights in nectar is therefore much lower than economists have been led to believe.

Few agricultural crops, to my knowledge, exhibit a higher year-to-year variance of yield than does the honey crop. Several natural factors contribute. Cold weather and rain discourage the bees from working, and winds alter their direction of flight. Also, the nectar flows of plants are susceptible to shocks of heat and cold.[13] The plants yielding most honey are mint, fireweed, and the legumes, such as alfalfa and the clovers. Fruit trees usually have low nectar flows, although orange blossoms (in California) are excellent. Indeed, the pollination of fruits, especially the cherry in early spring, may actually detract from the yield of honey: less honey may be in the hive after pollination than was there initially, owing to the bees' own consumption. Another reason for the low honey yield from fruit trees is the relatively short time that the hives are left in the orchards.

Cross-pollination is accidentally effected as the bees forage for nectar and pollen. Pollination services were not marketed before World War I, primarily because small farms had enough flowering plants and trees to attract wild insects. It was not until 1910 and the advent of modern orcharding, with its large acreage and orderly planting, that markets for pollination services began to grow rapidly.[14]

---

[11] According to a survey conducted by Robert K. Lesser in 1968, based on a sample of 30 out of 60 commercial beekeepers in the state of Washington, the total number of peak colonies is 14.6% higher than that of spring colonies. See Robert K. Lesser, "An Investigation of the Elements of Income from Beekeeping in the State of Washington" (unpublished thesis, School of Business Administration, Gonzaga University, 1969), p. 74.

[12] See, for example, A. I. and E. R. Root, op. cit., pp. 97–103; Eugene Keyarts, "Bee Hunting," *Gleanings in Bee Culture* (June 1960); pp. 329–33; U.S. Dept of Agriculture, *Protecting Honey Bees from Pesticides* (Leaflet 544, 1972); Carl A. Johansen, *How to Reduce Poisoning of Bees from Pesticides* (Pamphlet EM 3473, Washington State University, College of Agriculture, May 1971); Philip F. Torchio, "Pesticides," in *Beekeeping*, p. 97.

[13] See E. Oertel, op. cit.; C. R. Ribbands, *The Behaviour and Social Life of Honeybees* (1953) pp. 69–75 Roger A. Morse, "Placing Bees in Apple Orchards," *Gleanings in Bee Culture* (April 1960) pp. 230–3. Owing to its weather, Washington is not one of the better honey yielding states in the Union. Data made available to me by the U.S. Dept of Agriculture indicates that over the years (1955–71) Washington ranks 24th among 48 states in yield per colony and 20th in the total number of colonies. The U.S. Dept of Agriculture data, like those obtained by Lesser, provide no information on the different honey yields and pollination requirements of various plants and are therefore of little use for our present purpose. It should be noted that the U.S. Dept of Agriculture overall yield data are significantly lower than those obtained by Lesser and by me. See Robert K. Lesser, op. cit.

[14] See M. D. Levin, "Pollination," in *Beekeeping*, p. 77.

Today, the services are demanded not only for production of fruits but also for the setting (fertilizing) of seeds for legumes and vegetables. Evidence is incontrovertible that the setting of fruits and seeds increases with the number of hives per acre, that the pollination productivity of bees is subject to diminishing returns, and, despite some beekeepers' claims to the contrary, beyond some point the marginal productivity may even be negative.[15] There is also strong evidence that pollination yield will improve if the hives are placed strategically throughout the farm rather than set in one spot.[16] The closer a particular area is to a hive, the more effective will be the pollination within that area. Although each individual bee will forage only a few square yards, the bees from one hive will collectively pollinate a large circular area,[17] and this gives rise to a problem: given a high cost to control fully the foraging behavior of bees, if similar orchards are located close to one another, one who hires bees to pollinate his own orchard will in some degree benefit his neighbors. This complication will be further discussed in the next section.

In the state of Washington, about 60 beekeepers each own 100 colonies or more; at the peak season the state's grand total of colonies is about 90,000. My investigation, conducted in the spring of 1972, covered a sample of nine beekeepers and a total of approximately 10,000 spring colonies. (One of these beekeepers specialized in cut-comb honey and he will be treated separately in a footnote.) Table 3.1 lists the bee-related plants covered by my investigation. As seen from columns 3 and 4, some plants (such as cherry trees) require pollination services for fruit setting but yield no honey; some (such as mint) yield honey while requiring no pollination service; and some (such as alfalfa) are of a reciprocal nature. Note that when alfalfa and the clovers are grown only for hay, pollination services are not required, although these plants yield honey.

The practice of relocating hives from farm to farm, by truck, enables the beekeeper to obtain multiple crops a year, either in rendering pollination service or in extracting honey. However, while the maximum observed number of crops per hive per year is four and the minimum is two, my estimate is that a hive averages only 2.2 crops a year. More frequent rotation not only involves greater costs of moving and of standardizing hives, but abbreviates the honey yield per crop. In the southern part of the state, where the relatively warm climate permits an early working season, beekeepers usually begin by pollinating either cheery or almond (in California) in early spring. The hives may or may not then be moved northward

---

[15] Ibid., 9th Pollination Conference, Report, *The Indispensable Pollinators* (Ag. Extension Serv., Hot Springs, Ark., October 12–15, 1970); G. E. Bohart, "Insect Pollination of Forage Legumes," *Bee World* 41 (1960), pp. 57–64, 85–97; J. B. Free, Pollination of Fruit Trees," *Bee World* 41 (1960), pp. 141–51, 169–86; U.S. Dept of Agriculture, *Using Honey Bees to Pollinate Crops* (Leaflet 549, 1968); *Get More Fruit with Honey Bee Pollinators* (Pamphlet EM 2922, Washington State University, March 1968); *Protect Berry Pollinating Bees* (Pamphlet EM 3341, Washington State University, February 1970); *Increase Clover Seed Yields with Adequate Pollination* (Pamphlet EM 3444, Washington State University, April 1971); *Honey Bees Increase Cranberry Production* (Pamphlet EM 3468, Washington State University, April 1971).

[16] See, for example, Douglas Oldershaw, "The Pollination of High Bush Blueberries," in *The Indispensable Pollinators*, op. cit. (note 15), pp. 171–6; Roger A. Morse, op. cit. (note 13).

[17] There is, however, little agreement as to how far a bee could fly: estimated range is from one to three miles. For general foraging behavior, see M. D. Levin, op. cit. (note 14), p. 79; O. W. Park, "Activities of Honeybees," in Roy A. Grout (ed.) (1946) *The Hive and the Honeybee*, pp. 125, 149–206; C. R. Ribbands, op. cit. (note 13).

**Table 3.1**  Bee-related Plants Investigated (State of Washington, 1971)

| (1)<br>Plants | (2)<br>Number<br>of<br>beekeepers | (3)<br>Pollination<br>services<br>rendered | (4)<br>Surplus<br>honey<br>expected | (5)<br>Approximate<br>season | (6)<br>Number of<br>hives per<br>acre (range) |
|---|---|---|---|---|---|
| **Fruits and nuts** | | | | | |
| Apple and soft fruits[a] | 7 | Yes | No | Mid-April–mid-May | 0.4 to 2 |
| Blueberry (with maple) | 1 | Yes | Yes | May | 2 |
| Cherry (early) | 1 | Yes | No | March–early April | 0.5 to 2 |
| Cherry | 2 | Yes | No | April | 0.5 to 2 |
| Cranberry | 2 | Yes | Negligible | June | 1.5 |
| Almond (Calif.) | 2 | Yes | No | February–March | 2 |
| **Legumes** | | | | | |
| Alfalfa | 5 | Yes and no[c] | Yes | June–September | 0.3 to 3 |
| Red clover | 4 | Yes and no | Yes | June–September | 0.5 to 5 |
| Sweet clover | 1 | No[d] | Yes | June–September | 0.5 to 1 |
| Pasture[b] | 4 | No | Yes | Late May–September | 0.3 to 1 |
| **Other plants** | | | | | |
| Cabbage | 1 | Yes | Yes | Early April–May | 1 |
| Fireweed | 2 | No | Yes | July–September | n.a. |
| Mint | 3 | No | Yes | July–September | 0.4 to 1 |

[a] Soft fruits include pears, apricots, and peaches.
[b] Pasture includes a mixture of plants, notably the legumes and other wild flowers such as dandelions.
[c] Pollination services are rendered for alfalfa and the clovers if their seeds are intended to be harvested; when they are grown only for hay, hives will still be employed for nectar extraction.
[d] Sweet clover may also require pollination services, but such a case is not covered by this investigation.

in late spring, when apple and soft fruits (and some late cherry) begin to bloom.[18]

The lease period for effective pollination during spring bloom is no more than a week. But then, for a month or two between the end of fruit pollination and the beginning of summer nectar flow, the hives have little alternative usage. Since this period is substantially longer than the time needed for the beekeeper to check and standardize his hives for the honey crops, he will generally be in no hurry to move them and will prefer to leave them in the orchards with no extra charge, unless the farmer is planning to spray with insecticide. The appropriate seasons for the various plants listed in column 5 of table 3.1 may not, therefore, match the lengths of

[18] Following the practice of local beekeepers, we use the term "soft fruit" to refer to peaches, pears, and apricots, generally grown in the same area, and often in the same orchard, as apples. (By standard usage, the term refers only to the various berry plants.)

hive leases. Lease periods are generally longer for honey crops, for the collection of nectar takes more time.

The sixth column in table 3.1 indicates the various hive-densities employed. The number of hives per acre depends upon the size of the area to be serviced, the density of planting, and, in the case of fruit pollination, the age of the orchards. For the pollination of fruits, the hives are scattered throughout the farm, usually with higher densities employed in older orchards because the trees are not strategically placed to facilitate the crossing of pollen. The most popular choices are one hive per acre and one hive per two acres. It is interesting, and easily understood, that farmers demand significantly fewer hives for pollination than the number recommended by entomologists:[19] both are interested in the maximization of yield, but for the farmer such maximization is subject to the constraint of hive rentals. When bees are employed to produce honey only, the hives are placed together in one location, called an apiary, for greater ease of handling.[20] The relatively large variation in hive densities required if legumes are, or are not, to be pollinated is discussed in the next section.

Before we turn to an analysis of the pricing and contractual behavior of beekeepers and farmers, I must point out that the two government programs which support the beekeeping industry did not constitute relevant constraints for the period under investigation. The honey price-support program, initiated in 1949, involves purchase of honey at supported prices by the Commodity Credit Corporation.[21] For the period under investigation, however, the supported price was about 20 percent lower than the market price.[22] Section 804 of the Agricultural Act of 1970, effectuated in 1971 and designed to reimburse beekeepers for any loss due to pesticide sprays, has been largely ignored by beekeepers because of the difficulty of filing effective claims with the federal government.[23]

## II THE OBSERVED PRICING AND CONTRACTUAL BEHAVIOR

It is easy to find conclusive evidence showing that both nectar and pollination services are transacted in the marketplace: in some cities one need look no further than the yellow pages of the telephone directory. But the existence of prices does not in itself imply an efficient allocation of resources. It is, therefore, necessary to demonstrate the effectiveness of the market in dictating the use even of those resources – bees, nectar, and pollen – which, admittedly, are elusive in character and relatively

[19] See note 15 above.

[20] See, for example, W. P. Nye, "Beekeeping Regions in the United States," in *Beekeeping*, p. 17.

[21] See Harry A. Sullivan, "Honey Price Support Program," in *Beekeeping*, p. 136.

[22] From 1970 to 1972 the supported prices were near 11.5 cents per pound, whereas the market wholesale price was above 14 cents per pound. Between 1950 and 1965 were seven years in which the CCC purchased no honey, and two years of negligible amounts. See Harry A. Sullivan, op. cit. (note 21), p. 137.

[23] See 7 U.S.C. § 135 b, note (1970); Pub. L. no. 91–524 § 804. My judgment is based both on the behavior of beekeepers (see next section) after the initiation of the Act and on the complexity of relevant claim forms which I have at hand. In April 1972 beekeepers associations were still lobbying for easier claiming conditions.

insignificant in value. In doing so, I shall not attempt to estimate the standard sets of marginal values which an efficient market is said to equate: the burden of such a task must rest upon those who believe the government can costlessly and accurately make these estimates for the imposition of the "ideal" tax-subsidy schemes. Rather, I offer below an analysis based on the equimarginal principle. To the extent that the observed pricing and contractual behavior fails to falsify the implications derived from this analysis we conclude that (1) the observed behavior is explained, and (2) the observations are consistent with efficient allocation of resources.

## The analysis

The reciprocal situation in which a beekeeper is able to extract honey from the same farm to which he renders pollination services poses an interesting theoretic riddle. The traditional analysis of such a condition relies on some interdependent production functions, and is, I think, unnecessarily complex.[24] The method employed here simply treats pollination services and honey yield as components of a joint product generated by the hive. That is, the rental price per hive received by a beekeeper for placing his hives on a farm may be paid in terms of honey, of a money fee, or of a combination of both. The money fee or the honey yield may be either positive or negative, but their total measures the rental value of the hive.

The solution is illustrated in figure 3.1. We assume that the hives are always strategically placed. In figure 3.1(a) the curve $(\partial N/\partial h)_a$ depicts the value of the marginal nectar product of a farm in which beehives are used *only* for the extraction of nectar (as with fireweed, mint, or alfalfa grown only for hay), with the farming assets held constant. Given the market-determined rental price of OA per hive, constrained wealth maximization implies that OQ' of hives will be employed. In this case, the beekeeper will be remunerated only in honey, and will pay an *apiary rent* equal to area ABC (or DB per hive) to the farmer. The curve $(\partial P/\partial h)_b$, on the other hand, depicts the value of the marginal pollination product for a farm which employs hives for pollination *only* (as with cherry or apple orchards). Here the number of hives employed will be OQ, which again is the result of wealth maximization. With zero honey yield, the money pollination fee per hive is again OA, and the *orchard rent* is represented by the area AGH.

We now turn to the joint product case in Figure 3.1(b), where hives are used both for pollination and for the extraction of nectar (as in the setting of alfalfa and clover seeds). The curves $(\partial P/\partial h)_c$ and $(\partial N/\partial h)_c$ respectively are the values of marginal pollination and of marginal nectar products. Their *vertical* summation, the solid line $(\partial V/\partial h)_d$, is the total marginal value. Wealth maximization implies the employment of OQ" of hives, the point where the rental price per hive equals the

---

[24] In J. E. Meade, op. cit. (note 3), p. 53, this problem is set up in terms of the interdependent functions $x_1 = H_1, (1_1, c_1, x_2)$ and $x_2 = H_2 (1_2, c_2, x_1)$. I find Meade's analysis difficult to follow. Elsewhere, Otto A. Davis and Andrew Whinston employ the functions $C_1 = C_1 (q_1, q_2)$ and $C_2 = C_3 (q_1, q_2)$ in their treatment of certain "externalities." It is not clear, however, that the authors had the bee example in mind. See Otto A. Davis and Andrew Whinston, "Externalities, Welfare, and the Theory of Games," *J. Pol. Econ.* 70 (1962), p. 241.

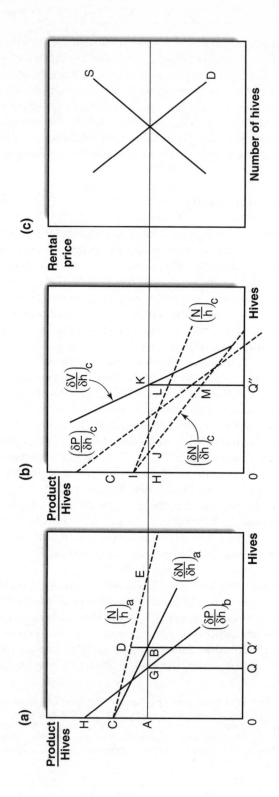

**Figure 3.1**  The supply of hives and demand for hives

aggregate marginal value. As drawn, area HIJ is smaller than area JKM. This implies that the value of the *average* nectar product, $(N/h)_c$ must pass below point K, as it does here at L. In this case the rental price per hive, KQ″, will consist of LQ″ in honey yield and KL in pollination fee. For this joint product situation, of course, it is possible to construct a case in which $(N/h)_c$ passes above point K, thus yielding an apiary rent. It is also possible to construct cases where the number of hives employed yields zero or negative marginal productivity, in either nectar or pollination. In other words, *zero or negative marginal productivity in one component of the joint product is consistent with efficient allocation of resources*.

Under open competition, there are large numbers of potential participants in each of the cases above. The aggregate total marginal value curve for the market, or the market demand for hives, is therefore the horizontal summation of a large number of the *solid* curves in Figures 3.1(a) and 3.1(b). Similarly, the market supply of hives is the horizontal summation of the marginal costs of producing and keeping hives of all actual and potential beekeepers. Both market curves are shown in Figure 3.1(c).[25] Assuming no costs for collating bids and asks or for forming rental contracts among all actual and potential participants, the price per hive, OA, is determined in the market. The Pareto condition is satisfied: the value of the marginal product of a hive is the same on every farm, and in turn equals the rental price and the marginal opportunity cost of producing the hive.

## Tests of implications

Before we derive and test some implications of the above analysis, it is necessary to point out the limitations of the information at hand. Since no attempt is made to estimate the marginal values or the elasticities of the marginal products, we will seek to confirm the marginal equalities with some observed average values. These include apiary rent, pollination fees, honey yields per hive, and the wholesale price of honey. We also have information on the number of hives employed on different farms, and some other numerical data. My choice of data for the honey yield per hive, however, must be qualified. The large fluctuations in yield from year to year and even from farm to farm caused by uncontrollable natural phenomena makes the use of the actual observed yields of a particular year, or even of a few years, irrelevant for our purposes. Take, for example, the exceptionally poor year of 1971 when, in many cases, the yield per hive was just one-third of that in a normal year. This windfall loss is irrelevant for decision-making (although the expected variance is relevant), and it cannot be attributed to market "failure." Lacking sufficient data to compute the honey yield per hive extracted from various plants over time, I resort to the expected yields as reported by beekeepers. Fortunately, their estimates for yields under comparable conditions-exhibit remarkable consistency.

An overall view of the pricing structure is shown in Table 3.2. Since a hive has different rental values for different seasons, we divide the time period into three

---

[25] More variables are usually used in the derivation of these curves, but for our present purpose little is gained by incorporating them.

**Table 3.2** Pricing schemes and expected honey yields of bee-related plants (State of Washington, 1970–1)

| Seasons | Plants | Surplus honey expected (pounds per hive) | Honey prices per pound (whole sale, 1970) | Pollination fees (range, 1971) | Approximate apiary rent per hive (range, 1970–1) |
|---|---|---|---|---|---|
| Early | Almond (Calif.) | 0 | – | $5–$8 | 0 |
| spring | Cherry | 0 | – | $6–$8 | 0 |
| | | | | | |
| Late | Apple and soft | | | | |
| spring | fruits | 0 | – | $9–10 | 0 |
| (major | Blueberry | | | | |
| pollination | (with maple) | 40 | 14¢ | $5 | 0 |
| season) | Cabbage | 15 | 13¢ | $8 | 0 |
| | Cherry | 0 | – | $9–$10 | 0 |
| | Cranberry | 5 | 13¢ | $9 | 0 |
| | | | | | |
| Summer | Alfalfa | 60 | 14.5¢ | 0 | 13¢–60¢ |
| and | Alfalfa | | | | |
| early | (with pollination) | 25–35 | 14.5¢ | $3–$5 | 0 |
| fall | Fireweed | 60 | 14.5¢ | 0 | 25¢–63¢ |
| (major | Mint | 70–75 | 11¢ | 0 | 15¢–65¢ |
| honey | Pasture | 60 | 14¢ | 0 | 15¢–65¢ |
| season) | Red clover | 60 | 14¢ | 0 | 65¢ |
| | Red clover | | | | |
| | (with pollination) | 0–35 | 14¢ | $3–$6 | 0 |
| | Sweet clover | 60 | 14¢ | 0 | 20¢–25¢ |

productive seasons: early spring, late spring, and the honey season (summer to fall). Surplus honey is not expected in the early spring season, although nectar may accumulate in the brood chamber and there may be a gain in brood strength. Most beekeepers in the state are idle during this season, and pollination is confined to almond in California or cherry in the southern part of Washington. The rental value of hives is the highest in the major pollination season of late spring (April to June), second highest in the major honey season, and lowest in the early spring (March).

The pollination fees listed in Table 3.2 are based on 1971 data, but they have remained roughly constant from 1970 to 1972. The wholesale honey prices, however, are based on 1970 and early 1971 data, as the unexpectedly low honey yield throughout the country in 1971 generated a a sharp rise in prices (from 14 cents a pound in April 1971 to 32 cents a pound in March 1972). The apiary rents are paid mostly in refined and bottled honey, and are therefore converted into money values according to 1970 retail honey prices. To maintain consistency with pollination fees, the apiary rents are computed per hive, although in the latter contracts the number of hives is not stipulated.

The following test implications are derived from our analysis.

Our first implication is that, at the same season and with colonies of the same strength, the rental price per hive obtained from different farms or by different beekeepers will be roughly the same whether the hive is employed for pollination, for honey production, or for a combination of both. By "roughly the same" I do not mean that hive rentals are invariable among different beekeepers. Rather, I mean that any differences which do occur are statistically no more significant than those for most other commodities in the market, and that there is a strong *negative* correlation between the pollination fee (hive rental in money) and the expected honey yield (hive rental in kind).

Data from the early spring season are not suitable to test this implication because during this period there are great variations in colony strength, in the gains in brood and unextracted nectar, and in distances traveled by beekeepers to deliver the hives.[26] Lacking sufficient information to make appropriate adjustments for these variations in calculating the rental price per hive, we concentrate on data from the late spring and summer seasons.

In contracting for pollination services, beekeepers offer discounts for larger numbers of hives and for less elaborate hive dispersals. Of the four beekeepers from whom detailed records are available, for example, each served from 10 to 14 farms of apples and soft fruits; their mean hive rentals in the major pollination season ranged from $9.20 to $9.68 and their coefficients of variation from 0.025 to 0.053.[27] To reduce the effects on price generated by discounts, we use the mean rentals for the above four beekeepers and the reported means from beekeepers who did not maintain records. Our data thus comprise separate observations of the mean hive rental of each beekeeper, of each different plant, and (for the summer season) of each different expected honey yield for the same plant. The latter separation is requisite because the expectation of honey yield varies greatly depending on whether pollination is, or is not, required in the case of such plants as alfalfa.

The coefficient of variation of the mean hive rentals among beekeepers who engaged in the pollination of apples (including soft fruits) and cherries (nine observations in total) is 0.035. The expected honey yield for these observations is zero. When we extend the computation to include cranberry, blueberry and cabbage pollination (13 observations in total), with expected honey yields converted into monetary terms and added to the pollination fees, the coefficient of variation is 0.042. We may meaningfully compare our coefficients of variations with those cited by George Stigler:[28] automobile prices (0.017) and anthracite coal prices (0.068).

---

[26] In the pollination of almond, for example, $5.00 is charged for a one-story hive and $6.00 to $8.00 for a two-story hive. On the one hand, Washington beekeepers have to travel to California to obtain this amount when they could have earned the same fee locally in the pollination of early cherry. On the other hand, however, the brood gain is greater with almond than with cherry; also, unextracted nectar in the brood chamber gains significantly in the case of almond but is likely to suffer a net loss with early cherry.

[27] An analysis of variance performed for these four beekeepers shows no significant difference in their mean rentals in the pollination of apple and soft fruits. However, the coefficient of variation of their means, 0.018, is lower than those computed from a larger body of data. This simply indicates a very low variation among the four who provided detailed records.

[28] George J. Stigler, "The Economics of Information," *J. Pol. Econ.* 69 (1961), p. 213.

Another, and more illuminating, way of testing our implication is through the relationship

$$x_0 = x_1 + x_2, \tag{1}$$

where $x_0$ is the total rent per hive, $x_1$ is the rent paid in money, and $x_2$ is the expected rent paid in nectar. During the major pollination season, $x_1$ is positive for all our observations, but during the summer honey season negative values for $x_1$ (that is, payments in apiary rents) are common. As noted earlier, $x_2$ may also be positive or negative, but it is generally either zero or positive for the late spring and summer seasons. In the major pollination season, the mean values of equation (1) are $9.65 = $9.02 + $0.64.

The variance of $x_0$ can be broken down to

$$\sigma^2_{x_0} = \sigma^2_{x_1} + \sigma^2_{x_2} + 2 \operatorname{Cov}(x_1, x_2). \tag{2}$$

With a total of 13 observations in late spring, the corresponding values are

$$0.166 = 1.620 + 2.317 - 3.771.$$

The variability in $x_1$ is almost entirely accounted for by the variability in $x_2$, as reflected by the large negative covariance term. The coefficient of correlation between $x_1$ and $x_2$ is $-0.973$.

Turning to the summer honey season, we have a total of 23 observations, covering mint (3), fireweed (2), pasture (4), sweet clover (1), red clover (6), and alfalfa (7). The mean values of equation (1) are $8.07 = $1.30 + $6.77. The values corresponding to equation (2) are

$$0.806 = 5.414 + 6.182 - 10.791.$$

Again, most of the variability in $x_1$ is strongly and negatively correlated with that of $x_2$. The remaining variance for $x_0$ (with a coefficient of variation of 0.111) is larger here than in the major pollination season. This can be explained as follows. First, high risks are associated with the expected honey yields, and beekeepers seem willing to settle for lower, but more certain, incomes. Since $x_1$ is more certain than $x_2$, beekeepers seem willing to accept a lower $x_0$ with a higher ratio of $x_1$ to $x_2$,[29] and the variability in this ratio is larger in summer than in spring. Similarly, they will accept a lower expected mean of $x_2$ for mint than for other honey crops, since mint is generally known to have the smallest variance in expected honey yield of any crop in the state.[30] A second, and more important, factor contributing to the larger

[29] This statement is drawn only from casual conversations with beekeepers; no attempt was made to seek refuting evidence.

[30] Inconclusive evidence indicates that hive rentals (paid in honey) obtained from mint is about 40 cents less than those obtained from other honey-yielding plants. Although available information is insufficient for us to compute the year-to-year variances of the honey yields of different plants, ranges of yields as recalled by beekeepers are larger than most agricultural crops.

variance of $x_0$ is the premium paid to beekeepers to assume the risk of pollinating crops (notably red clover) where the use of pesticide sprays on neighboring farms poses the danger of loss of bees. Since our information is inadequate to support adjustments for these factors, the resultant distortions must remain. Even so, the coefficient of correlation between $x_1$ and $x_2$ computed from the data is $-0.933$.

Second, the preceding evidence confirms that the rental prices of hives employed in different uses by different beekeepers lie on a roughly horizontal line. However, it does not confirm that these prices are equated to the marginal productivities. Refer to Figure 3.1, for example: the employment of hives might be at a point such as E rather than at G, B, or K. We now turn to some testable implications regarding the tendency toward the equalization of price and marginal productivity.

One obvious implication is that, if the employment of hives renders no valuable pollination services, then an apiary rent will always be observed. In the entire body of evidence available to me, there is not a single observation to the contrary,[31] and this means, referring to Figure 3.1(a), that the employment of hives is to the left of point E. It should be noted here that even in the absence of demand for pollination some is effected when bees forage for nectar from alfalfa and the clovers, but this is not to be treated as a service unless the seeds are harvested.

Less obvious implications can be obtained from the case of a farm where hives may be employed for nectar extraction only *or* jointly with pollination services. When we discussed the reciprocal case, as depicted in Figure 3.1(b), it was noted that either an apiary rent or a pollination fee may be paid. With simple manipulation, the following implications are evident:

1. If an apiary rent is paid in the case of a joint product, and if the marginal pollination product is positive, the number of hives employed per acre is necessarily greater than where bees are used only for nectar extraction on the same or a similar farm.
2. If a pollination fee is paid in the case of a joint product, the number of hives

Because honey from mint has an undesirably strong flavor that excludes it from the retail market, it is either sold to bakeries or used to feed bees during the winter. Quite understandably, onion honey shares the distinction of being much cheaper than any other. Generally rated as the best is orange honey, which commands a wholesale premium of about 1 to 2 cents a pound. Between the extremes, different varieties of honey have roughly the same value and are graded more by clarity than by taste.

[31] One beekeeper specializing in cut-comb honey reported that he pays apiary rents even though no surplus honey is expected, provided that gains in brood strength and in unextracted nectar are expected to be substantial, as when the hives are placed in a farm with maples. This beekeeper is excluded from our first test of implication because he did not engage in pollination and his colonies were of greater strengths.

Cut-comb honey is more expensive than ordinary honey because the comb wax, which goes with the honey, is about three times the price of honey per pound. Only honey of top grades (very clear) will be extracted. This observation is implied by the law of demand, since with the comb top-grade honey becomes relatively cheap. Implied by the same law also is that this beekeeper chooses to forgo pollination contracts so that a higher honey yield can be obtained (see evidence in implication test 2). Even during the major pollination season, when little honey can be expected, he prefers to place his hives in farms where the colonies will gain greater strength than would occur if they were used for pollination. For a related discussion on similar implications of the law of demand, see Armen A. Alchian and William R. Allen, *Exchange and Production: Theory in Use* (1969), pp. 78–9. These implications are accepted here in spite of the criticism in John P. Gould and Joel Segall, "The Substitution Effects of Transportation Costs," *J. Pol. Econ.* 77 (1969), p. 130.

employed per acre is necessarily greater than where bees are used only for nectar extraction on the same or a similar farm.

While both implications indicate a tendency toward point K (in Figure 3.1(b), we lack sufficient information regarding the marginal pollination product to test (1) above. But since in every available observation involving pollination and nectar extraction a pollination fee is paid, only implication (2) is relevant for our purposes.

The evidence, obtained from red clover and alfalfa farms, strongly confirms the implication. The density of hives employed is at least twice as great when the bees are used for both pollination service and nectar extraction as when used for nectar extraction only. As a rule, this increase in hive density leads to a sharp decrease in the expected honey yield per hive. In the typical case, the density of hives in alfalfa and clover farms for pollination services is about 2.5 times what would be employed for nectar extraction only, and the expected honey yield per hive is reduced by 50 percent. This indicates the marginal nectar product of a hive is close to zero and possibly negative. In one extreme case, in a red clover farm the hive density with pollination services is reported at about seven or eight times that for nectar extraction only; since the expected honey yield is then reduced to zero, the marginal nectar product of the hive is clearly negative! But, as noted earlier, zero or negative marginal product in one component of a joint product is consistent with efficient allocation of resources.

Third, it remains for us to show that the rental price of a hive is roughly equal to the marginal cost of keeping it. Lacking data on marginal cost, we will show that the price approximates the average cost, as implied by competition. We will make the comparison in terms of some general considerations. The expected annual income of a spring colony under a normal rate of utilization, as of 1970–1, is about $19.00. This includes rentals from a pollination crop, a honey crop, an occasional extra crop (for some hives), and a small amount from the sale of beeswax.[32] The costs of delivering or moving a hive and of finding and contracting the farmers for its use are estimated to total about $9.00 per year.[33] This figure is obtained as follows. Some beekeepers lease some of their hives to other beekeepers on a share contract basis; the lessor receives 50 to 55 percent of whatever income in money and in kind the lessee obtains from the farmers. Since the lessor could have contracted to serve the farmers himself and obtained the entire income of the $19.00, the fact that he has chosen to take 45 to 50 percent less indicates that $9.00 must approximate such costs. The interest forgone in keeping a hive is about $3.00 per year.[34] The cost of renewing

[32] In Lesser's investigation (see note 11) the actual mean annual income of a spring colony for the year 1967 was estimated to be $14.71, and the actual honey yields of that year were slightly larger than our expected honey yields. But in 1967 the price of honey was about 16% lower than that in 1970; and Lesser's estimate of pollination income per hive is about 37% lower than mine, owing both to a rise in pollination fees in recent years and to different samplings of beekeepers. According to Lesser's estimate, beeswax constitutes 4.4% of the beekeeper's total income.

[33] The moving costs cover labor, truck, and other hive-handling equipment. Depending on the time of the year, a complete hive (with supers) weights somewhere between 80 and 250 pounds.

[34] A complete hive, used but in good condition, sells for about $35.00. The borrowing rate of interest for the beekeepers is around 8%.

the colony strength in early spring is about $4.50, the price of a standard booster package of bees.[35] This leaves about $2.50 to cover the costs of depreciation of the hive value, the labor involved in checking and standardizing hives, space for keeping hives in the winter, and the equipment used for honey extraction.

## Characteristics of the contractual arrangements

Contracts between beekeepers and farmers may be oral or written. I have at hand two types of written contracts. One is formally printed by an association of beekeepers; another is designed for specific beekeepers, with a few printed headings and space for stipulations to be filled in by hand.[36] Aside from situations where a third party demands documented proof of the contract (as when a beekeeper seeks a business loan), written contracts are used primarily for the initial arrangement between parties; otherwise oral agreements are made. Although a written contract is more easily enforceable in a court of law, extra-legal constraints are present: information travels quickly through the closely knit society of beekeepers and farmers,[37] and the market will penalize any party who does not honor his contracts. Oral contracts are rarely broken.

Pollination contracts usually include stipulations regarding the number and strength of the colonies, the rental fee per hive, the time of delivery and removal of hives, the protection of bees from pesticide sprays, and the strategic placing of hives. Apiary lease contracts differ from pollination contracts in two essential aspects. One is, predictably, that the amount of apiary rent seldom depends on the number of colonies, since the farmer is interested only in obtaining the rent per apiary offered by the highest bidder. Second, the amount of apiary rent is not necessarily fixed. Paid mostly in honey, it may vary according to either the current honey yield or the honey yield of the preceding year.[38]

In general, contractual arrangements between beekeepers and farmers do not materially differ from other lease contracts. However, some peculiar arrangements resulting from certain complications are worth noting. First, because of the foraging behavior of the bees a farmer who hires bees may benefit his neighbors. Second, the use of pesticide sprays by one farmer may cause damage to the bees on an

---

[35] The nectar left unextracted in the brood chamber, which constitutes the major cost of overwintering, is not counted as part of income and therefore is not counted as part of the cost.

[36] Some beekeepers use just postal cards. The general contractual details reported below are similar to those briefly mentioned in Grant D. Morse, "How about Pollination," *Gleanings in Bee Culture* (February 1970), pp. 73–8.

[37] During my conversations with beekeepers, I was impressed by their personal knowledge of one another, including details such as the number of hives owned, the kinds of farms served, and the rents received.

[38] While we may attribute this behavior to the aversion of risks, the apiary contracts are not the same as share contracts. Rather, they resemble fixed-rent contracts with what I have called "escape clauses." For discussion of the "escape clause" and the stipulations of the share contract, see Steven N. S. Cheung, *The Theory of Share Tenancy*, chs 2 and 4 (1969). One impression I obtain is that apiary rents generally involve such low values in Washington that elaborate formations and enforcements of apiary contracts are not worthwhile. In further investigations of these contracts, states with higher honey yields are recommended.

adjacent farm. And third, fireweed, which yields good honey, grows wild in forests. Let us discuss each in turn.

## The custom of the orchards

As noted earlier, if a number of similar orchards are located close to one another, one who hires bees to pollinate his own orchard will in some degree benefit his neighbors. Of course, the strategic placing of the hives will reduce the spillover of bees. But in the absence of any social constraint on behavior, each farmer will tend to take advantage of what spillover does occur and to employ fewer hives himself. Of course, contractual arrangements could be made among all farmers in an area to determine collectively the number of hives to be employed by each, but no such effort is observed.

Acknowledging the complication, beekeepers and farmers are quick to point out that a social rule, or custom of the orchards, takes the place of explicit contracting: during the pollination period the owner of an orchard either keeps bees himself or hires as many hives per area as are employed in neighboring orchards of the same type. One failing to comply would be rated as a "bad neighbor," it is said, and could expect a number of inconveniences imposed on him by other orchard owners.[39] This customary matching of hive densities involves the exchange of gifts of the same kind, which apparently entails lower transaction costs than would be incurred under explicit contracting, where farmers would have to negotiate and make money payments to one another for the bee spillover.[40]

## The case of pesticide sprays

At the outset, we must remember that to minimize the loss of bees from insecticide usage is not necessarily consistent with efficient allocation of resources. The relevant consideration is whether the gain from using the pesticide is greater than the associated loss of bees, in total and at the margin. Provided that the costs of forming contracts permits, beekeepers and farmers will seek cooperative arrangements such that the expected marginal gain from using the pesticide is equal to the value of the expected marginal bee loss. In the absence of the arrangements, however, the total gain from using the pesticide may still be greater than the associated loss; the

[39] The distinction between an oral or an implicit contract and a custom is not always clear. A common practice in some areas is that each farmer lets his neighbors know how many hives he employs. Perhaps the absence of a court of law to enforce what could in fact be a highly informal agreement is the reason why farmers deny the existence of any contract among them governing the employment of hives.

[40] Since with a sufficiently high reward the notoriety of being a "bad neighbor" will be tolerated, the likelihood of explicit contracting rises with increasing rental values of hives. Alternatively and concurrently, with a high enough rental price of hives the average size of orchards may increase through outright purchases, or the shapes of the orchards may be so tailored as to match the foraging behavior of the bees. By definition, given the gains the least costly arrangement will be chosen.

Some beekeepers reported that there are peculiar situations where the foraging behavior of the bees forces a one-way gift, but these situations are not covered by the present investigation. Even under these rare situations, the absence of both contractual and customary restraints may not result in a different allocation of resources. See Steven N. S. Cheung, *The Theory of Inter-Individual Effects and the Demand for Contracts* (University of Washington, Institute of Economic Research).

greater the expected damage done to bees, the greater will be the gain from the cooperative arrangements.[41]

When a pollination contract is formed, the farmer usually agrees to inform the beekeeper before spraying his crop, but this assurance will not protect the bees from pesticide used on neighboring farms. In areas dominated by orchards which require pollination at roughly the same time, such as the apple-growing districts, this agreement will suffice, for no farmer will apply the spray during the pollination period. But in regions where adjacent farms require bee pollination at different times, or do not require it at all, a farmer with no present obligation to any beekeeper may spray his fields and inflict damages to the bees rented by other farms. In this situation, only cooperation over a large geographic area can avoid bee loss, and we find just such arrangements in the pollination of cranberries but not of red clover.

Cranberry farms near Seattle are usually found in clusters, and spraying is conducted shortly after the bloom, which may vary by as much as a week or two among neighboring farms. Although each cranberry grower agrees not to spray until the contracted beekeeper removes the bees from his farm, this does not protect bees which may still remain on adjacent farms. Therefore the beekeepers make a further arrangement among themselves to remove all hives on the same date, thus insuring that all the bees are protected.

Red clover presents a different situation. Since the plant is often grown in areas where neighboring farms require no bee pollination, the pesticide danger is reportedly high and beekeepers demand an additional $1.00 to $2.00 per hive to assume the risk. But just as the beekeepers cooperate with one another during cranberry pollination, a clover farmer could make arrangements with his neighbors. Given that neighboring farmers have the legal right to use pesticide, the clover farmer would be willing to pay them an amount not exceeding the beekeeper's risk premium if they would refrain from spraying during the pollination period. Although no such arrangements are observed, it would seem that the costs of reaching an agreement would be no higher than those encountered in the case of the cranberries, and we must infer, pending empirical confirmation, that the gain from using the sprays is greater than the associated loss. This would particularly apply when a single farm requiring pollination is located amidst a large number of farms which require spraying during that same period.

## The case of fireweed

I have at hand two types of apiary contract pertaining to fireweed, a honey plant which grows wild in the forest. The first is between a beekeeper and the Weyerhauser Company, owner of private timber land; the second is between a beekeeper and the Water Department of the City of Seattle. Two distinctions between them are worth noting. First, while both contracts stipulate 25 cents per hive, Weyerhaeuser asks a minimum charge of $100, and the Water Department a minimum of $25. In the apiary for fireweed honey, the number of hives used by a beekeeper is more than

---

[41] For a fuller discussion, see Steven N. S. Cheung, ibid.

100 but less than 400. Thus it happens that in the case of Weyerhauser, the apiary rent is independent of the number of hives, whereas with the Water Department it is dependent. The "underpriced" rent levied by the Water Department would have implied some sort of queuing except that a second unique feature is incorporated in its apiary contracts: no beekeeper is granted the exclusive right to the fireweed nectar in a particular area. The implication is that competition among beekeepers will reduce the honey yield per hive until its apiary rent is no more than 25 cents; while no beekeeper attempts to exclude entrants, the parties do seek a mutual division of the total area to avoid chaotic hive placement. Finally, fireweed also grows wild in the national forests and for this case I have no contract at hand. My information is that apiary rent is measured by the hive, is subject to competitive bidding among beekeepers, and has a reported range of 25 to 63 cents with the winner being granted exclusive right to a particular area.

## III CONCLUSIONS

Whether or not Keynes was correct in his claim that policy makers are "distilling their frenzy" from economists, it appears evident that some economists have been distilling their policy implications from fables. In a desire to promote government intervention, they have been prone to advance, without the support of careful investigation, the notion of "market failure." Some have dismissed in cavalier fashion the possibility of market operations in matters of environmental degradation, as witnesses the assertion of E.J. Mishan:

> With respect to bodies of land and water, extension of property rights may effectively internalize what would otherwise remain externalities. But the possibilities of protecting the citizen against such common environmental blights as filth, fume, stench, noise, visual distractions, etc. by a market in property rights are too remote to be taken seriously.[42]

Similarly, it has been assumed that private property rights cannot be enforced in the case of fisheries, wildlife, and whatever other resources economists have chosen to call "natural." Land tenure contracts are routinely taken as inefficient, and to some the market will fail in the areas of education, medical care, and the like.

Then, of course, there is the fable of the bees.

In each case, it is true that costs involved in enforcement of property rights and in the formation of contracts will cause the market to function differently than it would without such costs. And few will deny that government does afford economic advantages. But it is equally true that any government action can be justi-

---

[42] E. J. Mishan, "A Reply to Professor Worcester," *J. Econ. Lit.* 10 (1972), pp. 59, 62. As immediate refutation of Professor Mishan's claim, I refer the reader to a factual example: Professor John McGee has just purchased a house, separated from that of his neighbor by a vacant lot. That the space would remain vacant had been assured by the previous owner who (upon learning that a third party was planning to buy the lot and construct a house there) had negotiated with the neighbor to make a joint purchase of the ground, thus protecting their two households from the "filth, fumes, stench, noise, visual distractions, etc." which would be generated by a new neighbor.

fied on efficiency grounds by the simple expedient of hypothesizing high enough transaction costs in the marketplace and low enough costs for government control. Thus to assume the state of the world to be as one sees fit is not even to compare the ideal with the actual but, rather, to compare the ideal with a fable.

I have no grounds for criticizing Meade and other economists who follow the Pigovian tradition for their use of the bee example to illustrate a theoretical point: certainly, resource allocation would in general differ from what is observed if the factors were "unpaid." My main criticism, rather, concerns their approach to economic inquiry in failing to investigate the real-world situation and in arriving at policy implications out of sheer imagination. As a result, their work contributes little to our understanding of the actual economic system.

# 4

# The Fable of the Keys

## Stan J. Liebowitz and Stephen E. Margolis*

## I INTRODUCTION

The term "standard" can refer to any social convention (standards of conduct, legal standards), but it most often refers to conventions that require exact uniformity (standards of measurement, computer-operating systems). Current efforts to control the development of high-resolution television, multitasking computer-operating systems, and videotaping formats have heightened interest in standards.

The economic literature on standards has focused recently on the possibility of market failure with respect to the choice of a standard. In its strongest form, the argument is essentially this: an established standard can persist over a challenger, even where all users prefer a world dominated by the challenger, if users are unable to coordinate their choices. For example, each of us might prefer to have Beta-format videocassette recorders as long as prerecorded Beta tapes continue to be produced, but individually we do not buy Beta machines because we don't think enough others will buy Beta machines to sustain the prerecorded tape supply. I don't buy a Beta format machine because I think that you won't; you don't buy one because you think that I won't. In the end, we both turn out to be correct, but we are both worse off than we might have been. This, of course, is a catch-22 that we might suppose to be common in the economy. There will be no cars until there are gas stations; there will be no gas stations until there are cars. Without some way out of this conundrum, joyriding can never become a favorite activity of teenagers.[1]

The logic of these economic traps and conundrums is impeccable as far as it goes, but we would do well to consider that these traps are sometimes escaped in

* Earlier drafts benefited from seminars at Clemson University and North Carolina State University, and we would like to thank the participants at those seminars. We would also like to thank James Buchanan, Dan Klein, Bill Landes, Nancy Margolis, Craig Newmark, John Palmer, Gregory Rehmke, George Stigler, and Wally Thurman for their suggestions.

[1] This trap is treated more seriously in the literature on standards than in other economics literature. This reflects a supposition that foresight, integration, or appropriation are more difficult in the case of standards. The current literature fails to explain why these "externalities" are particularly relevant for standards. We will have more to say about this in forthcoming work.

the market. Obviously, gas stations and automobiles do exist, so participants in the market must use some technique to unravel such conundrums. If this catch-22 is to warrant our attention as an empirical issue, at a minimum we would hope to see at least one real-world example of it. In the economics literature on standards,[2] the popular real-world example of this market failure is the standard Qwerty typewriter keyboard,[3] and its competition with the rival Dvorak keyboard.[4] This example as noted frequently in newspaper and magazine reports, seems to be generally accepted as true, and was brought to economists' attention by the papers of Paul David.[5] According to the popular story, the keyboard invented by August Dvorak, a professor of education at the University of Washington, is vastly superior to the Qwerty keyboard developed by Christopher Sholes that is now in common use. We are to believe that, although the Dvorak keyboard is vastly superior to Qwerty, virtually no one trains on Dvorak because there are too few Dvorak machines, and there are virtually no Dvorak machines because there are too few Dvorak typists.

This article examines the history, economics, and ergonomics of the typewriter keyboard. We show that David's version of the history of the market's rejection of Dvorak does not report the true history, and we present evidence that the continued use of Qwerty is efficient given the current understanding of keyboard design. We conclude that the example of the Dvorak keyboard is what beehives and lighthouses were for earlier market-failure fables. It is an example of market failure that will not withstand rigorous examination of the historical record.[6]

## II  SOME ECONOMICS OF STANDARDS

Some standards change over time without being impaired as social conventions. Languages, for example, evolve over time, adding words and practices that are useful and winnowing features that have lost their purpose. Other standards are inherently inflexible. Given current technologies, it won't do, for example, for broadcast frequencies to drift the way that orchestral tuning has. A taste for a slightly larger centimeter really can't be accommodated by a sequence of independent decisions the way that increased use of contractions in academic writing can. Obviously, if standards can evolve at low cost, they would be expected to evolve into the forms that are most efficient (in the eyes of those adopting the standards).

[2] See, for example, Joseph Farrell and Garth Saloner, "Standardization, Compatibility, and Innovation," *Rand J. Econ.* 16 (1985), p. 70; Michael L. Katz and Carl C. Shapiro, "Network Externalities, Competition, and Compatibility," *Am. Econ. Rev.* 75 (1985), p. 424; and Jean Tirole, *The Theory of Industrial Organization* (1988).
[3] "Qwerty" stands for arrangement of letters in the upper lefthand portion of the keyboard below the numbers. This keyboard is also known as the Sholes, or Universal, keyboard.
[4] This is also sometimes known as the DSK keyboard, for Dvorak Simplified Keyboard (or the simplified keyboard). As explained below, the letters are arranged in a different order.
[5] Paul A. David, "Clio and the Economics of QWERTY", *Am. Econ. Rev.* 75 (1985), p. 332; and Paul A. David, "Understanding the Economics of QWERTY: The Necessity of History," in *Economic History and the Modern Economist* (William N. Parker ed. 1986).
[6] See Ronald H. Coase, "The Lighthouse in Economics," *J. Law and Econ.* 17 (1974), p. 357; Steven N. S. Cheung, "The Fable of the Bees: An Economic Investigation," *J. Law and Econ.* 16 (1973), p. 11. Our debt is obvious.

Conversely, an inappropriate standard is most likely to have some permanence where evolution is costly.

In a [1985] article on standards, Joseph Farrell and Garth Saloner present a formal exploration of the difficulties associated with changing from one standard to another.[7] They construct hypothetical circumstances that might lead to market failure with respect to standards. To refer to the condition in which a superior standard is not adopted, they coin the phrase "excess inertia." Excess inertia is a type of externality: each nonadopter of the new standard imposes costs on every other potential user of the new standard. In the case of excess inertia, the new standard can be clearly superior to the old standard, and the sum of the private costs of switching to the new standard can be less than the sum of the private benefits, and yet the switch does not occur. This is to be differentiated from the far more common invention of new standards superior to the old, but for which the costs of switching are too high to make the switch practicable. Users of the old standard may regret their choice of that standard, but their continued use of the old standard is not inefficient; would it not be foolish to lay all regrets at the doorstep of externalities?

Farrell and Saloner's construct is useful because it shows the theoretical possibility of a market failure and also demonstrates the role of information. There is no possibility of excess inertia in their model if all participants can communicate perfectly. In this regard, standards are not unlike other externalities in that costs of transacting are essential. Thus, standards can be understood within the framework that Coase offered decades ago.[8]

By their nature, this model and others like it must ignore many factors in the markets they explore. Adherence to an inferior standard in the presence of a superior one represents a loss of some sort; such a loss implies a profit opportunity for someone who can figure out a means of internalizing the externality and appropriating some of the value made available from changing to the superior standard. Furthermore, institutional factors such as head starts from being first on the market, patent and copyright law, brand names, tie-in sales, discounts, and so on, can also lead to appropriation possibilities (read "profit opportunities") for entrepreneurs, and with these opportunities we expect to see activity set in motion to internalize the externalities. The greater the gap in performance between two standards, the greater are these profit opportunities, and the more likely that a move to the efficient standard will take place. As a result, a clear example of excess inertia is apt

---

[7] Farrell and Saloner, op. cit. (note 2).

[8] Ronald H. Coase, "The Problem of Social Cost," *J. Law and Econ.* 3 (1960), p. 1. Of course, inertia is not necessarily inefficient. Some delay in settling on a standard will mean that relatively more is known about the associated technology and the standards themselves by the time most users commit to a technology. Recall the well-known discussion of Harold Demsetz, "Information and Efficiency: Another Viewpoint," *J. Law and Econ.* 12 (1969), p. 1, on the nature of efficiency. If a God can costlessly cause the adoption of the correct standard, any inertia is excessive (inefficient) in comparison. But it seems ill advised to hold this up as a serious benchmark. Excessive inertia should be defined relative to some achievable result. Further, some reservation in committing to standards will allow their creators to optimize standards rather than rushing them to the market to be first. If the first available standard were always adopted, then standards, like patents, might generate losses from the rush to be first. Creators might rush their standards to market, even where waiting would produce a better and more profitable product.

to be very hard to find. Observable instances in which a dramatically inferior standard prevails are likely to be short-lived, imposed by authority, or fictional.

The creator of a standard is a natural candidate to internalize the externality.[9] If a standard can be "owned," the advantage of the standard can be appropriated, at least in part, by the owner. Dvorak, for example, patented his keyboard. An owner with the prospect of appropriating substantial benefits from a new standard would have an incentive to share some of the costs of switching to a new standard. This incentive gives rise to a variety of internalizing tactics. Manufacturers of new products sometimes offer substantial discounts to early adopters, offer guarantees of satisfaction, or make products available on a rental basis. Sometimes manufacturers offer rebates to buyers who turn in equipment based on old standards, thus discriminating in price between those who have already made investments in a standard and those who have not. Internalizing tactics can be very simple: some public utilities once supplied light bulbs, and some UHF television stations still offer free UHF indoor antennas. In many industries, firms provide subsidized or free training to assure an adequate supply of operators. Typewriter manufacturers were an important source of trained typists for at least the first fifty years of that technology.[10]

Another internalizing tactic is convertibility. Suppliers of new-generation computers occasionally offer a service to convert files to new formats. Cable-television companies have offered hardware and services to adapt old televisions to new antenna systems for an interim period. Of interest in the present context, for a time before and after World War II, typewriter manufacturers offered to convert Qwerty typewriters to Dvorak for a very small fee.[11]

All of these tactics tend to unravel the apparent trap of an inefficient standard, but there are additional conditions that can contribute to the ascendancy of the efficient standard. An important one is the growth of the activity that uses the standard. If a market is growing rapidly, the number of users who have made commitments to any standard is small relative to the number of future users. Sales of audiocassette players were barely hindered by their incompatibility with the reel-to-reel or eight-track players that preceded them. Sales of sixteen-bit computers were scarcely hampered by their incompatibility with the disks or operating systems of eight-bit computers.

Another factor that must be addressed is the initial competition among rival standards. If standards are chosen largely through the influence of those who are able to internalize the value of standards, we would expect, in Darwinian fashion, the prevailing standard to be the fittest economic competitor. Previous keyboard histories have acknowledged the presence of rivals, but they seem to view competition as a process leading to results indistinguishable from pure chance.

---

[9] We may ask ourselves why new standards are created if not with the idea of some pecuniary reward. One would hardly expect nonobvious and costly standards to proliferate like manna from heaven.

[10] David, "Understanding," op. cit. (note 5). Additionally, see Herkimer County Historical Society, *The Story of the Typewriter: 1873–1923* (1923), which notes that in the early 1920s a single typewriter company was placing 100,000 typists a year.

[11] Arthur Foulke, *Mr. Typewriter: A Biography of Christopher Latham Sholes* (1961), p. 106, which notes: "Present old keyboard machines may be converted to the simplified (Dvorak) keyboard in local typewriter shops. It is now available on any typewriter. And it costs as little as $5 to convert a Standard to a simplified keyboard."

Consideration of the many complicating factors present in the market suggests that market failure in standards is not as compelling as many of the abstract models seem to suggest. Theoretical abstraction presents candidates for what might be important, but only empirical verification can determine if these abstract models have anything to do with reality.

## III   THE CASE FOR THE SUPERIORITY OF THE DVORAK KEYBOARD

Paul David introduces economists to the conventional story of the development and persistence of the current standard keyboard, known as the Universal, or Qwerty, keyboard.[12] The key features of that story are as follows. The operative patent for the typewriter was awarded in 1868 to Christopher Latham Sholes, who continued to develop the machine for several years. Among the problems that Sholes and his associates addressed was the jamming of the type bars when certain combinations of keys were struck in very close succession. As a partial solution to this problem, Sholes arranged his keyboard so that the keys most likely to be struck in close succession were approaching the type point from opposite sides of the machine. Since Qwerty was designed to accomplish this now obsolete mechanical requirement, maximizing speed was not an explicit objective. Some authors even claim that the keyboard is actually configured to minimize speed since decreasing speed would have been one way to avoid the jamming of the typewriter. At the time, however, a two-finger hunt-and-peck method was contemplated, so the keyboard speed envisioned was quite different from touch-typing speeds.

The rights to the Sholes patent were sold to E. Remington & Sons in early 1873. The Remingtons added further mechanical improvements and began commercial production in late 1873.

A watershed event in the received version of the Qwerty story is a typing contest held in Cincinnati on July 25, 1888. Frank McGurrin, a court stenographer from Salt Lake City, who was apparently the first to memorize the keyboard and use touch-typing, won a decisive victory over Louis Taub. Taub used the hunt-and-peck method on a Caligraph, a machine that used seventy-two keys to provide upper- and lower-case letters. According to popular history, the event established once and for all that the Remington typewriter, with its Qwerty keyboard, was technically superior. More important, the contest created an interest in touch-typing, an interest directed at the Qwerty arrangement. Reportedly, no one else at that time had skills that could even approach McGurrin's, so there was no possibility of countering the claim that the Remington keyboard arrangement was efficient. McGurrin participated in typing contests and demonstrations throughout the country and became something of a celebrity. His choice of the Remington keyboard, which may well have been arbitrary, contributed to the establishment of the standard. So it was, according to the popular telling, that a keyboard designed to solve a short-

---

[12] David, "Clio and the Economics of QWERTY," op. cit. (note 5).

lived mechanical problem became the standard used daily by millions of typists.[13]

In 1936, August Dvorak patented the Dvorak Simplified Keyboard (DSK), claiming that it dramatically reduced the finger movement necessary for typing by balancing the load between hands and loading the stronger fingers more heavily. Its inventors claimed advantages of greater speed, reduced fatigue, and easier learning. These claims have been accepted by most commentators, including David, who refers, without citation, to experiments done by the U.S. Navy that "had shown that the increased efficiency obtained with the DSK would amortize the cost of retraining a group of typists within ten days of their subsequent full-time employment."[14] In spite of its claimed advantages, the Dvorak keyboard has never found much acceptance.

This story is the basis of the claim that the current use of the Qwerty keyboard is a market failure. The claim continues that a beginning typist will not choose to train in Dvorak because Dvorak machines are likely to be difficult to find, and offices will not equip with Dvorak machines because there is no available pool of typists.

This is an ideal example. The number of dimensions of performance are few, and in these dimensions the Dvorak keyboard appears overwhelmingly superior. These very attributes, however, imply that the forces to adopt this superior standard should also be very strong. It is the failure of these forces to prevail that warrants our critical examination.

## IV  THE MYTH OF DVORAK

Farrell and Saloner mention the typewriter keyboard as a clear example of market failure.[15] So, too, does the textbook by Tirole.[16] Both works cite David's article as the authority on this subject. Yet there are many aspects of the Qwerty-versus-Dvorak fable that do not survive scrutiny. First, the claim that Dvorak is a better keyboard is supported only by evidence that is both scant and suspect. Second, studies in the ergonomics literature find no significant advantage for Dvorak that can be deemed scientifically reliable. Third, the competition among producers of typewriters, out

---

[13] This history follows David, "Clio and the Economics of QWERTY," op. cit. (note 5), but also see Wilfred A. Beeching, *A Century of the Typewriter* (1974), as an example of an account with the features and emphasis described here.

[14] David, "Clio," op. cit., p. 332. If true, this would be quite remarkable. A converted Sholes typist will be typing so much faster that whatever the training cost, it is repaid every ten days. Counting only working days, this would imply that the investment in retraining repays itself approximately twenty-three times in a year. Does this seem even remotely possible? Do firms typically ignore investments with returns in the range of 2,200 percent?

[15] Farrell and Saloner, op. cit. (note 2).

[16] Tirole, op. cit. (note 2), p. 405, states: "Many observers believe that the Dvorak keyboard is superior to this [Qwerty] standard, even when retraining costs are taken into account. However, it would be foolish for a firm to build this alternative keyboard and for secretaries to switch to it individually." Under some circumstances it might have been foolish for secretaries and firms to act in this manner. But this type of behavior hardly seems foolish in many real-world situations. For example, large organizations (federal, state, and local governments, Fortune 500 companies, etc.), often have tens of thousands of employees, and these organizations could undertake the training if the costs really are compensated in a short time. See notes 11 and 14 above.

of which the standard emerged, was far more vigorous than is commonly reported. Fourth, there were far more typing contests than just the single Cincinnati contest. These contests provided ample opportunity to demonstrate the superiority of alternative keyboard arrangements. That Qwerty survived significant challenges early in the history of typewriting demonstrates that it is at least among the reasonably fit, even if not the fittest that can be imagined.

## Gaps in the evidence for Dvorak

Like most of the historians of the typewriter,[17] David seems to assume that Dvorak is decisively superior to Qwerty. He never questions this assertion, and he consistently refers to the Qwerty standard as inferior. His most tantalizing evidence is his undocumented account of the U.S. Navy experiments. After recounting the claims of the Navy study, he adds "If as Apple advertising copy says, DSK 'lets you type 20 to 40% faster' why did this superior design meet essentially the same resistance as the previous seven improvements on the Qwerty typewriter keyboard?"[18]

Why indeed? The survival of Qwerty is surprising to economists only in the presence of a demonstrably superior rival. David uses Qwerty's survival to demonstrate the nature of path dependency, the importance of history for economists, and the inevitable oversimplification of reality imposed by theory. Several theorists use his historical evidence to claim empirical relevance for their versions of market failure. But on what foundation does all this depend? All we get from David is an undocumented assertion and some advertising copy.

The view that Dvorak is superior is widely held. This view can be traced to a few key sources. A book published by Dvorak and several coauthors in 1936 included some of Dvorak's own scientific inquiry.[19] Dvorak and his coauthors compared the typing speed achieved in four different and completely separate experiments, conducted by various researchers for various purposes.[20] One of these experiments examined the typing speed on the Dvorak keyboard, and three examined typing speed on the Qwerty keyboard. The authors claimed that these studies established that students learn Dvorak faster than they learn Qwerty. A serious criticism of their methodology is that the various studies that they compared used students of different ages and abilities (for example, students learning Dvorak in grades 7 and 8 at the University of Chicago Lab School were compared with students in conventional high schools), in different school systems taking different tests, and in classes that met for different periods of time. Still more serious is that they did not stipulate whether their choice of studies was a random sample or the full population of available studies. So their study really establishes only that it is possible to find studies in which students learning to type on Qwerty keyboards appear to have progressed less rapidly in terms of calendar time than Dvorak's students did on his

---

[17] For example, see Beeching, op. cit. (note 13), or Foulke, op. cit. (note 11).
[18] David, "Understanding," op. cit. (note 5), p. 34.
[19] August Dvorak, Nellie L. Merrick, William L. Dealy, and Gertrude C. Ford, *Typewriting Behavior* (1936).
[20] Ibid., p. 226.

keyboard. Even in this Dvorak study, however, the evidence is mixed as to whether students, as they progress, retain an advantage when using the Dvorak keyboard since the differences seem to diminish as typing speed increases.

In general, it is desirable to have independent evaluation, and here the objectivity of Dvorak and his coauthors seems particularly open to question. Their book is more in the vein of an inspirational tract than a scientific work. Consider the following (taken from their chapter about relative keyboard performances):

> The bare recital to you of a few simple facts should suffice to indict the available spatial pattern that is so complacently entitled the "universal" [Qwerty] keyboard. Since when was the "universe" lopsided? The facts will not be stressed, since you may finally surmount most of the ensuing handicaps of this [Qwerty] keyboard.
>
> Just enough facts will be paraded to lend you double assurance that for many of the errors that you will inevitably make and for much of the discouraging delay you will experience in longed-for speed gains, you are not to blame. If you grow indignant over the beginner's role of "innocent victim," remember that a little emotion heightens determination.[21]

> Analysis of the present keyboard is so destructive that an improved arrangement is a modern imperative. Isn't it obvious that faster, more accurate, less fatiguing typing can be attained in much less learning time provided a simplified keyboard is taught?[22]

The Navy study, which seems to have been the basis for some of the more extravagant claims of Dvorak advocates, is also flawed. Arthur Foulke, Sholes's biographer, and a believer in the superiority of the Dvorak keyboard, points out several discrepancies in the reports coming out of the Navy studies. He cites an Associated Press report of October 7, 1943, to the effect that a new typewriter keyboard allowed typists to "zip along at 180 words per minute" but then adds "However, the Navy Department, in a letter to the author October 14, 1943 by Lieutenant Commander W. Marvin McCarthy said that it had no record of and did not conduct such a speed test, and denied having made an official announcement to that effect."[23] Foulke also reports a *Business Week* story of October 16, 1943, that reports a speed of 108, not 180, words per minute.

We were able to obtain, with difficulty, a copy of the 1944 Navy report.[24] The report does not state who conducted the study. It consists of two parts, the first

---

[21] Ibid., p. 210.

[22] Ibid., p. 217.

[23] Foulke, op. cit. (note 11) p. 103.

[24] We tried to have the Navy supply us with a copy when our own research librarians could not find it. The Navy research librarian had no more success, even though she checked the Navy records, the Martin Luther King Library, the Library of Congress, the National Archives, the National Technical Communication Service, etc. We were finally able to locate a copy held by an organization. Dvorak International, and would like to thank its director, Virginia Russell, for her assistance. She believes that they obtained their copy from the Underwood Company. We would be more sanguine about the question of the document's history had it been available in a public archive. The copy we received was *A Practical Experiment in Simplified Keyboard Retraining – a Report on the Retraining of Fourteen Standard Keyboard Typists on the Simplified Keyboard and a Comparison of Typist Improvement from Training on the Standard Keyboard and Retraining on the Simplified Keyboard*, Navy Department, Division of Shore Establishments and Civilian Personnel, Department of Services, Training Section, Washington, D.C. (July and October 1944).

based on an experiment conducted in July 1944 and the second based on an experiment conducted in October of that year. The report's foreword states that two prior experiments had been conducted but that "the first two groups were not truly fair tests." We are not told the results of the early tests.

The first of the reported experiments consisted of the retraining of fourteen Navy typists on newly overhauled Dvorak keyboards for two hours a day. We are not told how the subjects were chosen, but it does not appear to be based on a random process. At least twelve of these individuals had previously been Qwerty typists, with an average speed of thirty-two words per minute, although the Navy defined competence as fifty words per minute. The typists had IQs that averaged 98 and dexterity skills with an average percentile of 65. The study reports that it took fifty-two hours for typists to catch up to their old speed. After completing an average of eighty-three hours on the new keyboard, typing speed had increased to an average of fifty-six net words per minute compared to their original thirty-two words per minute, a 75 percent increase.

The second experiment consisted of the retraining of eighteen typists on the Qwerty keyboard. It is not clear how these typists were picked or even if members of this group were aware that they were part of an experiment. We are not told whether this training was performed in the same manner as the first experiment (the Navy retrained people from time to time and this may just have been one of these groups). The participants' IQs and dexterity skills are not reported. It is difficult to have any sense whether this group is a reasonable control for the first group. The initial typing scores for this group averaged twenty-nine words per minute, but these scores were not measured identically to those from the first experiment. The report states that because three typists had net scores of zero words per minute initially, the beginning and ending speeds were calculated as the average of the first four typing tests and the average of the last four typing tests. In contrast, the initial experiment using Dvorak simply used the first and last test scores. This truncation of the reported values reduced the measured increase in typing speed on the Qwerty keyboard by a substantial margin.[25]

The measured increase in net typing speed for Qwerty retraining was from twenty-nine to thirty-seven words per minute (28 percent) after an average of 158 hours of training, considerably less than the increase that occurred with the Dvorak keyboard.

The Navy study concludes that training in Dvorak is much more effective than

---

[25] It is not an innocuous change. We are told that three Qwerty typists initially scored zero on the typing test but that their scores rose to twenty-nine, thirteen, and sixteen within four days (at 20). We are also told that several other typists had similar improvements in the first four days. These improvements are dismissed as mere testing effects that the researchers wish to eliminate. But the researchers made no effort to eliminate the analogous testing effect for the Dvorak typists. Truncating the measurements to the average of the first four days reduces the reported speed increases for the three typists with zero initial speed by at least thirteen, twelve, and fourteen. Assuming the existence of two other typists with similar size-testing effects, removing this testing effect would reduce the reported speed improvements by 3.6 words per minute, lowering the gain from 46 percent to 28 percent. The effect of the truncation at the end of the measuring period cannot be determined with any accuracy, but there is no testing effect to be removed at this stage of the experiment after many tests have been taken. While the apparent effect of these measurement techniques is significant, the indisputable problem is that they were not applied equally to the Qwerty and Dvorak typists.

retraining in Qwerty. But the experimental design leaves too many questions for this to be an acceptable finding. Do these results hold for typists with normal typing skills or only for those far below average? Were the results for the first group just a regression to the mean for a group of underperforming typists? How much did the Navy studies underestimate the value of increased Qwerty retraining due to the inconsistent measurement? Were the two groups given similar training? Were the Qwerty typewriters overhauled, as were the Dvorak typewriters? There are many possible biases in this study. All, suspiciously, seem to be in favor of the Dvorak design.

The authors of the Navy study do seem to have their minds made up concerning the superiority of Dvorak. In discussing the background of the Dvorak keyboard and prior to introducing the results of the study, the report claims: "Indisputably, it is obvious that the Simplified Keyboard is easier to master than the Standard Keyboard."[26] Later they refer to Qwerty as an "ox" and Dvorak as a "jeep" and add: "no amount of goading the oxen can materially change the end result."[27]

There are other problems of credibility with these Navy studies having to do with potential conflicts of interest. Foulke identifies Dvorak as Lieutenant Commander August Dvorak, the Navy's top expert in the analysis of time and motion studies during World War II.[28] Earle Strong, a professor at Pennsylvania State University and a one-time chairman of the Office Machine Section of the Amercian Standards Association, reports that the 1944 Navy experiment and some Treasury department experiments performed in 1946 were conducted by Dr. Dvorak.[29] We also know that Dvorak had a financial stake in this keyboard. He owned the patent on the keyboard and had received at least $130,000 from the Carnegie Commission for Education for the studies performed while he was at the University of Washington.[30]

But there is more to this story than the weakness of the evidence reported by the Navy, or Dvorak, or his followers. A 1956 General Services Administration study by Earle Strong, which was influential in its time, provides the most compelling evidence against the Dvorak keyboard.[31] This study is ignored in David's history for economists and is similarly ignored in other histories directed at general

---

[26] Navy, op. cit. (note 24), p. 2.

[27] Ibid., p. 23.

[28] See Foulke, op. cit.(note 1), p. 103.

[29] Earle P. Strong, *A Comparative Experiment in Simplified Keyboard Retraining and Standard Keyboard Supplementary Training* (U.S. General Services Administration 1956). However, Yamada, trying to refute criticisms of Dvorak's keyboard, claims that Dvorak did not conduct these studies, he only provided the typewriters. See Hisao Yamada, "A Historical Study of Typewriters and Typing Methods: From the Position of Planning Japanese Parallels," *J. Information Processings* (1980), p. 175. He admits that Dvorak was in the Navy and in Washington when the studies were conducted but denies any linkage. We do not know whom to believe, but we are skeptical that Dvorak would not have had a large influence on these tests, based on the strong circumstantial evidence and given Foulke's identification of Dvorak as the Navy's top expert on such matters. Interestingly, Yamada accuses Strong of being biased against the Dvorak keyboard (p. 188). He also impugns Strong's character. He accuses Strong of refusing to provide other (unnamed) researchers with his data. He also implies that Strong stole money from Dvorak because in 1941, when Strong was a supporter of Dvorak's keyboard, he supposedly accepted payment from Dvorak to conduct a study of the DSK keyboard without ever reporting his results to him.

[30] Yamada, op. cit.

[31] Strong, op. cit.

audiences. Strong conducted a carefully controlled experiment designed to examine the costs and benefits of switching to Dvorak. He concluded that retraining typists on Dvorak had no advantages over retraining on Qwerty.

In the first phase of Strong's experiment, ten government typists were retrained on the Dvorak keyboard. It took well over twenty-five days of four-hour-a-day training for these typists to catch up to their old Qwerty speed. (Compare this to the claim David makes about the Navy study's results that the full retraining costs were recovered in ten days.) When the typists had finally caught up to their old speed, Strong began the second phase of the experiment. The newly trained Dvorak typists continued training, and a group of ten Qwerty typists began a parallel program to improve their skills. In this second phase, the Dvorak typists progressed less quickly with further Dvorak training than did Qwerty typists training on Qwerty keyboards. Thus Strong concluded that Dvorak training would never be able to amortize its costs. He recommended that the government provide further training in the Qwerty keyboard, for Qwerty typists. The information provided by this study was largely responsible for putting Dvorak to rest as a serious alternative to Qwerty for those firms and government agencies responsible for choosing typewriters.[32]

Strong's study does leave some questions unanswered. Because it uses experienced typists, it cannot tell us whether beginning Dvorak typists could be trained more quickly than beginning Qwerty typists. Further, although one implication of Strong's study is that the ultimate speed achieved would be greater for Qwerty typists than for Dvorak typists (since the Qwerty group was increasing the gap over the Dvorak group in the second phase of the experiment), we cannot be sure that an experiment with beginning typists would provide the same results.[33]

Nevertheless, Strong's study must be taken seriously. It attempts to control the quality of the two groups of typists and the instruction they receive. It directly addresses the claims that came out of the Navy studies, which consider the costs and benefits of retraining. It directly parallels the decision that a real firm or a real government agency might face: is it worthwhile to retrain its present typists? The alleged market failure of the Qwerty keyboard as represented by Farrell and Saloner's excess inertia is that all firms would change to a new standard if only they could each be assured that the others would change. If we accept Strong's findings, it is not a failure to communicate that keeps firms from retraining its typists or keeps typists from incurring their own retraining costs. If Strong's study is correct, it is efficient for current typists not to switch to Dvorak.

Current proponents of Dvorak have a different view when they assess why the keyboard has not been more successful. Hisao Yamada, an advocate of Dvorak who is attempting to influence Japanese keyboard development, gives a wide-

---

[32] At the time of Strong's experiment, Dvorak had attracted a good deal of attention. At least one trade group had taken the position that, pending confirmation from the Strong study, it would adopt Dvorak as its new standard. See "U.S. Plans to Test New Typewriter," *New York Times*, November 11, 1955; "Revolution in the Office," *New York Times*, November 30, 1955; "Key Changes Debated," *New York Times*, June 18, 1956; "U.S. Balks at Teaching Old Typists New Keys," *New York Times*, July 2, 1956; and Peter White, "Pyfgcrl vs. Qwertyuiop," *New York Times*, January 22, 1956, 18.

[33] In fact, both the Navy and General Service Administration studies found that the best typists took the longest to catch up to their old speed and showed the smallest percentage improvement with retraining.

ranging interpretation to the Dvorak keyboard's failure. He blames the Depression, bad business decisions by Dvorak, World War II, and the Strong report. He goes on to say,

> There were always those who questioned the claims made by DSK followers. Their reasons are also manifold. Some suspected the superiority of the instructions by DSK advocates to be responsible, because they were all holders of advanced degree(s); such a credential of instructors is also apt to cause the Hawthorne effect. Others maintain that all training experiments, except the GSA one as noted, were conducted by the DSK followers, and that the statistical control of experiments [was] not well exercised. This may be a valid point. It does not take too long to realize, however, that it is a major financial undertaking to organize such an experiment to the satisfaction of statisticians . . . The fact that those critics were also reluctant to come forth in support of such experiment[s] . . . may indicate that the true reason of their criticism lies elsewhere.[34]

This is one nasty disagreement.[35]

Nevertheless, Yamada as much as admits that experimental findings reported by Dvorak and his supporters cannot be assigned much credibility and that the most compelling claims cited by Yamada for DSK's superiority come from Dvorak's own work. Much of the other evidence Yamada uses to support his views of DSK's superiority actually can be used to make a case against Dvorak. Yamada refers to a 1952 Australian post office study that showed no advantages for DSK when it was first conducted. It was only after adjustments were made in the test procedure (to remove "psychological impediments" to superior performance) that DSK did better.[36] He cites a 1973 study based on six typists at Western Electric, where, after 104 hours of training on DSK, typists were 2.6 percent faster than they had been on Qwerty.[37] Similarly, Yamada reports that, in a 1978 study at Oregon State University, after 100 hours of training, typists were up to 97.6 percent of their old Qwerty speed.[38] Both of these retraining times are similar to those reported by Strong and not to those in the Navy study. Yamada, however, thinks the studies themselves support Dvorak.[39] But unlike the Strong study, neither of these studies included parallel retraining on Qwerty keyboards. As the Strong study points out, even experienced Qwerty typists increase their speed on Qwerty if they are given additional training. Even if that problem is ignored, the possible advantages of Dvorak are all much weaker than those reported from the Navy study.

---

[34] Yamada, op. cit. (note 29), p. 189.

[35] Also see note 29 above.

[36] Yamada, op. cit. (note 29), p. 185.

[37] Ibid., p. 188.

[38] Ibid.

[39] Yamada interprets the Oregon study to support the Dvorak keyboard. To do so, he fits an exponential function to the Oregon data and notes that the limit of the function as hours of training goes to infinity is 17 percent greater than the typist's initial Qwerty speed. This function is extremely flat, however, and even modest gains appear well outside the range of the data. A 10 percent gain, for example, would be projected to occur only after 165 hours of training.

## Evidence from the ergonomics literature

The most recent studies of the relative merits of keyboards are found in the ergonomics literature. These studies provide evidence that the advantages of the Dvorak
is either small or nonexistent. For example, A. Miller and J. C. Thomas conclude
that "the fact remains, however, that no alternative has shown a realistically significant advantage over the Qwerty for general purpose typing."[40] In two studies
based on analysis of hand-and-finger motions, R. F. Nickells, Jr., finds that Dvorak
is 6.2 percent faster than Qwerty,[41] and R. Kinkhead finds only a 2.3 percent advantage for Dvorak.[42] Simulation studies by Donald Norman and David Rumelhart
find similar results:

> In our studies . . . we examined novices typing on several different arrangements of
> alphabetically organized keyboards, the Sholes [Qwerty] keyboard, and a randomly
> organized keyboard (to control against prior knowledge of Sholes). There were essen-
> tially no differences among the alphabetic and random keyboards. Novices type slightly
> faster on the Sholes keyboard, probably reflecting prior experience with it. We studied
> expert typists by using our simulation model. Here, we looked at the Sholes and Dvorak
> layouts, as well as several alphabetically arranged keyboards. The simulation showed
> that the alphabetically organized keyboards were between 2% and 9% slower than the
> Sholes keyboard, and the Dvorak keyboard was only about 5% faster than the Sholes.
> These figures correspond well to other experimental studies that compared the Dvorak
> and Sholes keyboards and to the computations of Card, Moran, and Newell . . . for
> comparing these keyboards . . . For the expert typist, the layout of keys makes surpris-
> ingly little difference. There seems no reason to choose Sholes, Dvorak, or alphabeti-
> cally organized keyboards over one another on the basis of typing speed. It is possible
> to make a bad keyboard layout, however, and two of the arrangements that we stud-
> ied can be ruled out.[43]

These ergonomic studies are particularly interesting because the claimed advantage of the Dvorak keyboard has been based historically on the claimed ergonomic
advantages in reduced finger movement. Norman and Rumelhart's discussion offers clues to why Dvorak does not provide as much of an advantage as its proponents have claimed. They argue,

> For optimal typing speed, keyboards should be designed so that:
>
> (1)   The loads on the right and left hands are equalized.
> (2)   The load on the home (middle) row is maximized.
> (3)   The frequency of alternating hand sequences is maximized and the frequency
>        of same-finger typing is minimized.

[40] A. Miller and J. C. Thomas, "Behavioral Issues in the Use of Interactive Systems," *Int. J. of Man-
Machine Stud.* 9 (1977), p. 509.
[41] Cited in Hisao Yamada, "Certain Problems Associated with the Design of Input Keyboards for
Japanese Writing," in *Cognitive Aspects of Skilled Typewriting* (William E. Cooper ed. 1983), p. 336.
[42] Cited in ibid., p. 365.
[43] Donald A. Norman and David E. Rumelhart, "Studies of Typing from the LNR Research Group,"
in *Cognitive Aspects of Skilled Typewriting* (William E. Cooper ed. 1983), pp. 45, 51.

The Dvorak keyboard does a good job on these variables, especially (1) and (2); 67% of the typing is done on the home row and the left–right hand balance is 47–53%. Although the Sholes (Qwerty) keyboard fails at conditions (1) and (2) (most typing is done on the top row and the balance between the two hands is 57% and 43%), the policy to put successively typed keys as far apart as possible favors factor (3), thus leading to relatively rapid typing.[44]

The explanation for Norman and Rumelhart's factor (3) is that during a keystroke, the idle hand prepares for its next keystroke. Thus Sholes's decision to solve a mechanical problem through careful keyboard arrangement may have inadvertently satisfied a fairly important requirement for efficient typing.

The consistent finding in the ergonomic studies is that the results imply no clear advantage for Dvorak. These studies are not explicitly statistical, yet their negative claim seems analogous to the scientific caution that one exercises when measured differences are small relative to unexplained variance. We read these authors as saying that, in light of the imprecision of method, scientific caution precludes rejection of the hypothesis that Dvorak and Qwerty are equivalent. At the very least, the studies indicate that the speed advantage of Dvorak is not anything like the 20–40 percent that is claimed in the Apple advertising copy that David cites. Moreover, the studies suggest that there may be no advantage with the Dvorak keyboard for ordinary typing by skilled typists. It appears that the principles by which Dvorak "rationalized" the keyboard may not have fully captured the actions of experienced typists largely because typing appears to be a fairly complex activity.

A final word on all of this comes from Frank McGurrin, the world's first known touch-typist:

> Let an operator take a new sentence and see how fast he can write it. Then, after practicing the sentence, time himself again, and he will find he can write it much faster; and further practice on the particular sentence will increase the speed on it to nearly or quite double that on the new matter. Now let the operator take another new sentence, and he will find his speed has dropped back to about what it was before he commenced practicing the first sentence. Why is this? The fingers are capable of the same rapidity. It is because the mind is not so familiar with the keys.[45]

Of course, performance in any physical activity can presumably be improved with practice. But the limitations of typing speed, in McGurrin's experiment, appear to have something to do with a mental or, at least, neurological skill and fairly little to do with the limitations on the speeds at which the fingers can complete their required motions.

## Typewriter competition

The Sholes typewriter was not invented from whole cloth. Yamada reports that there were fifty-one inventors of prior typewriters, including some earlier

---

[44] Ibid.
[45] George C. Mares, *The History of the Typewriter* (1909).

commercially produced typewriters. He states: "Examination of these material(s) reveal that almost all ideas incorporated into Sholes' machines, if not all, were at one time or another already used by his predecessors."[46]

Remington's early commercial rivals were numerous, offered substantial variations on the typewriter, and in some cases enjoyed moderate success. There were plenty of competitors after the Sholes machine came to market. The largest and most important of these rivals were the Hall, Caligraph, and Crandall machines. The Yost, another double-keyboard machine, manufactured by an early collaborator of Sholes, used a different inking system and was known particularly for its attractive type. According to production data assembled by Yamada,[47] the machines were close rivals, and they each sold in large numbers. Franz Xavier Wagner, who also worked on the 1873 Remington typewriter, developed a machine that made the type fully visible as it was being typed. This machine was offered to, but rejected by, the Union Typewriter Company, the company formed by the 1893 merger of Remington with six other typewriter manufacturers.[48] In 1895, Wagner joined John T. Underwood to produce his machine. Their company, which later became Underwood, enjoyed rapid growth, producing two hundred typewriters per week by 1898.[49] Wagner's offer to Union also resulted in the spin-off from Union of L. C. Smith, who introduced a visible-type machine in 1904.[50] This firm was the forerunner of the Smith-Corona company.

Two manufacturers offered their own versions of an ideal keyboard: Hammond in 1893 and Blickensderfer in 1889.[51] Each of these machines survived for a time, and each had certain mechanical advantages. Blickensderfer later produced what may have been the first portable and the first electric typewriters. Hammond later produced the Varityper, a standard office type-composing machine that was the antecedent of today's desktop publishing. The alternative keyboard machines produced by these manufacturers came early enough that typewriters and, more important, touch-typing were still not very popular. The Blickensderfer appeared within a year of the famous Cincinnati contest that first publicized touch-typing.

In the 1880s and 1890s typewriters were generally sold to offices not already staffed with typists or into markets in which typists were not readily available. Since the sale of a new machine usually meant training a new typist, a manufacturer that chose to compete using an alternative keyboard had an opportunity. As late as 1923, typewriter manufacturers operated placement services for typists and were an important source of operators. In the earliest days, typewriter salesmen provided much of the limited training available to typists.[52] Since almost every sale

[46] Yamada, op. cit. (note 41), p. 177.
[47] Ibid., p. 181.
[48] Beeching, op. cit. (note 13), p. 165.
[49] Ibid., p. 214.
[50] Ibid., p. 165.
[51] David, "Understanding," op. cit. (note 5), p. 38. Also see Beeching, op. cit., pp. 40, 199. Yamada, op. cit. (note 29), p. 184, in discussing the Hammond keyboard arrangement states: "This 'ideal' arrangement was far better than Qwerty, but it did not take root because by then Remington Schools were already turning out a large number of Qwerty typists every year." In 1893, Blickensderfer offered a portable typewriter with the Hammond keyboard.
[52] Herkimer County Historical Society, op. cit. (note 10), p. 78.

required the training of a typist, a typewriter manufacturer that offered a different keyboard was not particularly disadvantaged. Manufacturers internalized training costs in such an environment, so a keyboard that allowed more rapid training might have been particularly attractive.

Offering alternative keyboards was not a terribly expensive tactic. The Blickensderfer used a type-bar configuration similar in principle to the IBM Selectric type ball and, so, could easily offer many different configurations. The others could create alternative keyboard arrangements by simply soldering the type to different bars and attaching the keys to different levers. So apparently the problem of implementing the conversion was not what kept the manufacturers from changing keyboards.

The rival keyboards did ultimately fail, of course.[53] But the Qwerty keyboard cannot have been so well established at the time the rival keyboards were first offered that they were rejected because they were non-standard. Manufacturers of typewriters sought and promoted any technical feature that might give them an advantage in the market. Certainly shorter training and greater speed would have been an attractive selling point for a typewriter with an alternative keyboard. Neither can it be said that the rival keyboards were doomed by inferior mechanical characteristics because these companies went on to produce successful and innovative, though Qwerty-based, typing machines. Thus we cannot attribute our inheritance of the Qwerty keyboard to a lack of alternative keyboards or the chance association of this keyboard arrangement with the only mechanically adequate typewriter.

## Typing competitions

Typing competitions provided another test of the Qwerty keyboard. These competitions are somewhat underplayed in the conventional history. David's history mentions only the Cincinnati contest. Wilfred Beeching's history, which has been very influential, also mentions only the Cincinnati contest and attaches great importance to it: "Suddenly, to their horror, it dawned upon both the Remington Company and the Caligraph Company officials, torn between pride and despair, that whoever won was likely to put the other out of business!" Beeching refers to the contest as having established the four-bank keyboard of the Remington machine "once and for all."[54]

In fact, typing contests and demonstrations of speed were fairly common during this period. They involved many different machines, with various manufacturers claiming to hold the speed record.

---

[53] We should also take note of the fact that the Qwerty keyboard, although invented in the United States, has become the dominant keyboard throughout the world. Foreign countries, when introduced to typewriters, need not have adopted this keyboard if superior alternatives existed since there would not yet have been any typists trained on Qwerty. Yet all other keyboard designs fell before the Qwerty juggernaut. In France and some other countries, the keyboard is slightly different than the Qwerty keyboard used in the United States. The major difference is that the top left-hand keys are Azerty (that is also what these keyboard designs are called) and several letters are transposed, but most of the keys are identical.

[54] Beeching, op. cit. (note 13), p. 41.

Under the headline "Wonderful Typing," the *New York Times* reported on a typing demonstration given the previous day in Brooklyn by a Mr. Thomas Osborne of Rochester, New York.[55] The *Times* reported that Mr. Osborne "holds the championship for fast typing, having accomplished 126 words a minute at Toronto August 13 last." In the Brooklyn demonstration he typed 142 words per minute in a five-minute test, 179 words per minute in a single minute, and 198 words per minute for 30 seconds. He was accompanied by a Mr. George McBride, who typed 129 words per minute blindfolded. Both men used the non-Qwerty Caligraph machine. The *Times* offered that "the Caligraph people have chosen a very pleasant and effective way of proving not only the superior speed of their machine, but the falsity of reports widely published that writing blindfolded was not feasible on that instrument."[56] Note that this was just months after McGurrin's Cincinnati victory.

There were other contests and a good number of victories for McGurrin and Remington. On August 2, 1888, the *Times* reported a New York contest won by McGurrin with a speed of 95.8 words per minute in a five-minute dictation.[57] In light of the received history, according to which McGurrin is the only person to have memorized the keyboard, it is interesting to note the strong performance of his rivals. Miss May Orr typed 95.2 words per minute, and M. C. Grant typed 93.8 words per minute. Again, on January 9, 1889, the *Times* reported a McGurrin victory under the headline "Remington Still Leads the List."[58]

We should probably avoid the temptation to compare the Caligraph speed with the Remington speeds, given the likely absence of any serious attempts at standardizing the tests. Nevertheless, it appears that the issue of speed was not so readily conceded as is reported in Beeching's history. Typists other than McGurrin could touch-type, and machines other than Remington were competitive. History has largely ignored events that did not build toward the eventual domination by Qwerty. This focus may be reasonable for the history of the Remington Company or the Qwerty keyboard. But if we are interested in whether the Qwerty keyboard's existence can be attributed to more than happenstance or an inventor's whim, these events do matter.

## CONCLUSIONS

The trap constituted by an obsolete standard may be quite fragile. Because real-world situations present opportunities for agents to profit from changing to a superior standard, we cannot simply rely on an abstract model to conclude that an inferior standard has persisted. Such a claim demands empirical examination.

As an empirical example of market failure, the typewriter keyboard has much appeal. The objective of the keyboard is fairly straightforward: to get words onto the recording medium. There are no conflicting objectives to complicate the interpretation of performance. But the evidence in the standard history of Qwerty ver-

---

[55] *New York Times*, February 28, 1889, p. 8.
[56] Ibid.
[57] Ibid., p. 2.
[58] Ibid.

sus Dvorak is flawed and incomplete. First, the claims for the superiority of the Dvorak keyboard are suspect. The most dramatic claims are traceable to Dvorak himself, and the best-documented experiments, as well as recent ergonomic studies, suggest little or no advantage for the Dvorak keyboard.[59]

Second, by ignoring the vitality and variety of the rivals to the Remington machine with its Qwerty keyboard, the received history implies that Sholes' and McGurrin's choices, made largely as matters of immediate expediency, established the standard without ever being tested. More careful reading of historical accounts and checks of original sources reveal a different picture: there were touch-typists other than McGurrin; there were competing claims of speed records; and Remington was not so well established that a keyboard offering significant advantages could not have gained a foothold. If the fable is to carry lessons about the workings of markets, we need to know more than just who won. The victory of the tortoise is a different story without the hare.

There is more to this disagreement than a difference in the evidence that was revealed by our search of the historical record. Our reading of this history reflects a more fundamental difference in views of how markets, and social systems more generally, function. David's overriding point is that economic theory must be informed by events in the world. On that we could not agree more strongly. But ironically, or perhaps inevitably, David's interpretation of the historical record is dominated by his own implicit model of markets, a model that seems to underlie much economic thinking. In that model, an exogenous set of goods is offered for sale at a price, take it or leave it. There is little or no role for entrepreneurs. There generally are no guarantees, no rental markets, no mergers, no loss-leader pricing, no advertising, no marketing research. When such complicating institutions are acknowledged, they are incorporated into the model piecemeal. And they are most often introduced to show their potential to create inefficiencies, not to show how an excess of benefit over cost may constitute an opportunity for private gain.

In the world created by such a sterile model of competition, it is not surprising that accidents have considerable permanence. In such a world, embarking on some wrong path provides little chance to jump to an alternative path. The individual benefits of correcting a mistake are too small to make correction worthwhile, and there are no agents who might profit by devising some means of capturing a part of the aggregate benefits of correction.

It is also not surprising that in such a world there are a lot of accidents. Consumers

---

[59] See text in notes 30–43. There are several versions of the claim that a switch to Dvorak would not be worthwhile. The strongest, which we do not make, is that Qwerty is proven to be the best imaginable keyboard. Neither can we claim that Dvorak is proven to be inferior to Qwerty. Our claim is that there is no scientifically acceptable evidence that Dvorak offers any real advantage over Qwerty. Because of this claim, our assessment of a market failure in this case is rather simple. It might have been more complicated. For example, if Dvorak were found to be superior, it might still be the case that the total social benefits are less than the cost of switching. In that case, we could look for market failure only in the process that started us on the Qwerty keyboard (if the alternative were available at the beginning). Or we might have concluded that Dvorak is better and that all parties could be made better off if we could costlessly command both a switch and any necessary redistribution. Such a finding would constitute a market failure in the sense of mainstream welfare economics. Of course, this circumstance still might not constitute a market failure in the sense of Demsetz, which requires consideration of the costs of feasible institutions that could effect the change.

are given very little discretion to avoid starts down wrong paths. A model may assume that consumers have foresight or even that they are perfectly rational, but always in a very limited sense. For example, in the model of Farrell and Saloner, consumers can predict very well the equilibrium among the two candidate standards. But they are attributed no ability to anticipate the existence of some future, better standard. We are not led to ask how the incumbent standard achieved its status; as in David's telling, "It jes' growed."

But at some moment, users must commit resources to a standard or wait. At this moment, they have clear incentives to examine the characteristics of competing standards. They must suffer the consequences of a decision to wait, to discard obsolete equipment or skills, or to continue to function with an inferior standard. Thus, they have a clear incentive to consider what lies down alternative paths. Though their ability to anticipate future events may not be perfect, there is no reason to assume that it is bad relative to any other observers.

Finally, it is consistent that, in a world in which mistakes are frequent and permanent, "scientific approaches" cannot help but make big improvements to market outcomes. In such a world, there is ample room for enlightened reasoning, personified by university professors, to improve on the consequences of myriad independent decisions. What credence can possibly be given to a keyboard that has nothing to accredit it but the trials of a group of mechanics and its adoption by millions of typists? If we use only sterilized models of markets, or ignore the vitality of the rivalry that confronts institutions, we should not be surprised that the historical interpretations that result are not graced with the truth that Cicero asks of historians.

## REFERENCES

Beeching, Wilfred, *A Century of the Typewriter* (New York: St. Martin's Press, 1974).

Cheung, Steven N. S., "The Fable of the Bees: An Economic Investigation," *Journal of Law and Economics* 16 (April 1973) pp. 11–33.

Coase, Ronald H., "The Problem of Social Cost," *Journal of Law and Economics* 3 (October 1960) pp. 1–44.

Coase, Ronald H., "The Lighthouse in Economics," *Journal of Law and Economics* 17 (October 1974) pp. 357–76.

David, Paul A., "Clio and the Economics of QWERTY," *American Economic Review* 75 (May 1985); pp. 332–7.

David, Paul A., "Understanding the Economics of QWERTY: The Necessity of History," in *Economic History and the Modern Economist*, edited by W. N. Parker (New York: Basil Blackwell, 1986).

Demsetz, Harold, "Information and Efficiency: Another Viewpoint," *Journal of Law and Economics* 12 (April 1969), pp. 1–22.

Dvorak, August, Merrick, Nellie L., Dealey, William L. and Ford, Gertrude C., *Typewriting Behavior* (New York: American Book Co., 1936).

Farrell, Joseph, and Saloner, Garth, "Standardization, Compatibility, and Innovation," *Rand Journal* 16 (spring 1985), pp. 70–83.

Foulke, Arthur, *Mr. Typewriter: A Biography of Christopher Latham Sholes* (Boston, Mass: Christopher Publishing, 1961).

Herkimer County Historical Society, *The Story of the Typewriter: 1873–1923* (New York: Andrew H. Kellogg, 1923).

Katz, Michael L., and Shapiro, Carl, "Network Externalities, Competition, and Compatibility," *American Economic Review* 75 (June 1985), pp. 425–40.

Kinkhead, R., "Typing Speed, Keying Rates, and Optimal Keyboard Layouts," *Proceedings of the Human Factors Society* 19 (1975), pp. 159–61.

Landes, William M., and Posner, Richard A., "Trademark Law: An Economic Perspective." *Journal of Law and Economics* 30 (October 1987), pp. 265–309.

Liebowitz, S. J., "Tie-in Sales and Price Discrimination," *Economic Inquiry* 21 (July 1983), pp. 387–99.

Liebowitz, S. J., "Copying and Indirect Appropriability: Photocopying of Journals," *Journal of Political Economy* 93 (October 1985), pp. 945–57.

Mandeville, Bernard M., *The Fable of the Bees* (New York: Capricorn, 1962).

Mares, George C., *The History of the Typewriter* (London: Guilbert Pitman, 1909).

Margolis, Stephen E., "Two Definitions of Efficiency in Law and Economics," *Journal of Legal Studies* 16 (July 1987), pp. 471–82.

Miller, L. A., and Thomas, J. C., "Behavioral Issues in the Use of Interactive Systems." *International Journal of Man-Machine Studies* 9 (1977), pp. 509–36.

Navy Department, *A Practical Experiment in Simplified Keyboard Retraining – a Report on the Retraining of Fourteen Standard Keyboard Typists on the Simplified Keyboard and a Comparison of Typist Improvement from Training on the Standard Keyboard and Retraining on the Simplified Keyboard.* Department of Services, Training Section (Washington, D.C.: Navy Department, Division of Shore Establishments and Civilian Personnel, July 1944 and October 1944).

Norman, Donald A., and Rumelhart, David E., "Studies of Typing from the LNR Research Group," in *Cognitive Aspects of Skilled Typewriting*, edited by William E. Cooper (New York: Springer-Verlag, 1983).

Strong, Earle P., *A Comparative Experiment in Simplified Keyboard Retraining and Standard Keyboard Supplementary Training* (Washington, D.C.: U.S. General Services Administration, 1956).

Tirole, Jean, *The Theory of Industrial Organization* (Cambridge, Mass.: MIT Press, 1988).

Yamada, Hisao, "A Historical Study of Typewriters and Typing Methods: From the Position of Planning Japanese Parallels," *Journal of Information Processing* 2 (1980), pp. 175–202.

Yamada, Hisao, "Certain Problems Associated with the Design of Input Keyboards for Japanese Writing," *in Cognitive Aspects of Skilled Typewriting*, edited by William E. Cooper (New York: Springer-Verlag, 1983).

# 5

# Beta, Macintosh, and Other Fabulous Tales

*Stan J. Liebowitz and Stephen E. Margolis*

Can we rely on markets to move us in the right direction, either initially or when it is time to change? If, for example, a large number of us benefit from using the same word processor, can we change word processors when it's time to change? If we can, how do we?

[We have already] presented a simple statement of a problem as it is alleged in a good deal of academic and popular writing. If everyone uses A, yet each individual regards B as better, but only when many other people also use B, then we might find ourselves stuck with A. We argued that although this trap is certainly possible, interested parties are likely to respond in ways to disable this trap if it is actually causing significant harm.

Now, the mere possibility of such a trap should not be enough to spur us to action. Before we move to correct a possible harm, we need to establish empirically that the harm actually exists. Because reliable conclusions on these issues cannot be said to follow logically from agreed-upon economic principles and unassailable assumptions and restrictions, we must look at real-world cases.

In this chapter we examine a number of the standards or technology battles that are often cited as examples of this particular type of market failure. Of course, the most prominent of these claimed failures is the Qwerty keyboard. [ . . .] In this chapter we present the VHS-Beta history at some length, then consider several other cases.

Readers familiar with scholarly empirical work in economics may find our attention to case histories a bit out of the ordinary. Economists don't usually concern themselves much with individual cases: we tend to look at time-series of aggregate data – GNP and unemployment, the money supply or consumer expenditure – or at large data sets based on hundreds, thousands, or even larger numbers of companies, individuals, and products. This is because economists are usually looking for a pattern of behavior, a test for a theory that is held to apply *in general*. But theories of path dependence are different from such generalizing theories. In contrast, theories of third-degree path dependence and lock-in do not allege that these outcomes are the norm, or even that they are particularly common. Rather, they allege only that such path dependence is possible and perhaps that it is sufficiently likely to be important. Adherents of path dependence go somewhat further than this, arguing that it is likely to be common. But this argument does not come from the theory. Given that the theoretical result is a theorem about the possibility of lock-in, the empirical support, naturally enough, is a demonstration that the possible phenomenon has occurred. And also naturally enough, the empirical counterclaim involves calling into question these alleged demonstrations.

## VHS VERSUS BETA

After the typewriter keyboard, the VHS–Beta battle is the most often mentioned of alleged path-dependent market failures.[1] [. . .] We have used the names VHS and Beta in simple hypothetical examples of how the standards traps operate and how escapes are possible.[2] We turn now to the actual history of this standards battle, a history that is significant for several reasons. First, it incorporates structural features found in some of the models discussed here: in particular, it incorporates both economies of scale and ownership. Second, the actual history of the battle fails to support the claim that an inferior format dominated as a result of technological interrelatedness and economies of scale. Finally, it is a wonderful example of the foresight of the parties involved, and the tactics and strategies used to try to establish their standards.

The Ampex Corporation publicly demonstrated the first commercially viable videorecorder in 1956. These machines were sold for several years only to professional broadcasters. Eventually, Ampex concluded that transistors would replace tubes, and, having no experience with transistors, entered into an agreement with Sony to transistorize the videorecorder. In return, Sony received the rights to use Ampex-owned patents in machines designed for the home-use (nonprofessional) market, which Ampex was willing to cede.

The Ampex–Sony relationship quickly soured, however, and Ampex decided that it needed a Japanese partner to sell its recorders to the Japanese broadcast market. This time Ampex entered a partnership agreement with Toshiba. Other Japanese electronics producers that wanted to manufacture videorecorders then became Ampex's licensees. Eventually, various incompatible models of videorecorders coexisted in the marketplace, but none of these early machines proved successful in the home-use market.

In 1969 Sony developed a cartridge-based system called the U-matic for the home-use market. Because Matsushita, JVC (an independent subsidiary of Matsushita), Toshiba, and Hitachi all had such products in the works, Sony sought to bring in some partners to share the format in order to establish it as a standard. After Sony promised to make a few suggested changes to the machine, Matsushita, JVC, and Sony agreed to produce machines based on the U-matic specification (although Sony was to get the bulk of the eventual sales). The three companies also agreed to

---

[1] The example is most prominent in Arthur (1990).
[2] This history draws on Lardner (1987), chs 3, 4, and 10.

share technology and patents. Production of the U-matic began in 1971. Although it enjoyed some success in educational and industrial markets, high costs and excessive bulk led to its failure in the home-use market.

Attempts to break into the home-use market continued. In 1972 an American company came out with a product called Cartrivision that did many of the things that a Betamax was later to do (although it traded off picture quality for a longer playing time). Cartrivision was sold with a library of prerecorded programs. It failed when several technical problems arose, including the decomposition of the prerecorded tapes in a warehouse, which led to negative publicity. Philips produced a home recorder in 1972, but it never achieved much success. Sanyo and Toshiba joined forces to launch a machine known as the V-Cord, which also did poorly. Matsushita produced a machine called the AutoVision – a dismal failure. Of note for our story, Matsushita's management attributed this failure to the Auto Vision's short, thirty-minute tape capacity, a lesson that would later prove important. A Matsushita subsidiary, Kotobuki, introduced the VX-100 to the home-use market.

When Sony began selling Betamax in April 1975, it had a tape capacity of one hour. At the same time, JVC was also working on a machine known as the Video Home System, or VHS. As it had done earlier with the U-matic, Sony sought to cut through the clutter of competing formats and make Betamax the standard. Before introducing Betamax to the market, it once again offered its format to Matsushita and JVC, providing technical details of the Betamax, including an advance in azimuth recording that helped eliminate the problem of crosstalk. After lengthy discussions, dragging on for over a year, the three finally agreed to have a meeting to compare the Betamax, VHS, and VX machines. This meeting took place in April 1976 (a year after Sony had put Betamax on the market). Lardner (1987: 151–2) describes the meeting as follows:

> The first item on the agenda was the simultaneous playing, through all three [machines], of a "Sesame Street" type of children's program. . . . The Sony contingent's eyes were on the JVC machine. . . . What they saw was a considerably smaller machine than the Betamax. . . . Mechanically, too, VHS had a notable distinction: the use of a loading system called M-loading. . . . The basic concept had been tried in some of the early U-matic prototypes. . . . In other respects, JVC's and Sony's machines were strikingly similar. Both were two-head, helical-scanning machines using half-inch tape in a U-matic type of cassette. Both – unlike the V-cord, the VX, and indeed all the color videorecorders to date – used azimuth recording and countered the problem of cross talk by juggling the phase of the color signal. So the Betamax and the VHS were in a class by themselves as far as tape efficiency went.
>
> The real difference between them lay in how the two companies had chosen to exploit that advantage: Sony to make the cassette paperback size, and JVC to achieve a two-hour recording capacity . . . Eventually one of [the Sony people] said what all of the Sony representatives were thinking: "It's a copy of Betamax."

Needless to say, this apparent usurping of Sony's technological advances by JVC created bitterness between the one-time allies. Sony and Matsushita–JVC decided to go their separate ways.

The only real technical differences between Beta and VHS were the manner in which the tape was threaded and the size of the cassettes. The Beta format's threading offered some advantages for editing and special effects. But the larger cassette in the VHS format allowed more tape to be used, and for any given speed of tape, this implied a longer recording or playing time. For any given recording technique, slowing the tape increases recording time, but it also decreases picture quality. Because of its larger cassette size, VHS always offered an advantageous combination of picture quality and playing time. Otherwise, the differences between Beta and VHS were fairly trivial from a technical point of view. Our current perception of the differences is likely magnified by the advertising claims of each camp, the passage of time, and possibly by the fact that Beta still survives, reincarnated as a high-end broadcasting and videophile device.

The different choices of cassette size were based on different perceptions of consumer desires: Sony's managers, perhaps as a result of problems with the bulky U-matic, perhaps as a result of their many successes with portable devices, believed that a paperback-sized cassette, allowing easy carrying, was paramount. In contrast, Matsushita's managers, responding to the failure of the thirty-minute Autovision machine, believed that a two-hour recording time, allowing the taping of full-length feature movies, was essential.

This difference was to prove crucial. Sony was first to the market and enjoyed a virtual monopoly for almost two years. In an attempt to solidify its dominance of the U.S. market, Sony allowed its Beta machines to be sold under Zenith's brand name (Zenith being one of the major U.S. television manufacturers). To counter this move, Matsushita set up a meeting with RCA, which had previously concluded and publicly stated that a two-hour recording time was essential for a successful home videorecorder. By the time the meeting between Matsushita and RCA took place, however, Sony had announced a two-hour Betamax, Beta II. RCA proposed to Matsushita that it produce a machine that could record a football game, which implied a three-hour recording time. Six weeks later Matsushita had a working four-hour machine that used the same techniques to increase recording time that Sony had used in the Beta II.

RCA began selling VHS machines in summer 1977 (two years after Sony's introduction of the Betamax), dubbing its machine Selecta Vision. The advertising copy was simple: "Four hours. $1,000. Selecta Vision." Zenith responded by lowering the price of its Beta machine to $996. But within months VHS was outselling Beta in the United States. A Zenith marketing executive is quoted as saying, "The longer playing time turned out to be very important, and RCA's product was better styled."

The battle escalated. Sony recruited Toshiba and Sanyo to the Beta format, and Matsushita brought Hitachi, Sharp, and Mitsubishi into its camp. Any improvement in one format was soon followed by a similar improvement in the other. The similarity of the two machines made it unlikely that one format would be able to deliver a technological knockout punch. When one group lowered its price, the other soon followed. The two formats proved equally matched in almost all respects save one: VHS's longer playing time. When Beta went to two hours, VHS went to four. When Beta increased to five hours, VHS increased to eight. Of course, a consumer who wanted better picture quality could set either machine to a higher tape speed.

The market's referendum on playing time versus tape compactness was decisive and immediate, not just in the United States, but in Europe and Japan as well. By mid-1979 VHS was outselling Beta by more than two to one in the United States. By 1983 Beta's world share was down to 12 percent. By 1984 every VCR manufacturer except Sony had adopted VHS. Klopfenstein summarizes (our italics):

> Although many held the perception that the Beta VCR produced a better picture than VHS, technical experts such as Weinstein (1984) and Prentis (1981) have concluded that this was, in fact, not the case; periodic reviews in Consumers Reports found VHS picture quality superior twice, found Beta superior once, and found no difference in a fourth review. In conclusion, *the Beta format appeared to hold no advantages over VHS other than being the first on the market, and this may be a lesson for future marketers of new media products.*   (1989: 28)

How does this history address the theory and empiricism around path dependence? First, and most obviously, it contradicts the claim that the Beta format was better and that its demise constitutes evidence of the pernicious workings of decentralized decision making or sensitive dependence on initial conditions. Regarding the one aspect that clearly differentiated the two formats, tape length, consumers preferred VHS.

Second, even though the technical differences between the two formats were small, the advantage of longer recording times was sufficient to allow VHS to overcome Beta's initial lead. There might not have been any great harm had the market stayed with Beta, inasmuch as its recording time was up to five hours by the early 1980s. But consumers were not willing to wait those few extra years, and the market was responsive enough to make the switch to the better path.

Third, the history illustrates the role of ownership, strategy, and adopters' foresight in facilitating a change in paths. The formats were each owned, and both Sony and JVC–Matsushita expended considerable effort to establish their standards, indicating that they expected to capture some of the benefits of doing so. The ability of VHS to attract partners such as RCA and Matsushita indicates the market participants' ability to recognize the large potential gains from promoting a superior standard.

Although it is sometimes argued that the dominance of VHS resulted from the random association of VHS with a more aggressive licensing and pricing strategy, the pricing and promotion of the two formats were in fact closely matched. Sony was certainly no babe in the woods with regard to marketing consumer electronics. But consumers were apparently quick to identify a standard that they preferred and were confident that many others would do the same. Not only was the switch to VHS rapid, but it was also repeated in separate national markets. Thus, there is no evidence that the market choice was due to blunders, unlucky promotional choices, or insufficient investment by the owners of the Beta format.[3]

---

[3] In the economics literature of lock-in, the Beta-VHS story, very casually told, is often used to support the lock-in claim. Here, for example, is how Brian Arthur (1990) tells the story: "The history of the videocassette recorder furnishes a simple example of positive feedback. The VCR market started out with two competing formats selling at about the same price: VHS and Beta . . . Both systems were introduced at about the same time and so began with roughly equal market shares; those shares fluctuated early on because of external circumstance, 'luck' and corporate maneuvering. Increasing returns

An additional aspect of this standards battle further illustrates the richness of market behavior. Although the Beta format's advantages in editing and special effects were apparently relatively unimportant for home users, they were important for broadcasters. And the Beta format does survive in broadcasting, where editing and special effects are relatively more important. Broadcasters and home users do interact, of course, but mostly over the airwaves or cable. Their interaction does not generally involve much exchange of the cassettes themselves, and for those occasions when it does, broadcasters can keep some VHS equipment. But the high-performance, high-cost broadcasting machines that use the Beta format are one reason that many people assume that the Beta format offers higher quality.

The importance of Beta's survival in broadcasting is that there were really two standards battles, not one, and two different outcomes. Consumers got the format that they preferred, and broadcasters got the standard they preferred. This is really a story of coexisting standards. [. . .] The broadcasters are the minority that have strong preferences for a different standard. [. . .]

The Beta–VHS standards war is a rich example of a standards battle. It is *not*, however, a story of lock-in of the first product to market. Instead, it is a story of competing formats, consumers' switching when something better for them became available, and the coexistence of a minority standard that offers special benefits to a specialized group of users.

A final postscript on the Beta–VHS rivalry: one that indicates the dangers of lock-in stories. If a standard with a better picture were to come along but not be adopted, it might be tempting to suspect a potential case of lock-in. DVD might seem to fit this description, except that DVD is still thought likely to replace VHS. But if DVD should fail, we are likely to hear choruses of lock-in from the usual places. We should be slow to accept such a conclusion, however, since the market has already rejected a system with a higher quality picture that suffers no compatibility problems with VHS.

We are talking about SuperVHS, a system that, using special tape, can record and play back a picture with much higher resolution than ordinary VHS. SuperVHS machines can be purchased for about $350, which is somewhat higher than the price of a regular VHS machine with the same set of features normally found on SuperVHS (hi-fi, cable box control, and so forth). SuperVHS machines can play back regular VHS tapes, so there is no compatibility issue, and can even record regular VHS on regular tapes. With the special tapes, however, it has a picture that has 30–40 percent greater resolution. SuperVHS has been around for most, if not all, of the 1990s, so it has had plenty of time to generate market share, yet it clearly has failed to catch on.

Why has it failed? It cannot be due to lock-in, for there is no compatibility issue and no differential network effects. SuperVHS machines are part of the same network as regular VHS. Thus we must conclude that consumers are not willing to

on early gains eventually tilted the competition toward VHS: it accumulated enough of an advantage to take virtually the entire VCR market. Yet it would have been impossible at the outset of the competition to say which system would win, which of the two possible equilibria would be selected. Furthermore, if the claim that Beta was technically superior is true, then the market's choice did not represent the best outcome" (p. 92).

pay an extra $150 for SuperVHS. Improved picture quality is not, apparently, worth that difference. The difference in picture quality may be large in terms of technical specifications, but the typical consumer may not be able to see it. On ordinary television screens of twenty-seven inches or less, the fast speed of a regular VHS tape displays a picture about as good as the ordinary viewer can detect. Furthermore, regular VHS has a better picture than standard broadcast quality, which eliminates the value of SuperVHS for taping off the air. This is important because it tells us that even if Beta had a better picture than VHS, it might not have mattered as long as VHS's picture was good enough. After all, any difference between Beta and VHS is dwarfed by the difference between VHS and SuperVHS.

This story has implications beyond video recording. Just as the movement to a graphical operating system in computers did not take place until sufficiently powerful hardware became readily available and affordable (as we show in the next section of this chapter), the movement to a higher-quality video format (tape or broadcast HDTV) is likely to require affordable large-screen televisions that will make the enhanced picture quality worthwhile. Should DVD or HDTV, currently in their embryonic phase, fail in the market, that failure can be taken as a failure of markets or standards only if cheap large-screen televisions are readily available.

## COMPUTER OPERATING SYSTEMS: MAC VERSUS IBM

Among the popular examples of economic things that go bump in the night is the success of the DOS computer operating system. Macintosh, it is alleged, was far superior to command-line DOS, and even to DOS-based Windows, at least in its earlier versions. Yet Macintosh has garnered only a small share of the computer market and appeared, until quite recently, to be on the brink of extinction.

Because users clearly prefer a graphical user interface to a command-line interface, how did the DOS command-line interface manage to dominate personal computing when it and the Macintosh graphical user interface were competing head on? The usual story is that DOS was successful because DOS was successful. DOS had a large market share because there was a lot of software available for it, and there was a lot of software available for it because there were a lot of DOS-based machines in use. But it is also possible that DOS succeeded on its own merits.

First, DOS had a cost advantage over Macintosh. A graphical user interface requires considerably more computing power to get most jobs done, which significantly increased costs when that power was hard to come by. Furthermore, although Macintosh owners could see italics and boldface on screen, to print the screen as they saw it required a PostScript printer, and such printers cost in the vicinity of $1,000 more than ordinary laser printers. Second, command-line DOS was faster than Macintosh.[4] Macintosh owners had to wait for their screen displays to change,

---

[4] See the discussion of a graphical spreadsheet (Excel) *vis-à-vis* text-based spreadsheets in [Liebowitz and Margolis (1999, ch. 7)], where the speed penalty of the graphical product was rated as a fatal handicap.

whereas PC owners had almost instantaneous updates.[5] Third, although the graphical user interface allowed users to access and learn programs more easily, in many business settings a computer was used for only a single application. Only one program could run at a time, and hard drives were small or nonexistent at first. Many programs were copy-protected, usually requiring that the floppy disk be kept in the drive, so it was awkward to change programs. In that environment, the operator had very little interaction with the operating system interface, and once the operator had learned the application, there were few advantages of the graphical user interface. Finally, it was easier to create software for DOS machines, which is one reason that many applications packages became available so quickly in the DOS world.

The case for DOS in the 1980s, therefore, was much stronger than it appears from the vantage of the 1990s, with our multimegabyte memories and multigigabyte hard drives. Now that we routinely use computers that run 30 times faster than the old DOS machines, with 50 times the memory and 100 times the hard-drive capacity, the requirements of a graphical operating system seem rather puny. But they were enormous back in the 1980s.

As processors became faster, memory cheaper, and hard drives larger, the advantages of command-line DOS diminished. If we were still using DOS, we would certainly have an example of being stuck with an inferior product, one that offers smaller net benefits to consumers. But we are not still using DOS. Instead we are using a Mac-like graphical user interface. If someone went to sleep in 1983 and awoke in 2000 to see a modern PC, he most likely would think that the Macintosh graphical user interface had been colorized and updated, with a second button added to the mouse.[6] This modern Rip van Winkle might be surprised to learn, however, that the owner of the graphical user interface was not Apple, but Microsoft.

Although the movement from DOS to Windows was costly, it occurred quite rapidly. As in the other examples, the evidence is quite the opposite of lock-in: It demonstrates that markets, far from getting stuck in ruts, make rapid changes when there is a clear advantage in doing so. Because Windows also ran DOS programs, it lowered the transition cost.[7]

The competition between DOS and Macintosh demonstrates the importance of the distinction between a fixed standard and flexible standard. A fixed standard at

---

[5] The screen display on the PC required only 5 or 10 percent of the computer memory that was required by the Macintosh screen. Because this was constantly being updated when the screen changed, DOS screens tended to update instantaneously, whereas Macintosh screens had a noticeable lag and scrolling was much slower.

[6] The original graphical user interface, developed at the Xerox PARC research center, had a mouse with three buttons. The PC has two. The use of but a single button appears to be a matter of pride in the Macintosh community and is sometimes defended as optimal. Another point that rabid Macintosh users often made when pointing to the superiority of their operating system has to do with whether menus drop down automatically, or require a mouse click. To most users, these are minor differences compared with the chasms that separated graphical and textbased operating systems.

[7] If Apple had been interested in converting DOS users, they could have incorporated DOS compatibility in their operating system (purchasing or licensing a DOS clone such as DR DOS, for example) and porting their operating system to the Intel platform so as not to render obsolete a user's hardware. Apple apparently thought of themselves as a hardware company and did not actively pursue this strategy.

least allows for the hypothetical possibility that we get stuck – everyone would like to move but no one would like to go first. With a flexible standard, however, getting stuck is difficult to imagine. A flexible standard can evolve over time: It can add a new feature, or increase capacity, or adjust a parameter.

One important element in the success of the DOS-Windows platforms may well have been Microsoft's commitment to backward compatibility – evolution rather than revolution. In contrast, Macintosh computers were not compatible with earlier successful Apple products. This meant that the Macintosh did not have a base of carry-over users as early customers. Whether they stayed with Apple products or moved on to DOS, Apple customers faced an inevitable task of converting or abandoning files and applications.

Furthermore, Apple's behavior signaled customers that the company would not seek continuity in its operating systems in the future. In fact, Apple implemented, in fairly short order, two generations of incompatible operating systems – first the Lisa, and then the Macintosh.[8] Computer users, particularly commercial users, who found such abrupt changes to be disruptive took note of these policies. Commodore and Atari, which were also early adopters of graphical user interface operating systems, took approaches similar to Apple's.

The Windows system is often criticized for continuing to carry the vestiges of the dated DOS system. But, as in all interesting economic problems, benefits are usually accompanied by a cost. The benefit of continuity from DOS to the various versions of Windows was unavoidably accompanied by the cost of carrying over certain DOS features. In the remaining three sections, we see this interplay of these costs and benefits over and over again in the applications software market.

## METRIC VERSUS ENGLISH MEASUREMENT

George Washington, while president, spoke against the evils of metric. Did he know something we don't?

Washington was aware that the French had gone overboard in their adoption of metric. The switch to metric time in France after the revolution is a fascinating example of a case where the costs of switching were far greater than the benefits. The reason that metric time makes no sense is that is makes obsolete all clocks and provides no particular additional value. People do not often make calculations in time units, so having a system based on decimal units is of limited value. Metric time is rather like driving on the left or right side of the street – the choice is arbitrary, with little advantage for one over the other.

The costs of switching to metric measuring systems are nontrivial, and most Americans do not think that they outweigh the benefits. Tasks for which consum-

---

[8] This difference still separates the two companies. Apple, when it was switching to its recent Macintosh operating system (8.0), initially announced that it would not run software applications that were made to run under its older operating system (7.x). Microsoft, on the other hand, has been very careful about making Windows NT compatible with its Windows 95/98 operating system before it begins a serious migration of users, allowing five or six years for the process to be finished.

ers most commonly use a measuring system, such as finding out how hot or cold it is outside, purchasing meat at the supermarket, or determining the speed of your automobile, do not benefit from metric measurements. Thus, the failure to establish the metric system in the United States is a rational response to individual choices – not an indicator of a problem. This response contrasts sharply with the costly measures that have been implemented in Canada.

The metric system was adopted in Canada by government fiat in the 1970s. The change in standard happened only after considerable debate, and it is a high irony that one of the most persuasive arguments in this debate was that Canada needed to move quickly to stay on the same standard as the United States – where, at the time, there was some talk about a move to metric. In Canada, metric regulators went so far as to ban measurements in English units after the adoption of metric. Chaos in supermarkets and voter discontent quickly led regulators to allow the listing of both measurement systems, but metric continues to be the official measurement system in Canada. Nevertheless, to this day, English measurement is the de facto standard for many kinds of common measurement.

On the other hand, for many groups in the United States, such as scientists, metric is the standard. This is another example where the total number of people using a standard is less important than the particular individuals with whom one most closely interacts, and where two standards can coexist.

## BUREAUCRACY AND THE MYTH OF MITI

All of these examples – keyboards, VCRs, computers, and the metric system – are fables that circulate as evidence of a kind of after-the-fact Murphy's law of markets. If something happened, it probably went wrong. But there is an opposite myth that may be even more costly. It is the myth that we could have avoided these "disasters" by naming an omniscient, benevolent standards-dictator as an alternative to markets. Sometimes this savior is no more omniscient than a Monday morning quarterback: when he compares actual outcomes with a hypothetical ideal, it's obvious what should have happened. Often in these discussions, the wished-for arbiter of perfection is the government.

This is not to say that people don't harbor a good deal of cynicism about politics. But discussions of industrial policy often seem to incorporate a view that government, or the experts that it might draw upon, could figure out what technologies and standards are the best, even in the circumstances in which private parties are unable to sort these things out for themselves. It seems reasonable, however, to keep things even. There's no use in comparing real markets with a hypothetical, benevolent, and perfect government. Let's at least discipline ourselves to compare real markets with real government.

Now, governments are human institutions, and they are not omniscient. They can, however, do some very important things that private parties cannot manage. Even free-market types are usually willing to concede the utility of having a government that can record and enforce property rights, adjudicate contracts, and provide for the common defense. But governments can also fail. Even liberals acknowledge waste and fraud and misdirection of some government programs. For a better understanding of technology policy, what is required is not a litany of all the things that could happen, but some discussion of what has happened. For this, we do have a very good example: the Japanese Ministry of International Trade and Industry (MITI).

Only a few years ago, when the Japanese economy seemed to be a powerhouse that never made a misstep, MITI was often held up as an example of what the U.S. government needed to do, an example of successful industrial policy. Now, with Japan in recession, and the repercussions of underpriced capital and subsidized industry being sharply felt, we do not hear so much about MITI. In fact, MITI is a story of substantial misdirection, of damaging commitments to particular technologies, and damaging restraints on entrepreneurs who were thought not to be doing the right things. MITI's gaffes are now well known – wrong on transistors, which succeeded; wrong on supercomputers, which did not; wrong on the buildup of the steel industry; wrong on synthetic fuels; wrong on Honda; and wrong on HDTV.[9] Very simply MITI, which may well have had the best shot of any government agency at steering an economy toward the best bets, was no substitute for the interplay of multitudes of profit-seeking rivals competing with each other to find the best mousetrap.

## SOME OTHER EXAMPLES

Path-dependence advocates have sometimes claimed that the continued use of FORTRAN by academics and scientists is an example of getting stuck on the wrong standard.[10] But one doesn't have to peruse too many computer magazines to realize that FORTRAN has long ago been superseded by languages such as Pascal, C, C++, and now, perhaps, Java. Individuals continuing to use FORTRAN do so not because they want to be like everyone else, but because their cost of switching is too high. This is the opposite of the typical network-effects story. Network effects, as normally modeled, should have induced them to switch to mainstream programming languages years ago. This is a story of ordinary sunk costs, not of network "externality" or other market failure. This is another story where, network effects, if of consequence, are not related to the total size of the networks as much as they are to the small group of individuals who interact in their work.

Path-dependence proponents have also sometimes claimed that the gasoline-powered engine might have been a mistake, and that steam or electricity might have been a superior choice for vehicle propulsion. They advance this argument in spite of the fact that in the century since automobiles became common, with all of the applications of motors and batteries in other endeavors, and with all the advantages of digital electronic power-management systems, the most advanced elec-

---

[9] For a general discussion of the MITI, see Zinsmeister (1993).

[10] In case you think we are making this up in order to create a ridiculous straw man, see Arthur (1990). A recent Stanford economics Ph.D. dissertation (Kirsch 1998) was also devoted to examining this issue. Kirsch reports to us that he went into the project hoping to find great inefficiency in the use of the internal combustion engine, but his research forced him to conclude otherwise.

tric automobiles that anyone has been able to make do not yet equal the state of the art in internal-combustion automobiles as of the late 1920s.

A number of scholars have begun to examine other instances that have, at one time or another, been alleged to illustrate lock-in to inferior standards. For many years, economic historians argued that the small coal cars that were used in England were an example of what was called "technical backwardness." The mechanism for this backwardness was much the same as other lock-in stories. The stock of cars led to certain adaptations around the cars, which led to renewal of the stock of cars, and so on. Recently, however, Va Nee Van Vleck (1997) reconsidered this case. She found that the small coal car was in fact well suited to Britain's geography and coal-distribution systems. In a very different subject area, Larry Ribstein and Bruce Kobayashi (1996) have examined the possibility that the adoption of state laws locks in the features of the statutes that are adopted by the first states to pass legislation. They find very little persistence of these initial statutory forms.

Finally, software applications offer many instances in which one product replaces another. [. . .]

## REFERENCES

Arthur, W. B. (1990) "Positive feedbacks in the economy," *Scientific American* 262, pp. 92–9.

Kirsch, David A. (1998) "From competing technologies to systems rivalry: the electric motor vehicle in America, 1895–1915," Ph.D. dissertation (Stanford University, Calif.).

Klopfenstein, B. C. (1989) "The diffusion of the VCR in the United States," in M. R. Levy (ed.) *The VCR Age* (Newbury Park, Calif.: Sage).

Lardner, J. (1987) *Fast Forward* (New York: W. W. Norton).

Liebowitz, Stan J., and Margolis, Stephen E. (1999) *Winners, Losers and Microsoft* (Oakland, Calif.: The Independent Institute).

Ribstein, L., and B. Kobayashi (1996) "An economic analysis of uniform state laws," *Journal of Legal Studies* 34, pp. 131–99.

Van Vleck, V. N. (1997) "Delivering coal by road and by rail in Great Britain: The efficiency of the 'Silly Little Bobtailed Coal Wagons'," *Journal of Economic History* 57, pp. 139–60.

Zinsmeister, K. (1993) "Japan's MITI Mouse," *Policy Review* 64, pp. 28–35.

# 6

# Delivering Coal by Road and Rail in Britain: The Efficiency of the "Silly Little Bobtailed" Coal Wagons

*Va Nee L. Van Vleck\**

A recurring theme in economic history has been the allegedly slow conversion from older to newer technologies, especially in the instance of late-Victorian Britain. The small British coal wagon has been held up as an example of Britain's resistance to technological change. At best the "silly little bobtailed" coal wagon has been regarded as a curiosity; at worst it has been seen as further evidence of entrepreneurial failure.[1] It is unfortunate that the small coal wagon has not attracted systematic analysis in spite of the complaints of contemporaries and economic historians. The coal wagon was a technology common and central to the interests of the coal mining industry, the railways, and a multitude of coal users and which also exhibits network features. Presently, the persistence of the small coal wagon might be too readily categorized as another wrong decision that led to the larger British decline. This, too, would be a premature indictment.

The small coal wagon was neither a curiosity nor technological mistake. The coal wagon has been derided because it has been incorrectly modeled as one component in a system of bulk transport. Compared to its larger European and American cousins, the British coal wagon appeared clearly inefficient; and it seemed plain that larger coal cars could have allowed British railways to exploit economies of scale in transportation. But it is not so; I argue for an alternative view of the small

\* Va Nee L. Van Vleck was formerly Visiting Assistant Professor of Economics at Gustavus Adolphus College, Grinnell College, and Nebraska Wesleyan University and is currently an independent scholar in Modesto, CA. I would like to thank Deirdre McCloskey, the University of Iowa Economic History Seminar, and my former colleagues for their invaluable comments and encouragement. I have benefited from the advice and critiques of two anonymous referees and the Editor of the *Journal of Economic History*. Responsibility for any errors rests with me, of course.

[1] The adjectival phrase is owed to Thorstein Veblen, *Imperial Germany*, p. 130.

coal wagon, understanding it within a broader system of distribution in which the small wagon provided flexibility and substituted for the more expensive means of delivering coal by road. The little coal wagon was exactly the right type of technology to employ. It was not an example of technological backwardness.

## CRITICISMS OF THE COAL WAGON

Thorstein Veblen commented derisively on the small wagon in *Imperial Germany and the Industrial Revolution*. He pitied the British the increased competition from Germany and the United States. Britain had "shown the way," Veblen argued, but had later committed mistakes, failed to adopt innovations and new technologies, and stagnated.[2] Followers in industrialization learned from the mistakes of the leader, avoided them, adopted and adapted technologies, and grew faster. For example, the once innovative technologies of Britain's railways Veblen considered antiquated and a handicap; they ought to have been "junked" at the earliest possible opportunity.[3] The small railway car was Veblen's case in point. At the time when Belgian and German coal wagons carried 15 to 16 (long) tons – and American coal cars loaded 30 to 50 tons apiece – the British coal wagon typically carried only 10 to 12 tons of payload. Britain's coal wagons were small.

Veblen's acerbic pronouncements on British rolling stock crystallized later into three main criticisms: the coal wagon had too small a carrying capacity; there were too many of them; and they were owned by colliers, merchants, and manufacturers rather than solely by the railways, whose operating costs were directly affected by them.[4] Of some 614,000 mineral wagons enumerated in 1918, 62.5 percent were owned by collieries, 23.9 percent by merchants and other distributors, 8.2 percent by manufacturers, and the remaining 5.4 percent were held by the railways or by the Government.[5] The first and second criticisms above have been seen as natural consequences of the third: because of the multiplicity of owners, each with individualistic requirements, there were too many coal wagons; because of the multiplicity of owners, equipped with many wagons, railway competition devolved into "service" (quality) competition rather than economic (price) competition, and efficiency suffered.[6] Service was synonymous with small, frequent consignments in small wagons, that left unexploited economies of scale and unexploited opportunities for profit. So it is said.[7] No matter if the alleged economies of a larger coal

---

[2] Ibid., p. 132.

[3] Ibid., pp. 131–2.

[4] Prominent critics of the coal wagon after Veblen include Sherrington, *Economics*; Frankel, "Obsolescence"; Kindleberger, "Obsolescence"; David, "Landscape."

[5] U.K., Board of Trade, *Report*, pp. 5–6, 7. The survey was limited to owners of 30 or more wagons. the result being that the actual proportion of wagons held "privately" (nonrailway) is larger than the figures reported. (Later, in 1928, the number of coal wagons had risen to 753,000: 55.3 percent owned by collieries, 17.1 percent by other distributors, 4.3 percent by manufacturers, and 23.3 percent by railways. U.K., Standing Committee on Mineral Transport, *First Report*, p. 96.)

[6] See Cain, "British Railway Rates Problem" and "Private Enterprise"; Irving, "Profitability"; Lee, "Service Industries."

[7] The small coal wagon is arguably one of the original instances of path-dependence and technological "lock in." The crux of the matter is that two technologies coexisted; one purported to be clearly

wagon were large or small, real, or imagined, it is undeniable that there were some people – primarily railway sympathizers – who believed that the small wagon was the principal problem: "The economic problem is primarily that of moving a certain tonnage at the lowest possible cost, and unfortunately in Great Britain, as a result of the small size of wagons, much of that tonnage is deadweight."[8]

Regulation of the coal industry in 1930 and nationalization of the railways in 1947 finally placed all coal wagons under singular control – the government's. Even so, relatively small – 16-ton and later 20-ton – coal cars persisted. But if early small coal wagons were expensive in the sense that they required too many unproductive locomotive miles in marshaling and shunting, their advantages were, as we shall see, economizing on more expensive transportation resources: horses, hay and oats, trucks, and petroleum fuel.

## THE INEFFICIENCY COST OF SMALL WAGONS

Critics viewed the small wagon as a more cumbersome and expensive vehicle for transporting coal than a larger wagon would have been. A crude estimate, an upper bound, is needed to measure the implied inefficiency of the small coal wagon. Assume a fixed quantity of coal is transported either by 20-ton ("large") wagons or by 10-ton ("small") wagons. When the same per ton rate is applied to both modes – as it was – and the same load of coal is transported, total railway revenues are not different. Assuming that receipts are the same, the railways' incentive for larger wagons must lie in reducing *operating costs* per ton of payload. Contemporaries expected that the railway operating costs for one 20-ton wagon would have differed from the costs for two 10-ton wagons in the following ways: shunting and marshaling activity would be halved – working one wagon instead of two; rolling-stock maintenance would fall by one-quarter; and while tare weight would increase by only one-third to one-half, the payload per wagon doubled.[9]

To translate these anticipated engineering benefits into reasonable pecuniary economies, we need some detail on the railways' operating expenses. From 1899 to 1912 the average share of working expenditures incurred by the major departments of the British railways included the following: traffic expenses, 29.4 percent; locomotive power, 27.5 percent; ways-and-works maintenance, 15 percent; and rolling-stock maintenance, 8.3 percent. The remainder was made up of rates and taxes,

---

superior, and yet it is the allegedly inferior one that was most widely used. According to Veblen (and those who came after him) it was a choice dictated by history; small wagons were used because they were suited to the existing infrastructure, not because they were economical at the margin. Large wagons were supposedly economical *in toto* but were not adopted because they were incompatible with historical capital. The small coal wagon would appear to fit the spirit if not the letter of path-dependence as formulated by Arthur, "Competing Technologies", and David, "Clio," among others. (To date, critics of the small wagon have only implied its inefficiencies and have failed to account for any of its benefits.)

[8] Sherrington, *Economics*, vol. 2, p. 228.

[9] Fenelon, *Railway Economics*, p. 172; repeated by Kindleberger, "Obsolescence," p. 284; alternatively, see Irving, "Profitability," p. 62. The capacity-to-tare ratio compares the paying load to the empty wagon's weight. A higher ratio indicates a larger fraction of the wagon's loaded, gross weight is devoted to revenue-generating freight rather than to tare weight, which adds only to railway operating costs.

general charges, passenger duty, navigation operations, and miscellaneous.[10] The first four operating departments listed were the departments most likely to benefit from the use of larger wagons. A rough estimate of the purely operational benefits (per ton) from larger wagons weights the expected engineering economies of each department by their corresponding share of expenditures:

$$Estimated\ operating\ economy = \sum_{Dept\ i} Large\ Wagon\ Savings_i^* \cdot Expenditure\ Share_i.$$

The following relationships between the expected engineering benefits and the railways' operating costs were assumed: traffic expenses varied directly in proportion to the number of wagons; expenditures on locomotive power were proportional to the capacity-to-tare ratio; and rolling-stock maintenance varied inversely with the durability of the equipment.[11] Under these assumptions traffic expenses would have been at most halved with the replacement of two small wagons by one larger one; expenditures on locomotives could have been reduced by as much as half since percentage of tare weight was reduced, and fewer wagons were hauled; and rolling-stock maintenance was expected to fall by up to one-quarter.[12] The expected benefit from using only large wagons for mineral transport weights the operational savings by the share of traffic volume represented by coal and minerals:[13]

$$Estimated\ operating\ economy = 62\% \cdot [(0.5 \times 29.4\%) + (0.5 \times 27.5\%) + (0.25 \times 8.3\%)] = 19\%\ per\ ton.$$

This first approximation of the savings anticipated from the use of larger, 20-ton wagons is a 19 percent decrease in operating expenses per payload ton. Thus far it would seem clear that the use of large wagons was advantageous for the railways. However, 19 percent per ton is the largest realizable savings available to the railways if they could avoid bearing any capital costs necessary to make large wagons

---

[10] Irving, "Profitability," pp. 49, 60.

[11] Rolling-stock maintenance included superintendency and renewal and repair expenses as well as purchases of new rolling stock assets; locomotive power covered superintendency, wages, fuel, water, and lubricant expenses; and finally traffic expenses encompassed everything that did not fall into either previous category (nor into ways-and-works or miscellaneous). It was a hodgepodge of expenses that included salaries and wages for employees from clerks to *guards*; printing, stamps, advertising; *wagon covers, wages for shunting personnel, working of stationary engines, hoists and cranes, coal-tipping expenses,* railway clearing house expenses, and miscellaneous (Munby, *Inland Transport: Statistics,* p. 144). Ways-and-works maintenance does not appear in the estimate because the determining factor in rail and railbed wear is not the gross weight of the vehicle; it is the weight borne per axle. (See, for example, Kumar and Singh, "Threshold Stress Criterion.") A typical 10-ton wagon had an empty weight of roughly 6 tons; fully loaded, the small wagon would have carried 8 tons per axle. The larger 20-ton wagons were also constructed on *two* axles – not four – and empty they weighed 10 tons; thus, large wagons, fully loaded, would have carried 15 tons per axle. The increase in tons per axle essentially negates the benefit of fewer wagons (hence fewer axles). The estimate made omits this ambiguous net effect.

[12] This follows the assumptions of Fenelon, Kindleberger, and Irving (see note 9). In note 11 those expenses that would most likely be affected by a reduction in the number of wagons handled have been italicized. Further, the reduced number of wagons was expected to benefit the "traffic expenses" category, yet the greater weight per wagon could have increased some of these same costs (especially engines, hoists, cranes, and tippers).

[13] Bagwell, *Transport Revolution,* p. 115.

useful – such as rebuilding weighbridges or tipplers. Colliers and manufacturers faced the dismal prospect that the only certainty from adopting larger coal wagons was an increase in their capital costs for rebuilding and acquiring machinery compatible with the larger wagon.[14] On the face of it the collieries, merchants, and manufacturers had very little if anything to gain; therefore, to be induced into considering large wagons they would have expected a reduction in freight rates. The largest rate reduction they could have hoped for was the whole 19 percent from reduced railway costs.

Two overtures by private wagon owners to railway companies about the use of larger wagons, in return for a reduction in rates, have been curiously neglected in the coal wagon's standard history; they are as yet to be explained by transportation historians. First, in 1904 Sir Alfred Hickman offered a guarantee of two full trainloads per day, seven days a week, in his company's proposed 25- to 30-ton wagons in return for a reduced rate from the railway. The railway refused to adjust its rate.[15] Another proposal was made – to the Midland Railway – by Staveley collieries: Staveley would construct its newly sunk pits to accommodate 30-ton wagons if the Midland would reduce its rates for coal carried in the new wagons. The Midland declined, and presumably Staveley built to suit its existing rolling stock.[16] One historian suggested that the mindset of the railways contributed to these paradoxes: Hickman apparently "was completely mistaken in thinking that the railway companies wanted his local traffic or that of his fellow ironmasters."[17] Legally the railways could have given preferential rates so long as the rates were not unduly preferential, but demonstration of the basis for reduced freight then rested with the railways and their questionable account statistics.[18] That the railways were unwilling or unable to determine some acceptable division of the expected benefits suggests that any expected benefits were small – if there were any at all. (In truth, it does not appear that the railways themselves expected a 19 percent savings per ton from hauling coal in large wagons else they should have been moved to negotiate some reduction.)

---

[14] It is well understood that when otherwise independent investment decisions are technically interrelated the likelihood of new investment projects diminishes; this was Veblen's assertion that the large wagon was at a disadvantage from the outset. (Refer to Frankel, "Obsolescence"; Salter, *Productivity*.)

The infrastructure obstacle presumes that the hindered technology is more economical at the margin. Presumably 19 percent more economical in this case – but this is the wrong margin. Rather than address infrastructure directly I have taken a different approach: do the reduced variable costs (rail freight) save enough to offset the accompanying increases in other variable costs? If there were enough savings to "pay" for the other variable cost increases any remainder would "pay" toward new installation, and so forth. The reduced rail freight would not have been enough to offset the increases in other delivery-related variable costs, which then renders (amortized) capital-cost argument moot; see Salter, *Productivity*, p. 86.

For wagon owners there would have been a slight reduction in direct capital costs if two small wagons had been replaced by one 20-ton wagon, costing £110 in 1904 – rather than two new 10-ton wagons at £62 apiece; see Colliery Guardian, *Digest*, pp. 105, 117.

[15] U.K., Royal Commission on Coal Supplies, *Second Report*, p. 123 [#11624].

[16] Church, *History*, p. 85.

[17] Le Guillou, "Freight Rates," p. 112.

[18] Kahn-Freund, *Law*, p. 108. Railway statistics were notoriously ill-defined, which hindered meaningful analysis: "It never entered into the minds of those who compiled the existing form of accounts that any one should wish [to use them]" lamented Ackworth and Paish in 1912: Ackworth and Paish, "British Railways," p. 702.

Despite allusions to the contrary, there were high-capacity coal wagons running on Britain's rails at the time. There were 15- and 20-ton wagons, and a few even larger, in use in specialized and limited segments of the coal trade. Large coal wagons were employed primarily in moving coal to ports to be unloaded into steamers for coastal shipment south or for export. Gasworks, electrical works, iron and steel foundries, and the railways themselves all used large wagons. The common characteristic of these large-wagon users was they involved regular traffic of uniform coal in large quantities bound for a central site or single consumer. The characteristics of the rest of the coal trade were typically the opposite: intermittent traffic to any one particular coal buyer, covering numerous grades of coal, and collected from a few to a dozen different collieries. For example, the Stockport Cooperative Society deployed its 48 wagons from one depot to seven collieries; and Hall & Co., Ltd of Croydon (Surrey) – a coal dealer and builders' supplier – operated its 164 coal wagons out of 34 depots for its purchases from a dozen or so collieries.[19] Inland coal trains with their assortment of small wagons reflected the complexity of sources, types and sizes of coal, and final destinations.

The railways might have wished that the coal trade was a homogeneous monolith. It was not. Coal was bought from the collieries either on contract – typically stipulating monthly delivery quotas – or on the spot market by coal factors (wholesalers), merchants, and industrial users. A literal multitude of buyers and sellers were occupied in the coal market. The result was that coal trains were markedly heterogeneous. Enormous "wait order" sidings, located in coal districts or on the outskirts of large cities, were temporary repositories for hundreds or thousands of loaded wagons awaiting final despatch. The legacy was the shunting and marshaling necessary to form and reform the trains and the frequent deliveries of small consignments of coal. The expense of coal burned in the boilers of shunting and marshaling locomotives must have seemed to be railway profits gone up in smoke. To railway managers and investors alike the small wagon appeared to be a principal drain on profits; a 19 percent drain that might have been plugged if fewer, larger wagons had been used instead.

For their own part, the railways' use of large wagons was primarily limited to obtaining their own locomotive coal; the coal wagons they leased to customers were more often than not the small 10- or 12-ton wagons. And when it suited their purposes the railways were more than willing to publicly extoll the virtues of the small coal wagon. Such a case was when they wanted to sink the plans for revitalizing England's canal system and the bulk transport services it might have provided.[20] In 1910 Edwin A. Pratt wrote,

> the railway companies provide at many of their stations coal depots where the coal merchant can either discharge the coal into sacks or carts direct from the trucks [wagons] . . . and so deliver it at once to their customers; or else . . . store it alongside the lines, on a space allotted to them for the purpose at an annual rental, until they get

[19] Hudson, *Private Owner Wagons*, p. 59; Dobson, *Century*, pp. 167, 168.
[20] For a synopsis of the interplay of rail and waterborne transport (canals and coastal shipping) see Van Vleck, "Reassessing Technological Backwardness," ch. 3.

orders for it . . . They are able, also, under the system of small-truck [wagon] loads, delivered promptly as wanted, to deal in a larger variety of coal than if they had to order a large quantity of each kind.[21]

So even the railways recognized an economic advantages of the small coal wagon in the flexibility it permitted hundreds of their coal-merchant customers. The inland coal trade was not about volume or bulk. It hinged on speed and distribution, features coal merchants – and the railways – associated with small wagons rather than large ones.

Coal merchants said that they were not opposed to large wagons where economics deemed they were practical; though by their actions they demonstrated that the local coal trade was not one of those places.[22] Pratt was correct in noting that the small wagon was well suited to the inventory situation of most coal merchants. The typical merchant bought his coal in periodic, small lots that just filled a small wagon. For the fullest economies of large wagons to be realized, the large wagons had to be fully loaded. Twenty tons at a time was more than economical for some coal merchants to receive, constrained either by tying up their capital in coal stacked at the depot or by their capacity to deliver it from the railhead.[23] Rather than improve the capacity-to-tare ratio and reduce operating costs, as expected, large wagons carrying small quantities would have reduced the ratio and would have added to railway costs.

The matter of small versus large wagons is indirectly addressed by asking how cheap or expensive would coal have been under each possible transport technology: in large wagons or in small. Table 6.1 gives the breakdown of the retail price for coal as charged by nine Cooperative Societies in 1924. Cooperative Societies were consumer-owned enterprises that marketed primarily groceries and coal to the working classes. The single largest component was the pit price for coal graded to size at the colliery. Rail freight was the second largest component in the price; thus, it was assumed that coal could be made slightly cheaper if large wagons were employed and rail freight was reduced. Using the upper bound savings per ton (calculated earlier) and the share of rail freight in the price of coal, coal could have been at most 5 percent cheaper in the wholesale market and 3 percent cheaper in

[21] Pratt, *Canals*, pp. 51–2. Pratt had been hired by the railways to dissuade public sentiment for waterway transportation (Bagwell, *Transport Revolution*, p. 156).

[22] The idea that transportation customers were both greatly influenced by the modal choices available and themselves influenced the relative performance of different modes is not new. Rick Szostak has argued that the development of reliable and prompt transport modes in the prerailway era was a necessary condition for the success of the Industrial Revolution, which then fed back upon the transport sector; see Szostak, *Role*. In the current context, the factors of reliability, flexibility, and speed did not disappear with the coming of the railway; in fact, it is more likely that they were heightened so that the symbiosis of transport-provider and -customer was stronger than before.

[23] For more see Van Vleck, "Reassessing Technological Backwardness," ch. 2. The optimal lot size was simulated for differing sales volumes and obtains results consistent with the overall assessment of Britain's local coal trade. The small coal wagon is a historical instance of freight containerization – which has been credited with reducing break-bulk and other handling expenses in modern freight transport – yet is essentially ignored in its historical context.

[24] Using the figures from Table 6.1, rail freight accounted for roughly one-quarter of the wholesaler's expenses; hence, the wholesaler would have expected a reduction of 5 percent (= $0.25 \times 0.19$). Three percent in the retail market is obtained similarly (= $0.174 \times 0.19$).

**Table 6.1**   Components of the average retail price of coal, 1924

| | Price (d/ton) | | |
| --- | --- | --- | --- |
| Component | Mean | Standard deviation | Mean (percentage) |
| Pit price | 272.0 | 26.7 | 52.8 |
| Rail freight | 92.0 | 42.8 | 17.4 |
|    Railway wagon hire | 20.4 | 6.1 | 3.8 |
|    Short weight | 7.1 | 5.6 | 1.4 |
| Retail | | | |
|    Labor ("off loading") | 52.2 | 11.7 | 10.2 |
| Operating | | | |
|    Cart, rental | 26.0 | 9.2 | 5.1 |
| Costs | | | |
|    Sacks | 2.1 | 0.8 | 0.4 |
|    Rent, storage space | 1.4 | 0.8 | 0.4 |
|    Clerical | 8.1 | 2.5 | 1.6 |
|    Overhead (insurance) | 12.3 | 4.4 | 2.4 |
| Profit | 29.2 | 19.1 | 5.6 |
| Delivered price | 518.1 | 45.6 | 100.0 |

Columns may not sum due to rounding. Of the nine cooperative societies surveyed, two were from western England, two from Glasgow, and one was from each of the following: East Anglia, Hampshire, the Home Counties, the Midlands, and Lancashire.

*Source*: United Kingdom, Mines Department, *Retail Prices and Qualities of Household Coal*, Cmd 2185, pp. 6–7; a survey of nine Cooperative Societies.

the retail market.[24] It was hoped cheaper coal and reduced freight rates could revitalize British manufactures. What has been overlooked is that the rail rate with the small wagon was still cheaper than transporting freight by road and that imposing large coal wagons upon the existing distribution system would have pushed the expense of road freight higher, negating any rail economies that might have been realized.

## THE COSTS OF TRANSPORTING COAL ON THE RAILS AND ON THE ROAD

The figures in Table 6.1 are averaged across the nine Cooperative Societies surveyed. The rail freight as given reveals little about the rate per ton-mile, which was supposed to have been unnecessarily inflated by the "inefficient" small wagon. It is necessary to know what the rate per ton-mile was. Rail rates were quoted in pence per ton from specified points of origin to the various destinations; a standard rate corrected for distance, pence per ton per mile, was not. I have estimated the average rate for coal carriage by regression, run on available data from 1906, of the total freight charged per ton on miles hauled and miles-squared.[25] The estimated regression is given below:

$$Freight\ charged = 13.02 + 0.65 \cdot Miles + 0.0002 \cdot Miles^2 \qquad R^2 = 0.71.$$
$$\qquad\qquad\qquad (4.487)\ (0.163) \qquad\quad (0.0011) \qquad\qquad N = 172$$

The predicted rate is 0.65d per ton-mile and the relationship between freight and distance is essentially linear – long hauls were neither appreciably subsidized nor penalized. Curiously, the 0.65d rate estimated here is markedly *lower* than the rates typically reported for minerals traffic before World War I.[26] (The data are admittedly limited and, due to the nature of the source, cover routes where potential canal transport might have added an element of rate discrimination by the railways.)

Unlike the railways, merchants and some manufacturers were faced with two distinct components of transport costs: the freight to get the coal from the colliery to the railhead and cartage (road freight) to deliver it to themselves or their customers. The largest buyers received coal on a siding whereas other users relied either upon carrying their own coal or more often hired a coal merchant to supply the carting services. The railways had actively promoted the expansion of this inland coal trade, built sidings for manufacturers, and rented space to merchants and dealers for business in industrial, commercial, and household coals.[27] In the latter cases the coal had to be reloaded into a cart or truck and hauled away by horse power – animal or mechanical – a practice that continued through World War II. The limited adoption of large wagons by the merchants and manufacturers who owned them may have been a reflection of the resulting negative effects on the distribution and delivery costs for coal from the railhead – rather than mere stubbornness. The small coal wagon functioned as an integral part of local distribution and delivery of coal by horse and wagon and by motor lorry.

## Local delivery by horse-cart

In reconstructing the relationship between the rail-borne distribution and the local delivery of coal some details have been traditionally overlooked. Inelegant and common the horse and cart were quickly displaced from the pages of transportation history by the grandeur and power of the steam locomotive even if they were

[25] Data obtained from the U.K., Royal Commission on Canals, 1907 [*Second Report*], appendices 23 and 25. (Heteroscedasticity, as suspected, was confirmed by White's general test and White's standard errors are reported: White, "Heteroscedasticity-Consistent Covariance Matrix").

[26] Rates usually reported are some 30 percent higher, for instance 0.953d per ton per mile in 1906: Cain, "British Railway Rates Problem," p. 90. (Cain's rate was apparently drawn directly from railway records and his estimation method was not discussed.) The rate estimated here is not so different from rail rates for port-bound coal, 0.50 to 0.67d per ton per mile, Colliery Guardian, *Digest*, vol. 2, p. 114.

[27] Mitchell, *Economic Development*, p. 10.

not so quickly displaced from the streets.[28] Practically all coal for offices, small businesses, and houses was delivered at some point on its journey by horse-cart. The briefest summary of the local coal trade was implied in a question: "That is to say, you raise it, you put it into wagons, you send it by rail to a depot, and from the depot you distribute it to the consumer in your own horses and carts? – That is right."[29]

Quantitative evidence on the delivery of coal by horse-cart is scant, and what evidence there is relates to London.[30] T. C. Barker numbers the horses in London's coal trade in the early 1890s at 8,000; and prior to 1900 some 300 horses were worked out of London's King's Cross depot alone.[31] An important source has been the Committee on Retail Coal Prices of 1914 and 1915. The committee was given the task of determining the cause of the 35 percent increase in house-coal prices between June 1914 and February 1915. The committee collected evidence on railway congestion, horse and labor supplies, and profiteering and sought then to distinguish the effects of the war from inefficiency and opportunism. The report is most useful for the picture it provides of what was considered normal in the London coal trade. Using it as a snapshot of London's horse-carting trade some of the basic practices and costs can be quantified and an estimate of the carting rate made.

Horses were expected to deliver 24 to 36 tons of coal a week depending upon which market was being served: 24 tons in retail and 36 tons in delivery; earlier W. J. Gordon had given the figure of 30 tons per week per horse.[32] With six working days in the week, 4 to 6 tons per horse were to be delivered each day. It is doubtful that the whole amount was delivered in a single trip. A range of feasible horse-drawn loads is between a half-ton load per horse (the conservative figure used by Albert Fishlow) and 2 tons per horse per delivery (at the upper end according to Gordon). At 1 ton per horse per trip the retail trade would have required four trips per horse per day; the higher 2 tons per horse obtains two trips per day per horse.[33] The frequency of trips calculated here neatly mirrors the contemporary practice observed by Gordon of "two long journeys, or perhaps as many as four short ones" per day.[34] Large contract deliveries were probably carted by a team of horses so that there were effectively fewer deliveries performed per horse per day.

The rates charged for this carting were rarely of much interest and therefore rarely

[28] Thompson, "Nineteenth-Century Horse Sense," pp. 63–4; Barker, "Delayed Decline," p. 109. The history of horse-drawn transport has enjoyed a resurgence in more recent years, though it is still dwarfed by the sheer volume of history devoted to the railways. See, for instance, the collection of essays in Thompson, *Horses*; Gerhold, "Growth"; Langdon, "Horse Hauling"; Thompson, *Victorian England*; Turnbull, *Traffic*.

[29] U.K., *Report by the Committee Appointed by the Board of Trade to Inquire into the Causes of the Present Rise in the Retail Price of Coal*, p. 155 [#4547].

[30] The use of evidence from London is reasonably representative of the coal carting trade in general. The abundance of railway-owned, merchant-owned, and occasional trade horses present in London before World War I fairly approximates a competitive market: Turnbull, *Traffic*, pp. 136–7.

[31] Barker, "Delayed Decline," p. 103; Gordon, *Horse-World*, p. 130.

[32] U.K., Committee Appointed by the Board of Trade to Inquire into the Causes of the Present Rise in the Retail Price of Coal, *Minutes of Evidence*, p. 82 [#2305]; Gordon, *Horse-World*, p. 129.

[33] As used the term *delivery* suggests contract coal to large householders, small businesses, and manufacturers; *retail* was the street-by-street hawking of coal in small quantities per customer – usually 1 cwt. or less.

[34] Gordon, *Horse-World*, p. 132.

collected. Regrettably, no survey of delivery charges was conducted by the committee; although one exchange during the testimony is notably relevant:

> PROF. ASHLEY:   What do you charge for cartage? – It varies, according to distance, from 1s [12d] to 4s [48d].
>
> MR FLUX:   Is a shilling your minimum? – Yes.
>
> PROF. ASHLEY:   But most of your customers would dwell within the shilling radius, would they not? – I should think a fair average would be something like one side of the other of 2s [24d]. Of course I cannot give an exact figure.[35]

Comparable figures were given during subsequent testimony by representatives of the Cooperative Wholesale Society for overall cartage fees, 36d per ton in London and 30d per ton elsewhere.[36] In order to make a comparison of the expense of road freight versus rail freight the carting rate must be converted to a comparable ton-mile basis, which in turn depended on the average distance of a horse-cart's deliveries.

If the average speed of a laden horse-cart is two and a half miles per hour, at the upper extreme of two deliveries per day, the average market radius could have been as much as ten miles, one way.[37] The growing problem of traffic congestion suggests that the ten-mile distance is overstated; it is unlikely horse carts reached two and a half miles per hour in London or in other urban centers. Together, round-trip deliveries and traffic congestion stretch the calculated radius to its limit and thereby establish a lower bound on delivery charges. The minimum carting fee of 12d per ton and maximum of 48d per ton over a range of 10 miles obtains a road freight rate of some $3\frac{2}{3}$d per ton-mile. Compared to carting the small wagon mineral rate was cheap – even allowing for the moderate increases in rail rates at the time.[38]

Cartage was charged to cover horse feed, loading and unloading, a driver's wages, the costs of rescreening, weighing and bagging the coal, and the depreciation of horse and cart as principal components.[39] The labor and horse-feed components of cartage were the dominant costs, 43 percent and 40 percent. Table 6.2 details an example of the maintenance costs of a delivery horse and cart. The distance a horse could travel, the load drawn, and speed – hence the rate per ton-mile for road freight – were largely dependent upon how well the horse was fed.[40]

An average commercial horse consumed an estimated 1.4 tons of hay and 2.4 tons of oats in a year.[41] By 1892 the domestic supply of feedstuffs was insufficient

---

[35] U.K., *Report by the Committee Appointed by the Board of Trade to Inquire into the Causes of the Present Rise in the Retail Price of Coal*, p. 47 [#1164–6].

[36] Ibid., p. 122 [#3636].

[37] The two and a half miles per hour average speed was also used by Fishlow, *American Railroads*, p. 94, fn. 56. It is the same figure considered the "optimum working speed" for agricultural horses (Collins, "Farm Horse Economy," p. 77).

[38] See Munby, *Inland Transport Statistics*, p. 95.

[39] U.K., *Report by the Committee Appointed by the Board of Trade to Inquire into the Causes of the Present Rise in the Retail Price of Coal*, pp. 28–82 passim [#617, 856–64, 2275–6, 2291–2, and 2300–2].

[40] Other merchant costs – unloading railway wagons and loading carts, sacking coal, and driver's wages – did not vary with distance.

[41] Thompson, "Nineteenth-Century Horse Sense," p. 77 and "Horses," p. 60. More or less of these feedstuffs were consumed depending on the size of the horse, the intensity of employment, and the availability of other feed supplies.

**Table 6.2**    Weekly operating expenses for a horse cart, 1919

| Component | £ | s | d | Percentage of total |
|---|---|---|---|---|
| Wages (one laborer) | 3 | 3 | 0 | 42.9 |
| Hay and oats | 2 | 1 | 0 | 40.1 |
| Shoes | 0 | 6 | 0 | 4.1 |
| Harness | 0 | 5 | 0 | 3.4 |
| Cart | 0 | 5 | 0 | 3.4 |
| Stable | 0 | 5 | 0 | 3.4 |
| Insurance | 0 | 4 | 0 | 2.7 |
| **Total** | 7 | 7 | 0 | 100.0 |

*Source*: United Kingdom, *Findings by a Committee on Road Transport*, Cmd 549, 1920, p. 5.

for the growing population of private, agricultural, and commercial horses, so hay and oats were imported.[42] A rough estimate of the daily cost of hay and oats consumed by a working trade horse can be made using the feed ration orders issued during World War I. A working cart horse was allowed between 12 and 16 pounds of oats a day; rations on hay were introduced in 1918 after a particularly poor harvest: heavy horses received only 12 pounds of hay per day.[43] Taken together the hay and oat rations give what can be considered a minimum viable diet for commercial horses; and because horses were probably fed better during peacetime the estimated expense will be understated. F. M. L. Thompson has estimated the average price per ton for hay and oats in Britain in the 1900s at 66s and 129s.[44] Thus the average minimum feed bill per commercial horse per day is calculated to have been at least 15d per horse per day; in the United States a similar diet cost the equivalent of 4.9d per day.

In the consumer's eyes (and the coal merchant's, too) the total transportation cost of coal was the sum of the railway freight and the carting freight. Railway freight was 0.65d per ton-mile, obtained earlier. The delivery charge of 48d, assuming 4 tons per horse per day, and at most 10 miles per delivery, translates into a very conservative 1.2d per ton-mile as a lower bound carting rate. Now an expression for the full cost of distributed and delivered coal (in pence per ton) obtains:[45]

$$\text{Transport costs} = 31.23 + 0.65 \cdot (\textit{Railway miles}) + 1.18 \cdot (\textit{Cart miles}).$$

---

[42] Thompson, "Horses," pp. 68–9; Bagwell, *Transport Revolution*, p. 72. Large imports of hay were first noticed in 1892 with 61,237 tons; in the following two years imports increased threefold.

[43] U.K., *Statutory Rules and Orders*, p. 3; Thompson, "Horses," p. 72.

[44] Ibid., p. 60, table 4.1.

[45] The 1914–15 carting charge has been converted to 1906 pence using Feinstein's Gross Domestic Product Price Index; Feinstein, *National Income*, T132. The fixed cost term includes the railway fixed costs, estimated earlier, and the merchant's miscellaneous fixed delivery costs. Merchant fixed costs per ton were calculated from the nonfeed elements of Table 6.2, divided by the conservative delivery quota of 24 tons per horse per week, and similarly converted to 1906 pence.

**Table 6.3** Comparison of the relative prices of oats and petrol to coal in Britain, Germany, and the United States, 1913, 1920–7

| Year | Relative prices: oats to coal | | | Relative prices: petrol to coal | |
|---|---|---|---|---|---|
| | Britain | Germany | United States | Britain | United States |
| 1913 | | | 0.26 | 9.3 | |
| 1920 | | | 0.33 | 24.2 | 35.8 |
| 1921 | 0.14 | | 0.63 | 11.7 | 45.2 |
| 1922 | 0.12 | | 0.54 | 12.1 | 47.8 |
| 1923 | 0.13 | | 0.5 | 15.1 | 57.9 |
| 1924 | | | 0.45 | 13.4 | 65.4 |
| 1925 | 0.1 | 0.1 | 0.55 | 11.5 | 62.4 |
| 1926 | 0.11 | 0.09 | 0.55 | 11.8 | 61.3 |
| 1927 | 0.1 | 0.08 | 0.44 | 14.6 | 67.1 |

Spaces that are blank indicate that the ratio was uncalculable given the available price data.

*Sources*: British oat prices for 1921–3 are from International Institute of Agriculture, *Agricultural Problems (1927)* cited in Moeller, *German Peasants*, p. 182; British oat prices for 1925–7 are from Holt, *German Agricultural Policy*, p. 217; Dollar and Reichsmark prices were converted to shillings; British coal prices are from Mitchell, *British Historical Statistics*, pp. 748–9 (f.o.b. export prices); German oat prices are from *Statistisches Jahrbuch für das deutsche Reich* 1929, 1931, and 1933 cited in Holt, *German Agricultural Policy*, p. 217; German coal prices are from Jacobs and Richter, *Grosshandelspreise*, p. 63 (Rhineland-Westphalia series); U.S. oat and coal prices are from U.S., *Historical Statistics*, pp. 208 (oats), 511 (coal); oat prices were converted to a ton basis using a standard 38-pound bushel; British petrol prices are from Jenkins, *Oil Economist's Handbook*, pp. 133–4 (tax-free price); prices were converted to old shillings; U.S. gasoline prices are from American petroleum Institute, *Petroleum*, p. 49 (base price); the annual average was calculated from monthly data.

All assumptions have been made to reasonably understate the expense of horse-carts, especially the minimum diet and the long-market radius. From the perspective of the local coal merchant every ton-mile by horse-cart was twice as expensive as rail. The density of rail lines in Britain made it feasible – and ideal – to have the railways provide the bulk of the distribution services, depositing wagons of coal at hundreds of town and village depots for disposal by the local coal merchants and commercial purchasers. The short average hauls made by railways that might first have been understood as a consequence of Britain's economic geography – coal close at hand – are better understood as the result of substituting rail distribution for expensive road haul. Consider the first four columns of Table 6.3, which gives the relative price of oats to coal in Britain, Germany, and the United States. Clearly, oats were relatively expensive in Britain (and Germany) where a ton of coal translated into roughly the equivalent of one-tenth of a ton of oats. In contrast the relative price of horse feed in the United States was some fourfold cheaper; it was coal that was dear.[46]

Thus, Britain's density of the rail network and stations was advantageous to the widespread distribution that reduced the distances to be covered by horse and cart. Even in the age of steam the transportation system was dependent upon hay and oats. Merchants' practices – in particular the use of small railway wagons for distribution – economized on the quantities of horse-inputs per ton in delivery. This pattern persists into the era of the petrol-fueled motor lorry.

## Local delivery by motor vehicle

The horse and cart were eventually replaced by the motor vehicle, also an expensive mode for coal delivery relative to rail freight in Britain. (Motor lorries finally supplanted horse-carts in the 1950s.) The usual load per truck was between three and a half to five tons for delivery of small purchases, whereas six-ton trucks were reserved for "large" deliveries.[47] The advantage of the truck over the horse-cart was in the potential for more deliveries per day. Table 6.4 enumerates the 1919 operating expenses for two typical commercial trucks. The fuel economy of early road vehicles, especially heavy vehicles, was poor: a one and a half ton Crossley van got 14 miles to a gallon of petrol; a three-ton Leyland obtained only six miles per gallon.[48]

Petrol, like hay and oats, was an expensive energy source relative to coal in Britain, and petrol was the single largest variable cost associated with trucks. For a given load the minimum fuel-related operating cost per ton-mile can be approximated by multiplying the inverse of miles per gallon by the petrol price and dividing by the load carried. For example, in 1913 a gallon of petrol cost 21.12d, divided by the paltry six miles per gallon of a Leyland truck, and divided again by the three-ton capacity obtains a truck rate of 1.17d per ton-mile at the very least.[49] This approximation has been made assuming the best possible, albeit unlikely, scenario: every gallon of petrol was consumed during productive travel. The potential for idle time spent in local coal delivery was hardly trivial. Household coal was sold in sacks ranging from one-quarter to one cwt. (28 to 112 pounds); therefore, a truck with a three-ton load could conceivably have made up to 240 separate stops. At even as little as one minute per stop, the time spent standing – idling and consuming fuel – would be four hours per day. Larger coal sacks would have meant fewer stops – less idling – if the time spent handling the sack did not increase accordingly. Actual fuel-related operating costs may have been lower, if average loads were greater than the truck's rate capacity, or higher, due to idling and poorer fuel

[46] Though the magnitudes of these differentials curiously approximate the differentials in coal-wagon capacities (noted earlier) it is likely a coincidence; I am not suggesting a rigidly proportional correspondence. More detailed comparative efforts are beyond the bounds of this article but indicate a direction for future investigation.

[47] Charrington, "Road Distribution," p. 113.

[48] Robertson, *Wheels*, p. 37.

[49] Petrol prices are obtained from Jenkins, *Oil Economists' Handbook*, pp. 133–4.

**Table 6.4**   Weekly operating expenses for motor lorries, 1919

| Component | Three-ton lorry | | | | Five-ton lorry | | | |
| --- | --- | --- | --- | --- | --- | --- | --- | --- |
| | £ | s | d | Percentage | £ | s | d | Percentage |
| Wages (two laborers) | 6 | 16 | 0 | 38.0 | 6 | 16 | 0 | 35.1 |
| Petrol | 6 | 0 | 0 | 33.5 | 7 | 0 | 0 | 36.1 |
| Repairs | 1 | 10 | 0 | 8.4 | 2 | 0 | 0 | 10.3 |
| Tires | 1 | 0 | 0 | 5.6 | 1 | 0 | 0 | 5.2 |
| Oil | 0 | 12 | 6 | 3.5 | 0 | 12 | 6 | 3.2 |
| Garage | 0 | 12 | 0 | 3.4 | 0 | 12 | 0 | 3.1 |
| Grease | 0 | 1 | 6 | 0.4 | 0 | 1 | 6 | 0.4 |
| Insurance | 1 | 6 | 0 | 7.3 | 1 | 6 | 0 | 6.7 |
| **Total** | 17 | 18 | 0 | 100.0 | 19 | 8 | 0 | 100.0 |

Columns may not sum due to rounding.

*Source*: United Kingdom, *Findings by a Committee on Road Transport*, Cmd 549, 1920, p. 5.

economy, possibly compounded by overloading so that the net effect is ambiguous. Paradoxically then "[h]orses remained more efficient local carriers of low-cost freight, and of higher value goods, too, if collection and delivery involved much waiting time."[50]

Again, a more complete approximation of the coal merchant's view of full transport cost for coal can be made, final delivery made by motor lorry in this case. The approximation given has been converted to a 1913 base.[51]

$$Transport\ costs\ =\ F + 0.6 \cdot (Railway\ miles) + 1.17 \cdot (Truck\ miles).$$

The approximation was made for a Leyland truck with a three-ton load. The Leyland approximation is adequately representative. The fixed costs for the motorized coal merchant cannot be adduced, in this instance, because or the paucity of details available about the normal practice of motorized coal delivery; however, it is likely that the fixed costs would have been higher as motor vehicles involved larger initial outlays, higher wages for more highly skilled lorry drivers, and additional overhead to allocate.

Refer to the last two columns of Table 6.3; the pattern of the differential "cost" between road and rail transport in Britain and the United States is still evident: a ton of coal in the United States "bought" four to five times as much petroleum fuel

[50] Barker. "International History," pp. 7–8.
[51] The estimated 1906 rail freight was converted to 1913 pence using Munby's index of actual freight rates; Munby, *Inland Transport Statistics*, p. 95. (Use of a one and a half ton Crossley van would have yielded a slightly better per ton-mile truck rate but would have carried about the same load as a horse-cart, yet it was for heavier loads and unit deliveries that lorries were first used in the coal trade.)

in America as it did in Britain. (No petrol prices were forthcoming for Germany.) In any case coal was not carried inexpensively by motor vehicles either.[52]

## Large wagons, a costly counterfactual

The large wagons that there were on British rails were limited to the specialized pockets of coal trade already noted; because of their weight and dimensions many local facilities could not accommodate them. Marvin Frankel noted that these physical bottlenecks were only the most visible of obstacles to the larger wagon: "Yet the remedy is not a simple question of good sense. The terminal facilities, tracks, shunting facilities, and all the ways and means of handling freight on this oldest and most complete of railway systems, are all adapted to the bobtailed car."[53] In truth of fact, large wagons would have meant rebuilding colliery and terminal machinery though Frankel overstates the situation. And the local coal trade would have had to "rebuild" as well.

From the railways' vantage point large wagons would have afforded at most 19 percent savings on every ton of coal carried. But the 19 percent figure is too high. First, it was calculated as an upper bound; railway operating costs were probably not going to be reduced by so large a fraction. Second, the 19 percent benefits were calculated solely on railway economies and do not include the additional expenses incurred beyond the railhead. To obtain all of the 19 percent savings large wagons would have had to be fully loaded. Faced with a doubled consignment, coal merchants would have incurred additional labor costs for unloading – which was done by shovel – and bagging or loading carts, as well as additional costs for horses, carts, and hay and oats or trucks and petrol if the merchant sought to maintain delivery practices at the small wagon standard. Without more labor, more horses, or more trucks, the doubled consignment meant that double handling and storage (inventory) costs would increase.[54] If the large wagons were less than fully loaded, less than the 19 percent benefit obtains. If carrying half their capacity, then they were uneconomic on the basis of deadweight. Thus any savings the large wagon might have afforded were decidedly more modest than 19 percent per ton – perhaps even trivial.

Larger wagons were compatible with a distribution system that did not yet exist at the time when Veblen, Sherrington, and others were disgusted by the alleged inefficiency of small wagons.[55] Their singular view of coal transportation as lim-

[52] The extent to which the two pivotal assumptions – petrol was consumed in productive travel and trucks were not overloaded – which have opposing effects on cost, are realistic will be determined by future research into motor transport.

[53] Frankel. "Obsolescence," p. 311.

[54] Double handling refers to the additional time and labor of unloading coal from the railway wagon to the ground and then loading the coal from the ground to cart (or bag to cart) rather than unloading coal directly from wagon to cart (or bag to cart). If, to avoid double handling, coal dealers had left the coal in the wagons for storage, the slower clearing of wagons from depots and sidings would also work to diminish any anticipated benefits from larger wagons.

[55] The Railway Act of 1921 was an attempt to rationalize the excessive competition (services), the excess capacity, and the operating procedures of Britain's railways. This, too, was based on a myopic view of the role of rail freight. The proposed closure of redundant and "uneconomic" depots – in

ited to rail freight obscures the interrelatedness of the railways with road transport. Without the local collection and delivery made possible by horse-cart, the steam-powered railway themselves would have remained a technological curiosity. The railways depended acutely on horse transport and generated an ever increasing demand for carting services as their own volume of passengers and freight increased.[56] The Golden Age of the railways was also the Golden Age of horse-drawn transport.

Limiting factors to the continued expansion of horse-carting trade were the supply of horses and the supply of feedstuffs. Horses in the commercial sector typically started in the urban trade at the age of five.[57] Five years from foal to working town horse suggests that the short-run supply of horses was relatively inelastic – even when augmented by mature horses displaced by buses and motor cars in the transit and leisure sectors. Demand for horses exhausted domestically bred supply before 1900. Horses were brought in from Ireland and imported from Russia, western Europe, and the United States.[58] Tapping the international market for horses averted sudden drains on horses employed in British agriculture but still created an increase in the demand for feedstuffs with each additional animal.

At 1900 Britain's three and a half million horses consumed the annual output of some 15 million acres, near and far; town horses alone consumed up to 2 million tons of oats and 3 and a half million tons of hay.[59] By 1910 more acreage was planted to oats and barley than had been in the previous 50 years in Britain; yet it was not nearly enough to meet the dual and competing demands of horses and humans. Some years ago, Thompson conjectured that late-Victorian Britain (and the world) were very nearly on the cusp of unsustainable horse- and horse-feed demands.[60] The inelasticities of horse-drawn freight promised even higher rates for road freight if demand increased appreciably.

Substitution of truck transport was a possible solution, but it too was likely subject to inelasticities of supply. Little, if any, quantitative research has been done on economics of petrol or motor freight in Edwardian Britain. It remains at the level of a reasonable proposition that petrol supplies were relatively inelastic – at least in the short run. (Capacities for petroleum production and refining, transportation, and storage would not have been as quickly expandable as was the acreage devoted to hay and oats.) But elastic or inelastic, petroleum-based fuels were imported in the same way that horses, oats, and hay were imported. Imports it seems

---

combination with pressure to adopt large coal wagons – could only serve to exacerbate the merchant-specific costs discussed. Depot closings were in part rationalized on the basis that they would promote longer freight hauls and save the railways' operating costs; these longer rail hauls simultaneously meant longer distances to be covered by road transport.

[56] Thompson, *Victorian England*, p. 13 and "Horses," p. 71; Chivers, "Supply," p. 31; Barker, "Delayed Decline," p. 101.

[57] Chivers, "Supply," p. 37. Earlier practices of horse husbandry for the commercial trade are touched upon by Gerhold, "Growth", and Langdon, "Horse Hauling."

[58] Chivers, "Supply," p. 41.

[59] Thompson, *Victorian England*, p. 19 and "Nineteenth-Century Horse Sense," p. 78.

[60] Expansion of the horse population could have come only at the cost of diminished agricultural production for human consumption; Thompson, *Victorian England*, pp. 18, 19. At the time imports were a bitter tonic as Britain lost export markets to the very countries that would supply the horses, the oats and hay, and some of the petroleum products.

were inevitable: either food for human consumption or food and fuel for transportation. Priorities tended to favor food for the human population over the hay and oats and petrol needed to fuel the transportation sector – coal could be used for that. In hundreds of locomotive boilers it was.

## CONCLUSION

Contrary, then, to Veblen, Frankel, and the others Britain's probable binding constraints, delaying the large coal wagon, were not the colliery-machinery, track gauge, nor tunnels. They were instead the horse, hay and oats, trucks, fuel economy, and petroleum fuel. Road haulage was twice as expensive as the small-wagon rate. If large wagons had been in widespread use *more* rather than fewer horses and *more* rather than fewer trucks would have been needed for delivery. More horses would have meant either increased imports or bidding horses away from domestic agriculture, as well as increased imports of hay and oats. More trucks (or tractors for agriculture if horses were moved to the transport sector) would have meant larger imports of petrol. Larger and more visible imports, though economically founded, would not have been welcomed by popular opinion. Coal was the domestic energy source; coal meant domestic jobs; coal was the cornerstone of Britain's view of their economy.

Large-wagon enthusiasts were drawn to the nominally larger rail cars of the continent and the substantially larger American rail cars, but it is likely they were numb to their impracticality and inapplicability to conditions in Britain. In the simplest of terms, Britain was substituting its more generous endowment of coal – through more locomotive hours, miles, and more frequent trains – for horses and fodder and later trucks and petroleum fuel.[61]

Britain was rightly slow in adopting large wagons. The railways and coal merchants have been unfairly faulted for substituting service for engineering efficiency. My cost-benefit calculations do not condemn the small wagon as conclusively – nor advocate the large wagon as overwhelmingly – as the existing literature has suggested. Neither was the small coal car a curiosity – except to those who did not appreciate its function within the broader system of coal distribution and delivery. The British coal wagon may have been small and "bobtailed," but it was not "silly" economics.

## REFERENCES

Ackworth, W. M. and Paish, G. "British Railways: Their Accounts and Statistics," *Journal of the Royal Statistical Society* 75 (1912), pp. 687–730.

American Petroleum Institute, *Petroleum Facts and Figures* (Baltimore, Md.: American Petroleum Institute, 1930).

---

[61] Thompson said, "All this, it should be remembered, refers to a world served by highly developed railway systems in which coal had been substituted for oats as the fuel of the railway sector." Thompson, *Victorian England*, p. 19. His purpose was to demonstrate the importance of horse-drawn transport in general.

Arthur, W. Brian, "Competing Technologies, Increasing Returns, and Lock-In by Historical Events," *Economic Journal* 99 (March 1989), pp. 116–31.

Bagwell, Philip S., *The Transport Revolution from 1770* (London: Batsford, 1974).

Barker, T.C., "The Delayed Decline of the Horse in the Twentieth Century," in *Horses in European Economic History*, edited by F. M. L. Thompson (Reading: British Agricultural History Society, 1983).

Barker, T. C., "The International History of Motor Transport," *Journal of Contemporary History* 20 (1985), pp. 3–20.

Cain, Peter J., "The British Railway Rates Problem 1894–1914," *Business History* 20, no. 1 (1978), pp. 87–99.

Cain, Peter J., "Private Enterprise or Public Utility?" *Journal of Transport History*, 3rd ser., 1, no. 1 (1980), pp. 9–28.

Charrington, John, "Road Distribution and Depot Work," in *Coal: Production, Distribution, and Utilisation*, edited by P. C. Pope (London: Industrial Newspapers, 1949).

Chivers, Keith, "The Supply of Horses in Great Britain in the Nineteenth Century," in *Horses in European Economic History*, edited by F. M. L. Thompson (Reading: British Agricultural History Society, 1983).

Church, R. A., *The History of the British Coal Industry*, vol. 3, *1830–1913: Victorian Pre-eminence* (New York: Oxford University Press, 1986).

Colliery Guardian, *Digest of Evidence Given before the Royal Commission on Coal Supplies, 1901–1905* (London: Chichester Press, 1906).

Collins, E. J. T., "The Farm Horse Economy of England and Wales in the Early Tractor Age 1900–40," in *Horses in European Economic History*, edited by F. M. L. Thompson (Reading: British Agricultural History Society, 1983).

David, Paul A., "The Landscape and the Machine," in *Essays on a Mature Economy Britain after 1840*, edited by Donald N. McCloskey (Princeton, N.J.: Princeton University Press, 1971).

David, Paul A., "Clio and the Economics of QWERTY," *American Economic Review* 75, no. 2 (May 1985), pp. 332–7.

Dobson, C. G., *A Century and a Quarter* (London: Eden Fisher, 1951).

Feinstein, C. H., *National Income, Expenditure and Output of the United Kingdom 1855–1965* (Cambridge: Cambridge University Press, 1972).

Fenelon, K. G., *Railway Economics* (London: Methuen, 1932).

Fishlow, Albert, *American Railroads and the Transformation of the Ante-Bellum Economy* (Cambridge, Mass.: Harvard University Press, 1965).

Frankel, Marvin, "Obsolescence and Technological Change in a Maturing Economy," *American Economic Review* 45, no. 3 (June 1955), pp. 296–319.

Gerhold, Dorian, "The Growth of the London Carrying Trade, 1681–1838," *Economic History Review* 41 (August 1988), pp. 392–410.

Gordon, W. J., *The Horse-World of London* (London: Religious Tract Society, 1893; reprint, Newton Abbot: David & Charles, 1971).

Holt, John Bradshaw, *German Agricultural Policy 1918–1934* (New York: Russell & Russell, 1975; first published by the University of North Carolina Press, 1936).

Hudson, Bill, *Private Owner Wagons*, vol. 1 (Poole: Oxford Publishing, 1976).

Irving, R. J., "The Profitability and Performance of British Railways 1870–1914," *Economic History Review* 31, no. 1 (1978), pp. 46–66.

Jacobs, Alfred and Hans Richter, *Die Grosshandelspreise in Deutschland von 1794 bis 1934* (Berlin: Hanseatische Verlagsanstalt Hamburg, 1935).

Jenkins, Gilbert, *Oil Economists' Handbook* (London: Applied Science Publishers, 1977).

Kahn-Freund, Otto, *The Law of Carriage by Inland Transport* (London: Stevens, 1949).

Kindleberger, Charles, P., "Obsolescence and Technical Change," *Bulletin of the Oxford University Institute of Economics and Statistics* 23 (1961), pp. 281–97.

Kumar, S. and S. P. Singh, "Threshold Stress Criterion in New Wheel/Rail Interaction for Limiting Rail Damage under Heavy Axle Loads," *Journal of Engineering for Industry* 114 (August 1992), pp. 284–8.

Langdon, John, "Horse Hauling: A Revolution in Vehicle Transport in Twelfth- and Thirteenth Century England," *Past & Present* 103 (May 1984), pp. 37–66.

Le Guillou, M., "Freight Rates and their Influence on the Black Country Iron Trade in a Period of Growing Domestic and Foreign Competition, 1850–1914," *Journal of Transport History* 3 (1975), pp. 108–18.

Lee, Clive, "The Service Industries," in *The Economic History of Britain since 1700,* edited by Roderick Floud and Donald McCloskey, 2nd edn, vol. 2: *1860–1939* (Cambridge: Cambridge University Press, 1994).

Mitchell, Brian R., *Economic Development of the British Coal Industry 1800–1914* (Cambridge: Cambridge University Press, 1984).

Mitchell, Brian R., *British Historical Statistics* (Cambridge and New York: Cambridge University Press, 1988).

Moeller, Robert G., *German Peasants and Agrarian Politics 1914–1924* (Chapel Hill, N.C.: University of North Carolina Press, 1986).

Munby, D. L., *Inland Transport Statistics: Great Britain, 1900–1970* (Oxford: Clarendon Press, 1978).

Pratt. Edwin A., *Canals and Traders: The Argument Pictorial* (London: P. S. King and Son, 1910).

Robertson, Bruce, *Wheels of the RAF* (Cambridge: Patrick Stephens, 1983).

Salter, W. E. G., *Productivity and Technical Change* (Cambridge: Cambridge University Press, 1960).

Sherrington, C. E. R., *The Economics of Rail Transport in Great Britain,* 2 vols (London: Edward Arnold, 1928).

Szostak, Rick, *The Role of Transportation in the Industrial Revolution* (Montreal: McGill-Queen's University Press, 1991).

Thompson, F. M. L., *Victorian England: The Horse-Drawn Society* (London: Bedford College, University of London, 1970).

Thompson, F. M. L., "Nineteenth-Century Horse Sense," *Economic History Review,* 2nd ser. 29, no. 1 (1976), pp. 60–81.

Thompson, F. M. L., "Horses and Hay," in *Horses in European Economic History,* edited by F. M. L. Thompson (Reading: British Agricultural History Society, 1983).

Turnbull, Gerard, *Traffic and Transport* (London: George Allen & Unwin, 1979).

United Kingdom, Board of Trade, *Report on the Number, Capacity, and Construction of Private Traders' Railway Wagons in Great Britain at 1st August 1918* (London: HMSO, 1919).

United Kingdom, Mines Department, *Retail Prices and Qualities of Household Coal,* Cmd 2185 (London, 1924).

United Kingdom, Parliament, *Royal Commission on Coal Supplies. Second Report.* Minutes of Evidence and Appendices. Cd 1991. (London, 1904).

——*Royal Commission on Canals and Waterways. [Second Report] England and Scotland, Evidence and Appendices,* Cd 3718 (London, 1907).

——*Report by the Committee Appointed by the Board of Trade to inquire into the Causes of the Present Rise in the Retail Price of Coal Sold for Domestic Use,* Cd 7866 (London, 1915).

——Committee Appointed by the Board of Trade to Inquire into the Causes of the Present Rise in the Retail Price of Coal Sold for Domestic Use, *Minutes of Evidence with Appendix,* Cd 7923 (London, 1915).

——*Statutory Rules and Orders,* No. 954, Cd 8771 (London, 1917).

——*Findings by a Committee Appointed to Enquire into the Effect on Road Transport Rates Caused by an Alleged Existence of a Combine,* Cmd 549 (London, 1920).

United Kingdom, *Standing Committee on Mineral Transport, First Report to the Minister of Transport and the Secretary of Mines,* Cmd 3420 (London, 1929).

United States, Department of Commerce, *Historical Statistics of the United States: From Colonial Times to 1970* (Washington, D.C.: U.S. Government Printing Office, 1975).

Van Vleck, Va Nee L., "Reassessing Technological Backwardness: Absolving the 'Silly Little Bobtailed' Coal Car," Ph.D. diss. (University of Iowa, 1993).

Veblen, Thorstein, *Imperial Germany and the Industrial Revolution* (reprinted, New York: Augustus M. Kelley, 1964).

White, Halbert, "A Heteroskedasticity-Consistent Covariance Matrix Estimator and a Direct Test for Heteroskedasticity," *Econometrica* 48, no. 4 (1980), pp. 817–38.

# 7

# The Acquisition of Fisher Body by General Motors

*Ronald H. Coase*

## I  THE PREVAILING VIEW

The prevailing view of the events that led to the acquisition of Fisher Body by General Motors is that Fisher Body, which had a ten-year contract to supply bodies to General Motors, held up General Motors by adopting inefficient production arrangements (which increased Fisher Body's profits under its cost-plus pricing arrangement) and by refusing to locate its plants near the General Motors assembly plants. This led to a situation that was "intolerable" and that was brought to an end by General Motors acquiring Fisher Body. This consensus has come about because of the general acceptance of the account presented in an article by Benjamin Klein, Robert G. Crawford, and Armen A. Alchian and elaborated in subsequent articles by Klein.[1] As a result, the Fisher Body–General Motors case has been used as the standard example of a holdup in innumerable articles and books.[2] As Klein

---

\* At the meeting of the International Society for New Institutional Economics in 1997, I announced that the generally accepted version of the events leading to the acquisition of Fisher Body by General Motors was, in my view, wrong and that I was writing a paper on the subject. This led to my learning that Robert Freeland had also written a paper dealing with the Fisher Body–General Motors case. Freeland covers a wider range of topics than I do. I confine myself to the question of whether Fisher Body held up General Motors prior to the acquisition. Where there is an overlap in our papers there appears to be no substantial difference in our interpretation of events. This is also true of the independently written paper by Ramon Casadesus-Masanell and Daniel F. Spulber, which examines the relations between General Motors and Fisher Body in great detail.

[1] Benjamin Klein, Robert G. Crawford, and Armen A. Alchian, "Vertical Integration, Appropriable Rents, and the Competitive Contracting Process," *J. Law and Econ.* 21, (1978), p. 297; Benjamin Klein, "Vertical Integration as Organizational Ownership: The Fisher Body–General Motors Relationship Revisited," *J. L. Econ. and Org.* 4 (1988), p. 199, reprinted in *The Nature of the Firm: Origins, Evolution, and Development* ed. Oliver E. Williamson and Sidney G. Winter (1993); Benjamin Klein, "Why Hold-Ups Occur: The Self-Enforcing Range of Contractual Relationships," *Econ. Inquiry* 34 (1996), p. 444; Benjamin Klein, "Hold-Up Problem", in *The New Palgrave Dictionary of Economics and the Law*, ed. Peter K. Newman (1998), vol. 2, p. 241.

[2] For some books using the Fisher Body–General Motors case as an example of a holdup, see Jean Tirole, *The Theory of Industrial Organization* (1997), p. 3; Dennis W. Carlton and Jeffrey M. Perloff, *Modern Industrial Organization* (1994), p. 18; Oliver E. Williamson, *The Economic Institutions of Capitalism* (1985), pp. 114–15; Martin Ricketts, *The Economics of Business Enterprise* (1994), p. 200.

has said, this case is "[p]erhaps the most extensively discussed example in the economic literature of a hold-up due to the presence of specific investments."[3] Joel Trachtman, speaking of opportunistic behaviour, refers to the "classic example of Fisher Body and General Motors."[4] What economists have come to believe happened is well described in a recent article by Keith J. Crocker and Scott E. Masten:

> GM and Fisher Body initially agreed to a ten-year contract for the sale of metal auto bodies. Unanticipated increases in the demand for automobiles in the early years of the contract, however, led to frictions over price on sales exceeding those covered in the contract and the refusal of Fisher to locate production facilities closer to GM. Eventually, the tension between the two became intolerable and, by 1926, GM had acquired Fisher.[5]

I believe that the prevailing view gives a completely false picture of the events leading to the acquisition of Fisher Body by General Motors. There was no holdup. The situation never became "intolerable."

## II  MY VISIT TO THE UNITED STATES

In 1931, I was awarded a Sir Ernest Cassel Travelling Scholarship by the University of London. I decided to go to the United States for the year 1931–2, to study what I termed "lateral and vertical integration" in industry. What led me to choose this subject was that we seemed to lack any theory that would explain why production was organized in these different ways. I set out to find this theory. Although I visited universities, in the main I tried to find the answer to my question by visiting businesses and industrial plants.[6] At one stage, I considered the part that asset specificity might play in bringing about vertical integration. In a letter to my friend, Ronald Fowler, dated March 24, 1932, I said:

> Suppose the production of a particular product requires a large capital equipment which is, however, specialized insofar that it can only be used for the particular product concerned or can only be readapted at great cost. Then the firm producing such a product for one consumer finds itself faced with one great risk – that the consumer may transfer his demand elsewhere or that he may exercise his monopoly power to force down the price – the machinery has no supply price. Now this risk must mean that the rate of interest paid on this capital is that much higher. Now, if the consuming firm decides to make this product this risk is absent and it may well be that this difference in capital costs may well offset the relative inefficiency in actual operating.[7]

---

[3] Klein, "Hold-Up Problem," op. cit., p. 241.

[4] Joel P. Trachtman, "The Theory of the Firm and the Theory of the International Economic Organization: Toward Comparative Institutional Analysis," Nw. J. Int'l L. and Bus. 17 (1996–7), pp. 470, 521.

[5] Keith J. Crocker and Scott E. Masten, "Regulation and Administered Contracts Revisited," Lessons from Transaction-Cost Economics for Public Utility Regulation," J. Regulatory Econ. 9 (1996), pp. 5, 25.

[6] For a fuller account of my visit to the United States, see my lectures: R. H. Coase, "The Nature of the Firm: Origin, Meaning, Influence," J. L. Econ. and Org. 4 (1988), p. 3, reprinted in Williamson and Winter (eds), op. cit. (note 1). In later citations to these lectures, I will confine myself to citation of the book.

[7] Coase, op. cit. (note 6), p. 43.

Later, when I went to Chicago and discussed this analysis with Jacob Viner, he thought it was sound. But in the meantime I had discussed it with businessmen, and they were unimpressed. As I said in a letter to Fowler, dated May 7, 1932,

> My queries about the form of contracts for products requiring large capital equipment has shown me that contractual arrangements can be made to avoid this risk. Thus, the consuming firm may buy the particular equipment itself even though it is in another company's plant. There are a number of other contractual devices which tend to get over this difficulty.[8]

Unfortunately, I do not say in my letter what these other contractual devices were. My discussions with businessmen made me skeptical of the practical importance of asset specificity in bringing about vertical integration. When I visited the Ford Motor Company and General Motors in Detroit, it was with the belief that asset specificity of itself was not generally an important reason for vertical integration. In Detroit, I visited Ford and one of its suppliers; my recollection is that it was Kelsey-Hayes Wheel. At Ford I interviewed someone in the purchasing department (I thought the head) and "discussed the problems connected with contracting for supplies, purchasing schedules and the like for about an hour and a half."[9] I also visited General Motors. Unfortunately, I say nothing in my correspondence with Fowler other than that I paid them a visit. My recollection is that I was told that the reason for the acquisition of Fisher Body was to make sure that the body plants were located near the General Motors assembly plants.

After visiting Detroit, I went on to Chicago. While there I went to see the plant in Milwaukee of A. O. Smith, a producer of automobile frames whose main customer was General Motors. These heavy frames were then shipped to Michigan, hundreds of miles away. This led me to wonder why the location of the Fisher Body plants near the General Motors assembly plants was considered to be so important. There was also the problem of asset specificity. General Motors was the main customer of A. O. Smith, and much of the equipment in the latter's highly automated plan was specific for General Motors' automobiles. All of this suggested to me that contractual arrangements were able to handle the asset specificity problem in a satisfactory manner. In preparation for my lectures at Yale in 1987, I gathered more information about the relations between A. O. Smith and General Motors. I discovered that harmonious relations between them had continued for many decades. I had not made a similar investigation of the Fisher Body case. So I said that, although the problem could usually be handled in a satisfactory manner by contractual arrangements, as in the A. O. Smith case, "it seemed likely that this situation did sometimes lead to integration, and the acquisition of Fisher Body by General Motors might well have been an example of this."[10]

When my lectures were published in the *Journal of Law, Economics, and Organization*, I was surprised to find an article by Klein replying to my remarks, largely

---

[8]  Ibid., p. 45.
[9]  Ibid., p. 44.
[10]  Ibid., p. 46.

relying on what he claimed happened in the Fisher Body–General Motors case. I will be discussing Klein's views later. But I should make one comment now. He states that "Coase claims that before writing his classic paper he explicitly considered opportunistic behavior as a motive for vertical integration, in particular as it applied to the General Motors–Fisher Body case, and explicitly rejected it."[11] This is not an accurate account of the evolution of my ideas. Some carelessness in my writing may have been responsible for the misunderstanding. I had explicitly considered the problem of asset specificity before I visited General Motors. When I found, as a result of discussions with businessmen, that the problem could usually be satisfactorily solved through contractual arrangements – for example, the purchase of dies – I had concluded that vertical integration would not normally be the solution chosen. When I discussed with an executive of General Motors why they had acquired Fisher Body, I was told that it was to make sure that the body plants were located by the assembly plants. A subsequent visit to A. O. Smith made me skeptical about the need to locate the plants by the assembly plants, while the intimate and harmonious relations between A. O. Smith and General Motors strengthened my view that the asset specificity problem would normally be handled satisfactorily without vertical integration. My conclusion was that though the situation in the Fisher Body–General Motors case may have been as Klein described, it was an exceptional case. However, since the publication of my lectures and Klein's commentary, I became interested in finding out what exactly had happened in the Fisher Body–General Motors case. It soon became apparent that Klein's account was misleading, and I decided to make a more thorough investigation to discover what had happened. In 1996, with the aid of Richard Brooks as research assistant, I began to gather information on the events leading to the acquisition of Fisher Body by General Motors. A very different picture of these events emerged from that presented by Klein, Crawford, and Alchian.

## III   FISHER BODY AND GENERAL MOTORS

The tale of Fisher Body is the tale of the Fisher brothers. Fred (the eldest) had worked in his father's wagon and carriage business in Ohio but, in 1902, went to Detroit to work at the C. R. Wilson Carriage Works (which also made automobile bodies). There he was joined by five Fisher brothers. In 1907, he became superintendent. In 1908, the Fisher Body Company was formed, with Fred as its head and his five brothers occupying various positions in the firm. Shortly afterward, Louis Mendelssohn and Aaron Mendelson (hereafter referred to as the Mendelssohns) made a substantial investment in the firm. The business was very successful. Their automobile bodies were not simply an adaptation of carriages but were designed with the special needs of automobiles in mind. Although most automobiles in those days were open, the Fisher brothers realized that there would be a demand for closed bodies. They built 150 closed bodies for Cadillac in 1910. The same year, they formed the Fisher Closed Body Corporation, and in 1912 they created the Fisher

[11]  Klein, "Vertical Integration," in Williamson and Winter (eds), op. cit. (note 1), p. 213.

Body Company of Canada. In 1916, the three companies were merged to form the Fisher Body Corporation.[12] It was the largest body builder in the industry.[13] It made bodies for all the leading automobile manufacturers: Cadillac, Buick, Hudson, Chalmers, Studebaker, Chandler, Cleveland, and, of course, Ford.[14] Concerned that the two largest automobile makers, Ford and General Motors, might make their own bodies, thus leaving them to supply the smaller manufacturers that were left, the Fisher brothers considered entering the automobile business, and they set up in 1913 or 1914 the Hinckley Motor Company. They developed an engine, but to conceal their real objective they manufactured a truck engine that was used in World War I.[15] However, in November 1917, General Motors made a contract with them "to purchase substantially all their output at cost, plus 17.6 percent."[16]

General Motors was formed by William C. Durant. He had made a fortune in the carriage business and then decided to enter the automobile business. In 1904, he acquired the Buick Motor Company. In 1908, he formed the General Motors Corporation. Durant's approach was to grow by buying existing enterprises. He acquired several automobile companies – Olds (now Oldsmobile), Oakland (now Pontiac), and Cadillac – as well as firms producing parts and accessories. However, as Alfred Sloan has said, Durant "could create but could not administer."[17] In 1910, a downturn in sales resulted in Durant being unable to pay his employees or suppliers. General Motors was saved by a bank loan, but the bankers took over the management of the corporation, a task they carried out, as Sloan said, "efficiently though conservatively."[18] Durant, if a poor manager, was extremely enterprising. He formed a partnership with Louis Chevrolet and established the Chevrolet Motor Company. This prospered, and, using Chevrolet stock to acquire General Motors stock, Durant had, together with his own holdings, sufficient stock to be able to wrest control from the bankers in 1915.[19] In 1917, Durant formed a syndicate to buy General Motors stock with the aim of raising or maintaining its price (perhaps to facilitate the merging of Chevrolet and General Motors). However, the price of General Motors stock fell, and Durant found himself in financial difficulties.[20] Pierre du Pont, who had a personal investment in General Motors and who played a part in the events leading to the bankers' control of General Motors, was approached but was unwilling to advance any money at that time.[21] There was a suggestion that Fisher Body might take over General Motors since Fisher Body could raise money from the banks, but nothing came of this.[22] Finally, Durant, with the assistance of John Raskob,

---

[12] This account of the tale of the Fisher brothers is based on Arthur Pound, *The Turning Wheel* (1934), p. 288; and Testimony of Lawrence Fisher, Trial Transcript, vol. 2, pp. 958–1007, *United States v. Du Pont* 126 F. Supp. 235 (N.D. Ill. 1954).

[13] Pound, op. cit., p. 291.

[14] Testimony of Lawrence Fisher, *Du Pont*, 126 F. Supp. 235, p. 964.

[15] Ibid., pp. 991–2.

[16] Alfred D. Chandler, Jr., and Stephen Salsbury, *Pierre S. du Pont and the Making of the Modern Corporation* (1971), p. 465.

[17] Alfred P. Sloan, Jr., *My Years with General Motors* (1964), p. 4.

[18] Ibid., p. 8.

[19] Chandler and Salsbury, op. cit., pp. 440–2.

[20] Ibid., p. 448.

[21] Ibid., p. 449.

[22] Testimony of Lawrence Fisher, *Du Pont*, 126 F. Supp. 235, pp. 1006–7.

who was an executive at Dupont, approached the Dupont Company itself. They finally agreed to invest $25 million in General Motors. As part of the arrangement, it was agreed that du Pont would be in charge of the finances of General Motors while Durant would be responsible for its operations.[23]

## IV  THE ACQUISITION OF STOCK IN FISHER BODY BY GENERAL MOTORS

In 1917, as we have seen, Durant made a contract with Fisher Body by which General Motors would buy substantially all their output at cost plus 17.6 percent. This did not, however, remove General Motors' concerns over the future supply of bodies. The situation, as General Motors saw it, has been described by Alfred D. Chandler and Stephen Salsbury:

> The postwar expansion plans convinced Durant and the Finance Committee of the absolute necessity of having an assured control over General Motors' largest and most critical supplier. They simply could not afford to have the Fishers fail to renew their contract on acceptable terms. Any doubts . . . were quickly resolved when [it was] learned that automobile manufacturers in Cleveland (undoubtedly Willys-Overland) had opened negotiations to form a partnership with the Fishers in which they (the Fishers) would control.[24]

This account is essentially correct except that I would not give the same weight to the Cleveland negotiations in leading to the purchase of Fisher Body stock by General Motors. I will give the details.

In 1918, Durant sent Walter Chrysler to see Lawrence Fisher. Chrysler had been president of Buick and was working with Durant in New York. Later, of course, he would set up his own automobile company. Chrysler explained that the "closed body situation with General Motors was a very serious one . . . that [Durant] wanted to build plants in Flint and Lansing and Pontiac" and that he "wanted to enter into a deal with [the four younger Fisher brothers] to come with General Motors and set up [the] organization . . . to handle their closed body business." Lawrence Fisher replied that they "couldn't split the Fisher brothers."[25] It is not clear why Durant made this proposal. He must have known that the Fisher brothers would want to be treated as a unit. Possibly, the proposal was merely a way of sounding out the Fisher brothers about joining General Motors. At any rate, some months later, early in 1919, Durant got in touch with Fred Fisher (the eldest brother). At a meeting in New York, Durant made the same argument as had Chrysler. He said that he wanted to talk "about bringing the Fisher brothers into General Motors." Fred and Lawrence Fisher listened but gave no answer. As Lawrence Fisher said, "We were not interested at the time." Durant, however, was persistent and raised the question again about two months later. The situation with regard to bodies had become

---

[23] Chandler and Salsbury, op. cit., pp. 450–6.
[24] Ibid., p. 465.
[25] Testimony of Lawrence Fisher, *Du Pont*, 126 F. Supp. 235, pp. 987–8.

"more acute." In the meantime, Fisher Body received a very large order for closed bodies from Ford. The Fisher brothers this time decided to consider seriously the possibility of joining General Motors, and they talked with their associates, the Mendelssohns, who had a substantial stake in Fisher Body.[26] From the negotiations that followed, in which Pierre du Pont played a major role, an agreement emerged in September 1919. A complicating factor was that Fisher Body had made a tentative agreement with Willys-Overland in Cleveland to form a company to build automobile bodies. Fisher Body would own 51 percent of the shares and would provide the management. General Motors wanted this arrangement dropped, and this was done.[27]

The agreement between Fisher Body and General Motors was composed of the following elements:

1. The authorized common stock of Fisher Body, consisting of 200,000 shares, would be increased to 500,000 shares. General Motors would purchase 300,000 shares at $92 per share.

2. The 300,000 shares owned by General Motors together with 35,000 owned by the Fisher brothers would be deposited in a voting trust. The trust was to last for five years, and there were four trustees, two named by Fisher Body and two by General Motors. The trustees named by Fisher Body were Fred Fisher and Louis Mendelssohn and by General Motors, Durant and Pierre du Pont. No action of the voting trustees would be valid unless unanimous. This meant, in effect, that for five years the General Motors shares could not be voted in any way not desired by Fisher Body.

3. There would be fourteen directors of Fisher Body, seven to be nominated by the Fisher-Mendelssohn interests and seven by General Motors. Although General Motors owned 60 percent of the shares, they would be able to nominate only 50 percent of the directors.

4. An executive committee of Fisher Body would be created that would have complete charge of operations, except finances. This committee would consist of seven members, two nominated by General Motors and five by the Fisher-Mendelssohn interests. The finance committee would consist of five members, three nominated by General Motors and two by the Fisher-Mendelssohn interests.

5. It was provided that, for five years, at least two-thirds of the net earnings would be distributed as dividends until they should reach at least $10 per share.

6. A five-year employment contract was entered into with the four younger Fisher brothers. However, the two older brothers had an employment contract with Fisher Body that ended in 1926. The Fisher brothers wanted this contract to be modified so that the employment contracts of all the Fisher brothers would end in 1924. Durant did not like this change but finally agreed

---

[26] Ibid., pp. 989–91.
[27] Letter from Pierre S. du Pont to Fred J. Fisher (September 11, 1919), Govt Trial Ex. no. 425, *Du Pont*, 126 F. Supp. 235.

to it. The result was that all the Fisher brothers had the option of terminating their employment in 1924. The reason the Fisher brothers wanted this was that they were not sure how the partnership with General Motors would work out and wanted to be free, if it proved unsatisfactory, to enter the automobile business or to make some other business arrangement. When the arrangement was described by counsel as a "trial marriage," Lawrence Fisher agreed.

7. The Fisher brothers were to have paid to them, in addition to their salaries, 5 percent of the net profits of Fisher Body for five years.

8. General Motors agreed to give to Fisher Body such of its closed body business as Fisher Body was able to handle. The 1917 arrangements for pricing were to continue. The price to be paid by General Motors would depend on the grade of the work, but the average net profit to Fisher Body was to be 17.6 percent on cost. Durant had wanted this figure reduced to 15 percent but in the end agreed to 17.6 percent. It was, however, stipulated that General Motors could not be charged more than was charged to other customers for like products.

9. The contract for the supply of bodies would last ten years; that is, it would end in 1929.

10. It was agreed that Fisher Body would be free to work for customers other than General Motors.

The result of this agreement was that Fisher Body would be able to operate for five years essentially as an independent firm, notwithstanding that Dupont owned 60 percent of the common stock.[28] Even after 1924, the Fisher brothers would have considerable independence in running the Fisher Body Corporation.

## V   EVENTS LEADING TO THE COMPLETE OWNERSHIP OF FISHER BODY BY GENERAL MOTORS

In November 1920, Durant resigned as president of General Motors. This came about as the result of a crisis in his personal finances. After the slump in automobile sales in September 1920, Durant attempted to stabilize the price of General Motors stock by purchasing its stock on margin. Unable to meet the margin calls when the price fell and owing $20 million or perhaps more, he was rescued by the Dupont Corporation and J. P. Morgan. The bankers concluded that Durant was "totally incompetent to manage the corporation." Pierre du Pont concurred. As a result, he agreed to become president of General Motors.[29]

General Motors was dissatisfied with the 1919 arrangement. It had solved an immediate problem but had brought about an unsatisfactory long-term relationship with Fisher Body. The Fisher brothers tended to concentrate on their body-

[28] This account of the 1919 agreement is based on Govt Trial Ex. Nos. 424–30, *Du Pont*, 126 F. Supp. 235; Defendant's Ex. No. 101, *Du Pont*, 126 F. Supp. 235; and Lawrence Fisher's discussion of the agreement in Testimony of Lawrence Fisher Trial Transcript, Vol. 2, *Du Pont*, 126 F. Supp. 235. See also Chandler and Salsbury, op. cit., p. 465.

[29] Chandler and Salsbury, op. cit., pp. 482–91.

building business, and while they were efficient and their bodies were of high quality, they paid less attention to the needs of General Motors than General Motors would have liked. The result was that Pierre du Pont and later Alfred Sloan, who succeeded him as president of General Motors, were anxious to bring the Fisher brothers into a closer relationship with the General Motors organization.

In 1921, Fred Fisher was made a director of General Motors and in 1922, he was appointed a member of the executive committee of General Motors, as Chandler and Salsbury put it, "to ensure better communication with the Fisher Body Company."[30] Later in their book, Chandler and Salsbury were more explicit. It was hoped that placing Fred Fisher on the executive committee would "get him further involved in making the broad decisions about production, products design, output and pricing of General Motors products that inevitably affected the work of his own organization."[31] This attempt to bring about a closer relationship between Fisher Body and General Motors seems to have had some success. Lawrence Fisher, in his testimony in the Dupont antitrust suit, described Fred Fisher, although on the Fisher Body payroll, as devoting most of his time to his work with General Motors.[32] By 1922, the Fisher brothers seem to have given up the idea that they might sever their connection with General Motors at the end of the five-year period.[33] The "trial marriage" appears to have been a success. In fact, when, in 1924, their employment contracts expired, Charles and Lawrence Fisher joined Fred Fisher on the board of directors and the executive committee of General Motors, while Fred was also appointed to the finance committee. In 1925, Lawrence Fisher was made head of Cadillac, one of General Motors' most important divisions.

From 1924 on, it seems to have been understood that ultimately Fisher Body would probably merge with General Motors. Pierre du Pont, in a letter to Fred Fisher in July 1924, said this:

> I hope that you and your brothers will feel that Fisher Body and General Motors are really one and that the whole effort is so worthwhile and full of opportunity that you will take chances on associating yourselves permanently with the development. I see no trouble from awaiting the development of a contract between the two companies in order to determine relative values of shares, but so far, I have had some difficulty in picturing the situation whereby the Fisher brothers may stick together as a unit in the General Motors Corporation. However, we will straighten it out some way if we give constant attention to the matter.[34]

General Motors was anxious to acquire the 40 percent of the stock of Fisher Body that it did not own. Quite apart from the desire to bring the Fisher brothers even more closely into the General Motors organization, it was also concerned that the minority holding, through death or in some other way, might fall into other hands

---

[30] Ibid., p. 526.

[31] Ibid., p. 576.

[32] Testimony of Lawrence Fisher, *Du Pont*, 126 F. Supp. 235, p. 1003.

[33] Govt Trial Ex. No. 328, *Du Pont*, 126 F. Supp. 235.

[34] Letter from Pierre du Pont to Fred Fisher (July 28, 1924) (Longwood Manuscripts, Group 10, Series A, Papers of Pierre S. du Pont, Hagley Museum and Library, Greenville, Del.) (hereinafter Longwood Manuscripts).

with whom it might be difficult to deal.[35] The Mendelssohns and the Fisher brothers, for their part, were not anxious to sell their stock holdings to General Motors. The Mendelssohns were satisfied with their investment in Fisher Body and had no desire to change it to an investment in General Motors. The Fisher brothers still wanted to operate as a family firm, in which desire, as Chandler and Salsbury tell us, "they were emphatically supported by their strong-willed mother."[36] The Fisher brothers also thought that the price proposed by General Motors was too low. There were difficult negotiations. Finally, Fred Fisher and Pierre du Pont came to an agreement.

In May 1926, the Fisher Body Corporation was dissolved. General Motors acquired all of its assets and assumed all of its obligations and liabilities. In the notice sent out to the stockholders of Fisher Body it was stated that "Messrs. Fisher, Mendelssohn and other large shareholders, as well as all of the officers and directors of Fisher Body, approve and recommend this plan as being in the best interest of the stockholders." The notice also explained why they had concluded that it was in the best interest of the stockholders to accept the General Motors' offer:

> As the contract made with General Motors in 1919 has but a relatively short term remaining, your officers and directors have given serious thought to the future prospects of Fisher Body. In 1929, a new contract must be negotiated, or General Motors will be free either to build its own bodies or purchase them elsewhere. In view of these facts and in order to fully ascertain and provide for the conditions which might have to be met by Fisher Body upon the expiration of the present contract, many conferences have been had with officials of General Motors, and as a result of such conferences your Board of Directors received the offer [from General Motors].[37]

Stockholders of Fisher Body received two-thirds of a share of General Motors stock for each share of Fisher Body they owned. William Fisher was made head of the Fisher Body division and joined his three brothers on the board of directors of General Motors. In a letter to William Fisher welcoming him to the board, Pierre du Pont said that the "Fisher Body–General Motors combination is proving a very happy one, I think one of the best moves that has been made."[38] In a letter written to Pierre du Pont in January 1927, Fred Fisher referred to their disagreement over the value of Fisher Body stock: "If you recall my remarks made at the time you and I closed [the] transaction between General Motors and Fisher Body Corporation, I made the statement that there was considerable hidden value in regard to inventory and unabsorbed overhead." He then goes on to argue that the figures produced for the subsequent period by the accounting division of General Motors indicated that he had been correct.[39]

It will have been noticed that in my account of the events leading to the acquisition of Fisher Body by General Motors, there has been no mention of either a holdup

---

[35] Chandler and Salsbury, op. cit., pp. 576–7.
[36] Ibid., p. 576.
[37] Notice to Stockholders of Fisher Body Corporation (May 17, 1926), Govt Trial Ex. No. 855, *Du Pont*, 126 F. Supp. 235.
[38] Letter from Pierre du Pont to William A. Fisher (February 15, 1927) (Longwood Manuscripts).
[39] Letter from Fred Fisher to Pierre du Pont (January 19, 1927) (Longwood Manuscripts).

or the relations between Fisher Body and General Motors becoming intolerable. Indeed, it is ludicrous to suppose that the Fisher brothers, occupying the most senior positions in the General Motors organization, would have engaged in the practices injurious to General Motors that are described by Klein or, if they did, that they would have been appointed, reappointed, or given important additional responsibilities in the General Motors organization.

## VI THE BASIS FOR THE PREVAILING VIEW

The prevailing view about what happened in the Fisher Body–General Motors case was set out by Klein in the article "Hold-Up Problem" in the *New Palgrave Dictionary of Economics and the Law*. This is what he says:

> The [cost-plus] contract adopted by Fisher Body and General Motors was, like all contracts, not complete. What is unusual about this case, however, is that Fisher took advantage of the contractual incompleteness to hold up General Motors. Fisher was able to hold up General Motors because, after the parties signed their contract, the demand for closed automobiles increased dramatically. Fisher took advantage of the contractual incompleteness in the face of the large demand increase for automobile bodies to adopt an inefficient, highly labour-intensive production process. From Fisher's point of view there was no economic reason to make capital investments when, according to the contract, they could instead hire a worker and put a 17.6 percent upcharge on the worker's wage. In addition, Fisher used the contract to locate its body producing plants far away from the General Motors assembly plant. There was no economic reason for Fisher to locate their plant close to the General Motors assembly plant when according to the contract, they could profit by locating their plant far away from the General Motors plant and put a 17.6 percent upcharge on their transportation costs. The result was automobile bodies that were highly profitable for Fisher to produce, but very costly for General Motors to purchase.[40]

In the previous section, I said that given what we know about the relations of General Motors and the Fisher brothers, it was most improbable that the tale told by Klein was true. But can one show that, in fact, it was untrue? In the case of the location of the body plants, it is, I believe, very easy to show this. Richard Brooks examined the location of Fisher Body plants in the period 1921–5. No new body plants were built in the period 1919–21. In 1922, two body plants were built, one near the General Motors truck and Oakland plant in Pontiac, Michigan, and the other near the Chevrolet plant in St. Louis, Missouri. In 1923, body plants were built by Fisher Body in Flint, Michigan, near the Buick and Chevrolet plants; in Lansing, Michigan, near the Olds plant; in Janesville, Wisconsin, near the Chevrolet plant; in Oakland, California, near the Chevrolet plant; and in Buffalo, New York, near the Chevrolet plant. An assembly plant was also built near the Chevrolet plant in Cincinnati, Ohio. In 1925, a body plant was built in Tarrytown, New York, near the Chevrolet plant there. What is clear is that Klein's statement that Fisher Body

---

[40] Klein, "Hold-Up Problem," op. cit. (note 1), pp. 241–2.

located its plants "far away" from the General Motors assembly plants is completely untrue.[41]

The source on which Klein relies is Sloan's deposition and testimony in the Dupont antitrust case. Sloan made two references to the building of body plants by Fisher Body in the pages cited by Klein. In the first, Sloan was asked by counsel whether in the period before the acquisition there was a problem "to do with the location of the plants?" Sloan answered: "Yes . . . where there was a chassis assembly plant there had to be next to it a Fisher Body plant . . . And the Fisher brothers . . . rather questioned the desirability of their putting up large amounts of capital to establish these assembly plants."[42] In the second, counsel asked Sloan what he was referring to when he spoke of "a problem of assembly." He answered: "What I meant by that was that we were establishing throughout the country assembly plants . . . and where we had a chassis assembly plant, we had to have a Fisher Body assembly plant, but the Fisher Body Corporation was unwilling to put in an investment in these assembly plants. That handicapped us considerably."[43] It is evident that what Sloan was referring to was not a dispute over whether the Fisher Body plants should be located near the General Motors assembly plants but one over which organization should put up the capital required to do it. I know how this was handled in the case of the Fisher Body plant built near the Tarrytown Chevrolet plant. The cost was borne by General Motors.[44] No doubt this also happened for many of the other Fisher Body plants. Nor would this be surprising. My investigations in 1931–2 had taught me that it was normal for the expenditures for capital equipment dedicated to the use of one customer to be borne by that customer. That this was sometimes done by General Motors in financing the building of Fisher Body plants is made clear in a memorandum recording a discussion in 1922 among Pierre du Pont, two top executives of General Motors, and Fred Fisher on the Chevrolet assembly program. It records that "Fred Fisher suggested that these plants [to produce closed bodies] be built in Chevrolet property and leased to the Fisher Body Company." Again, after Fred Fisher had said "that possibly $5,000,000 for additional working capital and sundry improvements will be needed . . . but this can be taken care of by current borrowing," the memorandum states that after discussion, "it was agreed that it would be better for the Fisher Company not to issue further senior securities. To that end it would be better for General Motors Corporation to own the assembly plants, leasing them to the Fisher

[41] Fisher Body did have two plants "far away" from the General Motors assembly plants, but they hardly support Klein's thesis. In 1925, Fisher Body acquired a body plant in Fleetwood, Pennsylvania, as a result of its acquisition of the Fleetwood Body Corporation. And in 1924, it acquired a plant in Memphis, Tennessee, as part of the operations of the Fisher Lumber Corporation. It is described by Pound as a "wood working plant." See Pound, op. cit. (note 12), pp. 298–9.

[42] Deposition of Alfred P. Sloan, (April 28, 1952), *Du Pont*, 126, F. Supp. 235, pp. 189–90.

[43] Testimony of Alfred P. Sloan, (March 9, 1953), *Du Pont*, 126 F. Supp. 235, p. 2912. I should add that I fully accept Sloan's view that it was less costly to place the body plants near the assembly plants. The skepticism I felt about this after I visited the A. O. Smith plant ignored the difference in the cost of shipping bodies and frames or the possibility that economies of scale were more important in the production of frames than bodies. This error is perhaps excusable in an undergraduate, which I was at the time.

[44] See Minutes of the Executive Committee of General Motors (October 24, 1923) (General Motors' Law Library, Detroit, Mich.).

Company."[45] It is not without interest that it was Fred Fisher who suggested that the body plants be built on Chevrolet property.

While I had no doubt that the account given earlier about the location of the body plants was correct, it left me with a puzzle. I remembered being told, by an executive in General Motors in 1932, that the reason for the acquisition of Fisher Body was to make sure that the body plants were erected near the General Motors assembly plants. I found the solution to the puzzle in Robert Freeland's paper. He tells us that in late 1925, General Motors, as part of its expansion plan, wanted to close the Fisher Body plant in Detroit and build a new body plant in Flint, Michigan, near its assembly plant. The Fisher brothers objected. They wanted to expand their Detroit plant. There may have been a difference of opinion about the relative costs of handling the problem in these different ways, but, no doubt, even more important was that Fisher Body had customers other than General Motors, and it would have been less costly to supply them from Detroit rather than from Flint, a consideration that would not be present in the case of General Motors. It also has to be remembered that Fisher Body had large stockholders (the Mendelssohns) and perhaps others who had no interest in the fortunes of General Motors. No doubt there were other factors that influenced Fisher Body. The dispute ended when Fisher Body was acquired by General Motors. In November 1926, a new body plant went into operation in Flint, and in 1927 the Detroit plant was closed down.[46] It was undoubtedly this episode, which had happened only five or six years before, that the executive at General Motors had in mind when he told me in 1932 that the reason for the acquisition of Fisher Body was to make sure that the body plants were located next to the General Motors assembly plants.

Klein's other point is that Fisher Body adopted "an inefficient, highly labor-intensive production process." There is no mention of this in the Sloan testimony that Klein cites. I have argued in the previous section that, given the positions occupied by the Fisher brothers in the General Motors organization, it is most improbable that they would act in this way. There are other considerations that lead to the same conclusion. Fisher Body was supplying bodies to automobile manufacturers other than General Motors, and an inefficient production process would reduce their own profits from this business and make it less likely that they would secure it. Furthermore, since in many, perhaps most, cases, General Motors paid for the building of the body plants (which it also owned), it is most improbable that they would have been willing to do this for a plant using an inefficient production process. General Motors was not lacking in engineering talent. Furthermore, to the extent that Fisher Body was paying the capital costs, it needs to be remembered that General Motors nominated a majority of the members of the finance committee of Fisher Body, which would have had to approve such expenditures. I could say more, but there is little point in an extensive discussion of an improbable tale for which there is no supporting evidence.

---

[45] For an account of Fisher's finances in connection with the Chevrolet assembly program, see Longwood Manuscripts, file 624, box 1.

[46] Robert F. Freeland, "Creating Holdup through Vertical Integration: Fisher Body Revisited," *J. Law and Econ.* 43 (2000), p. 33.

The erroneous statement of the facts in the Fisher Body–General Motors case has misdirected the attention of economists and has stood in the way of the development of a more solidly based treatment of the problem of asset specificity. The view that I formed in 1932 and discussed in my Yale lectures was that the asset specificity problem was normally best handled by a long-term contract rather than by vertical integration and that "the propensity for opportunistic behavior is usually effectively checked by the need to take account of the effect of the firm's actions on future business."[47] This reexamination of the Fisher Body–General Motors case has not caused me to change my mind. It is true that I have said nothing about the role of reputation in the events discussed. However, I have no doubt that concern for their reputation would also have deterred the Fisher brothers from engaging in the kind of practices described by Klein.

I have not discussed human specificity. I leave the treatment of this subject to Freeland and others. However, I hope that those engaged in these studies will have some regard for the facts.

## REFERENCES

Carlton, Dennis W., and Perloff, Jeffrey M., *Modern Industrial Organization* (New York: HarperCollins College Publishers, 1994).

Chandler, Alfred D., Jr., and Salsbury, Stephen, *Pierre S. Du Pont and the Making of the Modern Corporation* (New York: Harper & Row, 1971).

Coase, R. H., "The Nature of the Firm: Origin, Meaning, Influence," *Journal of Law, Economics, and Organization* 4 (1988), pp. 3–47. Reprinted in *The Nature of the Firm: Origins, Evolution and Development*, edited by Oliver E. Williamson and Sidney G. Winter (New York: Oxford University Press, 1993).

Crocker, Keith J., and Masten, Scott E., "Regulation and Administered Contracts Revisited: Lessons from Transaction Cost Economics for Public Utility Regulation," *Journal of Regulatory Economics* 9 (1996), pp. 5–39.

Fisher, Lawrence, Direct Testimony. Trial Transcript, Vol. 2, pp. 958–1007. *United States v. E. I. du Pont de Nemours & Co., General Motors, et al.*, Civil Action 49C–1071, 126 F. Supp. 235 (N. D. Illinois 1954).

Freeland, Robert F., "Creating Holdup through Vertical Integration: Fisher Body Revisited," *Journal of Law and Economics* 43 (2000), pp. 33–66.

Klein, Benjamin, "Vertical Integration as Organizational Ownership: The Fisher Body–General Motors Relationship Revisited," *Journal of Law, Economics, and Organization* 4 (1988), pp. 199–213. Reprinted in *The Nature of the Firm: Origins, Evolution, and Development*, edited by Oliver E. Williamson and Sidney G. Winter (New York: Oxford University Press, 1993).

Klein, Benjamin, "Why Hold-Ups Occur: The Self-Enforcing Range of Contractual Relationship," *Economic Inquiry* 34 (1996), pp. 444–63.

Klein, Benjamin, "Hold-Up Problem," in vol. 2 of *The New Palgrave Dictionary of Economics and the Law*, edited by Peter K. Newman (New York: Stockton Press, 1998).

Klein, Benjamin, Crawford, Robert G. and Alchian, Armen A., "Vertical Integration, Appropriable Rents, and the Competitive Contracting Process," *Journal of Law and Economics* 21 (1978), pp. 297–326.

---

[47] Coase, op. cit. (note 6), p. 71.

Pound, Arthur, *The Turning Wheel: The Story of General Motors through 25 Years, 1908–1933* (Garden City, N.Y.: Doubleday, 1934).

Ricketts, Martin, *The Economics of Business Enterprise: An Introduction to Economic Organization and the Theory of the Firm* (New York: Harvester Wheatsheaf, 1994).

Sloan, Alfred P., Jr., *My Years with General Motors* (New York: Doubleday, 1964).

Tirole, Jean, *The Theory of Industrial Organization* (Cambridge, Mass.: MIT Press, 1997).

Trachtman, Joel P., "The Theory of the Firm and the Theory of the International Economic Organization: Toward Comparative Institutional Analysis," *Northwestern Journal of International Law and Business* 17 (1996–7), pp. 470–555.

Williamson, Oliver E., *The Economic Institutions of Capitalism: Firms, Markets, Relational Contracting* (New York: Free Press, 1985).

# 8

# The Fable of Fisher Body

## Ramon Casadesus-Masanell and Daniel F. Spulber*

The dismal science is enlivened occasionally by colorful fables that illustrate key points of economic theory.[1] The story of the acquisition of Fisher Body by General Motors (GM) is often used to point out the failure of market contracts as a result of asset specificity and opportunistic behavior. This story is influential because it plays a central role in both contract theory and the theory of the firm. Fisher Body provides a canonical example in Benjamin Klein, Robert Crawford, and Armen Alchian's work on vertical integration.[2] Oliver Williamson's transaction cost economics,[3] and Oliver Hart's property rights theory of the firm.[4] We demonstrate that the historical descriptions and interpretations of the Fisher Body acquisition given in the economics literature are largely inaccurate, which in turn casts some doubt on conclusions about opportunism in contracts that rely on those historical descriptions. The merger does not represent some immutable market failure but, rather, reflects economic considerations specific to that time that are not present today, as revealed by GM's current restructuring. We show that GM vertically integrated with Fisher Body to improve coordination between the two companies – particularly to assure GM adequate supplies of auto bodies, to synchronize the two companies' operations, and to provide GM with access to the executive talents of the Fisher brothers.

* We are grateful to Thomas G. Marx, general director of issues management at the General Motors Corporation, for his very valuable assistance. We also thank the Kettering/GMI Alumni Foundation Collection of Industrial History and the Hagley Museum and Library. We thank Marcus Alexis, Nabil Al-Najjar, Shane Greenstein, and Brain Uzzi for very helpful comments. We are grateful to Dennis W. Carlton and an anonymous referee for helpful suggestions that greatly improved the presentation. The opinions expressed are the responsibility of the authors.
[1] The Fisher Body account is yet another example of an alleged fundamental market failure that contradicts the historical record. We are indebted to earlier economic and historical analyses of other market-failure stories: Steven N. S. Cheung, "The Fable of the Bees: An Economic Investigation," *J. Law and Econ.* 16 (1973), p. 11; R. H. Coase, "The Lighthouse in Economics," *J. Law and Econ.* 17 (1974), p. 357; S. J. Liebowitz and Stephen E. Margolis, "The Fable of the Keys," *J. Law and Econ.* 33 (1990), p. 1.
[2] Benjamin Klein, Robert G. Crawford and Armen A. Alchian, "Vertical Integration, Appropriable Rents, and the Competitive Contracting Process," *J. Law and Econ.* 21 (1978), p. 297.
[3] Oliver E. Williamson, *The Economic Institutions of Capitalism* (1985).
[4] Oliver D. Hart, *Firms, Contracts, and Financial Structure* (1995).

The fable of Fisher Body originates in only three paragraphs of Klein, Crawford, and Alchian.[5] General Motors signed a ten-year contract with Fisher Body to purchase closed-car auto bodies and acquired a 60 percent interest in Fisher in 1919. According to Klein, Crawford, and Alchian, the contract provided price stipulations to protect the body company from being held up by GM, for Fisher Body had to make large specific investments in the presses and dies used to stamp the bodies. They assert that in the early 1920s, as the demand for closed bodies increased dramatically, the price provisions were insufficient to prevent Fisher Body from exercising opportunism and taking advantage of GM's contractual commitment. Klein, Crawford, and Alchian further state that the high prices charged for the bodies reduced GM's ability to compete and that the Fisher brothers refused to locate new body plants as requested by GM because they feared exposure to opportunistic behavior after the plants were built. By 1926, the story continues, the relationship became intolerable, and GM bought out Fisher Body.

The facts are different. The historical record indicates close collaboration and trust between the companies, which contradicts supposed contract failures. The extensive participation of the Fisher brothers in GM management beginning in 1921 also indicates an absence of the alleged opportunism by Fisher. The initial acquisition in 1919 was accompanied by substantial investment by GM in Fisher and a voting trust arrangement in which executives from the two companies had equal control over Fisher's board of directors, which contradict the need for property rights to exercise control. Moreover, Fisher Body did not price opportunistically under its manufacturing contract. Many Fisher Body plants already were located next to GM plants before 1926. Last, the supposed transaction-specific investment in metal presses and dies is inconsistent with Fisher's manufacturing technology, which was wood based and labor intensive and therefore flexible and not transaction specific. Talks regarding a full merger began as early as 1922. Thus, the 1926 acquisition of the remaining 40 percent of Fisher Body has little to do with asset specificity or contract failure.

Our analysis shows that the initial acquisition in 1919 and the completed merger in 1926 were driven primarily by a desire to enhance coordination between the two companies. The most important aspect of coordination for GM was an assurance of supplies of auto bodies, in the sense of Alfred D. Chandler, Kenneth J. Arrow, and Dennis W. Carlton.[6] The closed auto bodies made by Fisher represented quality and comfort and were a source of competitive advantage for GM in its competition with Ford. General Motors' vertical integration with Fisher was part of GM's extensive program of vertical integration with many other companies. Vertically integrating into auto body manufacturing allowed GM better to coordinate the management of inventories, production, and purchasing given the transportation, communications, and data-processing costs existing at that time. In light of Alfred P. Sloan's reforms aimed at interdivisional coordination, it is significant that Fisher Body was made a division of GM concurrent with the 1926 merger. Vertical

[5]  Klein, Crawford, and Alchian, op. cit.
[6]  Alfred D. Chandler, *Strategy and Structure* (1962): Alfred D. Chandler, *The Visible Hand* (1977); Kenneth J. Arrow, "Vertical Integration and Communication," *Bell J. Econ.* 6 (1975), p. 173; Dennis W. Carlton, "Vertical Integration in Competitive Markets under Uncertainty," *J. Indus. Econ.* 27 (1979), p. 189.

integration also achieved personnel coordination that gave GM access to the executive talents of the Fisher brothers.[7]

Our study confirms Ronald Coase's emphasis on transaction costs as a motivation for vertical mergers.[8] It also confirms his observation that asset specificity and opportunism in contracts fail in a fundamental way to explain vertical integration. Coase points out that in 1932, when writing his pathbreaking article "The Nature of the Firm," he contemplated the asset specificity hypothesis as a potential rationale for vertical integration. After a visit to GM in that year during which he learned about the Fisher Body merger and about the amicable relationship that GM enjoyed with its supplier of frames. A. O. Smith, Coase concluded that asset specificity coupled with self-interest were not powerful enough reasons for vertical integration.[9] Because it offers a Hobson's choice between contracts and vertical integration, the contracts literature identifies vertical integration between a company and its supplier as evidence of problems with market contracts. Coase rightly criticizes this approach, noting that "we are not surprised to see the man produce the rabbit out of the hat if we've just watched him put it in."[10]

Our finding that the desire for improved coordination rather than mitigation of opportunism was the principal motivating factor for the merger accords with the account of Alfred D. Chandler and Stephen Salsbury and that of Thomas G. Marx and Laura B. Peterson. Marx and Peterson and Susan Helper, John Paul MacDuffie, and Charles Sabel also discover problems with the Fisher Body story of Klein, Crawford, and Alchian.[11] Patrick Bolton and David Scharfstein point out that Hart's theory is incomplete in that it does not take into account the agency costs arising from delegation in decision making and thus does not adequately interpret the GM–Fisher Body case.[12] Bengt Holmström and John Roberts point out that many

---

[7] The Fisher Body Company was founded by the eldest two of the seven Fisher brothers. Fred and Charles (along with an uncle), for $50,000 on July 22, 1908, in Detroit, two months before the General Motors Company was founded. The seven brothers were Fred J. (1878–1941), Charles T. (1880–1963), William A. (1886–1969), Lawrence P. (1888–1961), Edward F. (1891–1972), Alfred J. (1892–1963), and Howard F. (born in 1902). There were also four Fisher sisters: Anna, Mayme, Loretta, and Clara. Four of the other brothers (William, Lawrence, Edward, and Alfred) joined the company and assumed operating positions. In 1912, Lawrence joined as superintendent of paint and trim; in 1913, Edward and Alfred joined after having completed drafting and design studies in New York; William joined in 1915. The youngest, Howard, managed the family real estate holdings. Louis Mendelssohn and Aaron Mendelson provided early financial backing and assumed the positions of treasurer and secretary, respectively. Roger B. White, "Body by Fisher: The Closed Car Revolution," *Automobile Q.* 29 (1991), p. 46.

[8] R. H. Coase, "The Nature of the Firm: Origin, Meaning, Influence," *J. L. Econ. and Org.* 4 (1988), p. 3.

[9] On that same occasion, Coase also visited an A. O. Smith plant, one of GM's main suppliers and the largest producer of automobile frames in the world. Coase relates how impressed he was with the level of automation and the degree of specificity of the assets involved in the production of automobile frames. Nevertheless, A. O. Smith had an amicable relationship with GM, and 45 years later GM was still one of A. O. Smith's main customers. Coase reasoned that the willingness to build a reputation for trustworthiness to promote future business invalidated the asset specificity/opportunism thesis.

[10] Coase, op. cit. (note 8), p. 43.

[11] Alfred D. Chandler and Stephen Salsbury, *Pierre S. du Pont and the Making of the Modern Corporation* (1971); Thomas G. Marx and Laura B. Peterson, "Asset Specificity, Opportunism, and the Vertical Integration of Body and Frame Production in the Automobile Industry" (unpublished manuscript, General Motors Corp., Detroit; 1993); Susan Helper, John Paul MacDuffie, and Charles Sabel, "The Boundaries of the Firm as a Design Problem" (unpublished manuscript, Columbia Univ. Law Sch., November 1997).

[12] Patrick Bolton and David Scharfstein, "Corporate Finance, the Theory of the Firm, and Organizations," *J. Econ. Persp.* 12 (Autumn 1998), p. 95.

observed ownership arrangements do not agree with the predictions of the property rights theory of the firm, suggesting that the theory neglects reputation effects.[13]

Because analyses of the Fisher Body acquisition in the economics literature have their roots in Sloan's testimony in *United States v. E. I. Du Pont*, it is worth reviewing the government's contention that GM's purchase of Fisher Body was carried out as a means of extending GM's market power. We observe that there is little empirical support for the allegation that GM's acquisition of Fisher Body was aimed at foreclosure.

The article is organized as follows. Section I reviews the portrayal of the Fisher Body acquisition in the economics literature. Section II evaluates the historical accuracy of the portrayal and interpretation of the Fisher Body acquisition. Section III examines vertical coordination as an explanation for the acquisition. Section IV shows that GM did not seek market power by acquiring Fisher Body. Section V concludes.

## I   THE FISHER BODY ACQUISITION IN THE ECONOMICS LITERATURE

The Fisher Body acquisition story has been used to illustrate at least three related theories in the economics literature. Klein, Crawford, and Alchian, Williamson, and Hart all contend that GM vertically integrated with Fisher Body in 1926 to counteract the body company's hold-up behavior under their long-term contract.[14] Klein, Crawford, and Alchian and Williamson illustrate opportunism in contracts by observing that the initial 1919 contract between GM and Fisher emerged because new production technology called for investments in relationship-specific physical assets that made spot contracting suboptimal.[15] Hart supports his property rights theory of the firm by an analysis of the GM–Fisher Body acquisition. According to Hart, the GM–Fisher Body acquisition combined ownership of complementary assets to enhance incentives to make relationship-specific investments.[16]

These works have inspired a substantial literature on contracting and the theory of the firm.[17] Since its first appearance in the economics literature, the historical

---

[13] Bengt Holmström and John Roberts, "The Boundaries of the Firm Revisited," *J. Econ. Persp.* 12 (Autumn 1998), p. 73.

[14] Klein, Crawford, and Alchian, op. cit. (note 2). Williamson, op. cit. (note 3); Hart, op. cit. (note 4).

[15] Williamson, op. cit., p. 114.

[16] Hart, op. cit., p. 7.

[17] See, for example, Kirk Monteverde and David J. Teece, "Appropriable Rents and Quasi-Vertical Integration," *J. Law and Econ.* 25 (1982), p. 321; Paul A. Grout, "Investment and Wages in the Absence of Binding Contracts: A Nash Bargaining Approach," *Econometrica* 52 (1984), p. 449; Sanford J. Grossman and Oliver D. Hart. "The Costs and Benefits of Ownership: A Theory of Vertical and Lateral Integration," *J. Pol. Econ.* 94 (1986), p. 691; Mathias Dewatripont, "Commitment through Renegotiation-Proof Contracts with Third Parties," *Rev. Econ. Stud.* 55 (1988), p. 377; Oliver Hart and John Moore, "Property Rights and the Nature of the Firm," *J. Pol. Econ.* 98 (1990), p. 1119; Tai-Yeong Chung, "Incomplete Contracts, Specific Investments, and Risk Sharing," *Rev. Econ. Stud.* 58 (1991), p. 1031; William P. Rogerson, "Contractual Solutions to the Hold-Up Problem," *Rev. Econ. Stud.* 59 (1992); Philippe Aghion, Mathias Dewatripont, and Patrick Rey, "Renegotiation Design with Unverifiable Information," *Econometrica* 62

accuracy of the Fisher Body story has been taken for granted. It is used frequently in academic discussions on contracting, vertical integration, and the theory of the firm to illustrate the economic implications of asset specificity and opportunism and the purported failure of market contracts.[18] Many economics and business textbooks refer at some length to the Fisher Body acquisition.[19] The Fisher Body story has become an essential ingredient in courses on contract theory, industrial organization, the economics of organization, and management strategy.

## Klein, Crawford, and Alchian's theory of vertical integration

Klein, Crawford, and Alchian argue that contractual incompleteness together with the presence of investments in specific assets open the door to contractual holdup. Anticipating holdup, parties to contracts invest in less specific assets, thus reducing gains from trade. Because boundedly rational agents cannot write complete contracts, the existence of appropriable quasirents opens the door for contract holdup. The bargaining power of the parties at the renegotiation stage is presumed to depend on the ownership of relationship-specific assets so that the parties will have an incentive to reduce investment in those assets, those lowering joint surplus. Assuming that opportunistic behavior is mitigated within firms, Klein, Crawford, and Alchian propose vertical integration as the solution to the problem of opportunism in market contracts.[20]

To illustrate their theory, Klein, Crawford, and Alchian observe that "[t]he original production process for automobiles consisted of individually constructed open,

(1994), p. 257; Georg Nöldeke and Klaus M. Schmidt, "Option Contracts and Renegotiation: A Solution to the Hold-Up Problem," *Rand J. Econ.* 26 (1995), p. 163; Aaron S. Edlin and Stefan Reichelstein, "Holdups, Standard Breach Remedies, and Optimal Investment," *Am. Econ. Rev.* 86 (1996), p. 478; Peter J. Buckley and Malcolm Chapman, "The Perception and Measurement of Transaction Costs," *Cambridge J. Econ.* 21 (1997), p. 127; and Yeon-Koo Che and Donald B. Hausch. "Cooperative Investments and the Value of Contracting," *Am. Econ. Rev.* 89 (1999), p. 125.

[18] See for example, Benjamin Klein, "Vertical Integration as Organizational Ownership: The Fisher Body–General Motors Relationship Revisited," *J. L. Econ. and Org.* 4 (1988), p. 199; Richard N. Langlois and Paul L. Robertson, "Explaining Vertical Integration: Lessons from the American Automobile Industry," *J. Econ. Hist.* 49 (1989), p. 361.

[19] These textbooks include the following: Jean Tirole, *The Theory of Industrial Organization* (1988), p. 33; Paul R. Milgrom and John Roberts, *Economics, Organization, and Management,* (1992), p. 137; Sharon M. Oster, *Modern Competitive Analysis* (1994), p. 209; Hart op. cit. (note 4) p. 7; David Besanko, David Dranove, and Mark Shanley, *Economics of Strategy* (1996), p. 146; Bernard Salanié, *The Economics of Contracts* (1997); James A. Brickley, Clifford W. Smith and Jerold L. Zimmerman, *Managerial Economics and Organizational Architecture* (1997), p. 56; Jeffrey Church and Roger Ware, *Industrial Organization: A Strategic Approach* (1999), p. 94; Salanié, for example, explains things as follows: "In the 1920s Fisher Bodies [sic] was producing car doors for General Motors; it therefore invested in some rather specialized machine tools and organized its production so as to respond best to the needs of General Motors. Clearly Fisher Bodies would have lost a considerable part of the value of its investments if it had left General Motors for another car maker. Therefore a contract signed in 1919 gave Fisher Bodies a ten-year exclusive dealing clause to protect it from being held up by General Motors. On the other hand, this gave Fisher Bodies the possibility of raising prices outrageously; to prevent this, the contract also contained a cost-plus clause. It turned out, however, that Fisher Bodies manipulated the price-protection clause by choosing a very low capital intensity and locating its plants far from those of General Motors. General Motors thus was effectively held up by Fisher Bodies and eventually bought it in 1926" (Salanié, op. cit., p. 181).

[20] Klein, Crawford, and Alchian, op. cit., pp. 298, 302.

largely wooden, bodies. By 1919 the production process began to shift toward largely metal closed-body construction for which specific stamping machines became important." Therefore, they continue, in 1919 GM entered into a ten-year contract with Fisher Body for the supply of closed auto bodies under which GM "agreed to buy substantially all its closed bodies from Fisher." According to Klein, Crawford, and Alchian, the goal of this exclusive dealing clause was to prevent GM from acting opportunistically by threatening to purchase bodies elsewhere and thus lowering the price after Fisher Body had made "specific investment in production capacity." In turn, to prevent Fisher Body from taking advantage of GM under the exclusive dealing clause, "the contract attempted to fix the price which Fisher could charge for the bodies supplied to General Motors . . . The price was set on a cost plus 17.6 percent basis (where cost was defined exclusive of interest on invested capital)." In addition,

> the contract included provisions that the price charged General Motors could not be greater than that charged other automobile manufacturers by Fisher for similar bodies nor greater than the average market price of similar bodies produced by companies other than Fisher and also included provisions for compulsory arbitration in the event of any disputes regarding price.[21]

Demand for closed automobiles increased dramatically in the years immediately following the manufacturing contract, and, according to Klein, Crawford, and Alchian, "these complex contractual pricing provisions did not work out in practice." Hence.

> General Motors was very unhappy with the price it was being charged by its now very important supplier, Fisher. General Motors believed the price was too high because of a substantial increase in body output per unit of capital employed. This was an understandable development given the absence of a capital cost pass-through in the original contract.

Moreover, they continue, "Fisher refused to locate their body plants adjacent to General Motors assembly plants, a move General Motors claimed was necessary for production efficiency." Klein, Crawford, and Alchian conclude that "[b]y 1924, General Motors had found the Fisher contractual relationship intolerable and began negotiations for purchase of the remaining stock in Fisher Body, culminating in a final merger agreement in 1926."[22] Thus, Klein, Crawford, and Alchian base their argument on the need for Fisher Body to make large relationship specific investments, Fisher Body's opportunistic pricing policies, and Fisher Body's unwillingness to locate its plants next to GM's plants.

---

[21] Ibid., pp. 308–9.
[22] Ibid., pp. 309–10.

## Williamson's transaction cost economics

Williamson examines the role of bounded rationality and uncertainty in the formation of contracts.[23] According to Williamson, asset specificity and opportunism by parties in contractual relationships create the need for more complex governance structures, including vertical integration of the buyer and seller. Williamson presents the relationship between GM and Fisher Body as a case study illustrating his theory of vertical integration.[24]

Williamson concludes that the relationship between GM and Fisher Body moved through three stages. In the first stage, the parties transacted through autonomous contracting, which was satisfactory while bodies were made mainly out of wood and did not require large specialized investments. The relationship entered a second stage as the technology of production shifted toward metal bodies. Large specific investments became necessary for production, and a larger mutual dependency developed. Hence, bilateral contracting became optimal. A pricing formula and dispute settlement by arbitration were instituted. The third and final stage in the relationship came about because "[u]nanticipated demand and cost realizations nevertheless placed this bilateral contracting relation under strain. Additional strains were in prospect, moreover, if Fisher Body were to accede to General Motors' request that site-specific investments be undertaken."[25]

In order to align operating and investment decisions in this important period of demand expansion, unified governance replaced bilateral governance. Williamson concludes that disagreement between the two corporations intensified as the degree of idiosyncracy of the assets involved in the relationship progressed. Williamson's explanation of the final 1926 merger is grounded on the same points made by Klein, Crawford, and Alchian: asset specificity, opportunism, and plant location. Williamson's interpretation of the 1919 contract hinges on bilateral dependency resulting from the effects of technological change on asset specificity. Williamson emphasizes that in the case of Fisher Body, specialized physical assets were needed to support the changes in auto body design that accompanied the "shift to the metal body era."[26]

---

[23] Williamson, op. cit. (note 3); and Oliver E. Williamson, "Transaction Cost Economics: The Governance of Contractual Relations," *J. Law and Econ.* 22 (1979), p. 233.

[24] Williamson, op. cit., p. 114, summarizes the relationship between Fisher Body and GM in four points: "1. In 1919 General Motors entered a ten-year contractual agreement with Fisher Body whereby General Motors agreed to purchase substantially all its closed bodies from Fisher. 2. The price of delivery was set on a cost-plus basis and included provisions that General Motors would not be charged more than rival automobile manufacturers. Price disputes were to be settled by compulsory arbitration. 3. The demand for General Motors' production of closed body cars increased substantially above that which had been forecast. As a consequence General Motors became dissatisfied with the terms under which prices were to be adjusted. It furthermore urged Fisher to locate its body plants adjacent to GM assembly plants, thereby to realize transportation and inventory economies. Fisher Body resisted. 4. General Motors began acquiring Fisher stock in 1924 and completed a merger agreement in 1926."

[25] Ibid., p. 115.

[26] Ibid.

## Hart's property rights theory of the firm

As in Klein, Crawford, and Alchian and Williamson, Hart maintains that parties underinvest in relationship-specific assets to reduce the impact of opportunism.[27] Hart shows that owning complementary assets creates outside options that increase the ex post bargaining power of parties to a contract. Owning a greater proportion of physical assets makes an agent less subject to holdup and more able to act opportunistically. Hart summarizes his theory as follows: "[O]wnership is a source of power when contracts are incomplete."[28] In Hart's property rights theory of the firm, physical assets will be allocated between the parties so that the resulting incentives to undertake ex ante specific investments induce the largest possible joint surplus. The more assets an agent owns, the greater his incentive to undertake relationship-specific investment, particularly in human capital.

Hart asserts that "[f]or a long time Fisher Body and GM were separate firms linked by a long-term contract. However, in the 1920s GM's demand for car bodies increased substantially. After Fisher Body refused to revise the formula for determining price, GM bought Fisher out." Without historical support, Hart observes that "GM wanted to be sure that next time around it would be in a stronger bargaining position; in particular, it would be able to insist on extra supplies, without having to pay a great deal for them."[29]

Why did GM and Fisher Body not write a better contract? Hart points out that it is costly to write complete contingent contracts. Hence, even the most detailed contract is open to renegotiation. Consequently, both companies would be less willing to undertake relationship-specific investments for fear of being held up by contract renegotiation. The proposed solution was to make GM the owner of Fisher Body's assets since doing so would confer residual control rights that would improve GM's future bargaining position. Hart notes that "[a]t an extreme, GM could dismiss the managers of Fisher Body if they refused to accede to GM's requests."[30] Speaking hypothetically, Hart suggests that by owning Fisher, GM would have greater incentives to undertake relationship-specific investments. Overall, Hart's interpretation of the merger emphasizes that GM and Fisher Body were independent companies prior to the merger, Fisher Body behaved opportunistically, and GM wished to be in a better bargaining position in future renegotiations.

## II   EVALUATION OF THE FABLE OF FISHER BODY

Given the influence of the Fisher Body story, it is important to examine whether or not the historical events support the analyses of Klein, Crawford, and Alchian, Williamson, and Hart. General Motors did enter into a ten-year manufacturing contract in 1919 for the purchase of bodies from Fisher Body at 17.6 percent above

---

[27] Hart, op. cit.
[28] Ibid., p. 29.
[29] Ibid., p. 7.
[30] Ibid., p. 7.

cost.[31] However, a number of significant aspects of the account in the economics literature are incorrect. First, the contractual relationship between GM and Fisher Body appears to have been amicable and characterized by trust, not "intolerable." Fisher does not appear to have priced auto bodies opportunistically. Second, the manufacturing agreement should be viewed in the context of the 1919 acquisition, earnings contract, and voting trust arrangements; the firms were not separate. Corporate governance arrangements accompanying the 1919 acquisition of Fisher Body by GM separated ownership from control, which contradicts the view that property rights were necessary for control. Third, after the 1919 acquisition, final merger talks between the two companies began as early as 1922, which suggests that they did not arise out of alleged problems with the contract in 1926. Fourth, the two companies coordinated plant locations and solved capacity problems prior to the merger.

Finally, Fisher Body's manufacturing technology focused primarily on wooden automobile bodies. This fact is highly significant because it shows that investments by Fisher were not transaction specific and thus did not require contractual protection. Woodworking technology was very flexible, allowing the company easily to change the styles of its auto bodies. Moreover, since the technology was wood based, the company did not have substantial transaction-specific investments in metal presses and dies.

## The contractual relationship with Fisher Body exhibited trust

Prior to the 1926 merger, the long-term relationship between the two companies, their extensive interaction, and their frequent exchange of information suggest an absence of opportunism. There are numerous specific indications of the amicable nature of contractual relations between the two companies.[32] General Motors's

---

[31] The ten-year duration of the manufacturing contract is confirmed by a May 17, 1926, letter to the stockholders of the Fisher Body Corporation from Louis Mendelssohn and William A. Fisher. Letter to the Fisher Body Corporation Stockholders (May 17, 1926), Govt Trial-Ex. No. 506. *United States v. E. I. Du Pont de Nemours & Co.; General Motors*, et al., Civil Action 49C-1071, 126 F. Supp. 235 (N.D. Ill. 1954); 353 U.S. 586 (1957); 366 U.S. 316 (1961). General Motors and Fisher Body had previously entered into a prior ten-year manufacturing contract on November 9, 1917, to purchase bodies at cost plus 17.6 percent, according to Lawrence H. Seltzer, *A Financial History of the American Automobile Industry: A Study of the Ways in Which the Leading American Producers of Automobiles Have Met Their Capital Requirements* (1928), p. 191; Roger B. White, "Fisher Body Corporation," in *The Automobile Industry, 1896–1920* (Encyclopedia of American Business History and Biography Series 1990). See also Chandler and Salsbury, op. cit. (note 11), p. 465. The contract was renegotiated with the same cost plus 17.6 percent formula in 1919, according to Seltzer, op. cit., p. 218; Chandler and Salsbury, op. cit., p. 465; and White, op. cit., p. 189. For other references to the presence of a ten-year manufacturing contract, see also Poor's *Manual of Industrials 1488* (1921); Arthur Pound, *The Turning Wheel: The Story of General Motors through Twenty-Five Years, 1908–1933* (1934), p. 291; Alfred P. Sloan, Jr., *My Years with General Motors* (1963), p. 15; and Al Fleming, "Body by Fisher," *Automotive News* 143 (1983). Chandler and Salsbury (p. 465) and White (p. 189) state that the contract was to be carried out for only five years until October 1924, coinciding approximately with the conclusion of the voting trust and other contractual arrangements for compensating the Fisher brothers.

[32] This interaction resembles the stylized cooperative relationship between a parent company and subcontractors described by Masahiko Aoki, "Horizontal vs Vertical Information Structure of the Firm," *Am. Econ. Rev.* 76 (1986), p. 971; Masahiko Aoki, "Toward an Economic Model of the Japanese Firm," *J. Econ. Literature* 28 (1990), p. 1.

national advertising campaigns mentioned Fisher's name, and all GM cars showed a distinctive plate reading "Body by Fisher." General Motors invested heavily in Fisher Body in 1919 and invested $4.5 million more in 1923, with Fisher Body expanding capacity to meet GM's demand. The increasing involvement of the Fisher brothers in GM's top management that began with Fred Fisher's membership in GM's executive committee shows good relations between the brothers and the top management at GM. The extensive participation of the Fishers in GM executive positions continued uninterrupted and expanded during the period between 1919 and 1926 and, indeed, continued for many years after the 1926 merger, providing evidence of the good relations between GM and the Fishers that preceded the merger.

Before the 1919 acquisition, Fisher Body required substantial capital investment to increase its scale to meet demand. Like many entrepreneurs and family businesses that obtain external capital investment, the Fisher brothers faced dilution of ownership as well as a corresponding loss of control. The sources of finance capital, such as the sale of equity shares or the creation of joint ventures, have important implications for corporate control. The close working relationship between Fisher Body and its principal customer, GM, and the structure of postacquisition control arrangements offered by GM were likely to have influenced Fisher Body's decision to accept GM's offer in 1919. The Fishers' trust of GM is indicated by their turning to GM as a partner. Fisher Body's good relations with GM continued, as shown by a 1926 letter to the former's shareholders, which notes that the 1919 manufacturing contract "has been exceedingly profitable to Fisher Body" and that about 90 percent of Fisher's business consists of bodies made for GM.[33] Also, according to Arthur Pound, Fisher Body accepted GM as an acquirer over two other car manufacturers because while the Fishers wanted to manufacture high-end quality bodies, they also were interested in expanding production. General Motors was growing rapidly and marketed automobiles on both ends of the product spectrum.[34]

Klein, Crawford, and Alchian's critical assertion that "[b]y 1924, General Motors had found the Fisher contractual relationship intolerable and began negotiations for purchase of the remaining stock"[35] is based on three *United States v. E. I. Du Pont* defendants' trial exhibits, numbered GM-32, GM-33, and GM-34.[36] What of these exhibits? Exhibit GM-32 is an October 1924 letter from Pierre S. du Pont to Harry McGowan, in which du Pont states that "[a]s it has not been possible for Alfred Sloan to give personal attention to all of the ramifications of the Corporation, I think the Messrs. Fisher are especially well adapted to assist him in ferreting out troubles promptly and applying remedies." The letter continues:

> Interestingly, two members of the Fisher family in General Motors will have a very beneficial effect in breaking up a line of separation of the two companies' interests that has not been altogether wholesome. From lack of knowledge, the two sides have tended to criticise each other, without good result. Hereafter the Fishers will better under-

---

[33] Letter to the Fisher Body Corporation Stockholders (see note 31).
[34] Pound, op. cit. (note 31), p. 291.
[35] Klein, Crawford, and Alchian, op. cit., p. 310.
[36] Defendants' Trial Ex. Nos. GM-32, GM-33 and GM-34, *Du Pont*, 126 F. Supp. 235.

stand General Motors problems and difficulties and, I think, General Motors men will better appreciate the Fisher problems.[37]

The letter goes on to list the many executive positions to which the Fishers will be appointed. Exhibit GM-33 is Harry McGowan's brief reply congratulating du Pont on bringing about more active participation by the Fisher brothers. Last, GM-34 is a letter from Sloan to J. J. Raskob, dated February 13, 1926, stating that "the protection of our competitive position requires that we make the most determined effort possible to work out Fisher Body situation along more constructive lines to the end that proper coordination can be effected."[38] He alludes to general operating issues but spends most of the letter on what is clearly the main issue: natural contention over the ratio at which GM stock is to be exchanged for Fisher Body stock. The negotiation concerns an earnings agreement, not the manufacturing contract. Sloan further observes in his letter that "Fred's [Fisher] whole attitude is so enthusiastically for General Motors, its present position and its future, that of course it makes it very much easier to deal with the problem than ever before."[39] These three exhibits do not support a claim of an intolerable contractual relationship with opportunistic behavior. Rather, they indicate a desire for merger based on the benefits of coordination.

Contrary to Klein, Crawford, and Alchian, Williamson, and Hart, there is little historical evidence that opportunism in pricing was a problem. General Motors was able to update pricing provisions because it had a controlling interest in Fisher Body dating back to 1919. Moreover, Chandler and Salsbury observe that when the 1919 earnings contract expired in 1924, GM and Fisher Body reached a new agreement that invalidated the old cost plus 17.6 percent pricing formula used for the previous seven years.[40] Sloan's testimony concerns pricing flexibility rather than high prices. Speaking of the years 1920–3 in his 1952 deposition, Sloan states that the pricing formula "became very restrictive; in other words, we were bound by a contract in which the minority interest was outstanding, which we had to respect. And it was a matter of great importance to us because we didn't have the *flexibility* in our price procedure that was necessary to meet commercial needs. It became absolutely necessary that we take over the 40 percent in order that we might coordinate the Fisher Company, integrate their operations more in line with our own."[41] This statement does not indicate the presence of opportunism or high monopoly prices. In fact, the suggested remedy involves the coordination of operations instead of pricing. Significantly, in that same deposition and again in testimony a year later, Sloan states that "I never saw the contract," referring to the 1919 manufacturing contract for the production of closed bodies.[42]

[37] Letter from Pierre S. du Pont to Harry McGowan (October 21, 1924), Defendants' Trial Ex. No. GM-32, *Du Pont*, 126 F. Supp. 235.

[38] J. J. Raskob was a director and the treasurer of the Du Pont Company. Chandler, *Strategy and Structure*, p. 126.

[39] Letter from Alfred P. Sloan, Jr., to J. J. Raskob (February 13, 1926), Defendants' Trial Ex. No. GM-34, *Du Pont*, 126 F. Supp. 235.

[40] Chandler and Salsbury, op. cit.

[41] Deposition of Alfred P. Sloan, Jr. (April 28, 1952), *Du Pont*, 126 F. Supp. 235, p. 188.

[42] Ibid., p. 187; Testimony of Alfred P. Sloan, Jr. (March 17, 1953), Trial Transcript vol. 5, *Du Pont*, 126 F. Supp. 235, p. 2908.

## General Motors' 1919 acquisition of Fisher Body separated ownership and control

In October 1919, GM acquired a 60 percent interest in the Fisher Body Corporation. At the same time, GM entered into the ten-year manufacturing contract with Fisher Body mentioned previously. Also, GM agreed to an earnings-sharing contract with Fred and Charles Fisher that paid 10 percent of net earnings to them as managers.[43] As part of the acquisition, GM established a voting trust arrangement that effectively separated the ownership of and the control over Fisher Body. The corporate control arrangement was closer to a collaborative joint venture than to a hostile takeover and indicates close cooperation at the highest levels of the companies.

As a result of the acquisition, Fisher Body increased its capitalization by issuing 300,000 new shares of common stock of no par value that GM bought at $92 per share.[44] General Motors paid approximately $5,800,000 in cash and $21,851,000 in five-year serial notes. In fact, if we include GM's pro rata share of the new Fisher stock issues, the total investment in Fisher Body was $32,151,825.

A five-year voting trust was established to hold the new stock, dated November 24, 1919; it terminated on October 1, 1924.[45] The voting trust had a five-year duration because the Fisher Body Corporation was organized under the laws of New York State, which then limited voting trusts to a period of five years.[46] The voting trust provided a device for owners of stock to control a corporation without tying up the money to hold the shares since the stock is transferred to the trust and the trust issues certificates that others can hold as stock.[47] In this case, holders of preferred stock transferred their certificates to the voting trustees and received a voting trust certificate. Voting trusts acted as holding companies and served as a means of unifying and allocating control rights and separating that control from property rights. Arthur S. Dewing defines a voting trust as an administrative device employed to maintain the executing or financial control of a corporation whereby "men owning little or none of the stock are able to control, absolutely, the policy of a corporation."[48]

The trustees were William C. Durant and Pierre du Pont from General Motors and Fred J. Fisher and Louis Mendelssohn from Fisher Body, thus giving Fisher

---

[43] This arrangement is mentioned in a letter from J. J. Raskob to William C. Durant (on file with the Kettering/GMI Alumni Foundation Collection of Industrial History, Flint, Mich.). The four younger brothers already had a contract for 5 percent of net earnings. A letter from Pierre du Pont to Harry McGowan (October 21, 1924) notes the expiration of the contract on October 1, 1924, referring to the payments received by the Fisher brothers. See Defendants' Trial Ex. No. GM-32, *Du Pont*. 126 F. Supp. 235.

[44] Chandler and Salsbury, op. cit. (note 11), p. 465; Seltzer, op. cit. (note 31), p. 191; Marx and Peterson. op. cit. (note 11), p. 8.

[45] The voting trust agreement covering stock of Fisher Body Corporation was between that company and Fred Fisher, Louis Mendelssohn, William C. Durant, and Pierre du Pont. See Govt Trial Ex. No. 429, Vol. 3, *Du Pont*, 126 F. Supp. 235. See also Poor's *Manual of Industrials*, op. cit., p. 1489.

[46] Harry A. Cushing, *Voting Trusts* (1927), p. 22.

[47] Harry A. Cushing, *Voting Trusts* (1915); Arthur Stone Dewing, *The Administration of Income* (The Financial Policy of Corporations Series, 5 vols, 1921).

[48] Dewing, op. cit.

Body half of the control of the trust.[49] In addition, Fisher Body's board of directors was restructured. Its final composition included fourteen members, half of them representing the interests of GM and the other half those of the Fisher family. Despite the 50/50 nature of this corporate control arrangement, the Fishers continued to manage their company. Thus, under the agreement the two companies were equally represented in both the voting trust and the board of directors. These arrangements show clearly the distinction between ownership and control. Significantly, even though GM owned 60 percent of Fisher Body, they exercised only 50 percent control. Even after GM completed its purchase of Fisher Body in 1926, the executive committee of the GM Corporation itself was split 50/50 between men from GM (Sloan, Donaldson Brown, and John L. Pratt) and three of the Fishers (Fred, Lawrence, and Charles) because the additional two members (du Pont and Raskob) were essentially inactive.[50]

Recall that Hart's property rights theory of the firm suggests that firms exist to consolidate ownership of physical assets in order to secure residual control rights.[51] The separation of ownership and control in the voting trust, the structure of Fisher Body's board of directors in 1919, and the control arrangements at GM after 1926 suggest, in contrast to Hart's interpretation of the motives for integration, that acquiring property rights to exercise residual control rights did not motivate the merger. After the initial 60 percent acquisition of Fisher Body by GM, the Fishers were owners of a minority interest in Fisher Body's assets but had substantial control rights as managers, directors, and members of the voting trust.

## Merger talks began at least in 1922

Contrary to any assertion that the 1926 merger resulted from contractual difficulties in the years immediately preceding, it should be emphasized that such a merger was contemplated much earlier. Indeed, Fisher Body's interest in a complete merger had arisen at least by 1922. Pierre du Pont, writing to Lammot du Pont on October 31, 1922, observes that

> [r]ecently, the Messrs. Fisher have brought up the question of their future relations with General Motors and have expressed a desire to become more intimately associated with the proposition as a whole and, with that end in view, have requested a study of relative values of General Motors and Fisher assets with a view to an exchange of Fisher Body common stock for General Motors shares.

---

[49] Pierre du Pont's contact with GM began in February 1914 after he invested $140,000 in common stock. By the end of the next year, half the value of du Pont's investment portfolio (outside chemicals) was in GM. On November 16, 1915, du Pont was named chairman of the board of directors of GM. He acted as a counselor to William C. Durant (president of GM from June 1, 1916, to November 30, 1920) and provided a sizable amount of funds to finance the 1918–19 expansion program, which included the purchase of Fisher Body. On November 30, 1920, du Pont succeeded Durant in office, held the appointment until May 10, 1923, and continued as chairman of the board until February 7, 1929. Pound op. cit. (note 31); Chandler and Salsbury, op. cit.

[50] Chandler and Salsbury, op. cit., pp. 465, 577.

[51] Bolton and Scharfstein, op. cit. (note 12), point out shortcomings in Hart's theory arising from his not considering the separation of securities ownership and management control at GM itself, although they do not consider the issues addressed here.

General Motors also was interested in a merger. Pierre du Pont stated that "a closer association with the Messrs. Fisher and closer cooperation between the two corporations would be of great benefit."[52] In autumn of 1922, Fred Fisher was elected a member of GM's executive committee, which was the first step in a progressive involvement of the Fishers in GM's top management.[53]

In 1924, there were additional merger talks between Pierre du Pont and the Fishers.[54] The voting trust and the earnings contract expired on October 1, 1924, and a new earnings agreement was reached. A key provision of that contract was that the Fisher brothers would be given ownership of shares in the Managers Security Company that were equivalent to the amount of shares given to those in similar executive positions at GM. Further, William Fisher would be the president of Fisher Body, Charles and Lawrence Fisher would also join GM's executive committee (with Charles spending time managing Fisher Body), and Edward and Alfred would be operating executives at Fisher Body.[55] Fisher Body's profit would be calculated in the same way as that of any other GM operating division instead of the earlier cost-plus formula.[56]

Merger talks began again a year later. General Motors' management was concerned that the remaining 40 percent interest of Fisher Body in the hands of the Fisher family, Louis Mendelssohn, and Aaron Mendelson could eventually be transferred or sold to some third party.[57] Also, during the years of expansion and reorganization at GM, both Sloan and du Pont had realized the value of having the Fishers devote their managerial attention to GM itself. They persuaded Lawrence Fisher to become general manager at Cadillac in 1925.

Fisher Body's interest in a merger was apparent. In explaining the proposed merger to its shareholders in 1926, Fisher Body noted that the ten-year manufacturing contract of 1919 "has but a relatively short term remaining . . . In 1929 a new contract must be negotiated, or General Motors will be free either to build its own bodies or purchase them elsewhere."[58] After a series of negotiations, GM completed its acquisition of Fisher Body on June 30, 1926. The transaction took place by exchange of securities at a ratio of 1.5 shares of GM per share of Fisher. The market value of the stock issued by GM for the transaction was $136 million, while Fisher's assets were listed at $92.3 million.

[52] Letter from Pierre S. du Pont to Lammot du Pont (October 31, 1922), Govt Trial Ex. No. 435, *Du Pont*, 126 F, Supp. 235.

[53] Sloan, op. cit. (note 31), p. 161; Chandler and Salsbury, op. cit., p. 526.

[54] According to Chandler and Salsbury, op. cit., p. 575, Fred Fisher agreed that more involvement in GM would be positive but did not accept complete integration because Fisher Body was a very profitable company and the Fishers did not want to see their family business completely absorbed by GM.

[55] Defendants' Trial Ex. No. GM-32, vol. 1, *Du Pont*, 126 F. Supp. 235.

[56] Chandler and Salsbury, op. cit., p. 576.

[57] Ibid.

[58] Letter to the Fisher Body Corporation Stockholders, Govt Trial Ex. No. 506, *Du Pont*, 126 F. Supp. 235.

**Table 8.1**   Fisher Body assembly plants

| Year | Plant | Floor (sq. ft) |
|------|-------|----------------|
| 1923 | Flint No. 2, Mich. | 266,443 |
|      | Lansing, Mich. | 622,234 |
|      | Buffalo, N.Y. | 150,692 |
|      | Norwood, Ohio | 182,167 |
|      | Jamesville, Wis. | 257,790 |
|      | Oakland, Calif. | 163,920 |
| 1925 | Tarrytown, N.Y. | 376,924 |
| 1928 | Atlanta, Ga. | 130,258 |
| 1929 | Kansas City, Mo. | 133,573 |

*Source*: Arthur Pound, *The Turning Wheel: The Story of General Motors through Twenty-Five Years, 1908–1933* (1934), pp. 298–9.

## Fisher Body plants were located close to General Motors' plants

By 1923 a schedule for the construction of body assembly plants was implemented. Plant location issues were essentially settled by 1924 before the original voting trust expired.[59] In 1923 and as a consequence of an increase in demand in 1922, Fisher Body added additional plants, increasing its body assembly capacity by 1,643,246 square feet. Flint body plant No. 1, with over 2 million square feet, was taken over from Durant Motors in 1926. In the three years immediately following the acquisition, Fisher's capacity increased by only 263,831 square feet. Table 8.1 shows Fisher's body assembly plant expansion during the period 1923–9.

Many Fisher Body plants were located adjacent to GM plants before 1926, as is demonstrated by table 8.1. For example, Fisher plants operated closely with adjacent Chevrolet plants in Flint, Michigan; Buffalo, New York; Norwood, Ohio; and Jamesville, Wisconsin; with Pontiac in Oakland, California; and with Oldsmobile in Lansing, Michigan.[60] A GM report from 1924 states that "[w]herever, in the United States and Canada, there is an important passenger car plant of Buick, Cadillac, Chevrolet, Oakland, or Oldsmobile, there is, or will be close by, a plant of Fisher Body, adequate to meet the demand for closed bodies of high quality."[61]

[59]   Marx and Peterson, op. cit. (note 11).

[60]   Pound, op. cit. (note 31), p. 289; White, op. cit. (note 7), p. 56. Helper, MacDuffie, and Sabel, op. cit. (note 11) point out the colocation of GM and Fisher Body plants.

[61]   *General Motors Corporation, Fisher Body: Its Contribution to the Automotive Industry* (1924). This is quoted by Helper, MacDuffie, and Sabel, which suggests that Klein, Crawford, and Alchian, op. cit., erred on the question of plant location by relying on Testimony of Alfred P. Sloan, Jr. (March 17, 1953), *Du Pont*, 126 F. Supp. 235. This testimony was taken almost three decades after the fact.

[62]   Michael Lamm and Dave Holls, *A Century of Automotive Style: 100 Years of American Car Design* (1996), p. 35.

## Fisher's productive assets were not relationship specific

Fisher Body did not make significant relationship-specific investments in metal presses to manufacture the bodies for GM because automobile bodies were mostly made out of wood, not metal. Fisher Body did not switch to the new metal production technology until the late 1930s, some two decades after the 1919 contract. Fisher's production technology in the 1910s, 1920s, and most of the 1930s was labor intensive. Thus, problems resulting from asset specificity could not have been a motivating factor in the acquisition and merger.

Michael Lamm and Dave Holls point out that "[f]rom 1905 through the mid-1930s, most car bodies were framed in wood and covered with sheet metal skins. This type of construction was called 'composite.' "[62] Although some rudimentary dies and presses were used for stamping the metal sheets that covered the wooden frames, these had been employed by Fisher Body long before 1919.[63] It was only in the late 1930s that Fisher, then a division of GM, began using large expensive dies and presses for the production of car bodies.

In fact, Fisher Body was the last major body producer to switch to metal-based technology. Lamm and Holls point out that "General Motors (Fisher) was the last major U.S. holdout to use composite body construction. The Fisher Brothers, of course, had grown up in the tradition of woodworking, which probably had a lot to do with their conservatism." They add that "General Motors kept building composite bodies until the 1937 model year."[64] As White relates: "By 1919, when GM purchased a majority of its stock, Fisher Body was the world's largest manufacturer of automobile bodies. The six Fisher brothers who then managed the corporation were specialists in closed-body construction and staunch advocates of the wood-and-steel body." White notes that "[i]n 1925 Chevrolet rejected an offer by Budd to build all-steel bodies. Six years later Fisher bodies still had hard-wood frames but also had steel or iron brace in place of wood at every joint; that type of construction continued in use for the next four years."[65]

The considerable reliance on wood in auto body construction is apparent. General Motors, in its 1924 report on Fisher Body, gives a good indication of the amount of wood used by Fisher: "Timberlands are located in many States. There are three saw mills, one of which is believed to be the largest hardwood mill in the United

---

[63] Ibid., pp. 63. 27. Lamm and Holls describe early sheet metal presses as follows: "By 1910, a few bodymakers, including C. R. Wilson and Fisher, were starting to use primitive drop presses to make sheet metal stampings. These presses consisted of a semi-steel female die and a lead male punch. The punch usually took its shape directly from the female die. Large loops were cast into the top surface of the lead punch, and it was lifted to the ceiling by ropes. Channels guided the punch to direct its drop into the female die. To make the actual stamping, workmen heated large sheets of steel in a gas furnace. When the metal was red-hot, they used tongs to hold the cherry-colored sheet over the female die. The male lead punch was then dropped from the ceiling and forced the sheet metal into the female die. The quality of sheet steel varied widely in that day, and it, wasn't unusual to have the stamped piece split as it took shape. Metal lubricants, more ductile sheets and a more consistent quality arrived with the advent of larger hydraulic and toggle presses." In fact, the first large presses were not invented until the late 1920s to early 1930s. See Karl Ludvigsen, "A Century of Automobile Body Evolution," *Automotive Engineering* 103 (1995), p. 51.

[64] Lamm and Holls, op. cit., p. 35.

[65] White, op. cit. (note 31), pp. 187, 191.

States. Annual capacity: 100,000,000 feet of hardwood lumber." On the basis of annual production, the report observes that "[t]he lumber in the bodies would build 10,000 seven-room dwellings."[66] Even in 1933, Fisher Body owned 222,000 acres of timberlands in Michigan and the southern states and 852,456 square feet of floor space in woodworking plants.[67]

The body production process was highly labor intensive. General Motors' 1924 report further indicates that "[e]very piece of wood in a closed body is glued, screwed and bolted into place. There are used 750,000 pounds of dry glue, 720 million screws, 17 million bolts."[68] The investments Fisher undertook in 1919 (and in the 1920s) to supply GM were neither large nor highly specific. Lamm and Holls describe the body manufacturing technology in the early years of automobile production:

> Unlike all-steel bodies, whose shapes were hard to revise because they required expensive dies and presswork, the styling of wood-framed bodies could be changed fairly easily by redesigning and reshaping the wooden frame members and then reforming the sheetmetal over them. For mass production, wooden pieces could be gang-sawed and shaped either by hand or with simple milling machinery. Jigs were made so that larger individual body parts, like roofs and door framing, could be built up as subassemblies. Complicated shapes, like rear wheelhouses, were sometimes made up from as many as 10 individual pieces of wood, which had to be glued and screwed together in special jigs. These subassemblies came together in ever-bigger jigs until they formed the framing for an entire automobile body.[69]

The flexibility of wood-based manufacturing shows an absence of asset specificity.

## III   THE ROLE OF VERTICAL COORDINATION IN THE FISHER BODY ACQUISITION

In this section, we show that GM merged with Fisher Body in order to achieve better vertical coordination in terms of assurance of auto body supplies and access to the executive talents of the Fishers. First, the bodies produced by Fisher offered competitive advantages because they were noted for their distinct quality and style. General Motors' 1919 annual report is clear: "Your Corporation was fortunate in assuring an enlarged supply of bodies through the acquisition of a majority interest in the Fisher Body Corporation, Detroit, Michigan, the largest builder of automobile bodies in the world." The report further observes, "The Fisher Body Corporation is expanding its Detroit facilities, thereby assuring your Corporation an adequate supply of bodies, particularly of the closed type, demand of which is increasing rapidly."[70]

Second, GM's interest in acquiring this important supplier was far from an isolated event. The 1919 purchase was part of William C. Durant's overall acquisition

---

[66] General Motors Corporation, op. cit. (note 61), pp. 6–7.
[67] Pound, op. cit. (note 31), p. 298.
[68] General Motors Corporation, op. cit. (note 61), pp. 6–7.
[69] Lamm and Holls, op. cit. (note 62), p. 35.
[70] General Motors Corporation, *Annual Report* (1919).

drive at GM. Mergers with suppliers were intended to achieve assurance of supplies in a rapidly growing and highly competitive market. This drive reflected the prevailing view of vertical integration in the strategic management and economics literature at that time.[71] Chandler's *The Visible Hand* documents the extensive vertical integration in American business between 1900 and 1917 and attributes the internalization of the market processes connecting mass production to distribution to efficiencies of the "visible hand of administrative coordination."[72] Earlier, Chandler observes that the strategy of the expansion of industry was based on a desire to assure more certain supply of stocks, raw materials, and other supplies.[73]

Third, the Fisher Body acquisition enhanced day-to-day coordination between the production of auto bodies and that of automobiles. Enhanced coordination was an essential element of the reforms put in place by du Pont and Sloan in the period from 1920 to 1924. With the 1926 merger, Fisher Body became a division of GM.

Fourth, the companies could better coordinate their personnel policies by creating an internal market for executives having the skills sought by Sloan. The Fisher Body acquisition gave GM access to the Fisher brothers as managers and directors. Sloan emphasizes the importance of incorporating the Fisher brothers into the operating organization of General Motors: "Because we needed talent of the highest order."[74]

## Auto bodies by Fisher offered competitive advantages

General Motors' acquisition of Fisher Body was motivated by the need to assure a supply of Fisher's auto bodies, which were a crucial competitive advantage for GM. As Sloan observes, "[T]he Fisher bodies were recognized throughout the trade as having that something added to them that was very distinguished and gave an appearance that other competitive bodies did not have."[75] Not only did the Fisher bodies have a reputation for quality and craftsmanship, but from the very first days, the Fisher brothers paid particular attention to the development and manufacture of closed-car bodies. This was risky because almost all automobiles were of the open type in the early 1900s. Their choice was well timed because by 1927 approximately 85 percent of all automobiles were of the closed type. The Fisher closed body represented comfort and luxury and was instrumental in GM's competition with Ford. Sloan calls the closed body the "last decisive element" in the competition with Ford.[76]

As early as 1910, Cadillac, which had been acquired by General Motors on July 1, 1909, placed an order with Fisher for 150 closed bodies. This was the largest order

---

[71] For example, Lawrence K. Frank, "The Significance of Industrial Integration," *J. Pol. Econ.* 33 (1925), pp. 179, 187, 191, argues that "coordinated operation calls for the ownership or control by some organization of all other stages" and suggests that "the price system, in so far as it affects the conduct of industry at least, is being rendered obsolete" due to vertical integration.

[72] Chandler, *Visible Hand*, op. cit., p. 34.

[73] Chandler, *Strategy and Structure*, op. cit., p. 37.

[74] Deposition of Alfred P. Sloan, Jr. (April 28, 1952), *Du Pont*, 126 F. Supp. 235.

[75] Ibid., p. 189.

[76] Sloan, op. cit. (note 31), p. 160.

**Table 8.2** Closed bodies as a percentage of total vehicles

| Year | Percent |
|------|---------|
| 1919 | 10 |
| 1920 | 17 |
| 1921 | 22 |
| 1922 | 30 |
| 1923 | 34 |
| 1924 | 43 |
| 1925 | 56 |
| 1926 | 74 |
| 1927 | 85 |

*Source*: Beverly Rae Kimes and Henry Austin Clark, Jr., *Standard Catalog of American Cars, 1805–1942* (3rd edn. 1996), p. 10; see also Ralph C. Epstein, *The Automobile Industry: Its Economic and Commercial Development* (1928).

of closed bodies ever made. In December 1910, the Fishers decided to organize the Fisher Closed Body Company to deal with similar orders. The Fishers proved to be skilled managers and experts in closed-body production technology. The Fisher enterprises grew fast: capacity in 1910 was 10 open bodies a day, in 1914 annual output was 105,000 closed and open bodies, and by 1916 yearly productive capacity was 370,000 bodies.[77] The number of Fisher plants grew from 4 in 1911 to 16 in 1918, to 44 in 1924.[78] Consolidated profits were $369,321 in 1913–14, $576,495 in 1914–15, and $1,390,592 in 1915–16.

The period 1916–19 was particularly successful for the Fishers, and their name became firmly associated in the public mind with a reputation for quality. On August 22, 1916, two months before GM incorporated, the Fishers merged the Fisher Body Company, the Fisher Closed Body Company, and the Fisher Body Company of Canada (created in 1912) into the Fisher Body Corporation, establishing the largest body-manufacturing company. Fisher Body's customers included Abbott, Buick, Cadillac, Chalmers, Chandler, Chevrolet, Church-Field, Elmore, E-M-F, Ford, Herreshof, Hudson, Krit, Maxwell, Oakland, Oldsmobile, Packard, Regal, and Studebaker.[79]

The crucial importance of the closed auto body is illustrated by table 8.2, which shows a dramatic shift in the industry from open-to closed-body production. The demand for Fisher's auto bodies increased rapidly, as shown by table 8.3, and greater growth was projected. Moreover, the proportion of Fisher bodies that were closed increased substantially from under a quarter to well over a half. The competitive value of closed bodies was reflected in Fisher's market share. In 1919, the Fisher Body Corporation held a 50 percent share of the U.S. market for closed bodies. By 1926, Fisher's share of the closed-body market rose to 60 percent. By 1925, Fisher

[77] General Motors Corporation, op. cit. (note 61), p. 5; Pound, op. cit. (note 31).
[78] White, op. cit. (note 7), p. 50.
[79] Ibid.; Fleming, op. cit. (note 31), p. 144.

**Table 8.3**  Fisher Body's output of bodies in the fiscal years ended April 30

| Year | Open | Closed | Total | Percent closed |
|------|------|--------|-------|---------------|
| 1919 | 103,449 | 31,318 | 134,767 | 23.24 |
| 1920 | 245,114 | 83,864 | 328,978 | 25.49 |
| 1921 | 112,401 | 87,796 | 200,197 | 43.84 |
| 1922 | 58,435 | 99,789 | 158,224 | 63.07 |
| 1923 | 202,867 | 217,632 | 420,499 | 51.76 |
| 1924 | 239,502 | 335,477 | 574,979 | 58.35 |

*Source*: General Motors Corporation, *Fisher Body: Its Contribution to the Automotive Industry* (1924).

Body was producing 40 types of closed bodies for Cadillac, Buick, Oakland, Oldsmobile, and Chevrolet.[80]

During the period 1920–1 Fisher Body supplied bodies for Cadillac and Buick and continued serving other non-GM automobile manufacturers such as Chandler and Cleveland. In 1922 demand for closed bodies increased dramatically, and all automobile manufacturers faced capacity constraints; for example, Ford Motor Company fell behind by 100,000 orders in late 1922. Fisher Body met GM's growing needs that year from a large new plant in Detroit and a newly acquired plant in Pontiac, Michigan.[81]

## Vertical and horizontal expansion at General Motors

General Motors' purchase and merger with Fisher Body were consistent with GM's pattern of growth and development. The General Motors Company, founded in September 16, 1908, by the director and general manager of the Buick Motor Car Company, William Crapo Durant, grew primarily by vertical and horizontal acquisition. General Motors obtained a complete or controlling interest in more than 20 automobile and parts-producing firms and was marketing 10 different brands of motor vehicles by 1910.[82] The company offered a large collection of diverse models as a means of pooling risk from fluctuating demand for specific makes.[83]

[80] White, op. cit., p. 48.
[81] Ibid., p. 55.
[82] Seltzer, op. cit. (note 31), pp. 36, 154; Pound, op. cit. (note 31), p. 119. Among the car-producing firms were Buick Motor Company, Cadillac Motor Car Company, and Olds Motor Works. Other acquisitions were Oakland Motor Car Company, Markette Motor Car Company, Cartercar Company, Elmore Manufacturing Company, Randolph Motor Car Company, Reliance Motor Truck Company, Rapid Motor Vehicle Company, Weston-Mott Company, Rainier, W. T. Steward Body Plant (assets), Michigan Motor Castings Company, Northway Motor & Manufacturing Company, Ewing Automobile Company, Dow Rim Company, Welch Motor Car Company, Michigan Auto Parts Company, Jackson-Church-Wilcox Company, Novelty Incandescent Lamp Company. Heany Lamp Companies, McLaughlin Motor Car Company, Champion Ignition Company. Brown-Lipe-Chapin Company, and Oak Park Power Company.

General Motors was incorporated in Delaware in October 13, 1916.[84] In the summer of 1917, Durant transformed GM into an operating company by turning all the subsidiaries into divisions. Durant began a new expansion program that included a capacity expansion plan and an increase in capitalization from $60 million to $100 million.[85] On May 2, 1918, GM bought the Chevrolet Motor Company and its subsidiaries.[86]

From its inception, GM followed a policy of increased self-manufacturing of components and parts.[87] Vertical integration was a driving force for Durant, who was committed to assuring the availability of auto parts.[88] For example, Durant formed the United Motors Corporation as a means of acquiring parts suppliers in May 1916 and merged the company into GM in the spring of 1918. Durant's policies continued under du Pont and Sloan. Pierre du Pont backed the unification of Durant's holdings under a single corporate umbrella and holding company, which was essentially complete by 1918 before the initial acquisition of Fisher Body took place.[89] Du Pont also established an executive committee consisting of the heads of all major divisions that had full authority and responsibility on all operating policies and a finance committee composed of Henry F. and Irénée du Pont, J. A. Haskell (a director and executive at Du Pont), Durant, and Raskob.[90]

[83] Seltzer, op. cit., p. 157. General Motors' substantial acquisition costs had serious consequences for the company. In the second quarter of 1910 the American economy entered in a recession and automobile sales dropped dramatically (ibid., p. 161); Carl H. A. Dassbach, *Global Enterprises and the World Economy: Ford, General Motors, and IBM. The Emergence of the Translational Enterprise* (1988), p. 107. In late September 1910, GM obtained a $15 million loan underwritten by a consortium of 23 banks headed by Lee, Higginson & Co. of Boston, J. & W. Seligman & Co., and the Central Trust Company of New York. A five-year voting trust was instituted with a majority of GM stock; the board was composed of three representatives of the syndicate, Anthony N. Brady (a large stockholder), and William C. Durant. See Seltzer, p. 164. This agreement effectively gave the bankers complete control over the board of directors. The bankers imposed conservative financial controls, dropping five of the eleven lines of motor vehicles, merging three into the GM Truck Company, and leaving untouched only Buick, Cadillac, Olds, and Oakland: Seltzer, pp. 37, 168. Durant's setback was only temporary. On November 6, 1911, together with the Chevrolet brothers, Durant founded the Chevrolet Motor Company. The success of this enterprise enabled him to acquire back a large proportion of GM shares. In 1916, Durant returned to direct GM after buying a controlling interest in the company and fully repaying the bankers' syndicate. Dassbach, p. 112.

[84] On August 1, 1917, the General Motors Corporation formally became an operating company. Seltzer, op. cit. (note 31), p. 178; Pound, op. cit. (note 31), p. 164; and Dassbach, op. cit., p. 121.

[85] On December 31, 1917, fixed-plant investment reached $38,657,835, more than double than in July 1916; inventories increased from $25,100,450 to $46,559,394; and reinvested profits in this period totaled $27,810,043. Seltzer, p. 179. See also Chandler and Salsbury, op. cit. (note 11), p. 464.

[86] Seltzer, op. cit., p. 180.

[87] C. C. Edmonds, "Tendencies in the Automobile Industry," *Am. Econ. Rev.* 13 (1923), p. 422.

[88] According to the *New York Times* Annalist (August 2, 1920): "It is said to be the dream of the genius behind the General Motors Corporation to make that company self-sustaining in every particular. W. C. Durant, his friends say, plans for the day when the General Motors pyramid will reach out into the ore fields and mine its own ore; when, over its own lines, which may be lines of motor trucks, it will bring the ore to its iron works, move it along to its steel-mills, distribute the steel to its own plants which will turn out the parts, take the parts to its assembly plants, and then send out the cars, trucks, and tractors to the sales agents, also part of the General Motors consolidation, for ultimate distribution to the users. And already there is the General Motors Acceptance Corporation which can finance the purchasers. A ranch or two for the leather upholstering and maybe an electric light plant might be added, if the Durant idea comes to realization, as those close to him expect it to, probably will be."

[89] Chandler and Salsbury, op. cit., p. 461.

[90] The finance committee was to set dividends and the salaries of top executives, to approve estimates for capital expenditures on an annual and semiannual basis, to authorize the regular budgets, and to make plans for the issuance of securities. Chandler, *Strategy and Structure*, p. 126.

The Fisher Body acquisition was part of an overall program of increased investments in 1919.[91] Coinciding with the postwar boom, GM's output in that year increased by almost 60 percent, while its profits of $60 million were four times the profits of the previous year. General Motors spent $20 million to expand existing car-producing plants, began work on a $20 million office building in Detroit, committed $20 million for a housing project for employees, and created the General Motors Acceptance Corporation to aid in financing distributors, dealers, and retail purchasers.[92] General Motors also acquired additional or new interests in nine parts-making firms and three other enterprises.[93]

Developments at GM following the initial acquisition of Fisher Body set the stage for the merger in 1926. The postwar recession created problems at GM that emphasized the need for internal coordination and that led to Durant's resignation as president on November 30, 1920.[94] Pierre du Pont succeeded Durant and served until May 10, 1923, when Sloan became president. Du Pont remained as chairman, and his work with Sloan imposed professional management based on market forecasts and financial analysis, which was critical to improving internal coordination.[95] In 2½ years, du Pont liquidated the least profitable groups and restructured the relationships among divisions while preserving decentralized administration.

General Motors' 1920 annual report identifies the development and integration into the GM organization of the Central Axle Division, Central Forge Division, Central Gear Division. Central Products Division, Michigan Crank Shaft Division, Muncie Products Division, Northway Motor and Manufacturing Division, Jaxon Steel Products Division, and Lancaster Steel Products Corporation. The report adds that GM has become the "producer of the greater part of its requirements of accessories"[96] through its ownership of the Harrison Radiator Corporation, Dayton Engineering Laboratories Company, Hyatt Roller Bearings Division, Klaxon Company, New Departure Manufacturing Company, Remy Electric Division, and Champion Ignition Company. By 1920, GM "had extended its scope so that not only all the engines used in its cars, but a large proportion of such units as gears, axles, crankshafts, radiators, electrical equipment, roller bearings, warning signals, spark plugs,

---

[91] After learning that Willys-Overland and another car manufacturer were holding negotiations with the Fishers to form a partnership that would give Fisher a controlling interest, Durant and du Pont decided to propose a closer association with their most important supplier. Chandler and Salsbury, op. cit., p. 465; Pound, op. cit., p. 291.

[92] Seltzer, op. cit., p. 192.

[93] Guardian Refrigerator Company (later Frigidaire, producer of electric refrigerators), the Dayton Products Company (producer of detonators, pressure indicators, and the like), and the Domestic Engineering Company (producer of Delco-Light power plant); ibid.

[94] A sudden decline in sales resulting from the postwar recession occurred in summer and fall of 1920. On top of the $79 million required to complete the expansion plans begun the previous year, large amounts of funds were needed to finance the inventories that had been accumulating because of deficient inventory management and the decline in sales. In March 1920, the executive committee approved a set of production guidelines with the objective of reducing inventories. General Motors was not able to generate enough cash flows to meet these obligations. Ibid., p. 198.

[95] Pound, op. cit., chs. 14 and 15. See also Seth W. Norton, "Information and Competitive Advantage: The Rise of General Motors," *J. Law and Econ.* 40 (1997), p. 245; Anthony Patrick O'Brien, "The Importance of Adjusting Production to Sales in the Early Automobile Industry," *Explorations Econ. Hist.* 34 (1997), p. 195.

[96] General Motors Corporation, *Annual Report* (1920), p. 7.

**Table 8.4**    Value of purchased components as a percentage of value of finished vehicles

| Year | Value finished vehicles ($) | Value purchased components ($) | Percent |
|---|---|---|---|
| 1922 | 1,787,122,708 | 982,952,384 | 55 |
| 1923 | 2,582,398,876 | 1,270,000,000 | 49 |
| 1924 | 2,328,249,632 | 900,321,000 | 39 |
| 1925 | 2,957,368,637 | 1,128,648,000 | 38 |
| 1926 | 3,163,756,676 | 823,394,000 | 26 |

*Source*: Lawrence H. Seltzer, *A Financial History of the American Automobile Industry: A Study of the Ways in Which the Leading American Producers of Automobiles Have Met their Capital Requirements* (1928), p. 57.

bodies, plate glass, and body hardware, were produced either by a General Motors unit or by a subsidiary."[97] General Motors' 1920 annual report states that the company "has become firmly entrenched in lines that relate directly to the construction of the car, truck or tractor."[98]

General Motors' vertical integration was focused on automobile components rather than on primary inputs.[99] The preference for vertical integration in the automobile industry at that time is illustrated by Ford's slogan "From Mine to Finished Car, One Organization," which indicates Ford's production of primary inputs. Seltzer points out in 1928 that "[a]n increasing measure of industrial integration has accompanied the concentration of [automobile] production in the recent years,"[100] with GM and other automobile producers manufacturing an increasing proportion of their products. For the automobile industry, the value of purchased components declined steadily as a percentage of the value of finished vehicles during the period 1922–6 (see table 8.4).

## Coordination and transaction costs

Related to the need for assurance of supplies, the GM acquisition of Fisher in 1926 was motivated by the desire to achieve least-cost coordination between the production of auto bodies and assembly, as noted by Sloan in his 1952 deposition. Chandler and Salsbury, and Marx and Peterson.[101] The key step in the coordination process was the conversion of Fisher Body Corporation into a division of GM at the time of the merger in 1926. By making Fisher Body a division, Sloan could integrate

[97]  Edmonds, op. cit. (note 87), p. 426.
[98]  General Motors Corporation, op. cit., p. 8.
[99]  Ibid.
[100]  Seltzer, op. cit., p. 57.
[101]  Deposition of Alfred P. Sloan, Jr. (April 28, 1952), *Du Pont*, 126 F. Supp. 235, p. 188; Chandler and Salsbury, op. cit. (note 11); Marx and Peterson, op. cit. (note 11).

auto body production into the newly created system of inventory and production management and interdivisional coordination.

In GM's 1921 reorganization, du Pont and Sloan created a unified central office for the corporation. They created an accessories group for units that sold more than 60 percent of their output outside the company and a parts group for units that sold 60 percent of their output within the company.[102] In 1922, Sloan established a general purchasing committee to coordinate purchasing across the divisions and to gain experience in such coordination.

In the mid-1920s Sloan instituted organizational reforms aimed at better coordinating GM's operating divisions. Information obtained from dealers improved dramatically, allowing better sales predictions, more efficient production scheduling, and better purchasing coordination.[103] General Motors also implemented an advanced management accounting system after 1921.[104] Seth Norton examines the effects of these changes on GM's performance and finds that GM's rate of return increased from 8.1 percent for the period 1918–25 to 13.5 percent for the period 1926–40, while GM's inventory-to-sales ratio declined significantly. Norton finds improved synchronization in GM's divisional sales and dealer sales in the period 1926–9 as compared to 1922–5.[105]

Improved demand information and production scheduling were used to enhance coordination of production with output of auto bodies through GM's interdivisional committees. Sloan explains the Fisher Body acquisition in terms of "operating economies to be gained by co-ordinating body and chassis assembly."[106] Emphasizing coordination by committee, Sloan implemented long-range inventory and production controls to reduce carrying costs and to meet demand more efficiently.

A critical aspect of coordination in auto assembly is guaranteeing that all components and parts are produced according to the correct technical specifications and that they are delivered precisely when needed.[107] Part designs must change frequently in conformity with the introduction of new products. Part deliveries must adjust to production schedules and demand fluctuations to avoid shortages or costly excess inventories. Divestitures and sourcing decisions by major automakers suggest that conditions in the automobile industry at the beginning of the twenty-first century favor divestiture of parts manufacturing and reliance on market contracts. However, understanding the Fisher Body acquisition requires examining the relative costs of arm's-length transactions versus those of internal coordination that were present in the 1910s and early 1920s.

According to Herbert Simon, authority relationships within the firm tend to facilitate such coordination.[108] Such relationships can respond to contingencies at less

---

[102]  Chandler and Salsbury, op. cit., p. 495.

[103]  Pound, op. cit. (note 31), p. 196; O'Brien, op. cit. (note 95).

[104]  See Thomas H. Johnson, "Management Accounting in an Early Multidivisional Organization: General Motors in the 1920s," *Bus. Hist. Rev.* 52 (1978), p. 490, and the extensive references therein.

[105]  Norton, op. cit. (note 95).

[106]  Sloan, op. cit. (note 31), p. 161.

[107]  Paul Milgrom and John Roberts, op. cit. (note 19), pp. 91, 556, discuss resource allocation problems with design attributes and with innovation attributes. They suggest that these types of resource allocation problems favor centralized coordination.

[108]  Herbert A. Simon, *Administrative Behavior* (1945), p. 139.

cost than external contracting by facilitating informal communication and flexibility. This difference may have been increased by a number of factors existing during that period that favored communication within the firm over market transactions. The state of the telecommunications technology made distant transmission of information across independent organizations very costly in comparison with reliance on internal managers.[109] Billing and invoicing were done manually and hence were expensive, labor-intensive operations. As a result, more data transmission and record keeping were necessary for interfirm transactions than for internal communication. Because air travel was still at the experimental stage and the interstate highway system had not yet been built, physical movement of personnel and merchandise was very costly, which suggests that reliance on delegated authority was more efficient than arm's-length transactions. In 1923, GM initiated the practice of frequent model changes.[110] New designs and modifications to existing models required further exchange of information with parts manufacturers.

Complete integration of the two companies after 1926 allowed for operating economies and more comprehensive sharing of common resources, especially managerial talent and financial assets, since GM's divisions shared financial, marketing, and administrative resources. Eva Flügge mentions that the organizational reforms instituted by Sloan called for greater integration, as the cost of adding one extra enterprise to the system was small (supposedly, because autonomous management was preserved) compared to the savings derived from using central organization to coordinate activities since duplication in administrative departments was reduced.[111] After the 60 percent acquisition in 1919, GM and Fisher Body shared financial, marketing, and administrative resources. The 1926 GM annual report anticipates that "[o]perating economies of important consequence will be developed through the ability to do those things which result in the lowest possible cost, many of which were impossible with the institutions operated separately."[112]

## Personnel coordination

General Motors was intent on having access to the executive talents of the Fisher brothers. Their experience in auto body manufacturing and their reputation for body styling were important features for GM. Sloan identifies the value of the Fishers as a motivating factor in the acquisition: "[T]he four Fisher brothers, who developed the Fisher body, were men of high level and competence in the manufacture and in the engineering of that type. They were particularly outstanding in the fact that they had the highest regard for quality."[113]

In the 1910s and 1920s, a number of factors favored the development of internal

---

[109] For example, in 1919 the Bell System announced plans for the introduction of machine switching (dial telephones) in its exchanges.

[110] Sloan, op. cit. (note 31), ch. 13.

[111] Eva Flügge, "Possibilities and Problems of Integration in the Automobile Industry," *Pol. Econ.* 37 (1929), p. 150.

[112] General Motors Corporation, *Annual Report* (1926), p. 10.

[113] Deposition of Alfred P. Sloan, Jr. (April 28, 1952), *Du Pont*, 126 F. Supp. 235, p. 189.

labor markets over external labor markets for managers. The high time costs of travel and underdeveloped communications already mentioned raised labor search costs. Specialized business education was relatively new (the Harvard Business School was founded in 1908). Writing in 1921, Frank H. Knight argued that "to find men capable of managing business efficiently and secure to them the positions of responsible control is perhaps the most important single problem of economic organization on the efficiency side."[114]

The problem of identifying talented managers was especially acute for GM. In 1923, Sloan implemented a number of important organizational reforms. General Motors introduced the multidivisional organizational form, with semiautonomous product-based divisions coordinated from a central office (the executive and finance committees). General Motors faced a shortage of individuals able to manage within this new organizational form. By 1923, the Fisher brothers had a great deal of valuable experience in the industry: Fred and Charles had 15 years, Lawrence had 11 years, Edward and Alfred had 10 years, and William had 8 years. They had distinguished themselves as outstanding managers knowledgeable in automobile markets and auto manufacturing technology. Also, they had worked closely with GM practically since its inception in 1908 and were familiar with GM's organization.

In October of 1924, Lawrence and Charles Fisher entered the GM executive committee, and Fred (who had been in the executive committee since 1922) was appointed to the finance committee. Together with Sloan and du Pont, Fred Fisher was one of only three men in both the executive and the finance committees; together with Sloan and Brown, he was one of only three men in both the executive and the operations committees.[115] In 1925 Lawrence was named general manager at Cadillac.[116]

Integration was the natural way to convince the Fishers to dedicate all of their time to GM. The brothers had been thoroughly devoted to the company they had founded 18 years before, and it would had been difficult to convince them to abandon its management in favor of GM without combining the two companies. The 1926 annual report mentions the importance of bringing the Fishers into closer relationship with GM:

> Many benefits will accrue through the consolidation of the two properties . . . Of even greater importance, is the bringing into the General Motors operating organization in closer relationship, the Fisher brothers, through whose constructive ability, foresight and energy the institution bearing their name has been built up to the dominating position it now holds.[117]

---

[114] Frank H. Knight, *Risk, Uncertainty and Profit* (1921).

[115] Chandler and Salsbury, op. cit., p. 577.

[116] Sloan further observes that the Fishers "were very capable people and we [General Motors] needed men of talent, and they had distinguished themselves in developing a very fine enterprise, and Fisher bodies were recognized as outstanding in quality, and we needed that kind of talent in General Motors at that time, and needed it badly, and I was very anxious to have them come in and help us in the broader problems of General Motors, feeling satisfied that our interest in Fisher Body would be properly taken care of by the remaining three brothers." Testimony of Alfred P. Sloan, Jr. (March 17, 1953), *Du Pont*, 126 F. Supp. 235, p. 2909.

[117] General Motors Corporation, op. cit., p. 10.

Following the 1926 merger, the Fishers were placed in various key managerial posts. Charles and Lawrence were appointed to the works managers committee and the sales committee, respectively. Fred entered the finance and the operations committees and continued in the executive committee. Together with Sloan, Fred Fisher was one of only two men belonging simultaneously to the three committees. William headed the Body Group that included the Fisher Plants plus accessory divisions. Last, Alfred represented the Body Group on the general technical committee and eventually rose to vice-president in charge of engineering.[118]

## IV   EVALUATION OF THE MARKET POWER MOTIVE

In *United States v. E. I. Du Pont*, the government questioned the purchase by Du Pont of a 23 percent stock interest in GM in the period 1917–19 based on Section 7 of the Clayton Act.[119] The government alleged, among other things, that GM's purchase of Fisher Body was intended to favor Du Pont and to foreclose other suppliers of Fisher Body.

The case was the first application of Section 7 to vertical integration. In a 1957 Supreme Court decision on appeal, Justice Brennan found that Fisher Body was acquired by GM because it resisted sales pressure from Du Pont to purchase products such as paints and fabrics. This conclusion appears to contradict the evidence in the case. Incredibly, Brennan maintains that the Fisher brothers continued to face such pressures and to hold out against it until 1947 or 1948, even after their company had been acquired and integrated into GM. Justice Burton, joined by Justice Frankfurter dissenting, points out that "the record affirmatively shows that the new products which Du Pont has sold to General Motors since 1926 have made their way, at General Motors as elsewhere, on their merits."[120]

A review of the case suggests that the Supreme Court decision has little basis in fact and no foundation in economic analysis.[121] The accusation that GM vertically integrated with Fisher Body to foreclose suppliers other than Du Pont is not justified either by the events of the period or by any economic motivation. Such an accusation forced Du Pont, GM, and Sloan to justify GM's acquisition of Fisher Body. As a consequence, it is not surprising that contractual difficulties might be mentioned among other explanations for a merger that took place over 30 years before.

Since the 1926 merger was vertical, it did not increase GM's market share in automobiles and thus could not be interpreted as an attempt to increase market power. In addition, double marginalization was not an issue in 1919 since the com-

---

[118]   Chandler and Salsbury, op. cit., p. 577; Pound, op. cit., p. 293.

[119]   *United States v. E. I. Du Pont de Nemours & Co., General Motors,* et al., 126 F. Supp. 235 (N. D. Ill. 1954); 353 U.S. 586 (1957); 366 U.S. 316 (1961). The 1957 decision was on appeal, and the 1961 decision was concerned with remedies related to the prior case.

[120]   353 U.S., p. 645.

[121]   As Roger D. Blair and David L. Kaserman, *Antitrust Economics* (1985), p. 327, point out, the "Supreme Court Decision did not rest on the empirical market facts as they existed during the 1917–19 period when Du Pont was in the process of acquiring the General Motors stock. Instead, it was based upon the market facts at the time of the suit, which was some 30 years later."

panies continued to transact on the basis of a cost-plus contract after the acquisition. Double marginalization did not trigger the 1926 buyout either, since from 1924 on the 17.6 percent markup over cost was eliminated and Fisher Body's profit was calculated by the same method used to compute that of any other GM operating division. The Fishers may have been concerned temporarily about the high prices charged by automobile manufacturers for closed cars since they thought it reduced the quantity demanded, thus lowering potential gains from scale economies. They considered entering automobile production but eventually chose not to as competition for closed-type cars intensified and prices fell.[122]

## V  CONCLUSION

Economic considerations and historical evidence suggest that enhancing coordination, rather than avoiding opportunism, stands out as the main reason for GM's merger with Fisher Body. Our analysis shows that asset specificity and contractual holdup do not adequately explain GM's vertical integration into automobile bodies. General Motors's purchase of a 60 percent controlling interest in Fisher Body in 1919 and vertical integration in 1926 were primarily motivated by the need to assure reliable supplies of the latter's auto bodies, which conferred unique competitive advantages. The acquisition and merger were consistent with GM's vertical integration into many types of automobile components manufacturing. By making Fisher one of its divisions in 1926, GM included the company in its system of interdivisional coordination of inventories, production, and purchasing.

The expansion of the automobile industry and the increased intensity of competition created a need for enhanced vertical coordination. As automobile buyers were becoming more sophisticated, GM began offering a larger number of models, as illustrated by its slogan "One car for every purse and purpose." This strategy required extensive exchange of information between the assembling plants and Fisher Body. The greater complexity of automobile production technology that accompanied the higher scale of operations increased the need for information transfer between the two companies. Interruptions in the regular flow of automobile bodies would have halted the entire automobile assembly line and the delivery of cars to dealers. General Motors' preference for vertical integration into components manufacturing over market procurement of parts reflected both the costs of carrying out market transactions and the difficulties in travel and communication that existed in the early part of the twentieth century. Vertical integration permitted GM to realize cost economies from coordinating production decisions and sharing resources.

The implementation of the new organizational reforms introduced by Sloan

---

[122] Pound, op. cit., p. 290. In 1913 Studebaker and Cartercar were selling closed "sedans" for about $2,000. In 1915 Ford introduced a closed version of the Model T that was sold for $975, but sales were very low for the first three years of production. In the late 1910s, Hudson, Overland, and other producers offered medium-priced closed cars. See White, op. cit. (note 7), p. 53. In 1921 the Hudson Motor Company sold a closed version of the Essex model at a price only $300 above the Essex touring car. Chandler and Salsbury, op. cit. (note 11), p. 575.

required managers capable of coordinating complex operations, making decisions in a decentralized organization, and using common resources effectively. Because there was a limited outside market for executives with these skills and since the Fishers had worked closely with GM, they were perhaps the best-qualified candidates for the posts Sloan had to fill. In addition, the Fishers brought crucial operational and manufacturing experience. By integrating Fisher Body into GM, Sloan was able to attract the Fisher brothers as managers and corporate directors.

General Motors's contractual relationship with Fisher Body prior to the final merger exhibited trust and cooperation rather than opportunism. Aoki sees some types of purchasing contracts as facilitating cooperation with suppliers along J-Firm lines.[123] The possibility that contracts enhance cooperation has important contemporary implications because GM is engaged in changing the vertically integrated structure that it originally established. General Motors' merger with Fisher reflected economic conditions in the early part of the century rather than immutable contractual holdup and market failure. Given technological changes in communications, data processing, and manufacturing, developments in the market for managers and skilled labor, and advances in the field of management strategy, the original motivations for GM's organization structure no longer apply. Jack Smith, GM's chairman, told *The Economist* in 1998, "As the world opened up to free trade, Sloan's system was not competitive."[124] Indeed, in 1999 GM spun off parts-manufacturing unit Delphi Automotive Systems Corporation to create the world's largest auto parts supplier with over 200,000 employees. Advising companies to consolidate asset ownership to avoid contractual opportunism on the basis of the fable of Fisher Body would not be well founded.

# REFERENCES

Aghion, Philippe, Dewatripont, Mathias, and Rey, Patrick, "Renegotiation Design with Unverifiable Information," *Econometrica* 62 (1994), pp. 257–82.

Aoki, Masahiko, "Horizontal vs. Vertical Information Structure of the Firm," *American Economic Review* 76 (1986), pp. 971–83.

Aoki, Masahiko, "Toward an Economic Model of the Japanese Firm," *Journal of Economic Literature* 28 (1990), pp. 1–27.

Arrow, Kenneth J., "Vertical Integration and Communication," *Bell Journal of Economics* 6, no. 1 (1975), pp. 173–83.

Berle, Adolf A., and Means, Gardiner C., *The Modern Corporation and Private Property* (New York: Harcourt, Brace & World, 1968).

Besanko, David, Dranove, David, and Shanley, Mark, *The Economics of Strategy* (New York: John Wiley, 1996).

Blair, Roger D., and Kaserman, David L., *Antitrust Economics* (Homewood, Ill.: Irwin, 1985).

Bolton, Patrick, and Scharfstein, David S., "Corporate Finance, the Theory of the Firm, and Organizations," *Journal of Economic Perspectives* 12, no. 4 (1998), pp. 95–114.

Brickley, James A., Smith, Clifford W., and Zimmerman, Jerold L., *Managerial Economics and Organizational Architecture* (Homewood, Ill.: Irwin, 1997).

---

[123]  Aoki, op. cit. (note 32).
[124]  Jack Smith, "The Decline and Fall of General Motors," *The Economist*, October 10, 1998, p. 63.

Buckley, Peter J., and Chapman, Malcolm, "The Perception and Measurement of Transaction Costs," *Cambridge Journal of Economics* 21 (1997), pp. 127–45.

Carlton, Dennis W., "Vertical Integration in Competitive Markets under Uncertainty," *Journal of Industrial Economics* 27, no. 3 (1979), pp. 189–209.

Chandler, Alfred D., *Strategy and Structure* (Cambridge, Mass.: MIT Press, 1962).

Chandler, Alfred D., *The Visible Hand* (Cambridge, Mass.: Harvard University Press, 1977).

Chandler, Alfred D., and Salsbury, Stephen, *Pierre S. du Pont and the Making of the Modern Corporation* (New York: Harper & Row, 1971).

Che, Yeon-Koo, and Hausch, Donald B., "Cooperative Investments and the Value of Contracting," *American Economic Review* 89 (1999), pp. 125–47.

Cheung, Steven N., "The Fable of the Bees: An Economic Investigation," *Journal of Law and Economics* 16 (1973), pp. 11–33.

Chung, Tai-Yeong, "Incomplete Contracts, Specific Investments, and Risk Sharing," *Review of Economic Studies* 58 (1991), pp. 1031–42.

Church, Jeffrey, and Ware, Roger, *Industrial Organization: A Strategic Approach* (Homewood, Ill.: Irwin/McGraw-Hill, 1999).

Coase, R. H., "The Nature of the Firm," *Economica* n.s. 4 (1937), pp. 386–405.

Coase, R. H., "The Lighthouse in Economics," *Journal of Law and Economics* 17 (1974), pp. 357–76.

Coase, R. H., "The Nature of the Firm: Origin, Meaning, Influence," *Journal of Law, Economics, and Organization* 4 (1988), pp. 3–47.

Cushing, Harry A., *Voting Trusts* (New York: Macmillan, 1915).

Cushing, Harry A., *Voting Trusts*, rev. edn (New York: Macmillan, 1927).

Dassbach, Carl H. A., *Global Enterprises and the World Economy: Ford, General Motors, and IBM: The Emergence of the Transnational Enterprise* (New York: Garland, 1988).

Dewatripont, Mathias, "Commitment through Renegotiation-Proof Contracts with Third Parties," *Review of Economic Studies* 55 (1988), pp. 377–89.

Dewing, Arthur Stone, *The Financial Policy of Corporations*, vol. 3: *The Administration of Income* (New York: Ronald Press, 1921).

Edlin, Aaron S., and Reichelstein, Stefan, "Holdups, Standard Breach Remedies, and Optimal Investment," *American Economic Review* 86 (1996), pp. 478–501.

Edmonds, C. C., "Tendencies in the Automobile Industry," *American Economic Review* 13 (1923), pp. 422–41.

Epstein, Ralph C., *The Automobile Industry: Its Economic and Commercial Development* (Chicago and New York: A. W. Shaw, 1928).

Fleming, Al, "Body by Fisher," *Automotive News* ("GM 75th Anniversary Issue"), September 16, 1983, pp. 143–51.

Flügge, Eva, "Possibilities and Problems of Integration in the Automobile Industry," *Journal of Political Economy* 37 (1929), pp. 150–74.

Frank, Lawrence K., "The Significance of Industrial Integration," *Journal of Political Economy* 33 (1925), pp. 179–95.

General Motors Corporation, *Annual Report* (Detroit: General Motors Corporation, 1919, 1920, 1921, and 1926).

General Motors Corporation, *Fisher Body: Its Contribution to the Automotive Industry* (Detroit: General Motors Corporation, 1924).

Grossman, Sanford J., and Hart, Oliver, D., "The Costs and Benefits of Ownership: A Theory of Vertical and Lateral Integration," *Journal of Political Economy* 94 (1986), pp. 691–719.

Grout, Paul A., "Investment and Wages in the Absence of Binding Contracts: A Nash Bargaining Approach," *Econometrica* 52 (1984), pp. 449–60.

Hart, Oliver, *Firms, Contracts, and Financial Structure* (Oxford: Clarendon Press, 1995).

Hart, Oliver D., and Moore, John, "Property Rights and the Nature of the Firm," *Journal of Political Economy* 98 (1990), pp. 1119–58.

Helper, Susan, MacDuffie, John Paul, and Sabel, Charles, "The Boundaries of the Firm as a Design Problem." Unpublished manuscript (New York: Columbia Law School, 1997).

Holmström, Bengt, and Roberts, John, "The Boundaries of the Firm Revisited," *Journal of Economic Perspectives* 12, no. 4 (1998), pp. 73–94.

Johnson, H. Thomas, "Management Accounting in an Early Multidivisional Organization: General Motors in the 1920s," *Business History Review* 52, no. 4 (1978), pp. 490–517.

Kimes, Beverly Rae, and Clark, Henry Austin, Jr., *Standard Catalog of American Cars, 1805–1942*, 3d edn (Iola, Wis.: Krause, 1996).

Klein, Benjamin, "Vertical Integration as Organizational Ownership: The Fisher Body–General Motors Relationship Revisited," *Journal of Law, Economics, and Organization* 4 (1988), pp. 199–213.

Klein, Benjamin, Crawford, Robert G., and Alchian, Armen A., "Vertical Integration, Appropriable Rents, and the Competitive Contracting Process," *Journal of Law and Economics* 21 (1978), pp. 297–326.

Knight, Frank, *Risk, Uncertainty and Profit* (Boston, Mass. and New York: Houghton Mifflin, 1921).

Kuhn, Arthur J., *GM Passes Ford, 1918–1938: Designing the General Motors Performance-Control System* (University Park, Pa.: Pennsylvania State University Press, 1986).

Lamm, Michael, and Holls, Dave, *A Century of Automotive Style: 100 Years of American Car Design* (Stockton, Calif.: Lamm-Morada Publishing, 1996).

Langlois, Richard N., and Robertson, Paul L., "Explaining Vertical Integration: Lessons from the American Automobile Industry," *Journal of Economic History* 49 (1989), pp. 361–75.

Liebowitz, S. J., and Margolis, Stephen E., "The Fable of the Keys," *Journal of Law and Economics* 33 (1990), pp. 1–25.

Ludvigsen, Karl, "A Century of Automobile Body Evolution," *Automotive Engineering* 103 (1995), pp. 51–9.

Marx, Thomas G., and Peterson, Laura B., "Asset Specificity, Opportunism and the Vertical Integration of Body and Frame Production in the Automobile Industry," Unpublished manuscript (Detroit, Mich.: General Motors Corporation, 1993).

Milgrom, Paul R., and Roberts, John, *Economics, Organization and Management* (Englewood Cliffs, N.J.: Prentice Hall, 1992).

Monteverde, Kirk, and Teece, David J., "Appropriable Rents and Quasi-Vertical Integration," *Journal of Law and Economics* 25 (1982), pp. 321–8.

Nöldeke, Georg, and Schmidt, Klaus M., "Option Contracts and Renegotiation: A Solution to the Hold-Up Problem," *Rand Journal of Economics* 26 (1995), pp. 163–79.

Norton, Seth W., "Information and Competitive Advantage: The Rise of General Motors," *Journal of Law and Economics* 40 (1997), pp. 245–60.

O'Brien, Anthony Patrick, "The Importance of Adjusting Production to Sales in the Early Automobile Industry," *Explorations in Economic History* 34 (1997), pp. 195–219.

Oster, Sharon M., *Modern Competitive Analysis* (New York: Oxford University Press, 1994).

Pound, Arthur, *The Turning Wheel: The Story of General Motors through Twenty-Five Years. 1908–1933* (Garden City, N.Y.: Doubleday, Doran, 1934).

Raskob, J. J., Letter to William C. Durant. September 4, 1919 (Kettering/GMI Alumni Foundation Collection of Industrial History, Flint, Mich.)

Rogerson, William P., "Contractual Solutions to the Hold-Up Problem," *Review of Economic Studies* 59 (1992), pp. 777–94.

Salanié, Bernard, *The Economics of Contracts: A Primer* (Cambridge, Mass.: MIT Press, 1997).

Seltzer, Lawrence H., *A Financial History of the American Automobile Industry: A Study of the*

*Ways in Which the Leading American Producers of Automobiles Have Met their Capital Requirements* (Boston, Mass. and New York: Houghton Mifflin, 1928).

Simon, Herbert A., *Administrative Behavior* (New York: Free Press, 1945).

Sloan, Alfred P., Jr., *My Years with General Motors* (Garden City, N.Y.: Doubleday, 1963).

Tirole, Jean, *The Theory of Industrial Organization* (Cambridge, Mass.: MIT Press, 1988).

*United States v. E. I. Du Pont de Nemours & Co., General Motors*, et al., Civil Action 49C-1071, 126 F. Supp. 235 (N.D. Ill. 1954); 353 U.S. 586 (1957); 366 U.S. 316 (1961).

White, Roger B., "Fisher Body Corporation," in *The Automobile Industry, 1896–1920*, pp. 187–92. Encyclopedia of American Business History and Biography (New York: Facts on File, 1990).

White, Roger B., "Body by Fisher: The Closed Car Revolution," *Automobile Quarterly* 29, no. 4 (1991), pp. 46–63.

Williamson, Oliver E., "Transaction Cost Economics: The Governance of Contractual Relations," *Journal of Law and Economics* 22 (1979), pp. 233–61.

Williamson, Oliver E., *The Economic Institutions of Capitalism* (Englewood Cliffs, N.J.: Prentice-Hall, 1985).

# 9
# Sharecropping
*Steven N. S. Cheung*

[. . .] Since under sharecropping a portion of every output unit produced is taken as rent, it yields the impression of being similar to an *ad valorem* excise tax – where part of every unit produced is "taxed" by the landowner (government). The distribution of output is not the same, it is believed, as with fixed rent or owner cultivation – where the tiller obtains the *entire* incremental product. Share tenancy, therefore, is said to result in less intensive (and less efficient) farming because the tenant's incentive to work or invest in land is reduced.[1]

It is not difficult to show that the application of the analysis of a tax to share tenancy (hereafter called the "tax-equivalent" approach) is erroneous. The hypotheses stemming therefrom fail on several counts. In the tax-equivalent approach, the writers generally fail to realize that the percentage shares and area rented under share tenancy are not mysteriously "fixed" but are competitively determined in the market. Furthermore, these writers fail to specify the nature of the system of land ownership upon which their hypotheses are constructed. Let me clarify.

First, though some classical economists discussed the division of land, they did not analyze it in a general equilibrium framework (see section A of this chapter). Since Marshall, the possibility of the landlord's allocating his total holdings to *several* tenants has been ignored (see section B of this chapter). While this is valid in analyzing an excise tax, under share tenancy the cost of land and the distribution of land are thereby neglected. Second, the percentage share has usually been taken as given. Under share tenancy, however, the rental percentage is a discretionary variable. Third, with a tax, the government is not contracting to maximize wealth. In other words, the tax-equivalent analysis fails to offer any explicit treatment of the terms in a share contract which the participating parties must *mutually* agree to abide by when the contract is formed.

We cannot analyze the way a person uses resources without first specifying the nature of his property rights. It is true that once the land size and the rental percentage are under contract to a tenant he prefers to work or invest less in land than

---

[1] It is interesting that oriental writers generally share the same view. [. . .]

if he cultivates his own land. But under private ownership of land, the landlord's incentive to maximize his wealth is not reduced. [. . .] It does not matter whether the landowner stipulates that the tenant is to invest more in land and charges a lower rental percentage or whether the landowner invests in land himself and charges the tenant a higher rental percentage: the investment will be made if it leads to a higher rental annuity.

Yet, it would be misleading to say that all earlier analysts of sharecropping were deceived by the tax-equivalent approach and invariably arrived at the conclusion of inefficient resource use. Some did so, some expressed doubt, and some seem to have abandoned the tax approach altogether. Indeed, a survey of the literature on the subject reveals that at times even their errors are most interesting and their insights are sometimes most profound.[2]

## THE CLASSICAL VIEW

Noting that sharecroppers "have been so long in disuse in England that at present I know no English name for them," Adam Smith wrote of the *metayers* (sharecroppers) in France, which he believed were successors of "the slave cultivators of ancient times."[3] Of the productive nature of the metayage system, Smith wrote:

> It could never, however, be the interest [of the metayers] to lay out, in the further improvement of the land, any part of the little stock which they might have saved from their own share of the produce, because the lord, who laid out nothing, was to get one-half of whatever it produced. The tithe, which is but a tenth of the produce, is found to be a very great hindrance to improvement. A tax, therefore, which amounted to one-half, must have been an effectual bar to it.[4]

Although the analogy to a tax which Smith drew might have led succeeding writers astray, the context in which he placed the discussion of the metayers is also significant. Smith did not focus on the metayage system itself: rather, in one full chapter he attempted to trace the development of land tenure arrangements with economic interpretations.[5]

According to Smith's view, the "slave" cultivators preceding the metayers were even less productive, because "a person who can acquire no property, can have no other interest but to eat as much, and to labor as little as possible."[6] Thus for more productive land use the metayers succeeded the "slaves." Since in his view the

---

[2] When the first draft of this study was written, I was unaware that share tenancy had been frequently analyzed. A subsequent survey of the literature convinced me that tracing the development of economic thinking on the subject would be worthwhile. The following section on the classical view is an expansion of a summary by D. Gale Johnson. See his "Resource Allocation under Share Contracts," *Journal of Political Economy* (April, 1950), pp. 112–14.

[3] Adam Smith, *Wealth of Nations* (1776, New York: Modern Library edition, 1937), p. 366.

[4] Ibid., p. 367.

[5] Ibid., book 3, ch. 2.

[6] Ibid., p. 365.

metayage system was also defective, Smith claimed that "by very slow degrees," the metayers were succeeded by "farmers . . . who cultivated the land with their own stock, paying a rent certain to the landlord."[7] Although Smith favored fixed-rent contracts (farmers) over sharecropping, he was nonetheless concerned with the "insecurity" of the farmers because of expiration of the lease: "The possession even of such farmers, however, was long extremely precarious, and still is so in many parts of Europe."[8] He advocated "the law which secures the longest leases against successors of every kind," but such a law was, to his knowledge, "peculiar to Great Britain."[9] In Smith's view, therefore, the British leasing arrangement – a freehold with a fixed rent and a lease for life – was more highly developed than those in other parts of Europe.[10]

Although the meaning of economic efficiency was not clarified until much later, Smith's idea of analyzing the development of land tenure systems on grounds of more gainful resource use is certainly an important one: however, the approach he used is not deep enough to yield fruitful results. Once property laws define a specific set of constraints on competition, there may exist several forms of contractual arrangements which imply the same resource use. [. . .] When these property laws are altered, the contractual arrangements may change. It follows that the appropriate approach in analyzing land tenure development is to trace the alterations in property laws: and not, as Smith did, to interpret (or advocate) the change in laws by tracing what might appear to be defective leasing arrangements.

Thus, Smith is in error. While his claim that "slave" cultivation is grossly wasteful may or may not be true, his view that, historically, for economic reasons sharecroppers have been gradually replaced by fixed-rent farmers, is wrong. One need only point out that share tenancy has not been replaced by fixed rent, and that in the United States similar share contracts predominate among leases of retail stores, beauty salons, gasoline stations, amusement park rentals, and even the much regulated oil and fishery industries. Indeed, the rarity of sharecropping in England as observed by Smith and later by Mill and Marshall might very well be the result of the freehold, under which a lease for life was enforced by law. Under a perpetual lease, the cost of enforcing a share contract may be so high as to make it undesirable, since tenancy dismissal is one effective device to insure against poor performance by sharecroppers.

It is, of course, difficult to evaluate Smith's influence over later writers on share tenancy. The tax-equivalent argument aside, what appears to have permeated the minds of subsequent English writers is the conviction that the British (fixed rent) system was more advanced and efficient than rental arrangements elsewhere. This conviction was reinforced by the famous *Travels* of Arthur Young.

Young was the secretary to the Honorable Board of Agriculture and Fellow of the

[7] Ibid., p. 368. As D. Gale Johnson points out: "Not only did Smith object to share renting, but he proposed that taxes be used to induce landlords to use other leasing arrangement." See Johnson, "Resource Allocation," p. 112: Smith, *Wealth of Nations*, pp. 779–88, esp. p. 783.

[8] Smith, *Wealth of Nations*, p. 368.

[9] Ibid., p. 369.

[10] Ibid., pp. 368–72.

Royal Society. Esteemed as an agricultural expert in England, he condemned the metayers almost every time they were mentioned in his *Travels in France during the Years 1787, 1788, and 1789*.[11] Of the metayage system, Young wrote:

> There is not one word to be said in favor of the practice, and a thousand arguments that might be used against it . . . In this most miserable of all the modes of letting land, the defrauded landlord receives a contemptible rent: the farmer is in the lowest state of poverty: the land is miserably cultivated: and the nation suffers as severely as the parties themselves . . . Wherever this system prevails, it may be taken for granted that a useless and miserable population is found.[12]

One hundred years later in 1892, however, a very different edition of *Young's Travels* appeared. The editor, Miss Betham-Edwards, author and officer of public information of France, took liberty to delete most of Young's condemnations of the metayers.[13] And to the only remaining statement that I could find – in which Young claimed that the metayage system "perpetuates poverty and excludes instruction" – Betham-Edwards added a footnote: "Complex as such an arrangement may appear at first sight, metayage must be counted as a factor of great importance in the agricultural prosperity of France."[14]

Betham-Edwards is not the only editor who challenged Young's judgment. Constantia Maxwell, who edited the *Travels* in 1929, made numerous corrections on Young's views in the lengthy "Editor's Notes."[15] Maxwell pointed out, with the support of many sources, that at Young's time in France there were government regulations on vine growing, heavy taxes, the aftermath of the wars of Louis XIV, and various political disturbances on the eve of the French Revolution. Certainly, Young was not ignorant of all this, and – even if we accept his view that French agriculture was "miserable" – it is difficult to understand why he blamed the metayers as the sole source of trouble.[16]

Young's condemnation of metayage notwithstanding, we find in his work one piece of evidence which seemingly is consistent with inefficient land use under

---

[11] Young's *Travels* was first published in 1792, and it has since gone through a number of editions. I have at hand a Dublin reprint dated 1793, vol. 2; an abridged version edited by Constantia Maxwell (Cambridge: Cambridge University Press, 1929); and Miss Betham-Edwards (ed.), *Arthur Young's Travels in France during the Years 1787, 1788, 1789* (London: George Bell and Sons, 1892).

[12] Young, *Travels*, Dublin edition, pp. 241–2. Young offered little analysis to support his claims, and one doubts his impartiality when he stated: "The *metayers* were so miserably poor, it was impossible for them to cultivate well. I started some observations on the modes which ought to be pursued: but all conversation of that sort is time lost in France" (Maxwell edition, pp. 202–3).

[13] Young, *Travels*, Betham-Edwards edition.

[14] Ibid., p. 18.

[15] Young, *Travels*, Maxwell edition, pp. 361–404.

[16] When Betham-Edwards wrote in her introduction to Young's *Travels* (p. vi) that "nothing has done more [than metayage] to improve the condition of the peasant and of husbandry within the last fifty years," she was not speaking of French agriculture at Young's time. Thus, Maxwell's editing method appears more appropriate. Maxwell's opinion on metayage is worth noting:

> It was not perhaps so much a cause of poverty however as a result, and that it was a system that worked rather better in practice than in theory is shown by the fact that it survived the Revolution, and is still a recognized form of land-holding . . . Even before the Revolution there were many French landlords who lived on excellent terms with their metayers, visiting them in their holdings and discussing agricultural matters with them. (Maxwell edition, p. xxx)

sharecropping: namely the low rent of land in France as compared with England.[17] According to the tax approach, nonland inputs committed to land under share rent are less than under fixed rent, and thus given the same area of land the rental payment to the landlord will be lower. According to standard economic theory, *ceteris paribus*, rent will be lower if (*a*) the land is less fertile (which Young discussed ambiguously), or (*b*) the cost of tenant inputs (or the wage rate) is higher (which Young would deny since the metayers were "miserably poor"). But other things were, in fact, not equal. In addition to the political instability and regulations on farming at that time, which might well have discouraged investment in land and thus led to lower rents, a more significant factor, perhaps, is the reportedly heavy taxes *imposed on the metayers*.[18] Given the metayers' alternative earnings, however trivial, a higher tax imposed on the occupation will require that the landowners charge a lower rental percentage in order to keep the metayers at work. And this implies a lower rent per acre of land.

Whereas Young might have allowed his emotion to run away with his judgment, some of his observations could have hinted to later writers that fixed and share rents yield the same intensity of nonland inputs should the constraints of competition be equal. In particular, Young observed that the share percentages varied from place to place, and that the division of farm size was related to population pressure.[19] Yet to my knowledge the only subsequent economists who elaborated further on the division of farms under share tenancy are Richard Jones and John Stuart Mill.

Writing in 1831, Jones duplicated not only Smith's thesis of the development of leasing arrangements, but also Smith's conclusions.[20] Jones, however, elaborated on the adjustment of labor input through land size divisions. With more information at hand, and acknowledging Young's observations, Jones wrote:

> While the metayer tenant pays nominally the same [rental percentage], his own share of the produce may be diminished in two modes: by his being subjected to a greater quantity of the public burthens: or by the size of his metairie being reduced. By this second mode of reduction, I am not aware that the French metayer suffered much.[21]

And he continued further when he came to the metayers in Italy:

> Metayers are always found ready to accept a subdivision [of land] . . . Their multiplication, as we have seen in the case of France, usually goes on till they are stopped by the smallness of their maintenance, or, as more often happens, by the policy of the

---

[17] See Young, *Travels*, Dublin edition, p. 239.

[18] Young's account of taxes is best seen in a chapter on the Revolution (*Travels*, Maxwell edition, pp. 327–60). On p. xxvi, Maxwell noted: "According to recent estimates 36 percent of the peasant's income disappeared in direct taxes to the State: 14 percent went on tithes payable to the Church; while 11 or 12 percent was consumed by seigneurial dues at Young's time."

[19] See ibid., pp. 296–7.

[20] Richard Jones, *An Essay on the Distribution of Wealth and on the Sources of Taxation*, part 1: *Rent* (London: John Murray, 1831). To my knowledge, no Part 2 was ever issued. That Jones shared Smith's view of landlease development is evident throughout the entire volume, and esp. on pp. 73–5.

[21] Ibid., p. 91.

proprietors refusing to subdivide lands, already supplied with labor beyond the point they deem most advantageous to themselves.[22]

Following this track one expects that Jones would go on to say that, at least in some cases, nonland inputs relative to land inputs were equally intensive (or output yields equally high) under metayage as under fixed-rent farming or owner cultivation. But he did not, and instead he concluded:

> If the relation between the metayer and the proprietor has some advantages when compared with ... the serf ... it has some very serious inconveniences peculiar to itself. The divided interest which exists in the produce of cultivation, mars almost every attempt at improvement.[23]

It is difficult to say whether Jones's conclusion contradicts his earlier statements. By improvement or what they called "stock" in the land, classical economists seem to mean "investment" in land, but exactly what they did mean is not clear. According to our convention, investment is the balancing of consumption over time: that is, present sacrifice for future benefit. A man is investing when he tills the soil today for corn tomorrow, pulls a weed, or removes a rock. The various time lengths of the investment returns are treated in a general framework. And it is conceptually the same whether the work is done by a man or a horse, or through the use of more fertilizers, better irrigation, or other assets. It is only within the framework of a timeless input–output model that we do not speak of investment. Under our convention, therefore, to say both that the intensity of labor input (which can be used to improve land) can be freely adjusted and also that "the divided interest mars almost every attempt at improvement" is contradictory indeed.

But to Jones and his contemporaries, and even to Mill and others after him, the concept of "improvement" or "investment" was ambiguous on two counts. First, they failed to distinguish farming inputs at *one moment* in time from investment *over time*. Thus it is not always clear whether they laid the blame on the product sharing or on the nonperpetual lease. Second, instead of viewing labor and nonlabor inputs as different physical entities performing different functions in production, they viewed them as different conceptually. To them, "labor" is "short" and nonlabor is "long," and "improvements" were made only by "capital" and not by "labor."

Even accepting their convention in vague terms, however, Jones might have seen that since "labor" could be adjusted so could "capital," or that "labor" could be traded for "capital." But Jones did not. Indeed, one cannot help but speculate that his abrupt conclusion was drawn not from logical reasoning, but from the preconception that the British system was superior. And it is a matter of conjecture whether Jones would have altered his conclusion had he considered the accounts on the Italian metayers written by Simonde de Sismondi some fifteen years earlier. Sismondi was himself a metayer landlord, and, of course, he wrote favorably of the system:

---

[22] Ibid., pp. 98–9.
[23] Ibid., p. 102.

> The system of cultivation by *metavers* . . . contributes, more than anything else, to diffuse happiness among the lower classes, to raise land to a high state of culture, and accumulate a great quantity of wealth upon it . . . Under this system, the peasant has an interest in the property, as if it were his own . . . The accumulation of an immense capital upon the soil, the invention of many judicious rotations, and industrious processes . . . the collection of a numerous population, upon a space very limited and naturally barren, shows plainly enough that this mode of cultivation is as profitable to the land itself as to the peasant.[24]

This exuberant endorsement of metayage is quite contradictory to Young's condemnations. But it was not until John Stuart Mill tackled the issue that arguments were taken from both sides.[25]

With an impressive coverage of the literature, Mill noted that "the metayer system has met with no mercy from English authorities."[26] He claimed "that the unmeasured vituperation lavished upon the system by English writers, is grounded on an extremely narrow view of the subject."[27] Mill's own analysis is essentially a modification of Jones's, and, more explicitly, he also treated labor input and improvement of land as two conceptually different things.

Mill quoted and accepted Smith's view that share rent is analogous to a tax, and therefore felt that the tenant would not be interested in making "improvements."[28] Thus, "the improvements must be made with the capital of the landlord," but "custom" is "a serious hindrance to improvement."[29] In regard to labor input, Mill's argument goes from "not enough" to a possibility of "too much," which may appear inconsistent at first sight:

> The metayer has less motive to exertion than the peasant proprietor, since only half the fruits of his industry, instead of the whole, are his own . . . I am supposing that this half produced is sufficient to yield him a comfortable support. Whether it is so, depends on the degree of subdivision of the land: which depends on the operation of the population principle . . . There is a landlord, who may exert a controlling power, by refusing his consent to a subdivision. I do not, however, attach great importance to this check, because the farm may be loaded with superfluous hands without being subdivided: and because, so long as the increase of hands increases the gross produce, which is almost always the case, the landlord, who receives half the produce, is an immediate gainer, the inconvenience falling only on the laborers.[30]

Two things should be noted. First, in this quotation Mill presupposed that no prevailing wage rate or alternative earning exists for the metayer tenant, and it is not

---

[24] J. C. L. Simonde de Sismondi, *Political Economy* [1814] (New York: Augustus M. Kelley, 1966), pp. 41–2.

[25] See John Stuart Mill, *Principles of Political Economy*, 4th edn (London: John W. Parker and Son, 1857), book 2, ch. 8, "Of Metayers."

[26] Ibid., p. 367. J. R. McCulloch was another noted "English authority" who wrote: "The practice of letting lands by proportional rents . . . is very general on the continent: and wherever it has been adopted, it has put a stop to all improvements, and has reduced the cultivators to the most abject poverty" (*Principles of Political Economy* (Edinburgh, 1843), p. 471).

[27] Mill, *Principles of Political Economy*, p. 380.

[28] Ibid., pp. 366–7.

[29] Ibid., p. 367.

[30] Ibid., pp. 365–6.

even clear whether the popular "subsistence" income is implied as a limit to the subdivision of land. Indeed, without explicitly stating the law of diminishing returns, it would be difficult to arrive at any kind of equilibrium.[31] Second, in regard to "improvements," Mill did not allow them to be made through adjusting the rental percentage – even though he was well aware of differing rental percentages.[32]

The lack of any definite conclusion by Mill stems from the fact that he did not claim to perform any economic analysis of the subject. He began by stating that the metayage system in Europe was regulated by custom and not by competition,[33] so that "when the partition of the produce is a matter of fixed usage, not of varying convention, political economy has no laws of distribution to investigate."[34] From whom did Mill get this "custom" idea? From Sismondi:

> This connexion [of input commitments] is often the subject of a contract, to define certain services and certain occasional payments to which the metayer binds himself: nevertheless the differences in the obligations of one such contract and another are inconsiderable: usage governs alike all these engagements, and supplies the stipulations which have not been expressed: and the landlord who attempted to depart from usage, who exacted more than his neighbor, who took for the basis of the agreement anything but the equal division of the crops, would render himself so odious, he would be so sure of not obtaining a metayer who was an honest man, that the contract of all the metayers may be considered as identical, at least in each province, and never gives rise to any competition among peasants in search of employment, or any offer to cultivate the soil on cheaper terms than one another.[35]

The contractual stipulations as described are implied by the theory of share tenancy, and as we shall see in greater detail, they are similar to those in China. But the statement that the metayage system "never gives rise to competition" is wrong. Indeed, the restraints on the contracting parties as visualized by Sismondi are restraints imposed by competition itself.

We may well ask: Why were the terms of a share contract viewed as "customary" and not determined by competition? The answer. I believe, is that *factor prices are not explicitly stated in a share contract.*[36] Under fixed rent or a wage contract, not only is the rental price of land or the wage rate explicitly stated, but also one party to the contract can buy freely any quantity of a resource by paying a high enough price. Under a share contract, where the pricing mechanism operates by adjusting the rental *percentage* and the *ratio* of nonland inputs to land, it not only yields an impression that market prices do not exist, but the mutually stipulated input intensity also yields an impression of "fixity." Sismondi and Mill were unable to see that, *ceteris paribus*, a reduction in farm size represents either a fall in the wage rate (or in the cost of nonland inputs) or a rise in the rental price of land: or that a fall in

---

[31] Note that the last statement in this quotation is quite different from Jones's view.
[32] See Mill, *Principles of Political Economy*, p. 363 and the second footnote on p. 364.
[33] Ibid., p. 363.
[34] Ibid., p. 364.
[35] Mill quotes Sismondi in ibid., pp. 363–4.
[36] This is drawn from my impression of their discussion of distribution. See, for example, Jones, *Distribution of Wealth*; Sismondi, *Political Economy*, ch. 3; McCulloch, *Principles of Political Economy*, pt 3: Mill, *Principles of Political Economy*, bk 2.

the rental percentage represents either a rise in the wage rate or a fall in the rental price of land. Furthermore, a change in relative factor prices in the market can be flexibly adjusted in a share contract through several dimensions, so flexibly that it may yeild an impression of inflexibility. For example, a 50 percent increase in the wage rate would appear significant in a wage contract: but, under a share contract, the same increase may be accounted for by lowering the rental percentage a trifle, reducing labor input a trifle. *and* expanding land size a trifle.

Thus, Mill was not able to settle the issue on theoretical grounds. But one must admit that, in light of the diversified arguments confronting him, the following judgment he made is of considerable wisdom:

> If the [metayer] system in Tuscany [Italy] works as well in practice as it is represented to do, with every appearance of minute knowledge, by so competent an authority as Sismondi: if the mode of living of the people, and the size of farms, have for ages maintained and still maintain themselves such as they are said to be by him, it were to be regretted that a state of rural well-being so much beyond what is realized in most European countries, should be put to hazard by an attempt to introduce, under the guise of agricultural improvement, a system of money-rents and capitalist farmers.[37]

## THE NEOCLASSICAL VIEW

Several analytical deficiencies stood in the way of classical writers in arriving at a general solution for resource use under share tenancy. Other than their conceptual ambiguities mentioned earlier, classical writers failed to treat land rent as part of production cost.[38] Furthermore, the marginal analysis required to reach an equilibrium was vague. These shortcomings did not handicap Alfred Marshall when he analyzed sharecropping. But whereas, before Marshall, Sismondi and Mill had not placed much weight on the tax-equivalent argument, Marshall renewed the thesis, presumably because the analogy to a tax under share rent fits rather neatly into his marginal analysis.[39] Even with such an approach. Marshall almost obtained the correct solution in a footnote.[40] [. . .]

It was with this analysis in mind that Marshall commented:

> When the cultivator has to give to his landlord half of the returns to each dose of capital and labor that he applies to the land, it will not be to his interest to apply any doses the total return to which is less than twice enough to reward him. If, then, he is free to cultivate as he chooses, he will cultivate far less intensively than on the English plan [fixed rent]: he will apply only so much capital and labor as will give him returns more than twice enough to repay himself: so that his landlord will get a smaller share even of those returns than he would have on the plan of a fixed payment.[41]

---

[37] Mill, *Principles of Political Economy*, pp. 380–1.

[38] At page proof, George J. Stigler informed me that Mill did recognize rent as a cost of production, whereas Marshall was reluctant.

[39] See Marshall, *Principles of Economics*, 8th edn, 1920 (London: Macmillan, 1956), pp. 534–7.

[40] Ibid., bk 4, ch. 3; bk 6, ch. 10, p. 536.

[41] Ibid., pp. 535–6.

What is important here is that Marshall saw that according to this analysis the share tenant will be getting a residual return and the landlord will be getting a smaller rental income than under fixed rent. What is strange is that Marshall did not question why the landlord does not choose instead a fixed rent contract or selling his landownership to the tenant outright.[42] And what is natural is that Marshall was reluctant to let the tenant's residual earning remain unexplained:

> If the tenant has no fixity of tenure, the landlord can deliberately and freely arrange the amount of capital and labor supplied by the tenant and the amount of capital supplied by himself to suit the exigencies of each special case.[43]

Marshall's view was that the metayer tenant "has practical fixity of tenure,"[44] and he referred to an article by Henry Higgs.[45] Higgs noted that the rental shares do differ, and that "rigid as *metayer* may at first sight seem to be, it is susceptible of considerable elasticity."[46] He nonetheless shared the "custom" idea with Sismondi and Mill. Higgs based his judgment on an empirical survey he had conducted in France, which unfortunately involved a sample of only a single farm.[47] It is the notion of "fixity of tenure," perhaps, that led Marshall to mention the possibility of adjustments only in a footnote:

> If the landlord controls the amount [of capital] freely and in his own interest, and can bargain with his tenant as to the amount of labor he applies, it can be proved geometrically that he will so adjust it as to force the tenant to cultivate the land just as intensively as he would under the English tenure [fixed rent]: and his share will then be the same as under it.[48]

Marshall provided no geometric proof, and it is an interesting conjecture whether he would have altered this footnote had he done so. This conjecture is interesting because the results he conceived are correct only in certain special cases, but as a matter of generality they are incorrect. They are incorrect because Marshall did not allow the rental percentage to vary.[49] [. . .] Given a certain (not any) rental percentage, and given that the landlord has been providing a sufficiently large amount of nonland "capital" input, then he may adjust the nonland inputs provided by either

---

[42] Marshall was aware, like other writers before him, that fixed rents and owner cultivators existed together with metayers in Europe. Various estimates on the frequency of metayer farms differ greatly.

[43] Marshall, *Principles of Economics*, p. 536.

[44] Ibid.

[45] Higgs, "'Metayage' in Western France," *The Economics Journal* (March, 1894), pp. 1–13.

[46] Ibid., p. 9 and n. 1.

[47] See ibid., pp. 9–13.

[48] Marshall, *Principles of Economics*, p. 536, n. 2.

[49] Though Marshall was aware that the rental percentage was not the same everywhere (p. 535, n. 1), he noted that for customary reasons variation of it "could seldom be done without an appearance of violence" (p. 533). No evidence of "violence" was offered. The theoretical difficulty Marshall encountered as a result of not varying the rental percentage was made evident when he wrote (p. 536, n. 2):

> If [the landlord] cannot modify the amount [of capital], but still control the amount of the tenant's labour, then with certain shapes of the produce curve, the cultivation will be more intensive than it would be on the English plan [fixed rent]: but the landlord's share will be somewhat less. This paradoxical result has some scientific interest, but little practical importance.

contracting party so that (*a*) the rental income under share rent is the same as under fixed rent and (*b*) the tenant's residual earning is exhausted – *without* varying the given rental percentage. As such, Marshall is correct. But suppose that the tenant is to provide *all* the nonland inputs, or that the landlord has been providing a part of the nonland inputs but the amount is too small; then, except by accident, the rental percentage must be varied (in addition to adjusting nonland inputs over land) to obtain the results Marshall visualized. To view the problem from another angle: given the ratio of nonland inputs to land that is consistent with wealth maximization, and given that the relative shares of nonland inputs contributed by the contracting parties are stipulated, there exists one and only one rental percentage which is consistent with equilibrium.[50] [. . .]

It should be noted that Marshall, like Smith, Jones, and Mill before him, attempted to "rank" various land tenure arrangements according to some notion of economic efficiency.[51] They did not tackle the issue by identifying a specific set of property right constraints subject to which several forms of land tenure arrangements may imply the same resource use. In their discussions of share tenancy, the freely alienable rights implicit in their analyses suggest that the constraint of private property rights was assumed.[52] But whereas Smith and Jones viewed a share lease, though wasteful, as transitional, Mill and Marshall laid the blame on "custom." Smith's prediction that fixed rents would replace share rents had failed to come true: and, as noted earlier, the terms of a share contract might yield the impression of being customarily fixed.

Among contemporary writers who performed similar "rankings" and also relied on the notion of "custom" are Rainer Schickele[53] and Earl O. Heady.[54] Schickele and Heady furthered the tax approach in their analyses of a share lease, but in a way somewhat different from Marshall. [. . .]

It is not clear what is meant by "custom" in its usage by Schickele and Heady in their discussions of land tenure. Whereas Mill had visualized "custom" only as something noncompetitive. Schickele and Heady referred to both "custom" and "competition" in their analyses of share tenancy. One interpretation is that by "custom" they meant a situation where the postulate of wealth or utility maximization

---

[50] [. . .] Note. however, that if several crops are grown, multiple rental percentages may exist in one share contract due to different factor intensities required for different crops. [ . . .]

[51] Marshall, *Principles of Economics*, bk 6, ch. 10.

[52] Transferability of rights among *individual* owners implies exclusivity in use, at least to some degree. Transfers of resource rights in the marketplace are not confined to outright transfers, but also include various leasing arrangements. A legal restriction on one form or another of these transfers may impose a higher cost of transaction, but still may not constitute a set of constraints different enough to affect resource use significantly. That freely alienable rights existed for the French metayage is evident in Young, *Travels*, Maxwell edition, "Editor's Notes."

When N. Georgescu-Roegen analyzed share tenancy, he referred to it as a form of land tenure under "feudalism." But we have yet to identify the property right constraint defining "feudalism." Georgescu-Roegen also employed the tax-equivalent approach and reached the conclusion that sharecropping was inefficient. See his "Economic Theory and Agrarian Economics," *Oxford Economic Papers* (February 1960), pp. 23–6.

[53] Rainer Schickele, "Effects of Tenure Systems on Agricultural Efficiency," *Journal of Farm Economics* (February 1941), pp. 185–207.

[54] Earl Heady, "Economics of Farm Leasing Systems, "*Journal of Farm Economics* (August 1947), pp. 659–78 [notes 55–8 omitted here].

does not apply. Yet without any such behavioral postulate, the meaning of competition cannot be defined. To complicate the matter, at times the postulate of maximizing behavior is implicit for the tenant but not for the landowner. This is explicitly stated by Charles Issawii in his analysis of share tenancy. [. . .] Issawii admitted that, in his analysis:

> It has been implicitly assumed throughout . . . that landlords do not respond readily to such economic motivations as the possibility of increasing their income by investment; if they did, the distinction between fixed rents and sharecropping would, naturally, lose most of its significance. In the past this assumption has, to a large extent, held true for most underdeveloped countries and, to a slightly lesser extent, it still holds true.[59]

This kind of analysis is quite popular in "underdevelopment" literature. And one wonders how an analyst following Marshall would fare should he discard the idea of custom. We find this in a study by D. Gale Johnson.[60] Johnson formalized Marshall's analysis in greater detail, and his equations led him to conclude:

> Under a crop-share lease, if the landlord's share of the crops is half, the tenant will apply his resources in production of crops until the marginal cost of crop output is equal to half the value of the marginal output. The same tenant, however, will conduct his livestock operations, where important costs are borne by the landlord and the receipts are not shared with him, in the usual manner. The landlord will not invest in land assets unless the value of the marginal product is twice the marginal cost.[61]

Johnson noted, however, that his analysis is based on "circumstances in which . . . the tenant and the landlord . . . each views his interest separately,"[62] which is similar to Marshall's supposition that the tenant "is free to cultivate as he chooses." This supposition, of course, renders the meaning of a *contract* nebulous. What is interesting here is that *even if we accept this supposition* Johnson's conclusion is founded on a set of constraints which are difficult to specify. This will be shown in the next section.

But Johnson was reluctant to accept the implication of inefficient resource use under a share contract, and he devoted one section to investigating other possible adjustments.[63] He found that, "though admittedly inadequate, the available evidence indicates that the crop-share contract yields at least as much, if not more, rent per acre than does the cash lease on comparable farms."[64] In an attempt to reconcile this apparent conflict between theory and fact, Johnson argued that with

[59] Charles Issawi, "Farm Output under Fixed Rents and Share Tenancy," *Land Economics* (February 1957), p. 76.
[60] Johnson, "Resource Allocation," pp. 111–23.
[61] Ibid., p. 111. Similar conclusions are also reached in Amartya K. Sen, "Peasants and Dualism with or without Surplus Labor," *Journal of Political Economy* (October 1966), pp. 445–6.
[62] Johnson, "Resource Allocation," p. 111.
[63] Ibid., v., pp. 118–21.
[64] Ibid., p. 118. In the associated footnote Johnson wrote:

> I have estimated net rents on crop-share-rented farms in Iowa from 1925 through 1946. From 1925 through 1934 net rents on share-rented farms averaged perhaps a dollar per acre less than on cash-rented farms. From 1935 through 1939 the net rents were roughly the same. From 1940 through 1946 net rents were at least four dollars an acre more on share-rented than on cash-rented farms.

a short-term lease the tenant is not really free to cultivate in anyway he sees fit.[65] Thus, the actual intensity of tenant input "will depend upon what he thinks 'he can get by with'."[66]

It is difficult to understand why Johnson did not discard his theoretical analysis and start anew – by considering that the contracting parties are *free* only to accept or not to accept a *contract*, and that they "*can get by with*" only as much as the restraints of competition allow. These choices are exactly the same as fixed rent and wage contracts, which are implied by the constraints of private property rights, and which Johnson had in mind. A theory constructed on these rights will reveal that the terms of a share contract are expressed through the market-determined rental percentage and ratio of nonland inputs to land. Yet on this point Johnson was in doubt:

> The process by which the landlord and tenant enter into a lease is not well understood. The price system does not function in the normal sense, for land is not necessarily rented to the tenant offering the highest rent payment. However, there is only a difference of modest degree in the role of price rationing in the share-rental market and in the cash-rental market.[67]

In the course of his analysis, Johnson had obtained – and abandoned – a condition which is quite sufficient to reveal the market terms of a share contract. Referring to the theoretical formulation, he wrote:

> Is it likely that a tenant operating under these conditions will allocate his resources in exactly the same way that he would if paying a cash rent independent of the actual output? The answer is apparently in the negative. There is only one average rent per acre for which the resource allocations will be the same under a variable-share proportion and a fixed rent per acre. And there is no reason to believe that this particular rent would emerge under competitive conditions.[68]

Why not? [...] The identity of the average rent under fixed and share contracts exists, in equilibrium, when rent per acre is at a maximum. This maximum rent per acre is unique because it is obtained when the marginal nonland cost equals the marginal product of nonland inputs. The associated land size per tenant, values of nonland inputs and rental percentage, will be the terms stipulated in the share contract. Thus, it is somewhat puzzling that Johnson also wrote:

> With a short-term lease renters are obviously aware that landlords have the alternative of renting their land for a cash rent independent of current output. Consequently, the tenant must plan to produce an average output per acre that will provide a rental payment, if yields are average, equal to the possible cash rent.[69]

The apparent contradiction between this and the earlier quotation can perhaps be reconciled as follows: In rejecting the theoretical identity of the average rent under

[65] Ibid., pp. 119–20.
[66] Ibid., p. 120.
[67] Ibid., p. 121.
[68] Ibid., p. 118.
[69] Ibid., p. 120.

fixed and share contracts, Johnson was following a model in which this identity cannot be obtained. In accepting the identity, empirically his observation led him to search for another interpretation. As we saw when we discussed Marshall, the theoretical identity can be derived only if the rental percentage is treated as a variable. My own impression of Johnson's insightful work is that he maintains that although share rent is less productive than fixed rent according to a model with considerable limitations they may nonetheless be identical in practice. For this reason perhaps, he called for "an empirical verification . . . of [the effects of] share leases upon resource allocation."[70]

[. . .]

## TESTS OF IMPLICATIONS

Just as D. Gale Johnson called for empirical confirmation of resource use under share tenancy in 1950, Chinese writers made a similar inquiry into tenant farming in general some twenty years earlier. Data on tenant farming was then assiduously compiled. In the late 1920s and early 1930s in China, attacks on farming under tenancy were common, and the desirability of *private* landownership was a subject of frequent debate. Lacking standardized economic theory to support their arguments, several Chinese organizations and independent writers resorted to empirical investigations. The debate on the tenancy issue was soon terminated by the Sino-Japanese War. And, with the exception of two noted works in the English language, both by John Lossing Buck, the greater part of these findings has since remained unknown.[74]

The aforementioned findings, inadequate as they may seem, constitute the most comprehensive body of evidence relating to agricultural land use *under unrestrained private property rights* that I could find. The Chinese experience, together with findings from elsewhere in Asia, will be applied in this section. [. . .] Note, however, that in every instance we use only data collected from periods and locations where the existing system of property rights conforms to the constraint on the basis of which the theory of share tenancy is derived. Therefore, the postwar farm land

[70] Ibid., p. 123 [notes 71–3 omitted].

[74] Under the auspices of the University of Nanking, Buck directed a forty-man team in the compilation of farming data in China during 1929–36. The original data, which appear to have passed unnoticed, are available in J. L. Buck (ed.), *Land Utilization in China – Statistics – A Study of 16,786 Farms in 168 Localities and 38,256 Farm Families in Twenty-two Provinces in China, 1929–1933* (Nanking: University of Nanking, 1937). During the preparation of this impressive volume. Buck wrote the noted *Chinese Farm Economy* (1930), and *Land Utilization in China* (1937), both of which have been distributed by the University of Chicago Press. However, Buck's earlier works are also important: *An Economic and Social Survey of 102 Farms near Wuhu, Anhwei, China* (Nanking, 1923); *An Economic and Social Survey of 150 Farms, Yehshan County, Hopei, China* (Nanking, 1926), and *Farm Ownership and Tenancy in China* (Shanghai: National Christian Council, 1927).

Surveys by independent writers aside, other organizations which have conducted surveys include the Department of Internal Affairs, the Real Estate Bureau, the National Government Statistics Department, the Executive Yuan, and the Legislative Yuan. I have found these independent findings generally consistent with one another.

reforms rule out the use of Asian agricultural data of the past twenty years in this part of the study.

Applying the implications of alternative theories of share tenancy to observations, we can perform several simple tests.

According to the standard theory of share tenancy [. . .], given the production function, the rental percentage depends upon the fertility of land and the alternative earning of the tenant. Specifically, we should observe a higher rental percentage if (*a*) the land is more fertile or (*b*) the cost of tenant inputs is lower.[75] Evidence confirming this hypothesis is strong.

According to an investigation which covers 641 sample farms in eleven localities in China (1921–5), J. L. Buck observed:

> As rent the tenant gives the landlord one-half of the grain and straw from wheat and rice land, two-fifths of the grain and straw from rice land only, and three-tenths of the grain and straw from poor land.[76]

Likewise, it was observed in Kweichow Province (1929–30) that:

> The rental shares depend on the fertility of land. On the average and roughly speaking, for upper grade land the rental share is 60 percent; for medium grade 50 percent; and for lower grade 40 percent.[77]

Casual observations aside, numerical data showing the same patterns were collected by the Legislative Yuan (China, 1930) and the Department of Internal Affairs (China, 1932).[78] The findings of the latter have been computed and placed in Appendix B, because they encompass twenty-two provinces in China with seven grades of land.

In Taiwan, a maximum rental of 37.5 percent of the annual yield was enforced by the government in 1949. This maximum percentage was uniform for all tenant contracts, regardless of whether the land involved was paddy field or dry field. The data reveal that 99.4 percent of the paddy fields under tenancy were affected by this share restriction: that is, the initial rental share was higher than 37.5 percent of the yield. However, only 50.9 percent of the dry fields under tenancy were affected by the same restriction.[79] This implies that higher rental percentages were generally associated with the more fertile paddy fields under a free market.

Also, Buck found that the rental percentage was higher when the landowner provided part of the farming inputs (i.e., the tenant cost was lower):

---

[75] [. . .]

[76] Buck, *Chinese Farm Economy*, p. 148. No further information is provided.

[77] Chinese National Government, *Shengching Route Economic Report* (1931), p. 102.

[78] See Legislative Yuan, *Statistical Monthly* (1930), 2.5; Department of Internal Affairs, *Public Reports of Internal Affairs* (1932), 2,1: 5, 1 and 2.

[79] [. . .] In Japan, the rental share restriction enacted in 1946 was a maximum of 25 percent of the yield for paddy, and 15 percent for upland fields, reflecting a recognition of the higher rental share for paddy fields under free market conditions. See Ministry of Agriculture and Forestry, *Agricultural Land Reform Legislation* (Tokyo, 1949).

The percentage of total receipts for the landlord varies from 24.6 percent . . . where small rents are demanded to 66.6 percent . . . where the cropper system prevails and where the landlord furnishes everything but labor and routine management.[80]

Similarly, according to another survey conducted by Ching-Moh Chen in four provinces (China, 1934), an average rental percentage of 55.98 was found in tenant farms where landowners provided seeds, fertilizers, and bullocks, as compared to an average of 46.37 percent when the tenants provided these nonland inputs.[81]

Furthermore, given the production function, the land space rented to each tenant depends upon the fertility of land and the tenant's alternative earning. Specifically, the farm size per tenant family will be smaller if (a) the land is more fertile or (b) the tenant's alternative earning is lower.[82] Again, supporting evidence is strong.

In Korea, the average farm size over a ten-year period (1929 through 1938) was 0.58 cho for paddy-field farms and 0.97 cho for dryland farms. In the same period and location, the prices of paddy fields were more than two and one-half times as high as those of dry fields, confirming that paddy fields were generally more fertile.[83]

According to another investigation conducted by Buck, which covers 16,786 sample farms in 168 localities in China (1929–33), we find (a) the average farm size in the more fertile rice region is 3.09 acres, as compared to an average size in the less fertile wheat region of 5.63 acres; and (b) of the seven types of crop fields listed, the smallest average size occurs in double-cropping rice fields (2.37 acres), which are generally most fertile.[84]

Turning to the tax-equivalent approach to analysis of share tenancy, [. . .] we may well ask: if the asserted equilibrium [. . .] were valid, what would we observe? The following is implied.

We would observe lower ratios of labor and other inputs to land in tenant farms than in farms under owner cultivation or in farms cultivated by hired farm hands. It also implies that hectare yields in tenant farms would be lower than in owner farms. But as Buck observed (China, 1921–5):

Contrary to the prevailing opinion that tenants do not farm as well as owners, a classification according to yields by different types of tenure shows no significant variation in yields for most localities, and for the few in which a difference does occur, it is

---

[80] Buck, *Chinese Farm Economy*, p. 149. The rental shares provided are averages of sample farms in each locality (eleven localities in China, 1921–5), and the 66.6 percent cited is purely incidental. See table 2 in ibid., p. 148.

[81] These averages are computed from Chen, *Land Rents of Various Provinces in China* (Shanghai: Commercial Press, 1936), pp. 102–3.

[82] [. . .]

[83] Andrew J. Grajdanzev, *Modern Korea* (New York: Institute of Pacific Relations, 1944). The average farm sizes are computed from data in table 2, p. 291, and the land prices are seen in table 5, p. 292.

[84] See Buck, *Land Utilization in China*, table 23, p. 197. With minor differences in magnitude, identical patterns are seen in tables 7 and 8, pp. 272–3. Note also that in ibid., p. 197, owner farms (average 4.22 acres) are larger than tenant farms (average 3.56 acres). This is because tenancy occurs more frequently on paddy fields than on dry land everywhere. See Sidney Klein, *The Pattern of Land Reform in East Asia after World War II* (New York: Bookman Associates, 1958), pp. 229 ff. See also Buck, *Statistics*, ch. 2, tables 23 and 26; ch. 7.

in favor of the tenant or part owner as often as for the owner . . . In some places, even, it is evident that the tenants farm better than the owners.[85]

Buck's data show the following crop indexes per acre: owner farms, 100 and 101; part-owner farms, 99 and 101; and tenant farms, 103 and 104.[86] Thirty years later, making no reference to Buck, James O. Bray echoed the same observation:

> Underdeveloped countries intent on technical progress in agriculture should recognize the fact that much of the most impressive gain in agricultural productivity occurred in areas of the United States where the dominant form of land tenure is a share rental arrangement between landlord and tenant.[87]

With respect to the intensities of farming, we find Japanese data (1932–8) showing that the average landholding per owner farmer is 2.22 tan, as compared to 2.10 tan per part-owner farmer and 1.93 tan per tenant farmer,[88] also denying the implication of the tax approach. The higher labor – land ratio in tenant farms can be explained by the somewhat higher proportion of paddy fields under tenancy.

We would observe, since the rental earning is lower with equilibrium [. . .] under the tax approach, that the market value of land under tenant cultivation is less than the value of land under owner cultivation. Again, evidence clearly denies this im-

---

[85] Buck, *Chinese Farm Economy*, pp. 156–7. Apparently failing to see that the rental percentage is a variable to insure efficient farming, Buck proceeded to discuss a program of "fair" rent.

[86] Ibid. Buck's finding is from a sample of 2,542 farms in fifteen localities, seven provinces. The slightly higher yields per acre in tenant farms are perhaps due to a higher proportion of paddy fields under tenancy, which Buck did not discern. For similar evidence, see Buck, *Farm Ownership and Tenancy in China*.

[87] Bray, "Farm Tenancy and Productivity in Agriculture: The Case of the United States," *Food Research Institute Studies* (1963), p. 25. Although Bray provided no formal theory of share tenancy, the traditional argument did not pass his intuition:

> The resource-efficiency argument is somewhat academic . . . Both tenant and landlord have an incentive to *try* to increase the marginal productivity of their own resources . . . neither wholly succeeds . . . For example, a landlord's suggestion that a third cultivation of the corn would pay (at no cost to him) may be met with the tenant's suggestion that the living room really would be improved by new wallpaper (at no cost to him).   (ibid., p. 27)

The lack of significant difference in resource use among different leases is also noticed by Walter G. Miller, Walter E. Chryst, and Howard W. Ottoson, "Relative Efficiencies of Farm Tenure Classes in Intrafirm Resource Allocation," *Research Bulletin* 461 (Iowa Agricultural and Home Economics Experiment Station, November, 1958), pp. 321–37. Evidence from the United States, however, is not heavily used in this study. This is because various government farm policies which result in different constraints on competition might have affected resource use under different contracts in different ways.

[88] These averages are computed from data in Andrew J. Grajdanzev. "Statistics of Japanese Agriculture," mimeographed (New York: Institute of Pacific Relations, 1941), table 17, p. 32. The findings are based on about ninety-five sample farms in each category. The same pattern is observed if "able-bodied man-units" are used instead of "number of members per family." [. . .]

Earl O. Heady and Earl W. Kehrberg conducted a survey (Iowa, 1949) with seventy-four selected pairs of cash-lease and share-lease farms. They found "no significant differences between share and cash leases" (p. 661) for the input intensities of farming. The authors, however, refused to accept the conflict between their theory and findings, and resorted to other factors which "might account for this lack of difference" (pp. 661–2). With the tax approach, they had concluded that, in theory, farming intensity under share rent is necessarily lower than under cash rent (pp. 658–60). See Heady and Kehrberg, "Relationship of Crop Share and Cash Leasing Systems to Farming Efficiency," *Research Bulletin 386* (Iowa State College Agricultural Experiment Station, May, 1952), pp. 635–83.

plication. We find that the values of land differ according to fertility grades and locations, and that "the value of land for the three types of tenure (owner, part-owner, and tenant) in most cases varies only a few dollars."[89] Also, with equilibrium [under the tax approach] we would observe that the actual rent received by the landowner is lower under share tenancy than under a fixed rent (rent per acre). As is shown in Appendix B, however, share rent is generally slightly higher than crop rent.[90] This slight difference, as I shall indicate later, might be explained as a payment to the landowner for his "risk" bearing under a share contract.

We would observe, as implied by the tax approach, that a higher rental percentage [. . .] would be associated with less farming inputs per unit of land in tenant farms. We find evidence to the contrary: tenant farms with higher rental percentages usually also display higher labor–land ratios.[91] This is due either to the land's being more fertile or to the tenants' alternative earnings being lower, a condition implied by our theory of share tenancy.

Finally, if the tax-equivalent approach were correct, we would observe that most, if not all, share tenants would rent land from several landlords. But this is rarely the case. Take Taiwan, for example. In 1949 there existed only 1.24 leases per tenant family.[92] This extra .24 lease can easily be explained by the use of marginal plots. [. . .] On the other hand, landowners issuing one or two hundred leases were regarded as common.[93]

## APPENDIX A: SOME COMMENTS ON THE HYPOTHESES OF DISGUISED UNEMPLOYMENT AND THE DUAL ECONOMY

A number of writers have attributed the small landholdings in Asia (and particularly in China) to family and social structure. Others have taken the crowded farming condition as evidence of disguised unemployment (where the marginal productivity of peasants is said to be zero or negative). Still others have claimed that whether or not the marginal productivity of peasants is zero, the productivity of labor is lower in agriculture than elsewhere. Various hypotheses of disguised unemployment and the dual economy have been developed in terms of family structure, of unlimited labor supply, of peculiar fixed-factor co-efficient production functions owing to the peasants' ignorance of farming methods, and of a "rock-bottom" subsistence theory. Some insist that it is

---

[89] Buck, *Chinese Farm Economy*, p. 156. No numerical data are provided.
[90] See also Legislative Yuan, *Statistical Monthly* (1930), 2,5.
[91] This is shown earlier in this section. [. . .]
[92] Computed from data in Sino-American Joint Commission on Rural Reconstruction, "JCRR Annual Reports on Land Reform in the Republic of China," mimeographed (1965), p. 35.
[93] Only a small amount of numerical data has been provided, and examples of landowners holding over one thousand leases are perhaps cases selected to emphasize the concentration of landownership. According to information provided in J. P. Gittinger, "Vietnamese Land Transfer Program," *Land Economics* (May, 1957), "before the land transfer program in Vietnam, 2,170 persons . . . have declared total holdings amounting to 976,602 hectares." Given that "the average tenant holding is approximately 2 hectares or perhaps slightly more," the average number of leases for each of these landowners was over two hundred.

the average product and not the marginal product which underlies farming decisions in underdeveloped areas.[1]

The hypotheses constructed on these premises are incorrect. First, to accept the phenomenon of crowded farming as social is to leave an economic question unanswered. Second, the existence of unlimited labor supply or labor "surplus" is an assertion which in fact has no empirical foundation. Third, it is presumptuous to say that the peasants are ignorant of farming methods, for competition will induce sophistication. It is far closer to the truth to say that it is the economic theorist who does not know. Fourth, the "rock-bottom" is soft and variable. Finally, lacking an explicit behavioral postulate, the average-product argument is inconsistent with wealth maximization under private ownership of resources.

The theory of share tenancy [. . .] provides a different explanation for higher ratios of labor to land in Asian agriculture: the peasants' landholdings are small because their alternative earnings are low. And their low earnings are due to the small area of arable land relative to labor force, together with the fact that farming skill and knowledge are not highly valued in other industries. Under private ownership of land, it is to the landowner's interest that no negative marginal effort is "disguised." Given the existing resources, crowded farming is the result of wealth maximization, not of "irrationality."

It is not difficult to show that "original" theorems or hypotheses intended to explain resource allocation in "underdeveloped" agriculture are unnecessary. For Asian agriculture, the aforementioned hypotheses can be readily dismissed in light of observations on land use and the analysts' neglect of the pertinent property right constraints.

First, let us take a closer look at the so-called overcrowded farming in Asia, which "overcrowding" cannot be denied by Western standards:

> The growing seasons of rice and cane crops overlap. At the time cane should be planted, the preceding rice crop is not yet ripe. This problem is solved by planting cane among the ripening rice plants one month before the latter are to be harvested. Because the distance between [cane] rows is 1.39 meters and between [cane] plants 0.4 meter, farmers often plant peanuts, sweet potatoes, cotton and soybeans between the rows of canes in summer. These interplanted crops are harvested in November or December before the canes grow tall.[2]

Examples as intricate as this are abundant.[3] But as J. L. Buck points out:

---

[1] The literature sharing these views is enormous. But see W. A. Lewis, "Economic Development with Unlimited Supplies of Labor," *Manchester School of Economic and Social Studies* (May 1954). For general discussion of these hypotheses, see Benjamin Higgins, *Economic Development* (New York: W. W. Norton, 1959), chs 11–17; C. H. C. Kao *et al.*, "Disguised Unemployment in Agriculture," in *Agriculture in Economic Development*, ed. C. K. Eicher and L. Witt (New York: McGraw-Hill, 1964): H. Myint, *The Economics of the Underdeveloped Countries* (London: Hutchinson, 1964); A. K. Sen, "Peasants and Dualism with or without Surplus Labor," *Journal of Political Economy* (October 1966).

[2] Tsung-han Shen, *Agricultural Development on Taiwan since World War II* (New York: Comstock, 1964), pp. 198–9.

[3] See, for example, F. H. King, *Farmers of Forty Centuries* (Emmaus, Pa.: Organic Gardening Press, 1900). As an observer in 1900, King, like J. L. Buck after him, took pains to understand farming techniques in Asia, though he mainly emphasized the intensive farming in his photograph-illustrated work. Oriental writers, however, are far less impressed with their farming methods. See, for example, Shen,

It is evident from this maze of detail on the actual use of land by crops in China, that, in spite of the intensive use of crops for human utilization directly rather than indirectly by first producing animal products, still greater production could be obtained.[4]

While Buck is amazed by the various methods of intensive farming and soil conservation in China, the flexibility of land use is frequently ignored by development economists. An unimaginative theorist, unfamiliar with the actual situation, might easily consider the crowded tilling wasteful, and hastily develop fancy theorems and policies to slay the dragon.

Evidence suggests that, before the agrarian reforms in Asia, the marginal product of agricultural labor was not only positive but also nowhere near zero. Take Taiwan, for example, where in 1948 the landholding per person in farming was about as small as one could find. [. . .] however, increases in labor and other inputs on tenant farms under the rental share restriction led to significant increases in outputs.

Indeed, the fact that common crops are grown confirms that the marginal product of labor is positive. This is so because the same land can be used to cultivate other crops, for example, vegetables. Vegetable crops have considerably higher market values than common crops, and they generally require eight times as much labor to cultivate.[5] Forgoing some common crops for vegetable planting will lead to increasing labor input, and a higher gross income. Yet only a small portion of cultivated fields has been used for vegetables in Asia.[6]

Zero marginal productivity of labor implies a condition where it is no longer possible to choose a more labor-intensive crop to obtain a higher income, which is refuted by the facts. It further implies that there exists no idle land margin or that it is impossible to adopt a faster crop rotation rate with increasing labor input and income, which is also refuted by the facts. It implies, too, that most dry fields are converted into paddy fields through the use of labor. And the list of refuting evidence goes on.

A second reason for rejecting the hypotheses of disguised unemployment and the dual economy lies in their neglect of the existing system of property rights. Under private ownership of land, disguised unemployment cannot be derived from standard economic theory, regardless of how crowded farming may be. Under common ownership, however, zero or negative marginal product of labor is consistent with the general body of economic theory.[7] This is so because competition among

---

*Agricultural Development on Taiwan*; Shen, *Agricultural Resources of China* (New York: Cornell University Press, 1951): and Nien-tsing Lu, *An Analysis of Farm Family Economy of Owner-Operators under the Land-to-the-Tiller Program in Taiwan* (Taipei: Research Department of the Bank of Taiwan, 1965).

[4] J. L. Buck, *Land Utilization in China* (Chicago: University of Chicago Press, 1937), p. 242.

[5] Estimates of labor intensity required for different crops are available in Lu, *Analysis of Farm Family Economy*, pp. 142–4; and in S. C. Hsieh and T. H. Lee, "The Effects of Population Pressure and Seasonal Labor Surplus on the Pattern and Intensity of Agriculture in Taiwan," mimeographed (1964). The market values for vegetables and other crops are available in Shen, *Agricultural Resources of China*, ch. 24; and Department of Agriculture and Forestry, *Taiwan Agricultural Yearbook*.

[6] See Shen, *Agricultural Resources of China*, ch. 24. See also the forty-eight observed systems of crop rotation listed in Lu, *Analysis of Farm Family Economy*, pp. 124–34.

[7] See, for example, H. Scott Gordon, "The Economic Theory of a Common Property Resource: The Fishery," *Journal of Political Economy* (August 1954). See also Anthony Bottomley, "The Effect of Common Ownership of Land upon Resource Allocation in Tripolitania," *Land Economics* (February 1963).

users will reduce the rental value of land to zero, thus equating the *average* product of labor with the wage rate (or alternative earning).

Suppose that, as development economists have taken for granted, empirical evidence did confirm that the marginal product of labor is lower in agriculture than in other industries. If their hypotheses are intended to interpret Asian experience in the past twenty years, as many of them are, then they are still incorrect. They are incorrect because private farm land ownership with free markets, conditions which their hypotheses have implicitly presupposed, have been rare in Asia since 1950. The various agrarian reforms in Asia [. . .] may in fact have led to "dual" economies. In particular, as analyzed in the second part of this study, the rental share restriction yields a condition where the marginal product of labor is lower in tenant farms than elsewhere. This result is derived entirely from standard economic theory.

The above discussion should not, however, be interpreted to mean that under private ownership of resources the marginal productivities of homogeneous labor must be equal everywhere at all times. The costs of information and of migration, and differentials in nonpecuniary gains and in the costs of living associated with different jobs, are sufficient to produce unequal marginal products of labor. These factors, of course, can be incorporated into the general body of economic theory. I object to the hypotheses of disguised unemployment and the dual economy on the grounds, rather, of their neglect of the flexibility of land use and of the pertinent property right constraints.

## APPENDIX B: RENTAL PAYMENTS OF FIXED AND SHARE CONTRACTS IN CHINA

In this appendix I seek to show two things: that rental percentages vary with land grades; and that share rents are generally slightly higher than fixed (crop) rents. The data, obtained from Chinese sources published in the 1930s, leave a great deal to be desired. I have been unable to determine in detail the methods by which the data were compiled, or even the exact numbers of samples. But my confidence in their reliability is enhanced by the fact that observations in different sources consistently exhibit the same patterns.

In table 9.1 rental percentages of seven different land grades in twenty-two provinces (China, 1932) are shown. They represent percentages of the main crops, obtained exclusively from share contracts. With a few exceptions, lower-grade lands are associated with lower rental percentages. According to another survey with similar details (twenty-three provinces and six grades of land, China, 1930), only two exceptions are found in a total of 124 observations.[1]

The lack of fuller information stands in the way of interpreting these exceptions. For example, the rental percentage depends not only on the fertility of land, but also on the amount of other nonland inputs provided by each of the contracting parties. Furthermore, some lands might grow more "minor" crops than others, and their sharing does not seem to have been appropriately included.

[1] See Legislative Yuan, *Statistical Monthly* 2.5 (1930).

**Table 9.1** Average rental percentages for seven grades of land in twenty-two provinces (China, 1932)

| Province | Grade A | Grade B | Grade C | Grade D | Grade E | Grade F | Grade G |
|---|---|---|---|---|---|---|---|
| Kiangsu | 51 | 49 | 49 | 49 | 49 | 48 | 47 |
| Chekiang | 50 | 49 | 47 | 43 | 41 | 38 | 36 |
| Anhwei | 42 | 42 | 37 | 41 | 39 | 37 | 35 |
| Kiangsi | 50 | 51 | 47 | 44 | 43 | 39 | 36 |
| Hupeh | 54 | 44 | 41 | 38 | 35 | 32 | 33 |
| Hunan | 54 | 52 | 48 | 46 | 44 | 39 | 37 |
| Szechwan | 69 | 55 | 52 | 47 | 43 | 39 | 37 |
| Hopeh | 56 | 53 | 51 | 50 | 48 | 46 | 44 |
| Shantung | 54 | 53 | 52 | 52 | 51 | 49 | 47 |
| Shansi | 57 | 54 | 54 | 52 | 49 | 47 | 44 |
| Honan | 56 | 57 | 55 | 54 | 53 | 53 | 51 |
| Fukien | 51 | 50 | 47 | 46 | 40 | 39 | 35 |
| Kwantung | 47 | 44 | 42 | 40 | 37 | 37 | 34 |
| Yunnan | 52 | 48 | 46 | 42 | 39 | 36 | 32 |
| Keichow | 57 | 53 | 50 | 47 | 42 | 39 | 35 |
| Liaoning | 49 | 45 | 41 | 40 | 37 | 32 | 29 |
| Chilin | 50 | 43 | 39 | 35 | 36 | 32 | 31 |
| Heklunkiang | 42 | 41 | 37 | 35 | 37 | 34 | 30 |
| Jeho | 49 | 46 | 46 | 44 | 43 | 40 | 33 |
| Chahayu | 54 | 51 | 50 | 49 | 45 | 40 | 31 |
| Suiyuan | 51 | 46 | 42 | 45 | 36 | 37 | 32 |
| Hsinkiang | 54 | 52 | 45 | 42 | 39 | 35 | 34 |

*Source*: Department of Internal Affairs, *Public Reports of Internal Affairs*, 2, vols 1 and 2 (1932).

In table 9.2, I intend to show that share rents are generally higher than crop rents because of the risk sharing. The figures are expressed as fixed monetary values. Not only do we find a few exceptions, but some of the differences appear unduly large. According to another survey of similar comparison (China, 1932),[2] in which fixed and share rents are expressed in *percentages* of the output yields, we find a few exceptions also (fixed rents being higher than share rents), but the differences are generally small.

In addition to the lack of fuller information on data compilation by which the exceptions and "erratic" differences may be explained, natural reasons are important. If fixed and share rents are to be compared, they must be expressed in the same dimensions, either both in fixed values or both in percentage values. However, share rents calculated and expressed in terms of *fixed* (monetary) values (as in table 9.2) will exhibit *lower* absolute rents with a *bad* harvest, and the converse with

[2] Department of Internal Affairs, *Public Reports of Internal Affairs* 2; vols 1 and 2 (1932). See also Legislative Yuan, *Statistical Monthly*, 2.5 (1930).

**Table 9.2** Fixed (crop) rents and share rents in annual crop values (yuan) per mow of Land (China, 1934)

| Province | Crop rent (yuan) | Share rent (yuan) | Province | Crop rent (Yuan) | Share rent (Yuan) |
|---|---|---|---|---|---|
| Summary average | 4.2 | 4.6 | | | |
| Kiangsu | 3.4 | 5.6 | Shensi | 3.1 | 3.0 |
| Chekiang | 4.6 | 5.9 | Kansu | 2.1 | 2.4 |
| Anhwei | 3.1 | 5.4 | Tsinghai | 1.1 | 1.8 |
| Kiangsi | 3.3 | 6.7 | Fukien | 5.7 | 6.0 |
| Hupeh | 2.8 | 5.6 | Kwantung | 7.5 | 6.1 |
| Hunan | 4.4 | 7.2 | Kwangsi | 6.6 | 6.5 |
| Szechwan | 7.1 | 8.3 | Yunnan | 7.5 | 7.6 |
| Hopeh | 3.1 | 3.3 | Kweichow | 5.0 | 4.5 |
| Shantung | 5.5 | 6.1 | Chahayu | 1.2 | 1.9 |
| Shansi | 1.7 | 1.8 | Suiyan | 1.8 | 1.5 |
| Honan | 4.4 | 2.5 | Ningsia | 6.1 | 4.2 |

*Source*: Department of Real Estates, *China Economic Yearbook* (1936), pp. G62–83.

a good harvest. On the other hand, fixed (crop) rents expressed in *percentage* values will exhibit *higher* percentage shares with a *bad* harvest, and the converse with a good harvest. Only in a normal year, *ceteris paribus*, can the risk premiums for share rents be accurately revealed. At any rate, the implication of the tax-equivalent approach, that the rental receipt under a share contract is necessarily lower than that under a fixed-rent contract, is refuted by evidence.

It is hoped that the risk premiums of different contractual arrangements will be investigated further.

## REFERENCES[1]

Betham-Edwards, Miss (ed.) *Arthur Young's Travels in France during the Years 1787, 1788, and 1789* (London: George Bell and Sons, 1892).

Bottomley, Anthony, "The Effect of Common Ownership of Land upon Resource Allocation in Tripolitania," *Land Economics*, February 1963.

Bray, J. O., "Farm Tenancy and Productivity in Agriculture: The Case of the United States," *Food Research Institute Studies* 4, no. 1 (1963).

Buck, John Lossing, *Chinese Farm Economy* (Chicago: University of Chicago Press, 1930).

—— *An Economic and Social Survey of 102 Farms near Wuhu, Anwhei, China* (Nanking, 1923).

—— *An Economic and Social Survey of 150 Farms, Yehshan County, Hopei, China* (Nanking, 1926).

—— *Farm Ownership and Tenancy in China* (Shanghai: National Christian Council, 1927).

[1] An asterisk indicates that the work is available only in Chinese; quotations from these sources are my translations.

—— *Land Utilization in China* (Chicago: University of Chicago Press, 1938).

—— (ed.) *Land Utilization in China – Statistics – A Study of 16,786 Farms in 168 Localities and 38,256 Farm Families in Twenty-Two Provinces in China, 1929–1933* (Nanking: University of Nanking, 1938).

*Chen, Ching-Moh, *Land Rents of Various Provinces in China* (Shanghai: Commercial Press, 1936).

*Chinese National Government, *Shengching Route Economic Report* (1931).

Department of Agriculture and Forestry, *Taiwan Agricultural Yearbook, 1948 Edition* (Taiwan: Provincial Government, 1948).

—— *Taiwan Agricultural Yearbook, 1949 Edition* (Taiwan: Provincial Government, 1949).

—— *Taiwan Agricultural Yearbook, 1950 Edition* (Taiwan: Provincial Government, 1950).

—— *Taiwan Agricultural Yearbook, 1951 Edition* (Taiwan: Provincial Government, 1951).

—— *Taiwan Agricultural Yearbook, 1952 Edition* (Taiwan: Provincial Government, 1952).

—— *Taiwan Agricultural Yearbook, 1953 Edition* (Taiwan: Provincial Government, 1953).

—— *Taiwan Agricultural Yearbook, 1958 Edition* (Taiwan: Provincial Government, 1958).

*Department of Internal Affairs, *Public Reports of Internal Affairs*, 2.1 (China, 1932).

*—— *Public Reports of Internal Affairs*, 5.1 and 2 (China, 1932).

*Department of Real Estates, *China Economic Yearbook* (Shanghai: Commercial Press, 1935).

Georgescu-Roegen, N., "Economic Theory and Agrarian Reforms," *Oxford Economic Papers*, February 1960.

Gittinger, J. P., "Vietnamese Land Transfer Program," *Land Economics*, May 1957.

Gordon, H. Scott, "The Economic Theory of a Common-Property Resource: The Fishery," *Journal of Political Economy*, August 1954.

Grajdanzev, Andrew J., *Modern Korea* (New York: Institute of Pacific Relations, 1944).

—— "Statistics of Japanese Agriculture," mimeographed (New York: Institute of Pacific Relations, 1941).

Heady, Earl, "Economics of Farm Leasing Systems," *Journal of Farm Economics*, August 1947.

Heady, Earl, and Kehrberg, Earl, "Relationships of Crop Share and Cash Leasing Systems to Farming Efficiency," *Research Bulletin 386* (Iowa State College Agricultural Experiment Station, May 1952).

Higgins, Benjamin, *Economic Development* (New York: W. W. Norton, 1959).

Higgs, Henry, "Metayage in Western France," *The Economic Journal*, March 1894.

Hsieh, S. C., and Lee, T. H., "The Effects of Population Pressure and Seasonal Labor Surplus on the Pattern and Intensity of Agriculture in Taiwan," mimeographed (1964).

Issawi, Charles, "Farm Output under Fixed Rents and Share Tenancy," *Land Economics*, February 1957.

Johnson, D. Gale, "Resource Allocation under Share Contracts," *Journal of Political Economy*, April 1950.

Jones, Richard, *An Essay on the Distribution of Wealth and on the Sources of Taxation*, Part 1: *Rent* (London: John Murray, 1831).

Kao, C. H. C. et al. "Disguised Unemployment in Agriculture," in *Agriculture in Economic Development*, ed. C. K. Eicher and L. Witt (New York: McGraw-Hill, 1964).

King, F. H., *Farmers of Forty Centuries* (Emmaus: Organic Gardening Press, 1900).

Klein, Sidney, *The Pattern of Land Tenure Reform in East Asia after World War II* (New York: Bookman, 1958).

*Legislative Yuan, *Statistical Monthly*, 2.5 (China, 1930).

Lewis, W. A., "Economic Development with Unlimited Supplies of Labor," *Manchester School of Economic and Social Studies*, May 1954.

*Lu, Nien-Tsing, *An Analysis of Farm Family Economy of Owner-Operators under the Land-to-the-Tiller Program in Taiwan* (Taipei: The Research Department of the Land Bank of Taiwan, 1965).

McCulloch, J. R., *Principles of Political Economy* (Edinburgh, 1843).

Marshall, Alfred, *Principles of Economics*, 8th edn (1920; London: Macmillan, 1956).

Mill, John S., *Principles of Political Economy*, 4th edn (London: John W. Parker and Son, 1857).

Miller, Walter G., Chryst, Walter E., and Ottoson, Howard W., "Relative Efficiencies of Farm Tenure Classes in Intrafirm Resource Allocation," *Research Bulletin 461* (Iowa Agricultural and Home Economics Experiment Station, November 1958).

Ministry of Agriculture and Forestry, *Agricultural Land Reform Legislation* (Tokyo: 1949).

Myint, H., *The Economics of the Underdeveloped Countries* (London: Hutchinson, 1964).

Schickele, Rainer, "Effect of Tenure Systems on Agricultural Efficiency," *Journal of Farm Economics*, February 1941.

Sen, Amartya K., "Peasants and Dualism with or without Surplus Labor," *Journal of Political Economy*, October 1966.

Shen, Tsung-han, *Agricultural Development on Taiwan since World War II* (New York: Comstock, 1964).

—— *Agricultural Resources of China* (New York: Cornell University Press, 1951).

Sino-American Joint Commission on Rural Reconstruction, "JCRR Annual Reports on Land Reform in the Republic of China," Composite volume, mimeographed (1965).

Sismondi, J. C. L. Simonde de, *Political Economy* (1814; New York: Augustus M. Kelley, 1966).

Smith, Adam, *Wealth of Nations* (1776; New York: Modern Library edition, 1937).

Young, Arthur, *Travels in France during the Years 1787, 1788, 1789*, vol. 2 (Dublin reprint, 1793).

—— *Travels in France during the Years 1787, 1788, and 1789*, ed. Constania Maxwell (Cambridge: Cambridge University Press, 1929).

# 10

# Predatory Price Cutting: The Standard Oil (N.J.) Case

## John S. McGee

> He [Rockefeller] applied underselling for destroying his rivals' markets with the same deliberation and persistency that characterized all his efforts, and in the long run he always won.
>
> **Ida Tarbell**

## I  INTRODUCTION

The purpose of this paper is to determine whether the pre-dissolution Standard Oil Company actually used predatory price cutting to achieve or maintain its monopoly. This issue is of much more than antiquarian or theoretic interest. Settling it is of direct importance to present antitrust policy. At the very least, finding the facts should aid in defining certain hazy notions that now figure in discussions of monopoly and its control.

The *Standard Oil* case of 1911 is a landmark in the development of antitrust law.[1] But it is more than a famous law case: it created a legend. The firm whose history it relates became the archetype of predatory monopoly.

It is sometimes said that *Standard Oil* was influential because it revealed deadly and reprehensible techniques by which monopoly on a heroic scale could be achieved and, probably more important, perpetuated. Historians tell us that the facts revealed in *Standard Oil* were in good part responsible for the emphasis that the antitrust laws came to place upon unfair and monopolizing business practices.

Perhaps the most famous of all of the monopolizing techniques that Standard is supposed to have used is local price cutting. Given the bad repute in which monopoly has long been officially held in [the United States], and the prominence of predatory pricing in *Standard Oil*, it is not surprising that the practice received special attention in the law. Monopoly was not new in 1911, but a predatory giant may have seemed novel. The vision of a giant firm that used a brutally scientific, and completely effective, technique for acquiring and maintaining monopoly must have aroused uncommon concern. Standard was invincible. Anything economists could say about the transience of monopoly must have seemed hopelessly unrealistic in

[1] *Standard Oil Co. of New Jersey v. United States*, 221 U.S. 1 (1911).

view of the vigor and success with which Standard was said to have prevented entry.

In any case, by 1914, in the Clayton Act, predatory price discrimination was included among a select group of business practices the character or effect of which called for explicit statutory prohibition. The Robinson-Patman amendment of 1936 lengthened the list, but certainly did not weaken the hostility toward local price cutting. Indeed, its legislative history and subsequent interpretation reveal a continuing dread of the device.

Predatory discrimination thus occupies a special and almost unquestioned place in law and economics. This has led to a certain amount of difficulty, especially in connection with the Robinson-Patman Act. Some critics claim that this statute unnecessarily restricts rivalry, thereby softening competition. Yet even the critics apparently fear that if we permit the helpful kind of discrimination we will encourage the lethal kind. Most are obliged to rely on the tenuous standard of intent to distinguish one kind from the other.

This fearful ambivalence, in which the spectre of *Standard Oil* figures prominently, may be responsible for the continuing, and somewhat fruitless, arguments about the proper role of a "good faith" defense under Section 2(B) of the Robinson-Patman Act. It may also account for the popular view that disciplinary price cutting makes cartelization easier and its benefits more lasting. It surely has influenced thinking about small firms that face large rivals.

For these reasons, a re-examination of *Standard Oil* may be worthwhile.


## II   PREDATORY PRICE CUTTING: SOME HYPOTHESES

According to most accounts, the Standard Oil Co. of New Jersey established an oil refining monopoly in the United States, in large part through the systematic use of predatory price discrimination. Standard struck down its competitors, in one market at a time, until it enjoyed a monopoly position everywhere. Similarly, it preserved its monopoly by cutting prices selectively wherever competitors dared enter. Price discrimination, so the story goes, was both the technique by which it obtained its dominance and the device with which it maintained it.

The main trouble with this "history" is that it is logically deficient, and I can find little or no evidence to support it.[2]

A brief examination of the logic of predatory price discrimination is helpful in interpreting the facts. In the beginning, oil refining in the United States apparently was competitive. Necessary capital was relatively slight, because of the modest quality demands imposed by consumer preferences and the primitive technologi-

---

[2] I am profoundly indebted to Aaron Director, of the University of Chicago Law School, who in 1953 suggested that this study be undertaken. Professor Director, without investigating the facts, developed a logical framework by which he predicted that Standard Oil had not gotten or maintained its monopoly position by using predatory price cutting. In truth, he predicted, on purely logical grounds, that they never systematically used the technique at all. I was astounded by these hypotheses, and doubtful of their validity, but was also impressed by the logic which produced them. As a consequence, I resolved to investigate the matter, admittedly against my better judgment; for, like everyone else, I knew full well what Standard had really done.

cal character of the refining process itself. The number of refiners was evidently large, since the Standard interests bought out more than a hundred of them. Standard Oil was not born with monopoly power: as late as 1870 it had only 10 percent of the refining business.

The usual argument that local price cutting is a monopolizing technique *begins* by assuming that the predator has important monopoly power, which is his "war chest" for supporting the unprofitable raids and forays. Evidently the technique could not be used until the Standard interests achieved the necessary monopoly power. Similarly, advantages from monopsonistic bargaining would not be available until the buyer attained considerable stature.[3]

A simpler technique did exist, and Standard used it. Unless there are legal restraints, anyone can monopolize an industry through mergers and acquisitions, paying for the acquisitions by permitting participation of the former owners in the expected monopoly gains. Since profits are thus expanded, all of the participants can be better off even after paying an innovator's share to the enterpriser who got the idea in the first place.

Under either competition or monopoly, the value of a firm is the present worth of its future income stream. Competitive firms can be purchased for competitive asset values or, at worst, for only a little more. Even in the case of important recalcitrants, anything up to the present value of the future monopoly profits from the property will be a worthwhile exchange to the buyer, and a bountiful windfall to the seller.

It is conceivable that Standard did not merge to the full size it wanted, but did achieve whatever size was necessary to use predatory techniques to grow the rest of the way. How would it go about using them? Assume that Standard had an absolute monopoly in some important markets, and was earning substantial profits there. Assume that in another market there are several competitors, all of whom Standard wants to get out of the way. Standard cuts the price below cost. Everyone suffers losses. Standard would, of course, suffer losses even though it has other profitable markets: it could have been earning at least competitive returns and is not. The war could go on until average variable costs are not covered and are not expected to be covered; and the competitors drop out. In the meanwhile, the predator would have been pouring money in to crush them. If, instead of fighting, the would-be monopolist bought out his competitors directly, he could afford to pay them up to the discounted value of the expected monopoly profits to be gotten as a result of their extinction. Anything above the competitive value of their firms should be enough to buy them. In the purchase case, monopoly profits could begin at once; in the predatory case, large losses would first have to be incurred. Losses would have to be set off against the prospective monopoly profits, discounted appropriately. Even supposing that the competitors would not sell for competitive value, it is difficult to see why the predator would be unwilling to take the amount that he would otherwise spend in price wars and pay it as a bonus.

Since the revenues to be gotten during the predatory price war will always be

---

[3] Example: railroad rebates. Although this subject lies outside the present inquiry, I am convinced that the significance of railroad rebates has also been misunderstood.

less than those that could be gotten immediately through purchase, and will not be higher after the war is concluded, present worth will be higher in the purchase case. For a predatory campaign to make sense the direct costs of the price war must be less than for purchase. It is necessary to determine whether that is possible.

Assume that the monopolizer's costs are equal to those of his competitors. The market has enough independent sellers to be competitive. Otherwise the problem of monopolizing it ceases to concern us. This implies that the monopolist does not now sell enough in the market to control it. If he seeks to depress the price below the competitive level he must be prepared to sell increasing quantities, since the mechanism of forcing a lower price compels him to lure customers away from his rivals, making them meet his price or go without customers. To lure customers away from somebody, he must be prepared to serve them himself. The monopolizer thus finds himself in the position of selling more – and therefore losing more – than his competitors. Standard's market share was often 75 percent or more. In the 75 percent case the monopolizer would sell three times as much as all competitors taken together, and, on the assumption of equal unit costs, would lose roughly three times as much as all of them taken together.[4]

Losses incurred in this way are losses judged even by the standard of competitive returns. Since the alternative of outright purchase of rivals would have produced immediate monopoly returns, the loss in view of the alternatives can be very great indeed.[5] Furthermore, at some stage of the game the competitors may simply shut down operations temporarily, letting the monopolist take all the business (and all the losses), then simply resume operations when he raises prices again. At prices above average variable costs, but below total unit costs, the "war" might go on for years.

Purchase has an additional marked advantage over the predatory technique. It is rare for an industrial plant to wear out all at once. If price does not cover average variable costs, the operation is suspended. This will often leave the plant wholly intact. In the longer run, it may simply be the failure of some key unit, the replacement of which is uneconomic at the present price level, that precipitates shut-down. In either case, physical capacity remains, and will be brought back into play by some opportunist once the monopolizer raises prices to enjoy the fruits of the battle he has spent so much in winning.

All in all, then, purchase would not be more expensive than war without quarter, and should be both cheaper and more permanent. It may at first be thought that predatory pricing more than makes up for its expense by depressing the purchase price of the properties to be absorbed. In effect, this requires that large losses reduce asset values less than smaller losses. This is not at all likely. Furthermore, assuming that the properties in question are economic,[6] it is unlikely that their

---

[4] Any assumption that the monopolizer's size gives him sufficient cost advantages rapidly takes us away from a predatory price cutting example and into the realm of so-called natural monopolies.

[5] It must not be supposed that, just because he enjoys profits elsewhere, anyone will be so stupid as to assume that it is costless to use them for anything but the best alternatives.

[6] If they are not, they need not concern us, since their extinction might be expected or welcomed under competition.

long-run market value will be much reduced by an artificially low price that clearly will not be permanent. The owners can shut down temporarily, allowing the monopolist to carry all of the very unprofitable business, or simply wait for him to see the error of his ways and purchase. Even if there is widespread bankruptcy, wise men will see the value to the monopolist of bringing the facilities under his control, and find it profitable to purchase them at some price below what the monopolist can be expected to pay if he must. Since the monopolist is presumably interested in profits, and has a notion of the effect of discount factors upon future income, he cannot afford to wait forever. Properties that a would-be monopolist needs to control can be an attractive investment.

Predation would thus be profitable only when the process produces purchase prices that are so far below competitive asset figures that they more than offset the large losses necessary to produce them. One empirical test, for those who suspect the logic, would be to examine prices paid for properties in cases where predatory pricing is alleged to have been practiced.

Some of the most strategic factors to be monopolized may be the skilled managerial and technical personnel of competitors. Reproducing them can be a much more formidable and longer job than the construction of physical facilities. But short of murder, the cost of which can also be expected to be high if undertaken in any quantity, the only feasible way of preventing their embarrassing and costly reappearance is to hire, retire, or share with them. None of these things can be accomplished well or permanently if these people are too much badgered in the process.[7]

There are two other crucial issues that must be examined, the first dealing with the extent to which monopolization is profitable; the second, with the necessary conditions for its success. Monopolization as such will be carried only so far as is necessary to maximize profits, since it inevitably involves certain expenses of planning, purchase, and rationalization. In the case of a vertically integrated industry the would-be monopolist will choose to monopolize the level that will produce the largest net profit. This requires choosing that one which is both cheapest to control and over which control is likely to endure. If a monopoly can be achieved at the refining level, for example, there is little sense trying to achieve one at the crude oil producing level, or marketing. Standard Oil of New Jersey achieved a refinery monopoly; anything more would have been redundant.[8]

This should not be taken to mean that the monopolist will not care what happens to the other levels; for he has every interest in seeing to it that the other levels are not monopolized by someone else. In marketing, for example, he would prefer that

---

[7] "[A]s Mr. Rockefeller and Mr. Archbold testified, most of the concerns which were brought together continued to be operated and managed by the former owners." Brief for the U.S., vol. 1, p. 19.

Further, "There are only a few cases in which the Standard interests, during this period [1872–80], acquired stock in concerns without taking the former owners in as stockholders of the Standard, or bringing them into the combination by leaving them a minority interest in the original concern." Ibid., p. 32.

[8] This abstracts from any cost reductions that integration may make possible. These have nothing to do with the problem at hand.

See Bork, "Vertical Integration and the Sherman Act," *U. of Chi. L. Rev.* 22 (1954), p. 157. Standard began producing crude oil in 1889, and by 1898 produced 33 percent of the total. By 1906, its share declined to 11.11 percent. Transcript of Record (Def. Exh. 266, vol. 19, p. 626).

the product be distributed as cheaply as possible, since he can then extract full monopoly revenues from the level in his control. This point is important in interpreting the facts of the *Standard Oil* case.

Obstacles to entry are necessary conditions for success. Entry is the nemesis of monopoly. It is foolish to monopolize an area or market into which entry is quick and easy. Moreover, monopolization that produces a firm of greater than optimum size is in for trouble if entry can occur even over a longer period. In general, monopolization will not pay if there is no special qualification for entry, or no relatively long gestation period for the facilities that must be committed for successful entry.

Finally, it is necessary to examine certain data that are often taken to be symptomatic of predatory price cutting, when in fact they may be nothing of the sort. Assume that a monopolist sells in two markets, separated effectively by transport costs or other impediments to free interchange, and that he has a complete monopoly in both. Elasticity of demand is assumed to be the same in both markets, and monopoly prices are identical. Assume that, for some unknown reason, entry occurs in one market but not in the other. Supplies are increased in the first and price falls; price in the second remains unchanged. There are now two different prices in the two markets, reflecting the existence of alternative supplies in the first. The theory of the dominant firm, maximizing by taking into account the outputs of his lesser rivals at various prices, appears to fit the case. An objective factfinder discovers that the monopolist is discriminating in price between the two markets. A bad theorist then concludes that he is preying on somebody. In truth, the principle established is only that greater supplies bring lower prices.

Compare this example with another. Assume that we have two separate markets, and that each is in short-run competitive equilibrium with firms earning super-normal returns. Assume that, for some reason, entry takes place in one market but not in the other. Supply increases and price falls in one but not in the other. From this evidence of price changes in both the monopoly and competition examples, the inference is simply that greater supplies lower prices. We should not infer from the price data that either case has anything to do with predatory price-cutting.

To sum up: (1) Predatory price cutting does not explain how a seller acquires the monopoly power that he must have before he could practice it. (2) Whereas it is *conceivable* that someone might embark on a predatory program, I cannot see that it would pay him to do so, since outright purchase is both cheaper and more reliable. (3) Because monopolization by any technique always involves some expense, a firm *qua* monopolizer will carry it to the one securest level in an integrated industry, not to all. (4) Actual variations in prices among markets may be accounted for in terms of variations in demand elasticities, but do not imply or establish that anybody is preying on anybody else.

## III  TESTING THE HYPOTHESES

The voluminous Record in the Standard Oil of N.J. dissolution suit furnishes a test of these propositions.[9]

The Record shows that: Standard established a refining monopoly.[10] Collusion among 100 to 200 different sellers was unstable. Standard achieved its monopoly position through merger and acquisition.[11] Although the Government alleged that Standard employed other techniques as well, it concluded that:

> Unquestionably the principal means used by the defendants to monopolize and restrain trade and commerce in petroleum has been the combination of previously independent concerns.[12]

> Standard acquired 123 refineries (many of which also did a marketing business), 11 lubricating oil works, 24 pipeline concerns, and 64 exclusively marketing concerns; a total number of 223.
>     Neither did these acquisitions all occur at an early date, about half of them, in number, occurred since 1879, and many important ones between 1890 and 1902.[13]

Of the refineries it acquired, Standard dismantled at least 75, and ultimately produced a greatly increased volume in only 20 separate installations.[14]

## 1  Price cutting against competing refiners

Standard's monopoly was in refining. Is there any evidence that predatory price cutting helped to achieve it?[15] To discover whether local price cutting played any

---

[9] The Transcript of Record consists of over 11,000 printed pages of exhibits and testimony; Appellants' briefs and oral argument covers more than 900 pages; Appellee's briefs and arguments almost 1,300 pages. The full record is thus more than 13,500 pages long. Unless otherwise noted, volume references are to the Transcript of Record.

[10] In 1879, Standard and those concerns "in harmony" with it, apparently refined from 90 to 95 percent of the U.S. output. See Vol. 6, p. 3303. It is not clear just what these data mean. Mr. Archbold testified that in 1870 Standard did about 10 percent of the refining business in the United States; and that for 1888 Standard's share was probably 75 percent. Ibid., pp. 3246–68. I think that much work remains to be done to determine how Standard's market position really changed over time. See e.g., vol. 2, pp. 783–4.

In any case, Standard's position in crude oil production was relatively small; it did very little retailing and did not perform all of its own wholesaling; several major railroads and the pipeline systems of Pure, Tidewater, Texas Co., Gulf, and others competed in the transportation of crude oil. Its strongest position was evidently in refining.

[11] "Q. Had you difficulty before you entered into relations with the Standard Oil Company to make money out of the business? A. The competition was always very sharp, and there was always someone that was willing to sell goods for less than they cost, and that made the market price for everything; we got up an association, and took in all the refiners until some of them went back on us, and that would break up the association; we tried that two or three times." Vol. 6, p. 3303.

See also Mr. Rockefeller's interesting testimony on the difficulty of effecting stable conspiracies. Vol. 16, especially pp. 3074–5.

[12] Brief for the United States, vol. 1, p. 169.

[13] Reply Brief for the United States, p. 62. See Appendix C, Sheets 1–11.

[14] Ibid., pp. 63–4.

[15] The first problem is to discover which companies were really refiners. Oddly enough, many of the

part in the many refinery acquisitions made by the Standard interests, I checked the whole Record for testimony about every refinery known to have been bought.[16] Furthermore, I have tried to check every alleged case of local price cutting involving competitive refiners that Standard did *not* buy. I can find few specific references to refiners in connection with allegations that Standard cut prices to drive out competitors. The following are the principal examples, including cases in which the marketing subsidiaries or branches of Standard's integrated competitors were involved. They are certainly the most significant ones.

### (a) "Suspect" cases involving acquisitions
### The Cleveland Acquisitions

During 1871–2 the Rockefeller interests purchased at least 17 Cleveland refineries.[17] I can find no real evidence that predatory price cutting or any other type of coercion figured in the acquisitions. According to Mr. Rockefeller, the consolidation of the Cleveland refineries was a blessing to all concerned, and arose

> In a most natural way . . . We were; [sic] neighbors, acquaintances, friends, having had our prosperity there together in the business in the good days; and beginning generally to recognize the changes that were coming, and the lessening of the chance of good returns from the refining business on account of the overproduction of refined oil, or the overproduction of the refinery construction.[18]

On the other hand, Mr. Lewis Emery, Jr., a long-time crude oil producer and refiner from Bradford, Pennsylvania, offered the following hearsay on the subject: "I talked with quite a number of them afterwards, and they said they thought the case was hopeless and they had arranged with the combination."[19]

Predatory price cutting had nothing to do with the acquisitions, according even to Mr. Emery's version. There is some question about Mr. Emery's testimony in any case: Emery was testifying, in 1908, about events that occurred 36 years earlier. Furthermore, he had evidently not been in Cleveland at this time and had no first-hand knowledge of the affair.[20]

---

firms mentioned in the record have "Refining Company" as part of their names, but were apparently not refiners at all. One example is Mr. Castle's Columbia Refining Co., wholly a marketing concern. Possibly the owners concluded that customers are better disposed towards marketers who make the products they sell.

[16] Brief for the United States, vol. 1, Appendices C and D; vol. 19, pp. 662–3; vol. 17, p. 3290.

[17] Reply Brief for the United States, Appendix C, Sheet 1.

[18] Vol. 16, p. 3065.

[19] Vol. 6, p. 2625. According to Emery, the refiners were pushed into consolidation because of the rail rate "preferences" given to Standard in the South Improvement Company program and the succeeding pool agreement of 1874. The South Improvement program apparently never became effective; and the contract of 1874, which Emery said sealed the doom of Pennsylvania independent refiners, simply *equalized* rail freight from Cleveland and Western Pennsylvania refineries. Ibid., pp. 2724, 2732. See testimony of Archbold, ibid., pp. 3244–5.

[20] Though it does not really prove anything, it is interesting that Emery was first of all a crude producer and like any raw materials supplier had little affection for the monopsony that faced him. He was also a successful politician during a period in which antitrust had great popular appeal. Ibid., p. 2642.

There are very good reasons to suppose that no kind of coercion figured in the Cleveland purchases. The stock records and a great deal of testimony confirm that Standard's usual practice during this time was to employ the managers and owners of the firms they absorbed, and often to make them shareholders as well. Victimized ex-rivals might be expected to make poor employees and dissident or unwilling shareholders.

## Mr. Emery's Own Experience

Lewis Emery entered the industry as a crude oil producer in 1865. By 1870 he became interested in the Octave Oil Company and Refinery. In 1875, Emery closed down the Octave, and in 1876 sold it to the Standard interests for $45,000.[21] Emery claimed that the railroad pool agreement of 1874 had squeezed him out along with other small Western Pennsylvania refiners. Predatory price cutting clearly had nothing to do with it.[22]

Whatever his reasons for selling the Octave, Mr. Emery was apparently not discouraged. For, in 1879, Emery and two partners formed Logan, Emery & Weaver, and started a new refinery at Philadelphia.[23] By 1880 the refinery was completed.[24] Nevertheless, he testified, his firm soon had trouble getting empty railroad cars.[25] Seven years later, Logan, Emery & Weaver sold out to Standard.[26] According to Emery, the original cost of the refinery, lands and wharves was $350,000. Standard bought the refinery for $275,000 and promptly dismantled it, though Emery claimed that the plant was "[f]irst class in every sense."[27] He did admit that refinery depreciation was commonly 10 to 15 percent per annum.[28] Emery said he sold because he could not get crude oil. The problem was, according to Emery, that Standard

---

[21] Ibid., pp. 2610, 2640. It was small, and must have been relatively high cost, since Standard dismantled it forthwith.

[22] See Note 19 above. Apparently even the railroad rebates, which Emery claimed built Standard, were also available to the small refiner: "[I]n the very early history of the Octave Oil Company, when we were shut down, we went to the railroads and they said they would give us 25 cents rebate . . . [p]er barrel on oil." Ibid., pp. 2772–3.

See also the testimony of Archbold (ibid., pp. 3244–5); and Josiah Lombard, an independent: "They gave . . . all shippers over that road a rebate of 10 percent, which we got with others." Vol. 1, p. 265. See also note 37 below.

[23] Mr. Emery was by this time a member of the Pennsylvania Legislature and remained in office for ten years thereafter. Vol. 6, p. 2642.

[24] Interestingly enough, Mr. Emery had borrowed $25,000 from – of all people – the Standard Oil Company. Ibid., p. 2643.

[25] Ibid. General rail car shortages were not infrequent during this period. Some oldtimers indicated that certain rail centers attracted refiners because they typically provided plenty of empty freight cars.

[26] Ibid., p. 2645.

[27] Ibid., p. 2646. Emery asked $750,000 for the refinery, but accepted $275,000. Ibid., p. 2768. Emery thought the plant was worth the money, "[b]ecause we had a large export trade, what independent refineries there were, and a very good opportunity to make a margin on our oils if we could get them there at the same price the Standard Oil Company did" (ibid.).

It is not clear whether Standard bought only the refinery for $275,000 or refinery, wharves, and real estate.

[28] Ibid., p. 2738.

and the crude oil producers had agreed to reduce crude output after the excessive production of 1887.[29]

Mr. Emery had also been interested in the Equitable Company, which built a crude oil pipeline in 1878, and sold it to the Tidewater interests for $178,000 in 1879. In 1889 Mr. Emery bought a small Bradford refinery for $5,000, commencing business with 250-barrel stills.[30] By 1908, output was 1,500 barrels per day. The Emery Manufacturing Company at Bradford, Pennsylvania thus had a much-enlarged refinery worth $250,000 to $400,000 and gathering lines worth $200,000. Sales had expanded from about $20,000 per year to between $480,000 and $600,000 per year. Standard's "predatory" tactics, if there were any, had apparently neither discouraged nor ruined Mr. Emery's own business.[31]

Furthermore, Emery became president of the United States Pipeline Company, which, in 1891, constructed a crude oil pipeline. The United States Pipeline Company later sold out to the Pure Oil Company.[32] When Emery sold the company, he took about $100,000 in Pure Oil Company stock, and retained a $15,000 interest in U.S. Pipeline. By 1893, Standard had bought a four-tenths interest in the United States Pipeline, but Emery and his colleagues frustrated their efforts to vote the stock.[33] In 1908, Emery's Philadelphia refinery had a capacity of 2,000 barrels per day, and his other oil interests were extensive. Emery clearly had a successful career, an important part of which consisted of selling companies to Standard and others. However rough the competitive storm may have been, Emery certainly weathered it well.

Emery's sole allegation of local price cutting concerns his Philadelphia marketing business, which he ultimately leased to Pure Oil Co. He admits he did not know who really started the Philadelphia price war.[34]

## Holdship & Irwin

In 1878 this Allegheny, Pennsylvania firm, with an output of 1,000 barrels of products per day, leased their refinery to Standard for five years.[35] Under the lease, the partners continued to run the refinery for Standard on a salary basis till 1883, when the lease expired and Holdship & Irwin resumed operation on their own account.[36] In 1886, they sold the refinery to Standard, with the understanding that they would

[29] Ibid., p. 2646. It seems strange that Standard, a large net purchaser of crude oil, would acquiesce in any scheme to increase the price of its principal raw material. In any case, abortive crude oil producers' cartels attempted, from time to time, to monopolize and shut in wells. See testimony of Rockefeller on the 1872–4 shut down. Vol. 16, pp. 3073 ff.; also testimony of Tarbell, vol. 3, p. 1430.

[30] With a probable daily output of 90 to 150 barrels.

[31] Vol. 6, pp. 2769–70.

[32] Emery summed up Pure Oil's business by saying that "Their money has been principally made in the production of crude oil" (ibid., p. 2718). According to Emery, Pure Oil's sales rose at least 15 percent to 20 percent between 1900 and 1908; dividends were 8 percent per annum.

[33] Ibid., pp. 2659–60.

[34] Ibid., pp. 2668–9. Emery did admit that he had cut Standard's prices, pp. 2785 ff.

[35] Ibid., p. 3013 – testimony of Lewis Irwin.

[36] Ibid., p. 3014.

not go back into the oil refining business. Mr. Irwin's testimony does not indicate that Standard used coercion of any kind.[37]

## The Empire Oil Works and the Globe Refining Co

In 1875 or 1876, Mr. David P. Reighard started the Empire Oil works in Pittsburgh. When Holdship & Irwin sold in 1886, Reighard also sold out to Standard.[38] Reighard stayed out of the oil business till 1887, when he built the Globe Refining Company at Pittsburgh.[39] He ran the Globe for 18 to 20 months, then sold out to Standard again. At the same time, Mr. Reighard sold a large Philadelphia refinery, which he was in the process of building.[40] The sale was no occasion for sadness, for as Mr. Reighard put it:

> Well, the reason I sold out was I found that the bonus that I asked those people (the Standard Oil) was as much as I could actually make on the profits for 15 or 20 years to come.[41]

Reighard sold for $1,224,800 in trust certificates and $50,000 cash.[42] Each of the last two refineries that Reighard sold to Standard had cost between $200,000 and $250,000. Thus it was that Mr. Reighard managed to build and sell three refineries to Standard, all on excellent terms.

## Woodland Oil Company (Mr. C. J. Castle)

Mr. Castle was an important government witness on predatory price cutting and other unfair competition. He had been an oil refiner, and was still a marketer of petroleum products when he testified. At this point we will deal only with Mr. Castle's early role as a refiner who sold out to the Rockefeller group.

In 1883, Mr. Castle and a partner started the Woodland Oil Company, a small Cleveland refinery.[43] They began with $8,000 to $10,000 capital. By 1886, book capital was $14,000, and Woodland sold to the Rockefeller interests for the same amount. Castle implied that one reason he sold was inability to get crude oil from the Standard Oil pipeline. But he did not allege that predatory price cutting played any

---

[37] Ibid. Irwin's testimony is also interesting on other grounds. (1) He claims that Standard accomplished considerable economies of scale (ibid., p. 3022). (2) In the period 1872–4, when both the railroad and oil industries were overbuilt and "demoralized," everyone in the oil business was getting rail freight rebates ("drawbacks"). In Irwin's words, "There were drawbacks and drawbacks within drawbacks . . . Everybody got drawbacks in those days" (ibid., pp. 3026–7).

[38] The Empire and Holdship & Irwin were co-owners of a pipeline system (ibid., p. 3131).

[39] It had 12 crude stills, each of 600 barrels capacity, and some pipelines (ibid., p. 3134).

[40] Ibid., p. 3136.

[41] Ibid., p. 3135.

[42] "Well, they didn't want us to take any certificates at all . . . I forced them, or went after them several times till I got them to give me some certificates." Ibid. The value given for the trust certificates was par value. Market value was higher. Vol. 17, p. 3332. The Government gives the "competitive value" of the two Reighard properties as $823,000. Reply Brief for the United States, Appendix C, Sheet 8.

[43] Capacity: 200 barrels per day. Vol. 6, p. 3060. By 1908, capacity of Standard's Whiting, Indiana refinery was 25,000–30,000 barrels per day.

part in the sale, and did not feel aggrieved at the price Standard paid for his property.[44] Indeed, after selling the refinery, he went to work for Standard and remained in their employ for about 14 years.

Castle told several other stories about Standard's predatory price cutting during the period in which he worked for them.[44a] Nevertheless, I think it is significant that when he left Standard in 1900 he was clearly unafraid: he immediately started a rival oil marketing firm.

## The Rocky Mountain Oil Company

Mr. E. M. Wilhoit's brief but pointed version of this affair clearly implies intent and ability to crush out competition. Wilhoit was employed by Standard at the time this incident took place, and claimed to know something about it. In his words,

> Before the Refinery got in operation, the Standard Oil made our fight on the Rocky Mountain Company and the Union Pacific went into the hands of a receiver and the Refinery was afterwards dismantled – went broke of course.[45]

On the surface, this incident is the nearest thing to predatory price cutting that I found in the Record. But there are reasons to suppose that there was something more here than meets the eye.

First, it is interesting that no complaint from the Rocky Mountain interests appears in the Record. Second, Continental – the Standard Company in the area – had entered into an agreement with the Florence Oil and Refinery Company and the United Oil Company, both located at Florence, Colorado.[46] Under the agreement, the two refiners sold their whole output of refined products to Continental. Prices were presumably attractive to the refiners, though, in view of the almost complete marketing monopoly of Standard in the area, quantities taken must have been limited.[47]

The United commenced refining oil about 1887 or 1888.[48] Sometime after Florence and United entered into the exclusive arrangement with Continental, shareholders of United and Florence started the Rocky Mountain Company at Pueblo, Colorado. A price war with Continental ensued. About 1894, after some two years of conflict, Rocky Mountain sold its crude oil properties to Western Oil Company, a producing subsidiary of United and Rocky Mountain. It is not clear what happened to the refinery itself, except that Rocky Mountain no longer ran it.[49]

---

[44] Ibid., p. 3029.

[44a] The relevant anecdotes are analyzed in the Marketing section of this paper.

[45] Vol. 3, p. 1216. The Government's position runs less to intent and causes, and more to a history of events. For, in Volume 2 of Brief for the United States, p. 157, the Government says: "parties connected with the United Company undertook to establish another refinery known as the Rocky Mountain . . . a violent price-cutting competition started in between the Standard's marketing company, the Continental, and this company . . . the Rocky Mountain Company failed and went out of business."

[46] Standard later came to own 17 percent of the stock of the United. Ibid. This may raise certain questions of minority shareholders' interests.

[47] The Government claimed that a little over 1 percent of the market was supplied by independents and "the marketing of oil in this territory is extremely profitable." Ibid.

[48] Vol. 1, p. 155.

[49] Ibid., p. 181.

What does this episode mean? Although the facts are not as ample as we would like, there is one hypothesis that is both logical and wholly consistent with what facts we do have: Standard had marketing facilities in the area, but no local supplies. Standard's refined products had to be brought in from Whiting, Indiana. The United-Florence interests had crude oil and refinery capacity. There may have been other competing refiners in the market as well.

Standard agreed to take certain quantities of refined products from United-Florence, at specified prices, in return for which the refiners agreed not to sell to anyone else. A restricted refinery output could be better for all concerned. But to get it, Standard would have to share monopoly gains with the refiners. In that way duplication of marketing facilities and refining capacity could be avoided.

In this case, as in other such sales arrangements, there must have been a temptation for the producers to sneak out a little more output on the side, in violation of the agreement, and thereby make supernormal returns on a larger output. That would be the best of all possible worlds: the monopoly price could be gotten from Standard on a limited quantity; in addition, a larger amount could be disposed of, on the side, at higher than competitive prices. Since United and Florence had an agreement with Standard for limited quantities, one way to chisel or to work their way into a larger share of the cartel profits would be to start a new firm. This they did in the form of the Rocky Mountain Company. Mr. Wesley H. Tilford, Treasurer of the Standard Oil Company of New Jersey, explained the purpose of Rocky Mountain in these words:

> They were not satisfied with the interest in the United and they built another refinery to take part of their own business.[50]

Mr. Henry M. Tilford, President of Continental since 1893, confirmed and elaborated Wesley Tilford's recollection of the incident:

> Early in 1891 or 1892 Mr. Daniel Eells came to our office, and had an interview with W. H. Tilford and myself in which he stated that he and some friends proposed to build a refinery in Colorado, and asked if the Continental Oil Company would take their output. He was told the Continental Oil Company was getting from the Florence Oil and Refining Company and the United Oil Company all the oil they could market in that vicinity. Some little time afterwards he came back to the office and said that the refinery had been built, and asked again if the Continental Oil Company could take the output, and he was advised that they could not, that the situation was the same as it was before . . . They commenced business and they commenced cutting prices.[51]

What happened after the reabsorption of Rocky Mountain is also consistent with the cartel hypothesis: the refiners *raised* the prices of refined products to Continental. Whatever their object, then, the net result was that United and Florence apparently emerged from the conflict with more favorable contract terms *vis-à-vis*

---

[50] Ibid., p. 156.
[51] Vol. 2, pp. 730–1.

Standard.[52] Tilford did not regard Rocky Mountain as having failed, but simply as having been reabsorbed by those who started it.[53]

With the passage of time, more refineries were built in the Rockies. By 1907, when Mr. Henry Tilford testified, refineries had been built in Sugar Creek and Evanston, Wyoming; Spring Valley, and Boulder, Colorado. At least two, those at Spring Valley and Boulder, were independent, and built between 1905 and 1906.[54] This suggests either that memories are short; or that those who were familiar with the episode did not regard the Rocky Mountain incident as a case of predatory price cutting.

## The 1895 purchases

James W. Lee, Vice President and Director of Pure Oil, testified that in the 1890s a group of Pennsylvania refiners sent emissaries to Standard to moderate the "destructive competition" that plagued them.[55] Standard offered to purchase their pipelines and facilities, for cost plus 12 percent. Whether for those terms or not, some of the group sold out, including Mr. Ramage.[56] It is interesting that none of those who sold out came forward to testify that they had been abused in any way.

Most did not sell, but banded together and formed the Pure Oil Company in 1895.[57] Pure Oil thus became the largest independent oil company in the United States. It was also a profitable one.[58]

Although Lee did not allege local price cutting, he claimed that Standard had squeezed the independent refiners by bidding up the price of crude oil in 1895.[59] As it turns out, however, since Standard was actually buying 90 percent of the crude oil in question, such a maneuver would have cost Standard a great deal more than those it was seeking to punish.[60]

## The Argand Refining Company

In spite of having "the regular severe competition of the Standard all the way through,"[61] this refinery was a profitable business. It earned "a little over $35,000"

---

[52] It may be that the cartel had more refiner members than United and Florence, for Tilford said "there were other people in the oil business selling oil to the Continental, and indirectly it affected them, of course." Vol. 1, p. 177, and see also p. 180.

[53] Ibid., p. 181.

[54] Vol. 2, pp. 731–2.

[55] Vol. 6, pp. 3169–70. Lee did not refer to local price cutting as a factor.

[56] Ramage evidently took some Standard stock, for he appears on the Standard stockholder lists. Messrs. Fertig and Burwell also sold.

[57] Consistent with logic, but not with a theory of predation, are Standard's persistent efforts to buy stock control in Pure Oil Company affiliates. Vol. 6, pp. 3176–9.

[58] Ibid., p. 3191.

[59] Ibid., pp. 3192–3.

[60] Ibid., pp. 3192–4. Apart from this elementary fact, quite acceptable and logical alternative explanations were given.

[61] Testimony of Cram, vol. 3, p. 1349. Earlier he had said: "Not anything more than ordinary competition in their business, I should judge . . . Well, I cannot say they cut on us particularly; they were a larger concern than we were and we followed their prices." Vol. 5, p. 2422.

a year, net, with 600 barrel still capacity and $50,000 beginning capital.[62] Dividends were paid regularly at the rate of 2½ percent per quarter.

Argand included among its stockholders several railroad officials.[63] According to Cram,

> There were no threats as to what they [Standard] would do if we didn't sell out. Our railroad stockholders became convinced that we would lose our railroad business, from which we derived half of our net profit.[64]
>
> The refinery was finally disposed of [to Standard] on a lease basis for $20,000 a year, for a period of ten years. It was afterwards adjusted on a cash basis on which our stockholders, on which the company, got $180,000.[65]

Predatory price cutting obviously had nothing to do with the sale.[66]

## Scofield, Shurmer and Teagle

This firm was one of the last large refiners purchased by Standard before its dissolution. SS&T had a refinery at Cleveland,[67] and sold about 200,000 barrels of refined products a year in Michigan, Illinois, Indiana, Iowa, Nebraska, Kansas and Missouri.[68] SS&T and Standard were old rivals, and had several clashes over the years. In 1876 Standard and SS&T ended one competitive struggle by signing a market-sharing contract. Under its terms Standard guaranteed a minimum profit to SS&T, in exchange for output limitation; and shared additional profits in specified proportions.[69] But in 1880, SS&T broke the contract, and, when Standard sought to enforce it, denounced the instrument as a tool of an unlawful monopoly.[70]

Nevertheless, when SS&T sold out, Walter Teagle joined Standard, as did the old staff. According to Walter C. Teagle, son of the head of SS&T, Standard continued to employ all but three SS&T employees after the acquisition.[71] Standard operated the

---

[62] Vol. 3, p. 1351. At that time, a still would be "run off" about once every two or three days at best. This would have made a 200 barrel per day output, or 73,000 barrels per year without allowance for down time and "turnarounds." Actual output was probably lower. See Vol. 5, pp. 2419–20.

[63] Vol. 3, p. 1349.

[64] Ibid., p. 1350. About half of the $200,000 capital stock was held by officials of the B&OSW and the Marietta & Columbus Northern Railroads. These railroads bought about one-fourth or one-fifth of Argand's output.

[65] Ibid., p. 1352. The sale apparently was consummated in 1897. Cram agreed to stay out of the oil business, as did some others. Vol. 5, p. 2424.

[66] It is curious that in his much earlier testimony Cram did not mention the possible loss of railroad business as a factor in the sale. Whereas in his later testimony he is not really hostile to Standard, and certainly does not claim local price cutting, Cram seems less happy with the sale. Perhaps he came to regret it. One possibility is that Cram felt aggrieved when the ample "stand-by" salaries Standard paid the managers under the original settlement gave way to a cash settlement to stockholders.

[67] According to Teagle, "We had a refinery at Cleveland, but the refinery at Cleveland was old and out of date, and the capacity of it was limited as compared with the sales end of our business. I don't suppose we refined, during the years immediately previous to our sale, over 35 to 40 percent of the refined oil products that we sold. Cleveland had ceased to be a refining center." Vol. 3, p. 1467.

[68] Ibid., p. 1468.

[69] Vol. 16, p. 3204.

[70] Ibid., p. 3205.

[71] Vol. 3, p. 1150. SS&T sold out in 1901 (ibid., p. 1153). After the dissolution Mr. Teagle became president of Standard Oil of New Jersey.

SS&T facilities under the style of Republic Oil Company till about 1905.[72] Claims that Standard operated SS&T as a "bogus independent" only strengthen the hypothesis that there was no coercion surrounding the sale. For it is impossible to keep a secret when those who must be relied on to keep it can injure their enemies by betraying it.

In any case, there is no evidence that predatory price cutting had anything to do with the SS&T acquisition, or with the terms on which Standard purchased it.[73]

## Summary

The record does not indicate that predatory price cutting forced any refiner to sell out. The only doubtful case is that of the Rocky Mountain Company and, in my opinion, this incident is no exception to the rule. Furthermore, there is no evidence that predatory price cutting was used to depress asset value of any of the more than one hundred-twenty competitive refineries that Standard bought.[74] So far as I can make out, Standard's purchase terms were generally very good, and sometimes lavish. Abstracting from purchases, the mortality rate in refining was evidently low after Standard achieved a monopoly position.

### (b) "Suspect" cases that did not result in merger or purchase

There remains the possibility that Standard used local price cutting to drive rival refiners to the wall without purchasing them. Perhaps Standard, without having to buy them out, simply exterminated them.

The following integrated refining firms at one time or another had local, or general, clashes with Standard. Standard did not buy, or merge with, any of these firms. Testimony about these incidents was often vague, which is not too surprising in view of the very long period covered.[75] There is also a large amount of pure hearsay, and many facts were hotly controverted.

### Fehsenfeld (the Red C interests)

Mr. W. H. Fehsenfeld was president of the Red C Oil Manufacturing Co. of Baltimore.[76] Red C was a marketing company, but Fehsenfeld was also president of Island Petroleum, a refiner.[77]

---

[72]  Ibid., pp. 1153 ff.

[73]  One independent oil man made the following observation about SS&T: "They had a plant that they maintained and they maintained it until they *succeeded* in selling out to the Standard." Vol. 2, p. 987. (Italics supplied.)

There is no real evidence that the "bogus" Republic waged predatory price cutting campaigns, either. See testimony of Crenshaw, for example, on the amicable settlement of one price cutting flurry in 1902: Vol. 3, pp. 1173–4.

[74]  See Mr. Lombard's testimony on the "very fair" prices Standard paid the refiners it bought out. Vol. 1, p. 250.

[75]  Testimony covered the period 1865 through 1908.

[76]  Vol. 5, p. 2302.

[77]  Ibid., p. 2330. Fehsenfeld was also President of the Columbia Oil Co., and Vice-President of both the Georgia Oil Co. and the Richmond Oil Co. All but Island were marketing companies. Island owned stock in the various marketing companies.

Fehsenfeld testified that up to about 1897, Red C and Standard competed in the South in the sale of barreled refined products. After 1897, Standard relied increasingly upon the tank wagon method of distribution. Red C continued to emphasize barrel distribution.[78] According to Fehsenfeld, Standard systematically offered price inducements to merchants to prevent Red C from making up carload shipments of 60 barrels, and sometimes induced Red C customers to countermand their orders.[79]

At one time or another, Red C faced competition from five different "bogus independents" operated by Standard.[80] According to Fehsenfeld, "[T]hey sold regardless of price, in order to secure our business."[81] On some occasions, at least, Red C clearly started the price cutting. Indeed, Red C evidently employed price cutting whenever it served their interests. As Fehsenfeld explained:

> I did certainly cut the price in order to get the business. . . . As occasion was necessary; that is to say, *in going into a territory we would have to offer some inducement.* . . . Sometimes I would sell – it would depend entirely upon the quality of the oil – at prices lower than the Standard or sell at prices higher than the Standard.[82]

According to C. T. Collings, Second Vice-President of the Standard Oil Company of Kentucky, Red C had always been a price cutter. Standard, on the other hand, found price cutting an unattractive policy. In Collings' words,

> Red C . . . had a way every once in a while of sending out one or two men, rushing them around over the South Carolina Field, and making up carload orders by cutting our prices from a half to one and a half cent a gallon . . . we had lost quite a good deal of business in years gone by by this system. . . . As you will see here in every one of those letters where their prices are mentioned, they are from half a cent to a cent and a half below our price . . . We didn't go down to their very low prices, except, I believe, in one case, and that was at Union, South Carolina. . . . We do not initiate the cut. We rely on our having been the pioneers in establishing the business, serving the trade with good oil in the most-up-to-date manner, and that if a competitor comes in there to get our business he must necessarily cut the price or offer some inducement in order to wean the trade away from us. Therefore, it is not necessary for us to cut prices.[83]

Although he said that thirty years of competing with Standard were hard, Fehsenfeld acknowledged that the Red C interests had grown steadily and prosperous since

[78] Red C did sell by tank wagons in and around Baltimore, and had various commission agents and jobbers over the country.
[79] Ibid., p. 2303.
[80] Ibid., p. 2311.
[81] Ibid., p. 2319.
[82] Ibid., p. 2341 (italics supplied).
[83] Vol. 12, pp. 895–6. See also vol. 13, pp. 1536–7. There is a great deal of corroborating testimony. See, for example, vol. 13, pp. 1306 ff., 1322 ff., 1362 ff., 1364–5, 1440. The Record is liberally sprinkled with evidence and anecdotes of competition between Red C and Standard. For example, see Vol. 5, pp. 2303, 2307, 2310, 2313, 2316, 2406–9, 2476; Vol. 10, pp. 1747–58, 1760–75; Vol. 12, p. 913; Vol. 13, pp. 1110–13, 1139–44, 1158 ff., 1167, 1239, 1250, 1305–7; Vol. 15, pp. 2443–4; Vol. 20, pp. 100–1, 146–48, 152–3, 156–68, 212 ff. In fact, much of Volumes 13 and 20 concerns this rivalry.

their modest beginning in 1878.[84] Before 1903, Standard twice tried to purchase the Red C group but failed.[85]

## Cornplanter Refining Company

Founded about 1888, Cornplanter was an old rival of Standard. Although there was a good deal of hearsay about Standard "attacking" Cornplanter over the years, it is clear that from time to time Standard and Cornplanter entered into agreements to avoid competition.[86] Mr. Todd, Cornplanter's Manager, testified that Standard had threatened Cornplanter with extinction, but that it never materialized.[87] Cornplanter was a Warren, Pennsylvania refiner, but, among other places, also sold in the St. Paul area.[88] The Manager of Standard's Whiting refinery told Todd that Cornplanter was selling too much kerosene in the St. Paul territory, and that if they did not agree to reduce output and regulate sales, Standard would run them out of business. Mr. Todd understood well the economics of local price cutting, for, as he testified:

> Well, I says, "Mr. Moffett, I am very glad you put it that way, because if it is up to you the only way you can get it [the business] is to cut the market, and if you cut the market I will cut you for 200 miles around, and I will make you sell the stuff," and I says, "I don't want a bigger picnic than that; sell it if you want to," and I bid him good day and left.[89]

The Standard threat never materialized.

Todd also testified that about 1898 a Standard Oil executive told him Standard's policy was to put all independents out of business.[90] Standard then launched a price cutting war against Cornplanter in New York. Todd said Standard started it, but acknowledged that Cornplanter had started a price cutting campaign around Boston.[91] The "war" was costly to both sides, and they entered into a market-sharing agreement for the Boston territory. Prices rose "from 6 to 10 cents in a very few days, and they remained there for a long time."[92] The agreement, first for three years and later renewed for five, remained in effect until about 1906. At that time, Cornplanter sold its Boston distribution facilities to the Gulf Refining Company, an aggressive independent concern.

Todd testified to other conflicts,[93] and still other agreements,[94] with Standard. In

---

[84] Vol. 5, p. 2333. Island was organized in 1901, when Red C integrated "backwards" into refining. Ibid., p. 2337. Island owned the controlling interest in the Richmond Oil Co.

[85] Ibid., p. 2329.

[86] See e.g. vol. 6, pp. 3209 ff.

[87] Ibid., p. 3212.

[88] Ibid., p. 3213.

[89] Ibid., p. 3214, and also p. 3227.

[90] Ibid., pp. 3215–16.

[91] Ibid., p. 3216. Cornplanter's gallonage trebled in Boston (ibid., p. 3231).

[92] Ibid., p. 3217. Cornplanter had acquired the Boston facilities when it bought out the New England Oil Company about 1897 (ibid., pp. 3228, 3230).

[93] Ibid., pp. 3220–1. See also testimony of Hopkins, vol. 3, p. 1030 about cutting Standard's prices.

[94] Vol. 6, pp. 3207–8, 3220, 3223–8.

spite of their difficulties with Standard, Cornplanter's capital had grown, in the twenty years of its existence, from $10,000 to $450,000. Todd admitted that they were still alive and, indeed, very healthy.[95]

## Crew-Levick

Crew-Levick had several refineries.[96] George J. Wolff, Baltimore manager, testified that a Standard "bogus" concern had waged war on them. Wolff admitted that he sometimes cut Standard's prices in Baltimore,[97] and acknowledged that Standard, whatever its motives, hadn't been able to kill Crew-Levick:

> Q:  You don't think you need any guardian for carrying on business against the Standard Oil Company, do you?
> A:  No by gosh! I don't.[98]

Crew-Levick had apparently done well in Baltimore, for as Wolff testified:

> Q:  From 1904 until recently you had a pretty steady increase, haven't you?
> A:  Yes, sir. The day I took charge I only sold 400 gallons, and that was all my own.
> Q:  And that would be about 2,000 gallons a week?
> A:  Yes.
> Q:  And now you sell about 20,00 gallons a week?
> A:  Yes, Sir.[99]

## Some other refining companies

Defendant's Exhibit 277 indicates that in 1908 there were 123 independent refineries in the United States.[100] Some were undoubtedly very small; some were not. The list includes firms which are major companies today and which were substantial even then. Pure Oil, Tidewater, Gulf, The Texas Company, Sun Oil Company, and Union Oil are perhaps the outstanding examples. By 1908, the Texas Company had a refinery of 12,000 barrels per day capacity; Gulf had two: one of 10,800, another of 41,600 barrels per day.[101] Pure, Tidewater, Gulf, and Texas each had large crude oil pipeline systems.

Standard owned about 31 per cent of Tidewater's common stock, and had various

---

[95] Ibid., p. 3221. Cornplanter had numerous other oil interests as well (ibid., pp. 3232 ff.). They marketed under several names, including Tiona Oil. There are many references to the competition of Cornplanter and Standard. See, e.g., vol. 20, pp. 45, 61–2, 114; vol. 6, pp. 3213–18; vol. 15, pp. 2383–7; Pet. Exh. 635.

[96] See vol. 20, pp. 105–6. Interestingly enough, they were operated under different names: Crew-Levick, the Glade Oil Works, the Muir Works, the Seaboard Oil Works.

[97] See e.g. vol. 20, pp. 118 ff. 122, 126, 131. See also vol. 16, pp. 2612 ff.

[98] Vol. 20, p. 126.

[99] Ibid., p. 109.

[100] Vol. 19, pp. 662–3.

[101] A 40,000 barrel per day refinery is of quite respectable size even today, and very large for its time. Testimony of Emery, vol. 6, pp. 2704, 2710–12.

agreements with that firm.[102] It also owned a substantial interest in the Pure Oil pipeline affiliate, but never achieved control.

There always had been some competing refiners.[103] At least 10 independent refineries which were built before 1890 were in continuous operation through 1908,[104] By 1895, there were 38 competing refineries.[105] By 1906, the figure had grown to 123.[106]

The Pure Oil Company, formed in 1895, is only one example of the growth and prosperity of independent refiners.[107]

## Refining: summary

I can not find a single instance in which Standard used predatory price cutting to force a rival refiner to sell out, to reduce asset values for purchase, or to drive a competitor out of business. I do not believe that Standard even tried to do it; if it tried, it did not work.

Standard bought many firms, and paid well to get them. Its purchases continued pretty much up till dissolution, and were apparently necessary to preserve the monopoly position it had built. In addition to purchasing many competitors, Standard entered into market-sharing and price-fixing agreements with still others.[108]

From the beginning of Standard's power, and throughout the period of its greatest strength, new firms sprang up and prospered; old firms survived and grew.

## 2   Price cutting involving jobbers and retailers

It is significant that far and away the largest amount of testimony about price cutting concerns the jobbing and retail levels. Most of the firms alleged to have been involved in price cutting by Standard were non-integrated marketers; the bulk of them were retail merchants and peddlers. Marketing affiliates of competing refiners have already been discussed.

Oil marketing, though different from what we know today, was changing. Before about 1890, refiners sold most of their products in barrels to jobbers, who then distributed the product locally.[109] About that time Standard began "tank wagon" delivery to grocers and other retailers. Under that system, Standard set up bulk stations to which it shipped barrels or tank cars of products, and from which it sent

---

[102]  See e.g. Archbold's testimony, vol. 17, p. 3321.
[103]  Vol. 1, pp. 243–4; vol. 3, p. 1467; vol. 5, p. 2542; vol. 6, pp. 2626, 2642, 2705, 3015, 3131, 3132; vol. 16, p. 3139; vol. 17, p. 3446; vol. 20, p. 31.
[104]  Vol. 5, p. 2542; vol. 6, pp. 2651, 2705, 2840, 3015, 3061, 3207; vol. 20, pp. 106–7.
[105]  Vol. 6, pp. 2690–712.
[106]  Vol. 2, p. 651; vol. 5, pp. 2543–5; vol. 6, pp. 2591, 2700, 2704, 2710, 2711–12; vol. 3, p. 1002 (Pet. Exh. 396); vol. 17, p. 3290; vol. 19, pp. 627 (Def. Exh. 269), 662; Brief for Appellants, vol. 1, appendix III, at 266.
For the more rapid growth of competition in the export trade, see vol. 8, p. 904 (Pet. Exh. 377). Competitors' greatest growth was in products other than kerosene. Brief for Appellants, vol. 2, pp. 102–3.
[107]  Pure's crude oil receipts more than doubled between 1900 and 1906 (vol. 3, pp. 1443, 1451). Another interesting example is the New York Lubricating Co. (vol. 2, pp. 532–3, 766–7, 773).
[108]  For some of the agreements, see vol. 1, pp. 175–6, 214–23; vol. 2, pp. 734, 738, 946, 950; vol. 3, p. 1130; vol. 17, p. 3321; vol. 12, p. 955.
[109]  Testimony of Archbold, vol. 17, pp. 3467–8.

out tank-wagons to serve retailers directly. A tank wagon was just what the name implies: a horse-drawn wagon with a wooden or iron tank mounted on it. Each tank wagon served 30 to 50 specified retail customers. Tank wagon drivers poured or pumped gasoline and kerosene into store-keepers' tanks, taking cash on delivery. Standard ultimately sold most of its products through the tank wagon channel.[110] Collings, of the Standard Oil of Kentucky, testified that as much as 90 percent of his sales were made in that way.[111] The remainder continued to go to jobbers and peddlers.

Peddlers usually called at a tank station and filled their own wagons. To reflect the savings on delivery, and the larger average purchase, peddlers usually paid ½ to 1 cent per gallon less than the tank wagon price.[112] Retail peddling wagons made 150 or more selling stops per day.

Jobbers were thus being displaced by an integrated marketing apparatus pioneered by Standard and imitated quickly by its competitors. Peddlers too, faced sweeping changes. Gas and electricity had begun to challenge the house hold kerosene market on which peddlers depended. The rise of the automobile was just beginning. These forces would ultimately make kerosene, then the principal product, a fourth-rate fuel.

At the same time these changes were taking place, refiners were groping for more efficient ways to market their products. Even as it was developing tank wagon delivery, Standard also experimented with its own peddling operations. It tried to keep its ownership of them secret. These constituted most of the "bogus independents" about which we have heard so often. Almost all the rest were jobbing concerns, generally small ones. They were never of great importance quantitatively.[113] And, for whatever it is worth, Standard was not the only company with "bogus" peddlers and jobbers.[114]

Standard gave several reasons for not advertising its connection with these firms. First, persistent public attacks on its monopoly and high profits had prejudiced some of the trade against buying Standard products.[115] Second, some of the mar-

---

[110] The proportion varied among the different territories. Barrel, jobber, and commission agent distribution were more important in very small communities, and in certain mountainous areas. As late as 1904, for example, Standard was still extending tank wagon service to small New York communities. In all areas, tank wagon delivery was coming to be the dominant method.

[111] Vol. 12, p. 896.

[112] Standard's competitors also granted these terms.

[113] More than half of the "bogus" concerns were strictly retail peddling outfits. Most were very small; they averaged, perhaps, two or three peddling wagons. In addition, most did not last very long. "They were an experiment in selling oil directly to the consumer, which largely on account of the necessity of giving credit, proved a failure." Brief for Appellants, vol. 2, at 192. See also vol. 13, pp. 1523–5. Most were gradually withdrawn as the equipment wore out. Those few that continued became "Can Departments" of the various Standard companies.

Furthermore, there is some question about just how secret these firms were supposed to be, and grave doubts about how secret they in fact were. Finally, the government, and witnesses for it, erroneously accused Standard of owning and operating firms that it did not really have anything to do with. For example see vol. 5, pp. 2412; vol. 12, pp. 779–80, 790–1; vol. 13, pp. 1218–20, 1279–83, 1307, 1533–5.

[114] There are many examples, including the firms operated by Mr. Castle, National Refining Co., Red C, Crew-Levick, and others.

[115] It is impossible to know how important this prejudice was, but it is clear that it existed. One possible symptom is the flavor of names adopted by some competitors: Antitrust Oil Co.; Freedom Oil; Uncle Sam Oil Co., etc.

keting concerns that it bought had substantial good will and better local market acceptance than Standard could economically create. Third, to break local retailer and peddler cartels and to meet the competition of other peddlers, from time to time Standard found it useful to run in a retail outfit selling at competitive prices. But to do these things without antagonizing its tank wagon customers, secrecy was useful.[116] Fourth, this approach permitted Standard to experiment with new personnel and marketing methods without abandoning the old, and without committing large resources.

As tank wagon distribution largely displaced barrel delivery to jobbers, Standard sought to extend integration further. As Mr. Squires put it:

> [W]e reached a point where it was felt that possibly another step nearer the consumer might be taken and save him money. It was learned that the retailer was making from 50 to 100 percent profit, and it was believed that we could save one-half of this to the consumer. To make this move required a great deal of care and caution, so that the trade which we were supplying might not be antagonized; also for the purpose of developing any impracticable features which in the end might prove it was not the proper course to pursue. Therefore a few towns were selected to make the experiment, and the towns quoted above were used for the purpose . . .
>
> But a very serious obstacle soon developed itself, namely, the giving of credit. The storekeeper gave credit to his customers, whereas with us they paid cash. This became such a factor as to make it almost impossible to sell the large quantity which was sought through this medium. Various ways were tried to see if it could not be overcome – like the sale of tickets by milkmen – but it did not work. Then credit was given, but our loss by bad debts was in itself sufficient to practically kill the enterprise. In addition to this we discovered that the expense due to wear and tear of the equipment was great. On account of loaning the cans to the consumer, being our property and not theirs, they did not take the proper care of them. More or less were damaged by carelessness and some were lost entirely. Therefore it was decided, after a very careful canvass of the experience of the different towns, to abandon the idea. Gradually from point to point the equipment was withdrawn, with the exception of two, namely, Youngstown and Cleveland, which have always been known by refiners as peddling points, due to the fact that a number of peddlers had been in existence there for years and the consumer had become familiarized with that means of delivery.[117]

Whether these were really Standard's motives, or merely clever rationalizations, is both imponderable and irrelevant. Suffice it to say that such a course of action is reasonable in light of the evolution of the industry. This evolution in fact accelerated after the 1911 dissolution when competition increased. It was not a creature of monopoly. After all, where are the kerosene peddlers today? The alternative explanation, that Standard sought to monopolize wholesale and retail distribution, is certainly less logical and is less consistent with the facts that we have.

---

[116] Collings: "We would much prefer selling to the dealer. That was the business that we were especially engaged in and prepared to take care of." Vol. 12, p. 887.

[117] Vol. 13, pp. 1523–4. Mr. Squire was not exaggerating retail margins, as the Record amply confirms. Whether margins were high because of retailer cartels or high costs does not matter. What does matter is that Standard, like any refiner, bad every interest in reducing them. See also vol. 2, pp. 757–8; vol. 3, p. 1109; vol. 5, pp. 2583, 2602, 2584.

In retailing, numbers were often very large, and entry was cheap and quick. Standard Oil never had, or apparently sought, a monopoly of retailing. It would have been pointless to try, and probably impossible to achieve. With a refining monopoly, Standard's interest in marketing should logically have been to keep it efficient and highly competitive.[118]

Of all the "levels" in the oil business, retailing would have been the most difficult for Standard to monopolize, and a monopoly there would have been the most transient of all. The reasons are simple. Kerosene retailers were of two sorts: grocers and other retail merchants, who kept tanks or barrels from which they filled customers' oil cans; and peddlers, who operated one or more wagons which went house-to-house on regular routes, much like the milkman of today and the iceman of old.

The skills and resources devoted to refined oil peddling were neither expensive, scarce, nor specific. A wagon, horse, driver, and some cans or a tank made a peddler.[119] A large peddling concern might have two or three wagons. The resources could, and did, move quickly out of oil pedding and back again, lured by the prospects for gain.

Similarly, entry into grocery retailing and general merchandising has never been difficult. Very early in the game, Mr. Rockefeller realized that a private monopoly of crude oil was impossible.[120] He must have realized that a retailing monopoly was even more hopeless. Only governments succeed for very long in monopolizing activities of that kind. Furthermore, Standard evidently concluded that its interests could usually best be served by letting someone else perform the retailing function.

Thus it was that before the dissolution jobbers and retailers were exposed to evolutionary forces at work in the industry at large. These changes persisted, indeed probably accelerated, after the dissolution.[121] In addition, jobbers and retailers were subject to all the ills and quarrels that characterize petty trade, where size was small and numbers large. It is not surprising, therefore, that most complaints about price cutting involved non-integrated marketers.[122]

---

[118] A monopolist in manufacturing would prefer that marketing have zero costs and be competitive. In that way, the maximum monopoly returns could be extracted from manufacturing.

[119] Shea testified that he entered the peddling business in 1892 with $25.00 of his own money, $25.00 borrowed capital, and a borrowed horse. He grew rapidly, and branched off into jobbing as well as retailing. "I would imagine that we are doing about 30 times as much business as we were in 1892 when we first started." Vol. 5, pp. 2493.

[120] Rockefeller's description of the ill-fated crude producers' agreement of 1872 is classic:

I could not state how long it was in existence or said to be operative, but the high price for the crude oil resulted, as it had always done before and will always do so long as oil comes out of the ground, in increasing the production, and they got too much oil. We could not find a market for it.

[O]f course any who were not in this association were undertaking to produce all they possibly could; and as to those who were in the association, many of them men of honor and high standing, the temptation was very great to get a little more oil than they had promised their associates or us would come. It seemed very difficult to prevent the oil coming at that price . . . There was a limitation beyond which we, as refiners and merchandizers in the oil, could not go. We were their servants in passing on to the consumer the refined product, and the limitation was there in what we could at that time sell. Vol. 16, p. 3074.

[121] In 1911, for the first time, gasoline sales passed kerosene.

[122] Standard claimed that its tank wagons served 37,000 towns in the United States. The number of jobbers and peddlers must also have been large.

It is clearly impossible to review here all of the incidents involving jobbers and retailers. The record is filled with many very similar examples, and commenting on each of them is an unnecessary and uneconomic task.[123] For present purposes, it is enough to review some of the more important and representative cases. The incidents can conveniently be divided into three categories: (*a*) alleged price cutting which involved competing marketers, but which had no particular outcome; (*b*) alleged price cutting accompanied by purchase of competing marketers; (*c*) alleged price cutting accompanied by the disappearance of competing marketers. Alleged incidents of the first class are numerous, but do not support a theory of predatory monopolization. Examples of the second and third class would be more useful for such a theory, but are very scarce.[124]

Only a few representative incidents will be discussed in detail; others will be cited.

## (a)  Price cutting with no specified outcome

The bulk of evidence, and assertion, established only that Standard sold at different prices within the same community or among communities; and that the lower prices often resulted from greater competition.[125]

## Hisgen Brothers

A typical example of a marketing firm that complained about local price cutting is Hisgen Brothers. The type of evidence presented is also representative of this whole class of incidents.

Hisgen started selling axle grease in 1889.[126] In 1900, they began retailing and wholesaling kerosene, which they purchased from independent refiners. They complained that in 1901, when they started selling kerosene in various small towns along the Hudson River, Standard cut prices to run them out. Prices elsewhere were said to have remained high. Standard's records indicated that their kerosene prices actually rose during the time Hisgen said Standard was cutting in the six

---

[123] To a remarkable degree, the record is freighted with casual hearsay, petty complaints of small traders, and countless unimportant charges and countercharges. This is probably attributable to the nature of the proceedings under which testimony was taken. Witnesses appeared before an Examiner, not a judge, who felt that he had no power to rule on the admissibility of evidence. A large amount of the Government's testimony came from ex-employees of Standard, most of whom had been discharged or resigned under pressure. Several admitted grudges against Standard management. Some of these witnesses were testifying about Standard operations of which they had no direct knowledge, e.g., vol. 5, pp. 2347, 2364, 2381; vol. 15, p. 2472.

[124] Because firms often were both jobbers and peddlers, and testimony about them was often scant, it is impossible to segregate the incidents into those involving jobbers or peddlers. Such a distinction would have little value in any case.

[125] See, for example, vol. 8, pp. 905–1011 (Petitioner's Exhibit 379–96); vol. 10, pp. 1624–59 (Pet. Exh. 628–35). But compare vol. 8, pp. 664; vol. 10, 1624; vol. 21, pp. 133 (Pet. Exh. 962). See also, vol. 2, p. 937; vol. 3, p. 1046; vol. 5, pp. 2484, 2490–1; vol. 17, pp. 3620–2, 3628; vol. 20, pp. 229–31, 233.

[126] Vol. 4, p. 1795. By the second year business trebled, and kept on increasing. By 1900 sales were $80,000 to $100,000. Hisgen twice ran for Governor of Massachusetts on an antitrust (anti-Standard Oil) platform. Vol. 4, pp. 1800, 1841, 1848–49, 1852.

towns involved.[127] Six grocers testified that it was Hisgen, not Standard, who started price-cutting.[128] In any case, Hisgen admitted that he sometimes did cut Standard's prices,[129] and was very vague about Standard's cuts against him.[130] Later episodes around Springfield, Massachusetts show that, at least part of the time, Hisgen initiated price cuts against Standard.[131]

Quite apart from the question of who started the price wars, Hisgen apparently did well. During 1904, for example, Hisgen Brothers did 21 percent of the oil business at Springfield, and increased their share to 30 percent in 1905.[132] After 1900, they greatly enlarged their territory and business and apparently prospered in the process.[133]

## (b) Price cutting and purchasing

There were several allegations that Standard used local price cutting to force independent marketers to sell out. For the most part, the evidence was simply that there was price cutting and someone affected by it sold out to Standard. In a few cases, the testimony was somewhat more pointed. The following are the most important and relevant examples.

[127] Vol. 12, pp. 713, 813–15. At one time prices did decline, allegedly because of price cutting by Tiona, marketing subsidiary of Cornplanter Refining Co. (ibid., p. 716).

[128] Vol. 12, pp. 780–2, 812–13, 818–19, 822–4, 826–7, 830–1, 833–5; vol. 4, pp. 1894–5, 1963–6.

[129] Vol. 4, pp. 1813–15, 1856 ff. 1888–9, 1898, 1977–8. See also ibid., pp. 1932–7, 1952, 1964–72; vol. 12, pp. 729–37, 782–8, 810–17, 822–37.

[130] Vol. 4, pp. 1861, 1874.

[131] In 1904 Hisgen began selling at 10½¢ per gallon, undercutting Standard by ½¢. Part of the following decline was attributed to a general price reduction over a wide territory; part to further cutting by Hisgen. In 1905, Hisgen stopped cutting, and Standard's prices rose. Vol. 10, p. 1636.

[132] Brief for Appellants, vol. II, p. 177. See also vol. 12, pp. 782–5, 809–10; vol. 10, p. 1636.

[133] Vol. 4, pp. 1836–44.

There are numerous other examples of this class of incidents. See, for example: *H. C. Boardman*: in 1904, when Standard fired him, Boardman opened a marketing business in Augusta (vol. 5, p. 2189). Prices fell (ibid., pp. 2169–71). Boardman captured and held one-third of the trade. In his words: "If I could get a third of the trade, I was satisfied. I recognized the fact that the Standard had to live, too, and needed the money, and so I thought I would let them live. So I kept it at 11 cents" (ibid., p. 2171).

In 1906 Boardman opened up a tank station in Denmark, South Carolina. While he was erecting tanks, Standard cut prices (ibid., p. 2175). But, cut as they would, Boardman got about 40 percent of the business. Although he was largely confined to one territory, and therefore should, so we are told, have been particularly vulnerable to "discriminatory sharp-shooting," Boardman prospered. His trade was profitable from the start; by 1908 he had 75 percent of the Augusta lubricating oil business, and one-third of the refined oils trade (ibid., pp. 2171, 2181). Boardman started business with a capital of $3,000, including tanks and a wagon. The first year his sales were $40,000, the second year, $50,000, and the third year $60,000. "I have never had a month yet that I haven't made a nice profit, even from the first month" (ibid., p. 2181).

*C. J. Castle*: vol. 6, pp. 3040, 3044–6, 3055–7, 3067–8, 3088; vol. 13, pp. 1483, 1517–18.

*St. Louis Oil Co*: vol. 2, pp. 891, 894, 896, 899, 900. For a similar case, see vol. 15, pp. 2411–15, 2425; vol. 20, pp. 229–33.

*E. M. Wilhoit*: vol. 3, pp. 1037–8 pp. 1269–70. "In going into a new territory I cut usually the Standard price" (ibid., p. 1227).

*Cooper Brothers*: vol. 5, pp. 2358–9, 2392–2400; vol. 15, pp. 2434, 2453, 2472–3, 2542–6.

*Testimony of Maxon and Kercher*: vol. 5, pp. 2459–70; vol. 6, pp. 2811–13, 2815–33. But see vol. 12, pp. 922–3, 969.

# G. T. Wofford

From 1898 to 1902, Mr. Wofford was chief clerk and assistant to the Manager in the Birmingham headquarters of the Standard Oil Company of Kentucky.[134] He testified that Standard gave rebates to induce countermands or requirements contracts. Collings denied these allegations.[135] About the end of 1902, Wofford and some associates started the Southeastern Oil Company – a marketing firm – in Birmingham. According to Wofford, Kerosene prices fell steadily from 14 cents to 11 cents per gallon. Southeastern lost money, and sold out to Standard about 1904. There are several convincing reasons why this is *not* a case of successful predation: first, Wofford admitted that it was not Standard's price-cutting on kerosene that made the business unprofitable: "We made a reasonable profit on that particular grade of oil, but we lost money on the general business."[136] Second, Standard claimed, and there is some evidence to support it, that Southeastern solicited the sale to Standard.[137] Third, there was even some testimony that Standard did not actually cut prices before Southeastern sold out.[138]

Fourth, the Government claimed that Standard's Birmingham business was profitable during 1903.[139]

# People's Oil Company

E. N. Wooten, an ex-Standard employee, testified that from 1892 to 1898 Standard cut prices severely at Atlanta to kill off the People's and the Commercial, and that both were forced to sell out to the Standard.[140] Collings denied that Standard started a price war or tried to drive them out.[141] There is both indirect and direct evidence that they were not *forced* out. First, Wooten said the sales were secret, and secrets cannot usually be kept when parties are aggrieved. Second, People's was a *customer* of Standard. Third, the former owner of People's explicitly denied that she was forced out or underpaid.[142] Fourth, Wooten acknowledged that the value of People's and the Commercial had not been higher at any time than when they sold out.[143]

---

[134] Vol. 5, p. 2150.

[135] Ibid., pp. 2155–6; vol. 12, p. 908.

[136] Vol. 5, p. 2156.

[137] Vol. 12, p. 848.

[138] Ibid., pp. 847–8, 908.

[139] Brief for the United States, vol. 2, p. 486. After the sale, Wofford went on to establish another successful oil marketing firm.

[140] Vol. 5, pp. 2096–103. Commercial was owned by the Peerless Refining Company of Cleveland. Standard claimed to have fired Wooten because of his alleged "drug habit." Vol. 12, p. 906.

[141] Ibid., pp. 897–901.

[142] Vol. 18, p. 253 (Def. Exh. 92½).

[143] Vol. 5, p. 2149. Another example is the purchase of two wholesale marketing organizations started by a Mr. Joseph. According to Cooke, a Government witness: "[T]he Standard was anxious to get a location . . . and they realized there was hardly room for two companies (it was not a large town), and they went to Joseph and offered to buy him out; and I must say for the Standard Oil Company, they were very fair and equitable with him because they gave him a darned sight more than the old trap was worth" (ibid., p. 2531).

## Testimony of Mr. Castle

Castle testified that while employed by Standard, he forced an independent Port Huron, Michigan dealer – Mr. Campfield – to sell out to Standard sometime after 1889.[144] Correspondence indicated that Castle was supposed to rebate to dealers to keep the Port Huron kerosene price depressed to 6 cents per gallon to combat Campfield.[145] It is not clear who started the price cutting, and I can find no further evidence about the incident. There is no doubt that Castle employed rebates extensively in the Ohio territory;[146] that is why Standard claimed they fired him. Castle also testified that he forced a Cuyahoga Falls peddler named Blackburn to sell out.[147] For one who claimed to have waged war so long and widely, even the results that Castle claimed appear slender, indeed.[148]

## (c) Price cutting and business extinction

There remains the possibility that marketers were exterminated rather than purchased. The evidence is scanty and unconvincing.

## Decline of Cleveland peddlers

According to Castle, in 1903, when Standard sent peddling wagons into Cleveland, the independent peddlers were doomed.[149] Whereas before that time independent peddlers flourished, their numbers declined drastically:

> [A]t that time peddlers were getting a pretty good rebate and the retail prices hadn't been brought down. They were doing pretty well there for a start . . . After they brought these wagons on . . . [I]t made the margin very small, and it had the effect that up to this time there are very few peddlers in the business, at the present time. Out of probably two hundred and fifty at that time, I don't think you could find fifty now.[150]

Joseph agreed to stay out of the oil business, but soon came back, put up another bulk plant, and started cutting prices.

Q: And the Standard met his cut?
A: Well, you wouldn't expect them to take bank shots all the time, would you?" (Ibid.)

Joseph sold out again.

[144] Vol. 6, pp. 3059–60.

[145] Vol. 10, pp. 1894–5 (Pet. Exh. 836, 837).

[146] Vol. 3, pp. 1362–3; vol. 6, pp. 3030, 3037–8, 3039–45, 3071; vol. 10, p. 1886 (Pet. Exh. 829); vol. 13, pp. 1511–15, 1576.

[147] Vol. 6, p. 3044. At p. 3041, he says an unnamed peddler at Columbiana, Ohio also was forced to sell. The Columbina affair arose out of price-cutting by Freedom Oil, vol. 13, pp. 1511–15, as did many incidents in Ohio (vol. 6, pp. 3040, 3044).

[148] Mahle, a former Standard stenographer, claimed that Blaustein tried to run Fivel, a peddler, out of Norfolk (vol. 5, pp. 2211–12, 2360–2). Blaustein denied that, but admitted buying Fivel's wagon and supplies (vol. 15, pp. 2434–9). Farquaharson said Blaustein ultimately bought Fivel out for $50 more than the "excessive" figure at which he first offered to sell (vol. 5, p. 2211. See also vol. 2, pp. 725–7; vol. 5, pp. 2100–2, 2107, 2279; vol. 12, pp. 902–5; vol. 15, pp. 2445–7, 2549–52, 2544.

[149] Vol. 6, pp. 3054–6, 3108–19; 3124, 320, 3206; see also vol. 3, pp. 1507–10.

[150] Vol. 6, p. 3056.

Squire, of Standard, offered a different and more sensible explanation:

> [I]n 1902 there were 115 peddlers, with no natural-gas meters in use. In 1903 there
> were 90 peddlers, with 16,194 natural-gas meters in use. In 1904 there were 80 ped-
> dlers, with 30,165 natural-gas meters in use. In 1905, there were 78 peddlers, with
> 46,819 natural-gas meters in use. In 1906 there were 61 peddlers, with 66,743 natural-
> gas meters in use. In 1907 there were 43 peddlers, with 77,646 natural-gas meters in
> use. In 1908 there were 40 peddlers, with 83,976 natural-gas meters in use.[151]

Natural gas, of course, was used both for heating and lighting.

## The Mahle testimony

Mahle gave a great deal of hearsay testimony. For example, he said that three oil
dealers in the Baltimore territory had been run out of business by Standard: Tough-
Rutherford, McNeil, and the Purse family at Seaford, Delaware. I cannot find any
evidence on the first two, but the allegation with respect to Purse is erroneous. The
Seaford Company was a Crew-Levick concern, not a Standard "bogus" company,[152]
and the Purse family said it was Red C price-cutting that drove them out.

## Other incidents

H. C. Boardman worked for Standard in Augusta, Georgia from 1886–1904, and
testified that during that period Standard cut prices to drive out competitors.[153]
Boardman said that one marketer, J. T. Thornhill, "finally abandoned business";
and that other major integrated competitors of Standard withdrew from the territory. These allegations were controverted.[154] Even Boardman admitted that Standard cut prices only "as last resort."[155]

Maywood Maxon, once a Standard employee, testified that in 1899 an unnamed
independent oil dealer at Paris, Illinois was forced out of business after a year of
rebating and price war.[156] Collings denied the whole affair.[157] In another instance,
Kercher claimed that a peddler named Wagner left the business.[158]

C. M. Lines testified that he ran a string of bogus peddling wagons for Standard
between 1900 and 1903.[159] He said he thought that these concerns lost money.[160] George
Lane, who had worked for Lines, said that in Youngstown Lines made a "drive" on

---

[151] Vol. 13, p. 1532.

[152] Vol. 13, pp. 1218, 1278–9, 1281, 1283, 1307. Cf. vol. 5, p. 2412; vol. 13, pp. 1219–20.

[153] Vol. 5, pp. 2163–7.

[154] See e.g. vol. 12, p. 910; vol. 5, p. 2163. Boardman himself was a little vague: "I don't know whether
they sold out, but the impression was that they sold out to the Standard" (vol. 5, p. 2166). Boardman
claimed that Tidewater, Crew-Levick, and Blodgett, Moore & Co., all withdrew.

[155] Ibid., p. 2164.

[156] Vol. 3, pp. 1291, 1293, 1294, 1313. Maxon obviously wanted revenge on Standard (ibid., p. 1294).

[157] Vol. 12, p. 890, see also vol. 5, pp. 2466–9.

[158] Vol. 6, pp. 2832–3. But see vol. 10 p. 1846 (Pet. Exh. 798). Kercher was an admitted perjurer. He also
had a grudge against Standard, and apparently tried to blackmail them (vol. 6, pp. 2949 ff., 2969 ff., 2990).

[159] Vol. 6, pp. 3201 ff.

another peddler's business, and drove everybody out of business except the man he was after.[161] On the other hand, Vahey, the peddler who was alleged to be the object of Lines' warfare, testified that he did a land office business when the Standard group attacked him.[162] Far from going out of business, he apparently flourished.

## Marketing: summary

This testimony is voluminous, controverted, and confusing. Many exhibits were ambiguous, and some are of dubious authenticity. Several conclusions stand out, however:

1.  If Standard's object was to monopolize marketing – and that would have been irrational to begin with – they failed. For, if we abstract from the decline of kerosene peddling that followed the growth of natural gas in Cleveland, I can find less than 10 small oil dealers whose sale or disappearance appears to have anything to do with local-price cutting. And that is a liberal estimate of the evidence. Some of the firms were nameless; allegations were often vague; most claims were disproved; some, while not controverted, were never really proved. In many cases, probably most of them, the independents clearly initiated price cuts.

    The "possible" cases are, therefore, really unexplained cases. Most of them involved peddlers, among whom I would expect failures to be relatively numerous in the absence of predatory practices.

    "Fatalities," from all causes, were apparently not very numerous in petroleum retailing and wholesaling, which is surprising in the light of the usual experience in petty trade. There were a fair number of purchases, but fewer than one might have expected.

2.  Standard's correspondence and directives to salesmen show that they were intent on getting business that paid, but were not going to give away anything to get it.[163] Salesmen were cautioned to "be as economical in getting

---

[160]  Ibid., p. 3205.

[161]  Vol. 3, pp. 1356–61.

[162]  Vol. 3, pp. 1366–7. Though just a peddler, Vahey was no fool. He claimed that when a Standard employee threatened to put him out of business, he replied that "I was positive it would take him at least two years to put me out of business and maybe he couldn't do it then" (ibid., p. 1367). For another alleged instance see Nicolai Brothers (vol. 13, p. 1196).

[163]  Standard's salesmen and agents had to fill in "Form 29" requesting permission to cut prices, e.g., vol. 3, pp. 1021–2; vol. 12, p. 962. Permission was often withheld (vol. 10, pp. 1758–9; Pet. Exh. 690). See vol. 12, pp. 688, 845, 907. Standard's employees by and large appear to have learned what they were told. As one Waters-Pierce man put it: "Our goods was [sic] just as good or [a] little better than our competitors and I thought we should get as much for them as possible. [Cutting price] might increase the gallonage, but I figured we would lose money" (vol. 3, p. 1170).

Wilmer also testified that Standard expected its salesmen to get the business at remunerative prices, for "[a]nyone could give goods away" (vol. 13, p. 1250). Metzell, a competitor's salesman, agreed that "[t]hey are getting all they can" (vol. 5, p. 2418). Wilhoit knew that Standard's profitability rested on high prices, not low ones. As he put it, "[I]f I could market my goods at such prices as the Standard Oil Company get for them regularly, I would not want but one year's business at their regular prices, if I got twenty-five percent of the business. One year would be all I want to retire on at their regular price. We don't get their regular price" (vol. 3, p. 1038).

this business as possible";[164] were denounced for cutting prices when it was not necessary[165] and for selling too much oil at special prices.[166]

3. It is interesting that most of the ex-Standard employees who testified about Standard's deadly predatory tactics entered the oil business when they left the Standard. They also prospered.

4. Standard apparently had a shrewd and hard marketing organization. It had every interest in distributing as cheaply as possible, and tried to achieve that result.[167]

## IV  CONCLUSIONS

Judging from the Record, Standard Oil did not use predatory price discrimination to drive out competing refiners, nor did its pricing practice have that effect. Whereas there may be a very few cases in which retail kerosene peddlers or dealers went out of business after or during price cutting, there is no real proof that Standard's pricing policies were responsible. I am convinced that Standard did not systematically, if ever, use local price cutting in retailing, or anywhere else, to reduce competition. To do so would have been foolish; and, whatever else has been said about them, the old Standard organization was seldom criticized for making less money when it could readily have made more.

In some respects it is too bad that Standard did not employ predatory price cutting to achieve its monopoly position. In doing so it would surely have gotten no greater monopoly power than it achieved in other ways, and during the process consumers could have bought petroleum products for a great deal less money. Standard would thereby not only have given some of its own capital away, but would also have compelled competitors to donate a smaller amount.[168]

It is correct that Standard discriminated in price, but it did so to maximize profits given the elasticities of demand of markets in which it sold. It did not use price

---

[164] Vol. 10 p. 1840 (Pet. Exh. 790).

[165] "I have also corresponded with our agents in the South Carolina field and they fully understand we want to retain our business and would reduce our market ½ cent per gallon rather than see the business go to the other oil companies, but I have impressed upon their minds that we do not want to put this reduction into effect unless it is absolutely necessary" (vol. 10, pp. 1758–9: Pet. Exh. 690).

[166] Vol. 12, p. 1019.

[167] Collings said that the incidents in Standard of Kentucky territory were in large part caused by excessively high dealer prices that Standard was in the process of breaking down (Vol. 5, p. 2462; vol. 12, pp. 886–9, 923–7). According to Collings, a peddler working on a 4¢ per gallon margin can do well: As he put it:

> So that at 4 cents a gallon it will be about, at 150 gallons a day, $6 a day. A man with one horse and wagon that can make $6 a day is doing very well . . . [W]e figure that from 2 to 3 cents over the tank-wagon price was a fair price for the peddler. They could make a good living out of that . . . And where they tried to hold up the customer to a fancy profit above that we used our efforts in one way or another to get them to bring it down, the object being, of course, to increase the consumption of oil. We felt, of course, that if they held the price up to 15 or 20 cents a gallon for oil, people would be more economical in the use of it.

> Ibid., p. 890. See also ibid., pp. 917–18. Cooke, a Government witness, testified that the effect of Standard's Capital City Wagons was to force peddlers to charge reasonable prices to consumers.

discrimination to change those elasticities. Anyone who has relied upon price discrimination to explain Standard's dominance would do well to start looking for something else.[169] The place to start is merger.

It should be quite clear that this is not a verdict of acquittal for the Standard Oil Company; the issue of monopoly remains. What this study says is that Standard did not achieve or maintain a monopoly position through price discrimination. The issue of whether the monopoly should have been dissolved is quite separate.

I think one further observation can tentatively be made. If the popular interpretation of the *Standard Oil* case is at all responsible for the emphasis that antitrust policy places on "unfair" and "monopolizing" business practices, that emphasis is misplaced.[170] This limited study suggest that what businessmen do *to* one another is much less significant to monopoly than what they find it useful to do together to serve their common interest.

---

[168] This, of course, ignores certain moral issues. Economics is not a particularly useful tool for dealing with them.

[169] In arguing against the Defendant's motion for adjournment to prepare its case, Government Counsel may have admitted what I have concluded: "What is there, then, to prepare for in this case? Simply the question of unfair competition. The Examiner can see from the testimony that has already been taken that that is not a great task; that it won't take any particular time for them to prepare to meet that testimony" (vol. 6, p. 3333).

[170] The Standard Legend may also be responsible for the strained analogy often drawn between business and war. Analogies to chess strike me as being equally weak. Chess is a competitive game which one player wins, while the other loses. Successful quasi-monopoly seeks to avoid the competitive game, since all players lose as soon as they begin playing it.

# 11

# Another Look at *Alcoa*: Raising Rivals' Costs Does Not Improve the View

*John E. Lopatka and Paul E. Godek**

## I   INTRODUCTION

The government monopolization case some fifty years ago [in 1937] against the Aluminum Company of America is well known to antitrust aficionados. Judge Learned Hand declared that Alcoa, by expanding so as to maintain an overwhelming share of the U.S. market for virgin aluminum, had committed the offense of monopolization. For many years now, Judge Hand's standard of antitrust liability has stood condemned. The consensus has been that Alcoa committed no economic wrong.

Recently, however, the case has been prominently cited to illustrate a different approach to analyzing supposedly predatory practices – raising rivals' costs (RRC). Proponents of this approach argue that much of antitrust analysis, in fact all of the analysis of exclusion, should be redefined to focus explicitly on whether a firm's transactions raise the costs of its competitors and, thereby, cause prices to rise. While they do not endorse Judge Hand's reasoning, they do believe that the facts of *Alcoa* demonstrate an array of "exclusionary" practices, including the naked purchase of exclusionary rights.

We believe that RRC methodology is seriously flawed as a useful approach to antitrust problem solving. Regardless of how *Alcoa* is analyzed, however, the facts of the case do not indicate an antitrust violation, assuming that the antitrust laws promote efficiency. We intend to demonstrate that *Alcoa* deserves its infamy.

* We thank Don Boudreaux, Frank Easterbrook, Joe Kattan, Andrew Kleit, John Peterman, Rick Warren-Boulton, and an anonymous referee for their thoughtful suggestions on earlier drafts but, of course, we assume all responsibility for the final version.

## II  ALCOA

Alcoa was formed in 1888, and, until 1909, its aluminum production was protected by patents.[1] After its patents expired, it maintained a large share of the aluminum market, its output growing with demand. For many years it remained the only producer located in the United States. Between 1912 and 1934, Alcoa's domestic production grew from about 42 million pounds of ingot to 327 million pounds.[2] Thus, in 1912 it sold nearly 91 percent of the virgin ingot in the United States, and, in all but three years between then and 1938, its share exceeded 80 percent. For the last five years of this period, its share exceeded 90 percent.

The U.S. government sued the company in 1937. Trial lasted two years and two months, the testimony ending in 1940. Portending the voluminous nature of future antitrust cases, the record filled more than 58,000 pages, 155 witnesses testified, and 1,803 exhibits were introduced. In 1941, District Judge Francis G. Caffey dismissed the complaint.[3]

With the Supreme Court unable to muster a quorum to hear the appeal, Congress passed a statute designating the Court of Appeals for the Second Circuit the appellate court of last resort for the case.[4] Judge Learned Hand delivered the opinion of the court in 1945, reversing the judgment for Alcoa.[5] He acknowledged that Alcoa might not have violated section 2 of the Sherman Act in that "it may not have achieved monopoly; monopoly may have been thrust upon it." He continued: "The successful competitor, having been urged to compete, must not be turned upon when he wins." But he concluded that Alcoa failed to come within this exception from liability for "those who do not seek, but cannot avoid, the control of a market." Judge Hand wrote:

> It was not inevitable that [Alcoa] should always anticipate increases in the demand for ingot and be prepared to supply them. Nothing compelled it to keep doubling and

---

[1]  For descriptions of the history of Alcoa, see the district and appellate court opinions in the monopolization case, as well as Charles C. Carr, *Alcoa: An American Enterprise* (1952); Donald H. Wallace, *Market Control in the Aluminum Industry* (1937); Merton J. Peck, *Competition in the Aluminum Industry: 1945–58* (1961), pp. 5–21; George D. Smith, *From Monopoly to Competition: The Transformation of Alcoa: 1888–1986* (1988).

[2]  In 1912, the government charged that Alcoa had violated the antitrust laws by entering into an international market-division agreement with a foreign producer and several agreements with domestic suppliers that contained restrictive provisions. See *United States v. Aluminum Co. of America*, June 7, 1912 (W.D. Pa.), printed in *Decrees & Judgments in Federal Antitrust Cases: July 2, 1890–January 1, 1918* (Roger Shale ed. 1918). The vertical restraints at issue appeared to have limited commercial significance and are of little relevance to the questions addressed in this article. In any event, less than a month after the charges were filed, Alcoa accepted a consent order that vitiated the challenged agreements and enjoined the firm from entering into like transactions in the future. The appellate court in the later monopolization case viewed Alcoa's actions prior to the consent decree as irrelevant, and so it offered market share statistics beginning in 1912. For an informative discussion of many of the arrangements challenged in the 1912 proceeding, see Carr, op. cit., pp. 78–80.

[3]  *United States v. Aluminum Co. of America*, 44 F. Supp. 97 (S.D.N.Y. 1941).

[4]  At that time, an appeal from the final judgment of a district court in a civil antitrust suit brought by the United States lay only with the Supreme Court. 15 U.S.C.A. § 29 (1973). The provision was repealed in 1974. See 15 U.S.C.A. § 29 (Supp. 1990).

[5]  *United States v. Aluminum Co. of America*, 148 F. 2d 416 (2d Cir. 1945).

redoubling its capacity before others entered the field. It insists that it never excluded competitors; but we can think of no more effective exclusion than progressively to embrace each new opportunity as it opened, and to face every newcomer with new capacity already geared into a great organization, having the advantage of experience, trade connections and the elite of personnel.[6]

Thus, Judge Hand found that Alcoa had illegally monopolized merely by maintaining a size sufficient to serve most of the U.S. market for virgin aluminum.

The economic perversity of Judge Hand's standard is well understood.[7] The initial supplier of a valuable new product will necessarily have a large market share. By Judge Hand's reasoning, if that supplier expands output so as to maintain its market share, it violates the antitrust laws. In effect, the supplier is told to restrict output and raise price in order to induce entry.

If Alcoa cannot rationally be condemned for growing, can it be condemned for something else? Adherents to RRC analysis, most notably Thomas Krattenmaker and Steven Salop, assert that Alcoa succeeded in acquiring power over price principally by foreclosing competitors from two necessary inputs – electricity and bauxite. Raising-rivals'-costs analysis rests upon the proposition that, by raising the costs of a sufficient number of its competitors by a significant amount, a firm can raise its price and earn economic profits, thereby reducing efficiency.[8] Suppose that the cost of a particular input represents a substantial proportion of the cost of a product and that the supply of the input is not perfectly elastic. If a firm can profitably foreclose a significant amount of the supply that it is not using itself in making the product, the market price of both the input and the product will increase. Price in the output market continues to be determined by marginal cost, but marginal cost is higher than it would have been, output is lower, and the predator reaps a share of the resulting inframarginal rents.

This analysis resembles the discredited foreclosure theory of a bygone era. According to that theory, a firm that contracts with a supplier for its requirements of widgets forecloses its competitors from the widgets purchased. Since supply dwindles, the argument went, price must increase. Price, of course, does not increase – the reduction in available supply is exactly offset by the reduction in demand that is satisfied by the contractual purchases. Krattenmaker and Salop recognize the flaw in the old foreclosure theory and insist that their analysis avoids this fallacy.[9]

---

[6] Ibid., pp. 429–31.

[7] See, for example, Richard A. Posner, *Antitrust Law: An Economic Perspective* (1976), p. 214: Robert H. Bork, *The Antitrust Paradox: A Policy at War with itself* (1978), p. 170.

[8] For descriptions of the RRC approach and its application to specific issues, see Thomas G. Krattenmaker and Steven C. Salop, "Anticompetitive Exclusion: Raising Rivals' Costs to Achieve Power over Price," *Yale L. J.* 96 (1986), p. 209: Thomas G. Krattenmaker and Steven C. Salop, "Exclusion and Antitrust," *Regulation* 11 (1987), p. 29; Thomas G. Krattenmaker and Steven C. Salop, "Competition and Cooperation in the Market for Exclusionary Rights," *Am. Econ. Rev.* 76 (1986), p. 109; Thomas G. Krattenmaker and Steven C. Salop, "Analyzing Anticompetitive Exclusion," *Antitrust L. J.* 56 (1987), p. 71; Steven C. Salop and David T. Scheffman, "Raising Rivals' Costs," *Am. Econ. Rev.* 73 (1983), p. 267; Steven C. Salop and David T. Scheffman, "Cost Raising Strategies," *J. Indus. Econ.* 36 (1987), p. 19; Janusz A. Ordover, Garth Saloner and Steven C. Salop, "Equilibrium Vertical Foreclosure," *Am. Econ. Rev.* 80 (1990), p. 127.

[9] See Krattenmaker and Salop, "Anticompetitive Exclusion," op. cit., pp. 231–4.

The predator does not simply deny its competitors the units of an input that it uses but denies them units that it does not need. This is "direct foreclosure," which the predator accomplishes either by paying suppliers not to sell to its competitors, called the "naked purchase of exclusionary rights," or by purchasing more than it uses and withholding the excess from its rivals, referred to as "overbuying."[10]

The RRC analysts may identify, in theory, a sphere of anticompetitive harm that is not fully captured by conventional antitrust analysis. In theory, a firm that does not have a sufficient share of an output market to raise price above marginal cost can, through vertical transactions, increase input costs to competitors, produce a welfare-reducing price increase in the output market, and reap profits. But theoretical possibility alone is not enough to validate the use of an analysis in practice. As an approach to antitrust problem solving, raising-rivals'-costs methodology fails if it produces no net gain relative to traditional antitrust analysis.[11] Arguments have been made that the methodology fails this test for a number of reasons.[12] It exaggerates the likely profitability to the predator of the postulated strategy. It understates the reach of conventional antitrust analysis. It does not adequately take efficiencies into account. It requires quantitative assessments of competitive effects that are beyond the normal capabilities of courts and enforcement agencies. And it ignores its own potential strategic use for anticompetitive ends.

If RRC analysis is to overcome these criticisms, it cannot stake its claim on its application to *Alcoa*. Alcoa allegedly raised its rivals' costs by increasing the prices of electricity and bauxite.[13] These were the only two inputs in aluminum production whose strategic acquisition by Alcoa could possibly have affected the price of aluminum. Alcoa's activities with respect to these goods and the likely effects of those activities are discussed separately below.

---

[10] The direct-foreclosure branch of RRC analysis posits that rivals' costs are raised through the predator's purchases of exclusionary rights in the input market. A second branch posits that input costs are raised by inducing collusion among input suppliers. See ibid., pp. 238–41. These authors suggest (but only halfheartedly) that Alcoa may have raised rivals' costs by inducing collusion: the suggestion can be dismissed. See ibid., p. 241, n. 106.

[11] See Frank H. Easterbrook, "Allocating Antitrust Decisionmaking Tasks," *Geo. L. J.* 76 (1987), p. 305.

[12] See Wesley J. Liebeler, "Exclusion and Efficiency," *Regulation* 11 (1987), p. 34; Timothy J. Brennan, "Understanding 'Raising Rivals' Costs'," *Antitrust Bull.* 33 (1988), p. 95; Easterbrook, op. cit., pp. 314–16; Malcolm B. Coate and Andrew N. Kleit, "Exclusion, Collusion, and Confusion: The Limits of Raising Rivals' Costs" (Working Paper no. 179, Federal Trade Common. Bur. of Economics 1990); Donald J. Boudreaux, "Turning Back the Antitrust Clock: Nonprice Predation in Theory and Practice," *Regulation* 13 (Fall 1990), p. 45; Donald J. Boudreaux and Thomas J. DiLorenzo, "Raising Rivals' Costs: Competition or Predation?" (unpublished manuscript, George Mason Univ., Dept Economics, 1989); New Zealand Business Roundtable, "Antitrust in New Zealand: The Case for Reform" (September 1988), p. 36; Charles F. Rule, "Claims of Predation in a Competitive Marketplace: When is an Antitrust Response Appropriate?" Remarks of the Assistant Attorney General, Antitrust Division, before the 1988 annual meeting of the American Bar Assn (August 9, 1988).

[13] Krattenmaker and Salop, "Anticompetitive Exclusion," op. cit., pp. 236–7. The authors imply that Alcoa may have foreclosed competitors by also raising the costs of inputs other than electricity and bauxite. They comment that, apart from electricity, "Alcoa's excess accumulation of scarce inputs, *notably bauxite*," drove up the price of the remaining available inputs (ibid., emphasis added). The inference appears to be that Alcoa overbought other scarce inputs, but the authors identify none, and no other input appears to have been scarce. As the district court noted, "In order to produce aluminum it is necessary . . . only to have bauxite and water power." See 44 F. Supp. at 144.

## Electricity

Without a doubt, aluminum production requires vast amounts of electricity. Using the technology of the day, aluminum was produced by combining electricity and bauxite in fairly stable proportions: four tons of bauxite plus 22,400 kilowatt hours of electricity yielded one ton of aluminum.[14] In 1940, the aluminum industry was the largest single user of electric energy in the United States.[15] Nevertheless, Alcoa controlled but a tiny percentage of the input. Exactly how small that percentage was depends on how one defines the input market.

By the end of 1938, there were 4,088 electric generating plants in the United States owned by 1,632 establishments.[16] These plants produced 117 billion kilowatt hours of electricity during 1938, and 45 billion kilowatt hours of this total, or 38.5 percent, was generated by hydroelectric plants.[17] By the end of 1938, existing hydroelectric plants had a capacity of 11 million kilowatts. At about the same time, there were an estimated 1,883 undeveloped waterpower sites in the country. These had an estimated annual average potential output of 276 billion kilowatt hours and an estimated capacity of 53 billion kilowatts. The estimated capacity of undeveloped waterpower sites suitable for aluminum production at existing dams of the same type as those owned by Alcoa was between 7,425,000 and 8,250,000 kilowatts. At the end of 1937, Alcoa controlled 306,000 kilowatts of developed electric-energy capacity and a small amount of undeveloped waterpower. By 1940, Alcoa had 360,000 kilowatts of developed waterpower capacity.[18]

Aluminum production requires electricity but not necessarily electricity produced by any particular method. Alcoa occasionally used steam-generated electricity, fueled by coal and natural gas, and at that time German producers used steam exclusively to generate power and made more aluminum than Alcoa.[19] If the total amount of electricity controlled by Alcoa were measured against the total amount of electricity produced in the United States, Alcoa's share would be minute, its purchases obviously incapable of adversely affecting its rivals' cost of power.

Nevertheless, electricity generated by water was usually much cheaper than that

---

[14] See 44 F. Supp. at 116, 123. The district court's opinion recites that ten kilowatt hours of electricity are needed to make one pound of aluminum; 2,240 pounds equals one long ton.

[15] Carr, op. cit., p. 88, citing Nathaniel H. Engle, Homer E. Gregory, and Robert Mossé, *Aluminum – an Industrial Marketing Appraisal* (1945).

[16] See 44 F. Supp. at 123.

[17] The *kilowatt hour* is a measure of *quantity* of electricity consumed. The *kilowatt* is a measure of the *rate* at which energy is delivered or consumed. It could be stated as "kilowatt hours per hour." Thus, the capacity of an electric facility can be measured in kilowatts, or the maximum rate at which it can deliver electricity. See Edwin Vennard, *The Electric Power Business* (2nd edn, 1970), pp. 14–21.

[18] See 44 F. Supp. at 123. In 1937, Wallace, op. cit., p. 141, claimed that "the number of power sites which are economically suitable for aluminum production is quite limited" but offered no point of reference or empirical support for the observation. Of course, the subsequent development of the domestic aluminum industry proved him wrong.

[19] 44 F. Supp. at 124. Carr, op. cit., p. 88, reported that, before the turn of the century, Alcoa used coal and natural gas to run steam engines, but that, though the fuel cost was low, "electricity generated by steam engines did not seem to be the answer. As early as 1893 the search for cheap electricity had definitely pointed the way to the one source of electric energy which seemed best suited to aluminum production – water power."

produced otherwise. Let us assume, then, that the relevant input-product market was hydroelectric power. The power-transmission technology of the time no doubt limited the area in which a producer could economically sell, but many large customers, such as aluminum makers, were mobile and therefore were able to locate near the cheapest energy source.[20] Thus, owners of hydroelectric power sites could compete for mobile customers that demanded low-cost electricity, and the owners of the hydroelectric sites that permitted production at the lowest cost were able to capture economic rents.

The owner of a natural source of low-cost power will earn economic rents, whoever that owner is. Alcoa owned some low-cost power sites and presumably earned rents as a consequence. The fact that Alcoa was an owner, however, would have had no anticompetitive effect on the price of power or the cost of aluminum production. For example, suppose that Alcoa sought out and acquired a waterpower site that was particularly well suited to hydroelectric generation for aluminum production and that they denied the resource to rivals. Competitors would have to search out the next-best waterpower source. Competitors' costs would increase to the same extent that Alcoa's would fall. But that is obviously not an anticompetitive result. Indeed, productive efficiency increases as the lower-cost input is employed, regardless of who develops it, even if the price of the output remains unchanged.

With this in mind. Alcoa's shares of various hypothetical power markets can be calculated from the data presented above. If the amount of Alcoa's waterpower capacity in 1940 is measured against the total developed waterpower capacity in the United States, Alcoa's share is 3.27 percent. If the denominator consists of the capacity of developed hydroelectric plants and undeveloped sites suitable for aluminum production at existing dams similar to Alcoa's, its share is at most 2 percent. If the denominator consists of developed waterpower capacity and the estimated capacity of all undeveloped hydroelectric sites, Alcoa's share is 0.0007 percent.

Perhaps, however, developed sites should be excluded from the market. The new demand of an aluminum-production plant could be so great that no developed site could supply sufficient power to make aluminum production feasible. If, then, the denominator consists only of the estimated capacity of undeveloped hydroelectric sites suitable for aluminum production at existing dams like Alcoa's, the firm's share is between 4.4 and 4.8 percent. Thus, the largest possible share of a plausible energy-input market that Alcoa could have had is 4.8 percent. Alcoa's purchases could not have had a significant effect on any rival's cost of power, for the supply of electricity was simply too great. But even these market-share statistics are deceptively large for two reasons.

First, under RRC methodology, the question is not the amount of an input purchased and used by a firm. That amount, however large, shifts the input-supply curve up and to the left but also shifts the demand curve down and to the left an offsetting amount, so that the market price of the remaining input supply is

---

[20] For example, Carr, op. cit., p. 90, writes: "In placing an aluminum reduction works at Niagara Falls, (Alcoa) was inaugurating a policy Nature has imposed upon it, one of locating its aluminum reduction operations whenever possible near sources of hydroelectric energy. This custom has prevailed for a half century."

unaffected.[21] Only purchasing inputs that would not be used or making stark commitments to withhold inputs from the firm's rivals could possibly have an anticompetitive effect on the input's cost. And Alcoa apparently used virtually all of the waterpower capacity it developed.[22] Even if Alcoa had acquired some waterpower rights that it did not intend to use itself, that would have represented only a small percentage of its already-insubstantial share of the input market.[23]

Second, these market shares are based on available water power in the United States. Firms could produce aluminum in Canada, as Alcoa did, if not elsewhere, and ship it into the United States, Alcoa controlled some waterpower in Canada, but its holdings presumably accounted for an even smaller share of suitable Canadian hydroelectric sites than its share in the United States.[24]

Krattenmaker and Salop allege that Alcoa drove up the price of power to rivals by purchasing from electric utilities naked exclusionary-rights agreements to refuse to sell power to other aluminum producers. They define a naked exclusionary-rights agreement as a transaction in which the purchaser acquires merely the promise that the seller will not sell to the purchaser's competitors; "no goods or other commodities are to be exchanged."[25] It is an agreement "in which the purchaser obtains solely the naked right to exclude rivals from the inputs without a requirement that it purchase quantities of the input as well."[26] They allege that the agreements with the electric utilities were "naked" because Alcoa bought no electricity from the firms, only their promises not to sell to rivals.[27]

Alcoa did indeed enter into a total of eleven covenants that prohibited two companies from furnishing power for aluminum production to firms other than Alcoa.[28] The transactions, however, did not involve "only the companies' promises not to sell electricity to other aluminum producers," as claimed.

By 1893, Alcoa was searching for sources of cheap electricity, near which it would construct aluminum-reduction plants.[29] In that year, it contracted with the Niagara Falls Power Company in New York for the purchase of direct electric current and

[21] See Krattenmaker and Salop, "Anticompetitive Exclusion," op. cit., pp. 231–4.

[22] The district court found that all of Alcoa's developed waterpower capacity "was either used by Alcoa or sold or exchanged by an economical method which avoided waste." See 44 F. Supp., p. 124. See also ibid., p. 126.

[23] For example, the district court does not explain just how Alcoa "sold or exchanged" the waterpower it did not use. Moreover, the market shares are based on Alcoa's control of developed waterpower capacity, but, at least in 1937, Alcoa also had "a comparatively small amount of undeveloped water power" (ibid., p. 123). Thus, there may have been some increment of incipient power capacity that was not reflected in the defined market and that Alcoa did not intend to use. Within the RRC paradigm, this increment and the waterpower sold and not consumed by Alcoa would constitute the maximum amount of input by which Alcoa could have engaged in "direct foreclosure."

[24] The district court noted the extent of Alcoa's Canadian waterpower rights but cited no evidence of the total amount of developed and undeveloped waterpower in that country (see ibid., p. 124).

[25] Krattenmaker and Salop, "Anticompetitive Exclusion," op. cit., p. 227.

[26] Ibid., p. 235.

[27] Thus, "Alcoa reportedly purchased exclusionary covenants from power companies from which Alcoa did not purchase any electricity. The contracts involved only the companies' promises not to sell electricity to other aluminum producers, not the sale of electricity to Alcoa . . . In other words, Alcoa purchased only market power, not electric power. Such contracts are 'naked' exclusionary rights agreements" (ibid., p. 227). See also Krattenmaker and Salop, "Exclusion and Antitrust," op. cit., pp. 29–30.

[28] See 44 F. Supp. pp. 136–8.

[29] See Carr, op. cit., pp. 88–91.

soon thereafter began operating an aluminum-reduction facility at that site. In 1896, it stopped buying direct current from the company and started buying "mechanical power" instead; Alcoa installed its own generators to convert the mechanical power into electrical energy. Between 1895 and 1905, Alcoa and the Niagara Falls Power Company entered into a series of five power purchase contracts that contained restrictive covenants.[30]

Similarly, by 1899, Alcoa had located a source of inexpensive power at Shawinigan Falls in the wilds of Quebec.[31] It contracted with the Shawinigan Water & Power Company (SWPC) to purchase energy in the form of water in the forebay. Alcoa built its own power-conversion plant and aluminum-production facility at the location. It purchased additional water energy in 1907 and immediately constructed a second power house. Alcoa and the SWPC entered into a total of six contracts that contained restrictive covenants; the first began in 1899, and the last expired by its terms in 1940.[32]

Alcoa, therefore, never purchased commitments from electric utilities to withhold power from competitors that were unattached to power or incipient power purchases. Indeed, the government did not even allege "naked" exclusion. In describing the two locations involving exclusive covenants, the Justice Department's complaint stated that Alcoa "purchase[d] substantial quantities of mechanical power" in one instance and was purchasing power for a "subsidiary's new plant" in the other.[33] That Alcoa paid firms only for exclusionary rights is nowhere intimated. Indeed, it is difficult to take the idea seriously. Had Alcoa made such a deal, we imagine that it soon would have been swamped with similar offers from other power companies, for entry barriers into the trade of not selling waterpower were probably low. The case for anticompetitive exclusion based on Alcoa's bauxite transactions is no better.

## Bauxite

Aluminum is extracted (or reduced) from natural substances through a series of chemical processes.[34] At the time of *Alcoa*, aluminum was recognized as one of the most plentiful metallic elements, constituting an estimated one-twelfth of the solid portion of the earth to a depth of ten miles.[35] It could be extracted from various ores, including bauxite, alunite, and leucite, as well as common clay.[36] In fact, those in the aluminum industry were fond of the expression "every clay bank is an aluminum mine."[37] Nevertheless, the cost of aluminum production was distinctly

---

[30] See 44 F. Supp., pp. 136–7.
[31] See Carr, op. cit., pp. 91–2.
[32] See 44 F. Supp., p. 138.
[33] Bill in Equity of the United States, no. 85–73, paragraphs 84, 85 (April 23, 1937).
[34] For a good, simple description of the aluminum-making process, see Rhea Berk et al., *Aluminum: Profile of the Industry* (1982), pp. 6–15.
[35] See Carr, op. cit., p. 62. See also Ferdinand E. Banks, *Bauxite and Aluminum: An Introduction to the Economics of Nonfuel Minerals* (1979), p. 3.
[36] See 44 F. Supp. pp. 109–10. See also Banks, op. cit., pp. 3–5: Berk et al., op. cit., pp. 20–30.
[37] See Carr, op. cit., p. 63.

lowest when the feedstock was bauxite, a claylike material of varying color and texture discovered in 1821 near the village of Les Baux, France.[38] Bauxite exists in different grades of quality, and aluminum could be refined most economically from what was termed aluminum-grade bauxite.[39]

Let us make the conservative and reasonable assumption that the relevant input-product market is aluminum-grade bauxite. The geographic market, however, is problematic. At the time in question, aluminum-grade bauxite had been found in seven states, though almost all of the known reserves were in Arkansas. Outside of the United States, the ore's supply was considered "practically inexhaustible."[40] In particular, France, Hungary, Italy, Suriname (Dutch Guiana), British Guiana, Yugoslavia, Russia, the Dutch East Indies, and Greece were major producers. By 1949 at least, additional large reserves had been located in Jamaica, Africa, and the islands off the coast of French Guinea.[41]

American bauxite production started in 1889, the year after Alcoa began producing aluminum.[42] But for the first fourteen years of its history, Alcoa bought alumina, an intermediate substance in the refining process, and extracted aluminum from that. It bought most of its requirements from the Pennsylvania Salt Manufacturing Company but, even then, imported some from France. In 1888, Merrimac Chemical Company was importing bauxite from Ireland and, by treating it with sulfuric acid, was refining aluminum salts from the ore. Later, it purchased bauxite domestically but continued to import largely from France, where it could obtain the ore at a cheaper price. Even after commercial mining of bauxite began in the United States, Alcoa continued to import bauxite from South America and, for a time after 1924, imported ore from Italy and Yugoslavia.[43] In the 1920s, a would-be competing domestic aluminum producer was prepared to import bauxite from South America.[44] And, at least by 1949, Alcoa's competitors owned substantial reserves in Jamaica.[45]

During the relevant period of the complaint, 1909–41, substantial quantities of bauxite were imported: about 60 percent was produced domestically and 40 percent was imported. From 1909 to 1923, the annual import share ranged from 0 to 22 percent, with trivial amounts imported from 1915 to 1919. In 1924, imports grew

[38] Ibid., pp. 65, 73.

[39] See 44 F. Supp. pp. 116–17; Carr, op. cit., pp. 71–3.

[40] 44 F. Supp. p. 117.

[41] See Carr, op. cit., pp. 65–7. Since then, the production of bauxite in the United States has become a trivial percentage of the world total. The U.S. Bureau of Mines estimated that domestic production accounted for 0.6 percent of the world total in 1989 and that the United States' net import reliance for all grades of bauxite in that year was 97 percent. See U.S. Department of the Interior. Bureau of Mines, *Mineral Commodity Summaries* (1990), pp. 28–9. The bureau has stopped releasing domestic production statistics but has estimated the net import reliance to be 98 percent for 1990. See U.S. Department of the Interior, Bureau of Mines, *Mineral Commodity Summaries* (1991), pp. 22–3.

[42] See Carr, op. cit., p. 66.

[43] See ibid., pp. 61, 65; Wallace, op. cit., p. 139.

[44] See 44 F. Supp. p. 121 (in 1924, a Mr. Moore attempted to buy bauxite land located in South America from Mr. Uihlein, who owned an aluminum concern); Wallace, op. cit., p. 137 (the Uihleins were able to obtain satisfactory bauxite in South America). At about the same time, another would-be competitor thought he would have no trouble procuring bauxite, but it is not clear whether he had in mind a foreign or domestic source. See *Perkins v. Haskell*, 31 F.2d 53, 60 (3d Cir. 1929).

[45] See Carr, op. cit., pp. 66–7.

significantly to 37 percent, and, from 1925 to 1941, they usually exceeded 50 percent, reaching 68 percent in 1932.[46]

It is not likely, therefore, that domestic bauxite constituted a relevant economic market. In an international market of "practically inexhaustible" supply, Alcoa's total accumulation of bauxite could have neither conferred monopoly power on the firm nor had an anticompetitive effect on the costs of its competitors.[47]

In the United States, Alcoa apparently owned about one-half of the aluminum-grade bauxite reserves estimated to exist in 1940. One witness at trial estimated that there were about 10.3 million tons of bauxite in the country, of which Alcoa owned about 4.9 million tons and "quite a number" of others owned 5.4 million tons; another estimated the total to be about 11.5 million tons, of which Alcoa owned 6 million tons.[48] The judge rejected the government's allegation that Alcoa owned "more than 90 percent" of domestic aluminum-grade bauxite deposits, finding that the government's estimate was based on a flawed methodology and that its two witnesses on the subject were not credible.[49]

In the unlikely event that the United States represented a relevant input market for bauxite, then a share of approximately 50 percent might be enough to satisfy a necessary condition of the asserted anticompetitive foreclosure. But just how a firm can profitably raise competitors' costs by "overbuying" an input is not at all clear. With little elaboration. Krattenmaker and Salop assert that the strategy can succeed (1) if the firm uses the input less intensively than does its rivals; (2) if it alone is vertically integrated into a fraction of its input needs; (3) if its input price is lower than the price to its rivals because it has a long-term, fixed price contract or superior bargaining skills; or (4) if marginal costs rise faster than average costs.[50]

The claim that overbuying can be a profitable method of predation is counterintuitive, and the brief comments offered by Krattenmaker and Salop do not dispel the skepticism.[51] At the very least, the technical conditions necessary for profitable overbuying are likely to be extremely narrow. The only condition the authors mention that seems to hold any promise of a plausible explanation is an

---

[46] Data source is U.S. Bureau of the Census, *Historical Statistics of the United States: Colonial Times to 1970* (1975), p. 605.

[47] Wallace's conclusions are ambiguous. "It is unquestionable that there exist at present [1936] large tonnages of good bauxite in various parts of the world which are not owned by aluminum companies or producers of alumina. Some of these deposits are accessible to cheap transport." See Wallace, op. cit., p. 140. He points out that members of the Uihlein family, who wanted to produce aluminum and who later were witnesses for the United States in *Alcoa* (44 F. Supp. at 121), "were able to obtain satisfactory bauxite in South America" (ibid., p. 137). And he comments, "[E]xcellent bauxite in fairly accessible locations in the tropics still remain to be discovered. It would not appear that the costs of exploration are very great, since the ore usually occurs on the surface" (ibid., p. 141). Yet he concluded that acquisitions of ore reserves since World War I by established firms "greatly enhanced the difficulty of the problem facing potential entrants" (ibid.).

[48] Ibid., pp. 118–19.

[49] Ibid., pp. 116–18.

[50] See Krattenmaker and Salop, "Anticompetitive Exclusion," op. cit., p. 238.

[51] Krattenmaker and Salop do not refer to any previous work in explaining their specific theory of overbuying. Perhaps they are tacitly deriving it from Nelson's insight that an increase in marginal costs in a competitive industry can lead to an increase in rents, which is set forth in one of the articles they cite for general support. See Richard R. Nelson, "Increased Rents from Increased Costs: A Paradox of Value Theory," *J. Pol. Econ.* 65 (1957), p. 387. But Nelson does not discuss overbuying, and Krattenmaker and Salop do not explain how his observation leads to their conclusion.

advantage in an input's intensity of use, such as could be created using different production technologies. In *Alcoa*, however, competitors would have been free to employ the same technology as Alcoa, for Alcoa's patents had expired and the production process was well known.

Assuming without theoretical proof that overbuying can be a profitable strategy, it can only occur, as its name implies, when a firm purchases an input that it will not use to produce its output. But firms normally attempt to insure an adequate supply of necessary inputs, and that requires obtaining the right to an amount that exceeds the quantity being used at any single moment in time. Whether an input is "overbought," therefore, depends on the current rate of use and judgments about the future.[52] In general, overbuying can never become a useful target of antitrust scrutiny unless it can in practice be distinguished from buying "just enough," a task we doubt can be effectively performed, particularly because the theory itself is unclear. In *Alcoa*, the firm acquired rights to a sufficient volume of domestic bauxite to last eight years at its 1939 rate of consumption, a rate that was surely expected to increase.[53] The best that can be discerned from such a record is that Alcoa's purchases of bauxite were not excessive in any relevant economic sense.[54]

In sum, a direct-foreclosure variant of RRC analysis could conceivably apply to Alcoa's bauxite purchases, though only through overbuying – no one alleges that Alcoa purchased naked exclusionary rights to bauxite. The evidence suggests, however, that the input market included foreign ore, that Alcoa's purchases were therefore incapable of significantly raising prices, and that Alcoa did not buy excess quantities in any event.

## III   ANCILLARY RESTRICTIONS IN SUPPLY CONTRACTS

Although Alcoa never obtained naked promises from power utilities to refuse to sell to its competitors, the facts nevertheless raise an interesting question, Why did Alcoa procure covenants from its suppliers not to sell to other aluminum companies? Certainly Alcoa may have believed that, before making site-specific investments in electric generation and additional aluminum-production facilities, it had to make sure that sufficient power would be available at an attractive price. In other words, it may have wanted to protect itself from postcontractual opportunism.[55] A more likely method of obtaining security, however, would seem

[52] See Krattenmaker and Salop, "Anticompetitive Exclusion," op. cit., p. 282 n. 228.

[53] 44 F. Supp. p. 120. Certainly the rate of aluminum production did soar. See Berk et al., op. cit., p. 32: Peck, op. cit., p. 8.

[54] Judge Caffey dismissed the government's bauxite charges. See 44 F. Supp., p. 121. On appeal, Judge Hand noted that Judge Caffey had relied in part on the testimony of certain witnesses in concluding that Alcoa had bought only the volume of bauxite it intended to use. He continued, "It would be hard to imagine an issue in which the credibility of the witnesses should more depend upon the impressions derived from their presence." See 148 F. 2d p. 433. He concluded that "it seems plain to us that we should be unwarranted in declaring" Judge Caffey's findings on witness credibility clearly erroneous. See 148 F.2d p. 433. Of course, Judge Caffey's determination that Alcoa had not overbought bauxite was based on objective evidence as well as statements of intent.

[55] See Benjamin Klein, Robert G. Crawford, and Armen A. Alchian, "Vertical Integration, Appropriable Rents, and the Competitive Contracting Process," *J. Law and Econ.* 21 (1978), p. 297.

to have been a contractual provision that guaranteed the desired quantity at a specified price. Perhaps only the demand of another aluminum plant represented a serious threat to its supply. Alcoa might have entered into the restrictive convenants as a form of guarantee because the transaction costs associated with a restrictive covenant were less than those associated with a conventional guarantee.

Possibly Alcoa's decision to build production facilities at a particular waterpower site created the prospect of positive externalities. Other firms might have been able to free ride on Alcoa's investments in locating favorable water power sources or in constructing the infrastructure necessary to produce aluminum. Alcoa would have had an incentive to internalize the benefits that flowed from its investments, and it may have come close to achieving this purpose by purchasing hydroelectric companies. But even when it chose an arrangement short of full vertical integration, at the very least it would have had an incentive to prevent competitors from appropriating any of the value of its investments because only those firms could injure it through sales in aluminum markets. It may have sought to thwart this kind of appropriation by using restrictive covenants.[56]

We can only speculate about the efficiencies that the restrictive covenants could have produced. The effects of an agreement between a firm and its supplier not to supply its competitors will often be difficult to prove. To be sure, the inference of an anticompetitive effect is strongest when the commitment is unconnected to a presumptively productive transaction, but, even then, the inference is rebuttable. For example, suppose a firm sets out to locate the best source of some input. After an expensive search, it locates two good sources and chooses one. If a competitor can free ride on the search and contract with the other source, the value of the search declines, and the incentive to search would decline. An agreement with the unchosen source not to supply competitors could prevent the free ride. Of course, such an arrangement could have anticompetitive effects, and some transaction short of a convenant not to sell to competitors might be sufficient to protect the investment. In the end, though, the welfare effects even of the stark, unconnected promise not to sell to rivals are ambiguous.

Moreover, after 100 years, naked exclusion has yet to be identified in any antitrust case. Krattenmaker and Salop could only point to the Alcoa convenants as examples, and those agreements were not naked.[57] The real challenge is to assess the competitive significance of covenants that are connected to other transactions – such agreements *are* reported.

The concept of a naked purchase of exclusionary rights is derivative of, though not identical to, the antitrust doctrine of ancillary restraints. Circuit Judge William Howard Taft delivered the classic statement of that doctrine over ninety years ago

[56] One possibly anticompetitive explanation can be rejected. Alcoa did not attempt to impose costs on rival aluminum companies that had incurred sunk costs by denying them the waterpower adjacent to the plants these rivals had constructed. Assuming that the imposition of sunk costs on a competitor can ever have an anticompetitive effect, no rival company had facilities in the locations that Alcoa selected for its plants.

[57] The authors have observed that, aside from the *Alcoa* case and cases alleging misuse of government process, "a naked exclusionary rights contract is not mentioned, to our knowledge, in any reported antitrust case" (see Krattenmaker and Salop, "Anticompetitive Exclusion," op. cit., p. 228).

in the *Addyston Pipe* case,[58] and the Supreme Court largely used the formulation eighty-one years later in *BMI*.[59] In general, the doctrine provides that an agreement restricting competition is lawful if it is ancillary to some other, legitimate transaction. Thus, the naked purchase of an exclusionary right is likely to be illegal, although not a single case of it has been found. But a restriction that a supplier agrees to in the context of a broader transaction nevertheless may fail the ancillary-restraints test if it does not promote the purpose of the main transaction or if the main purpose of the entire transaction is illegitimate – for example, the acquisition of monopoly power. The question should always be whether the restriction serves some productive economic function.

Sometimes the evidence suggests that a restriction is designed to produce market power, even though the restraint is connected to another, usually lawful, transaction. The *American Can* case involved this kind of restriction.[60] Around the turn of the century, a group of promoters formed the American Can Company to monopolize the market for packers' cans, which are hermetically sealed containers used to hold food products. During a two-year period, it acquired ninety-five leading producers of packers' cans, representing at least 90 percent of the country's can-making capacity, excluding production solely for internal consumption, at prices that ranged from two to twenty-five times the value of the businesses' tangible assets. With few exceptions, the sellers agreed not to engage in can making for fifteen years within 3,000 miles of Chicago.[61]

American Can also attempted to deny any surviving or new competitors machinery to make cans. Only a few commercially significant can machinery shops existed then. American Can entered into exclusive-supply arrangements with three of them. It agreed to pay the largest manufacturer, the E. W. Bliss Company, $25,000 per quarter in exchange for a promise that Bliss would not produce certain can-making machinery for any company other than American Can for six years.[62] American Can also agreed to purchase all of the machinery produced by the Adriance Machine Company for six years at $75,000 a year. It also guaranteed the Ferracute Machine Company a profit of $10,000 per year for six years in return for an exclusive-supply relationship.[63]

---

[58] *United States v. Addyston Pipe & Steel Co.*, 85 F. 271 (6th Cir. 1898), modified and aff'd. 175 U.S. 211 (1899). Bork has commented that, given the time it was written, *Addyston Pipe* "must rank as one of the greatest, if not the greatest, antitrust opinions in the history of the law" (Bork, op. cit., p. 26).

[59] *Broadcast Music. Inc. v. Columbia Broadcasting System. Inc.*, 441 U.S. 1 (1979).

[60] *United States v. American Can Co.*, 230 F. 859 (D. Md. 1916), appeal dismissed without consideration. 256 U.S. 706 (1921). We thank the referee for directing our attention to this case. For discussions of the case and the history of the industry, see Simon N. Whitney, *Antitrust Policies: American Experience in Twenty Industries* (1958), pp. 196–226; Charles H. Hession, "The Tin Can Industry," in *The Structure of American Industry*, ed. Walter Adams, rev. edn 1954, pp. 403–42.

[61] 230 F. pp. 865, 868–9.

[62] Though it is possible that American Can bought no machinery from Bliss for the duration of the agreement, it is much more likely that it did. American Can represented a huge demand for can-making machinery, and Bliss was the largest manufacturer of it. Moreover, American Can did purchase machines from two other makers who agreed to restrictive covenants. The restriction on other sales by Bliss, therefore, was almost certainly connected to a supply transaction.

[63] Ibid., pp. 874–5. American Can claimed that Bliss was infringing its patents, but Bliss denied the charge. American Can also induced Bliss to breach contracts to supply other can makers and paid the litigation costs and judgments for Bliss in the resulting suits brought against the firm (ibid.).

There is little doubt that American Can was attempting to monopolize the can market. The covenants not to compete contained in the purchase agreements with acquired can producers were unquestionably designed to further that objective, as were the restrictions on sales to rival can manufacturers contained in the supply agreements with can-machinery makers. Of course, one would predict that, absent entry barriers, such a scheme was bound to fail. And indeed, when the industry became aware that the plan was afoot, new can makers began popping up, either hoping to be purchased at a premium or expecting to thrive under the monopolist's umbrella.[64] Indeed, the Continental Can Company, which would become a powerful competitor, entered the industry in 1904. American Can could not profitably acquire all the upstarts. Similarly, the can-machinery firms found ways to evade their restrictions on sales to rivals, and new, good machine shops emerged.[65] Nevertheless, however constrained the monopoly profits were, American Can's conduct would violate any sensible monopolization standard, and the restrictive contractual provisions would fail the ancillary-restraints test. The court found an antitrust violation but concluded that the intervening emergence of competition rendered any immediate remedy inappropriate.[66]

In most cases, however, it will not be nearly so easy to conclude that a restriction connected to a supply transaction serves no productive function. Indeed, we predict, with no empirical proof, that most such restrictions will pass a rational ancillary-restraints test. In any event, the evidence in *Alcoa* strongly indicates that the electric-utility covenants served a productive function because the anticompetitive potential was so remote.

## IV  CONCLUSION

As a paradigm for assessing exclusionary conduct, *Alcoa* fell into disrepute because it failed to distinguish between efficient and anticompetitive activities. Recently, however, some have attempted to resuscitate the case. They cite it to support a new approach to exclusion: raising-rivals'-costs analysis. The heart of this analysis is the concept of exclusionary-rights agreements, and the centerpiece of that concept is the naked promise to exclude. It is through exclusionary-rights agreements that a firm supposedly raises input costs to competitors and gains power over price. *Alcoa* is the only reported decision that purportedly involved a naked agreement, but, in fact, *Alcoa* involved no such thing, and the concept of naked exclusion remains an inhabitant only of the realm of imagination. Ancillary exclusion certainly takes place, but determining its welfare effects when it does occur is usually a difficult task. The RRC methodology may have identified in theory a sphere of anticompetitive conduct that is not captured by conventional monopolization analysis. That is hardly enough, however, to commend its adoption as a preferable approach. Compelling concerns remain that the approach, in practice, would do

[64] Ibid., pp. 868, 879–80.
[65] Ibid., p. 875.
[66] Ibid., p. 904.

more harm than good. The proponents of the approach can draw no succor from *Alcoa*, for the case demonstrates none of the anticompetitive scenarios attributed to it. *Alcoa* remains a perversity.

## REFERENCES

Banks, Ferdinand E., *Bauxite and Aluminum: An Introduction to the Economics of Nonfuel Minerals* (Lexington, Mass.: Lexington Books, 1979).

Berk, Rhea, Lax, Howard, Prast, William, and Scott, Jack, *Aluminum: Profile of the Industry* (New York: McGraw-Hill, 1982).

Bork, Robert H., *The Antitrust Paradox: A Policy at War with Itself* (New York: Basic Books, 1978).

Boudreaux, Donald J., "Turning Back the Antitrust Clock: Nonprice Predation in Theory and Practice," *Regulation* 13 (1990), pp. 45–52.

Boudreaux, Donald J., and DiLorenzo, Thomas J., "Raising Rivals' Costs: Competition or Predation?" Unpublished manuscript (Arlington, Va: George Mason University, Department of Economics, 1989).

Brennan, Timothy J., "Understanding 'Raising Rivals' Costs'," *Antitrust Bulletin* 33 (1988), pp. 95–113.

Carr, Charles C., *Alcoa: An American Enterprise* (New York: Rinehart, 1952).

Coate, Malcolm B., and Kleit, Andrew N., "Exclusion, Collusion and Confusion: The Limits of Raising Rivals' Costs," Working Paper no. 179 (Washington, D.C.: Federal Trade Commission, Bureau of Economics, October 1990).

Easterbrook, Frank H., "Allocating Antitrust Decisionmaking Tasks," *Georgetown Law Review* 76 (1987), pp. 305–20.

Hession, Charles H., "The Tin Can Industry," in *The Structure of American Industry*, edited by Walter Adams, rev. edn (New York: Macmillan, 1954).

Klein, Benjamin, Crawford, Robert G., and Alchian, Armen A., "Vertical Integration, Appropriable Rents, and the Competitive Contracting Process," *Journal of Law and Economics* 21 (1978), pp. 297–326.

Krattenmaker, Thomas G., and Salop, Steven C., "Anticompetitive Exclusion: Raising Rivals' Costs to Achieve Power over Price," *Yale Law Journal* 96 (1986), pp. 209–93.

Krattenmaker, Thomas G., and Salop, Steven C., "Competition and Cooperation in the Market for Exclusionary Rights," *American Economic Review* 76 (1986), pp. 109–13.

Krattenmaker, Thomas G., and Salop, Steven C., "Analyzing Anticompetitive Exclusion," *Antitrust Law Journal* 56 (1987): 71–89.

Krattenmaker, Thomas G., and Salop, Steven C., "Exclusion and Antitrust," *Regulation* 11 (1987), pp. 29–33.

Liebeler, Wesley J., "Exclusion and Efficiency," *Regulation* 11 (1987), pp. 34–40.

Nelson, Richard R., "Increased Rents from Increased Costs: A Paradox of Value Theory," *Journal of Political Economy* 65 (1957), pp. 387–93.

New Zealand Business Roundtable, "Antitrust in New Zealand: The Case for Reform" (September 1988).

Ordover, Janusz A., Saloner, Garth, and Salop, Steven C., "Equilibrium Vertical Foreclosure," *American Economic Review* 80 (1990), pp. 127–42.

Peck, Merton J., *Competition in the Aluminum Industry, 1945–1958* (Cambridge, Mass.: Harvard University Press, 1961).

Posner, Richard A., *Antitrust Law: An Economic Perspective* (Chicago: University of Chicago Press, 1976).

Rule, Charles F., "Claims of Predation in a Competitive Marketplace: When is an Antitrust Response Appropriate?" Remarks of the Assistant Attorney General, Antitrust Division, before the 1988 Annual Meeting of the American Bar Association, August 9, 1988.

Salop, Steven C., and Scheffman, David T., "Raising Rivals' Costs," *American Economic Review* 73 (1983), pp. 267–71.

Salop, Steven C., and Scheffman, David T., "Cost-raising Strategies," *Journal of Industrial Economics* 36 (1987), pp. 19–34.

Smith, George D., *From Monopoly to Competition: The Transformation of Alcoa: 1888–1986* (New York: Cambridge Publishers, 1988).

U.S. Bureau of the Census, *Historical Statistics of the United States: Colonial Times to 1970* (Washington, D.C.: Government Printing Office, 1975).

U.S. Department of the Interior, Bureau of Mines, *Mineral Commodity Summaries 1990* (Washington, D.C.: Government Printing Office, 1990).

U.S. Department of the Interior, Bureau of Mines, *Mineral Commodity Summaries 1991* (Washington, D.C.: Government Printing Office, 1991).

Vennard, Edwin, *The Electric Power Business*, 2nd edn (New York: McGraw-Hill, 1970).

Wallace, Donald H., *Market Control in the Aluminum Industry* (Cambridge, Mass.: Harvard University Press, 1937).

Whitney, Simon N., *Antitrust Policies: American Experience in Twenty Industries* (New York: Twentieth Century Fund, 1958).

# 12

# How Much Did the Liberty Shipbuilders Learn? New Evidence for an Old Case Study

*Peter Thompson**

## I  INTRODUCTION

Numerous empirical studies of productivity growth have shown a tendency for productivity to rise with cumulative output, particularly at early stages of production (see Dutton and Thomas 1984; Jovanovic and Nyarko 1995 for examples). To engineers and managers, this phenomenon is known as the start-up curve, but economists most often refer to it as the learning curve, or learning by doing. Implicit in economists' choice of terminology is the judgment that a causal relationship has been found: producers learn from experience and cumulative production is a good measure of experience. However, numerous difficulties involved in measuring the sources of productivity growth raise the possibility that much of what has been attributed to learning by doing in empirical studies may instead be measurement error.

Several careful studies of apparent learning curves lend credence to this concern. Lazonick and Brush (1985) examine productivity in a nineteenth-century cotton mill, concluding that David's (1973) earlier attribution of productivity growth to learning was mistaken. Bell and Scott-Kemmis (1990) muster a variety of qualitative evidence to suggest that productivity growth in the wartime airframe and ship-building industries was due to numerous factors other than on-the-job learning.

* Financial support was received from a Research Initiation Grant at the University of Houston. I am grateful to Richard Peuser and Becky Livingstone of the National Archives, Washington, D.C., for invaluable assistance in locating uncatalogued records; to Anna Hickman for hospitality during data collection; to Jim Bessen, Margaret Byrne, Boyan Jovanovic, Steven Klepper, Sam Kortum, and Christian Murray for extremely helpful discussions. Peter Pumphrey provided much needed advice on engineering aspects related to fractures. I am also indebted to Lars Hansen and an anonymous referee for suggesting numerous improvements.

Mishina (1999) provides quantitative evidence that capital investments mattered for wartime productivity growth at Boeing's Plant No. 2. Most recently, Sinclair, Klepper and Cohen (1999) find that variations in productivity growth rates across more than one thousand products of the specialty chemicals division of a modern Fortune 500 company are largely attributable to variations in process R&D, rather than to variations in rates of learning by doing.

This paper brings new evidence to bear on a classic case study in learning: the Liberty shipbuilding program of World War II. The main contributions of this paper rest on a new, disaggregated data set constructed from contemporary worksheets, reports and correspondence contained in the Records of the U.S. Maritime Commission (USMC) and the Records of the U.S. Coast Guard currently housed at the National Archives. Extensive data collected at the level of the individual ship include a quantitative measure of vessel quality, and shipyard data include new information on investment in physical capital.

The empirical analysis focuses on two omissions in previous research: investment in physical capital, and variations in product quality. First, I show that capital deepening was much more extensive than has been assumed. Ship construction was well under way before the shipyards themselves had been completed, and additional capital investments accounting for almost two-thirds of the terminal capital stock were undertaken well into the ship construction program. Second, part of the measured increase in productivity was secured at the expense of quality. Incentive payments for fast work led to poor supervision and defective welding. As a result, over thirteen percent of the Liberty fleet developed fractures, which in some instances caused the affected ship to sink. I link productivity to the probability that a Liberty ship developed fractures, suggesting that a trade-off of quantity for quality was made.

The contribution of capital investment to measured productivity growth was much larger than the contribution of quality changes to productivity mismeasurement. The former accounts for as much as half of the measured increase in labor productivity, while the latter induces mismeasurement equivalent to only about 5 percent of observed productivity growth. As a corollary to the larger role attributed to capital, the inclusion of the capital investment data diminish the importance of learning. Without capital data, a *ceteris paribus* doubling of cumulative output is estimated to increase monthly output by 41 percent; the inclusion of capital reduces this estimate to about 22 percent. These findings are subject to two caveats. First, comovements in capital and standard measures of experience make it quite difficult to separate their effects reliably. Second, my empirical analysis continues to omit other sources of productivity growth – among them, training, R&D, and new technology – which may have also played an important role. If, as Rosenberg (1976) has suggested, coefficients on conventional measures of experience are biased because they are correlated with omitted variables, the inclusion of capital investment has reduced, but not eliminated, that bias.

## II  THE LIBERTY SHIP MIRACLE

In 1941, the USMC embarked on a massive expansion of the merchant marine fleet under the auspices of the Emergency Shipbuilding Program. The standard Liberty ship, an all-welded cargo ship with a displacement of 7,000 tons, was the centerpiece of this program. Over a four-year period, 16 U.S. shipyards delivered a total of 2,699 ships, by far the largest production run of a single ship class. Of these, 119 vessels – tankers, colliers, and aircraft and tank transporters – were modifications to the standard Liberty ship design. In addition, a small number of the standard Liberty cargo ships were converted to hospital ships, troop carriers, or training ships. In some cases, the Emergency Shipyards carried out these conversions; in others, the ships were delivered to the navy incomplete.

A revolutionary aspect of the Liberty shipbuilding program was that a substantial portion of ship construction was undertaken off the ways (the berths in which the keel is laid and from which the ship is eventually launched). Most yards had a linear "conveyor belt" plan. Steel plates and shapes entered a holding area in the yard on its inland side, and passed through a large prefabrication area where major sections of the ship were constructed. The sections were then transported on rails or by moveable cranes to one of the ways, where large cranes lifted them onto the hull for final assembly. Welding constituted the bulk of this work. A Liberty ship contained almost 600,000 feet of welded joints, and welding labor accounted for about one-third of the direct labor employed in construction.[1] Once the main structures were completed, the vessel was launched and moved to the outfitting docks nearby. Another keel was typically laid on the vacant way within twenty-four hours. At the outfitting dock, final painting, joinery and electrical work were completed, and rigging and lifeboats were added. The same day that final outfitting was completed, the ship was delivered to a representative of the USMC, boarded by its crew, and sent to join one of hundreds of convoys crossing the Atlantic or the Pacific.

Output at the shipyards was primarily constrained by the number of ways at the yard, and the length of time that a ship spent on the ways before it was launched. Prefabrication of major components of the ships reduced considerably the time ships spent on the ways, greatly increasing the productive capacity of the yards. One ship was launched only four days and fifteen hours after its keel was laid.[2] Labor productivity was also remarkably high by pre-war standards, as the new prefabrication techniques allowed many tasks to be carried out more conveniently

---

[1] Statistics and Reports Unit (1944). Bunker (1972) describes the production process at the Kaiser Permanente Yard in Richmond, Calif. At that yard, 61 percent of the ship was prefabricated, with more than 152,000 feet of welding conducted in preassembly areas. A total of 97 prefabricated sections, each weighing up to 250 tons with "all interior fittings – even mirrors, bunk ladders, postholes, washbasins and radiators – already installed," were transported between the preassembly areas and the ways.

[2] This was the *Robert E. Peary*, built in November 1942 at Kaiser Permanente's no. 2 yard in Richmond, Calif. At the time, Permanente's average construction time was almost 50 days. The construction of the *Robert E. Peary* was a propaganda effort designed to show that the USMC could always produce ships faster than they could be destroyed. In fact it could not, because there was neither enough steel nor sufficient capacity to manufacture engines at this pace. See Bunker (1972) for an account of the special circumstances under which the *Robert E. Peary* was built.

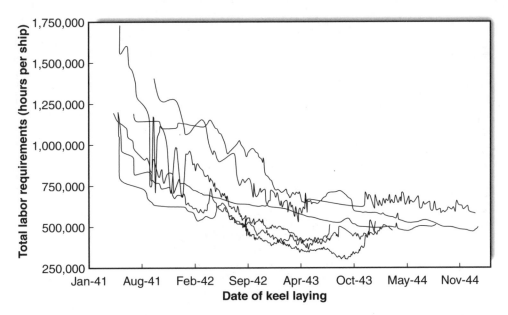

**Figure 12.1**   Standard Liberty ships labor productivity, six yards. The six yards are those for which capital data are available, and which form the focus of study in this chapter. See Searle (1945), Lane (1951), or Lucas (1993) for graphs of other yards. All ships delivered incomplete or modified are excluded.

in inland work areas. For example, metal plates could be held in positions that allowed for automatic welding or that made manual welding easier.

Economists have been interested in the Liberty ship program primarily because of the dramatic increases in labor productivity that were observed over a very short period of time. The phenomenal increase in labor productivity experienced during the Emergency Shipbuilding Program, first brought to the profession's attention by Searle (1945), is now well known. Over the course of three years, labor productivity on Liberty ships rose at an average annual rate of 40 percent. Production time fell even more rapidly. While the first ships produced in each yard required more than sixth months from keel laying to delivery, only thirty days were required by late 1943 (see figures 12.1 and 12.2). For over fifty years, economists have attributed these dramatic gains to learning by doing.

Rapping (1965) is most closely associated with the learning-by-doing interpretation of productivity growth in the Liberty ship program. Rapping proposed a yard-specific production function of the form

$$y_{it} = Ae^{\lambda t} W_{it}^{\alpha} L_{it}^{\beta} Y_{it}^{\gamma}, \tag{1}$$

where $Y_{it}$ is annual deliveries of yard $i$, $W_{it}$ is the number of ways in operation at time $t$ (his proxy for the stock of capital), $L_{it}$ is the annual rate of physical labor

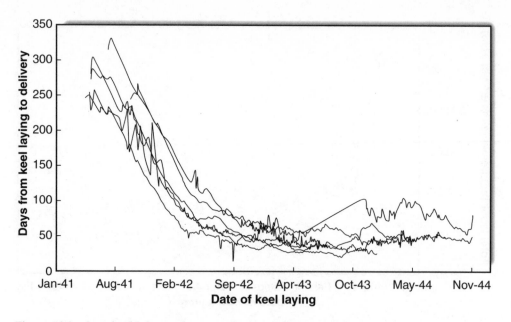

**Figure 12.2**   Standard Liberty ships production speed, six yards

input in hours, and $Y_{it} = Y_{it} - 1 + y_{it-1}$ is cumulative yard output. Rapping estimated the parameters of the production function using pooled annual data for fifteen yards, obtained from Fischer (1948). His analysis was in line with earlier findings by Searle. Each doubling of cumulative output was associated with an increase in annual deliveries of between 7 percent and 27 percent (the point estimates of $\gamma$ ranged from 0.11 to 0.34). depending on specification, with a mean of 17 percent. Moreover, this apparent learning effect was robust to the inclusion of calendar time, which had no significant impact on productivity. Argote, Beckman, and Epple (1990), using monthly data also constructed from Fisher's statistical summary, reached even stronger conclusions about the importance of learning. Estimating the same specification as (1), they obtained a value for $\gamma$ of 0.44. Thus, each doubling of cumulative output was associated with a 36 percent increase in monthly deliveries.

## III   THE MISSING DATA: CAPITAL INVESTMENT

The absence of data on capital has encouraged the perception that none of the increase in productivity at the yard level can be attributed to the familiar mechanism of capital deepening. Rapping (1965) and Argote, Beckman and Epple (1990) used the number of authorized ways in each yard as a proxy for the capital stock, a measure that exhibits almost no variation over time for individual yards. I now have substantial evidence that the number of ways is in fact a crude proxy for capital. Table 12.1 provides three measures of infrastructure per way for seven large

yards. Crane capacity – the major constraint on the size of prefabricated components – varied from 22 tons to 46 tons per way; expenditures on machinery and
equipment varied from $286,000 to $811,000 per way; and the size of prefabrication
areas varied from 14,200 square feet to 66,400 square feet per way. It is evident that
the four yards with above average productivity had significantly more infrastructure than the three least productive yards.

## Authorizations for increased capital

Of course, differences across yards do not show that capital can account for increases in productivity over time. If capital were constant over time, yard dummies
control for differences in capital. However, not all investment was carried out at
the time that the yards were constructed. USMC (1945) notes, for example, that no
new shipyards were established during the fiscal year July 1943 to June 1944, but
$31,142,777 was expended during that period for additional facilities in existing
yards. Importantly, none of these funds was used to construct additional ways.

Figure 12.3 plots Maritime Commission authorizations for capital investment at
the six yards for which adequate data are available. New capital authorizations
at Calship (panel b) followed a typical pattern. On January 10, 1941, the Commission approved expenditures of $4.8 million to build six ways and supporting

**Table 12.1**  Selected facilities per way for seven yards

| | Crane capacity (tons per way) | Equipment (thousand $ per way) | Prefabrication plant (square feet per way) |
|---|---|---|---|
| **A**  Four yards with above average productivity in twelfth round | | | |
| Calship | 34.3 | 679 | 27.7 |
| North Carolina | 44.7 | 765 | 30.2 |
| Oregon | 46.5 | 689 | 66.4 |
| Permanente | 40.0 | 593 | 53.7 |
| **Four-yard average** | **41.4** | **682** | **44.5** |
| | | | |
| **B**  Three yards with below average productivity in twelfth round | | | |
| Bethlehem-Fairfield | 34.0 | 811 | 33.4 |
| New England | 22.4 | 579 | 17.2 |
| Todd-Houston | 24.7 | 286 | 32.7 |
| **Three-yard average** | **27.0** | **558** | **27.7** |

Productivity comparisons are made for the twelfth round of the ways. Planners at the
USMC typically thought in terms of "rounds of the ways." The first ship produced on a
particular way belongs to the first round, the second ship to the second round, and so on.
It has long been standard practice to compare productivity across yards by averaging over
all ships built in a yard at a particular round of the ways, even though the dates at which
each yard reached that round varied.

*Source*: Fischer, 1948, table 1.

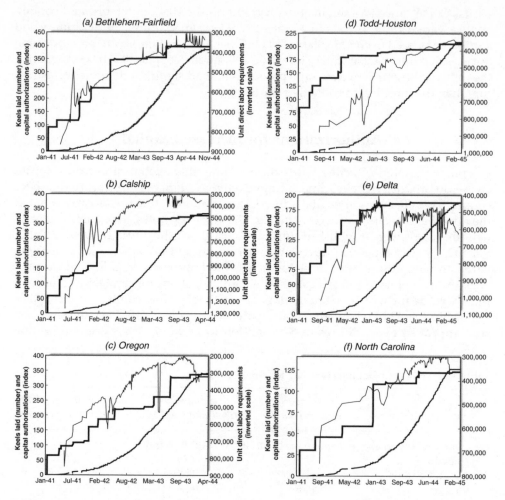

**Figure 12.3**   Capital, experience, and unit labor requirements, six yards

production facilities, adding another eight ways and supporting facilities on April 10 for an additional cost of $4.3 million. However, these expenditures account for only one third of total investment during the program. On January 16, 1942, investments of $2.8 million were approved for additions to the prefabrication plant and expanded electrical and automatic welding facilities. These expenditures were approved after nineteen keels had been laid, and five ships had been launched. On June 16, 1942, another $1.9 million was approved to install new cranes that would enable the yard to pre-assemble larger components, and to install additional welding equipment on ways and pre-assembly platforms. Fifty keels had already been laid prior to this investment. Additional authorizations, between May 1941 and January 1943, accounted for a further $8.2 million expansion of capital. Finally, $4.7 million of new capital was authorized in April 1943. Intended to facilitate conversion of the yard to production of the more complex Victory cargo ships, the additional capital was also available for Liberty ship production.

The reader should note that Figure 12.3 can mislead in several ways. First, all appearances to the contrary, the panels do not show a stronger relationship between capital authorizations and labor productivity than between cumulative output and labor productivity. In fact, capital and experience are each equally capable of providing good within-sample predictors of productivity. Second, delays between investment authorization and the installation of new capital imply that Figure 12.3 overestimates the speed with which capital was expanded. Third, the graphs show frequent large but short-lived shocks to labor productivity. The new ship-level information allows most of these to be explained by design modifications (most large negative shocks), and ships delivered incomplete for subsequent conversion by the navy (most large positive shocks). One interesting exception is the large negative shock to productivity experienced by Oregon in April 1943. This shock represent eight vessels on which construction was started by another yard in Vancouver; the ships were towed to Portland and completed there.

## Time-to-build delays

Time-to-build delays were substantial and clearly had a significant impact on labor productivity. In each yard, construction on the first round of Liberty ships began while the yard itself was still being built. Because prefabrication buildings and cranes were often not installed when a yard began ship construction, a large proportion of the production of first- and second-round ships took place on the ways. The result was that the earliest ships in each yard spent longer on the ways, they were produced using more labor-intensive techniques than were ships produced after the yard was completed, and labor productivity was lower.

There are no direct data on how long it took to complete construction of new yard, nor on how many ships were affected, but both were clearly substantial. In August 1942, for example, Admiral Vickery, vice-chairman of the USMC, testified to the Truman Committee that "it had been our experience from the yards we had put in that it takes about a year to put a yard in and get really producing" (Senate 1942, p. 251). If this was generally true, productivity on as many as the first ten ships produced in each yard may have been adversely affected by time-to-build delays.

Similarly, there are no direct data on the extent to which productivity was affected. However, construction progress reports for South Portland Shipbuilding Corporation provide some illustration. The yard laid its first Liberty ship keel on September 24, 1941, yet on January 7, 1942 only five of seven cranes in the construction plans had been delivered and only three of these were operational. Four ships were being constructed at the time, on ways 1 through 4, but the keels on ways 2 and 3 were being constructed largely from manual welding. While the effect on labor productivity is not known,[3] we do know that the ships produced on ways 1

---

[3] The establishment of South Portland was so disorganized that its management was soon replaced, at which time the yard changed its name to the New England Shipbuilding Corporation. Probably because of the disorganization, audited productivity data were not collected for the first eight ships.

and 4 were launched 233 and 221 days after keel laying, while the ships on ways 2 and 3 took 256 and 272 days.[4] Evidently, production techniques were different for the first round of the ways, and it would be wrong to attribute to learning by doing all the productivity increases observed as yards progressed from the first to the second round. In fact, Lane (1951, p. 232) simply notes that the first round of ships "was often built while the yard was still under construction" and disregards them in making his productivity comparisons.

## Investment decisions: did experience play a role?

Capital deepening over the life of the Liberty ship program was extensive, and is clearly correlated with cumulative output. Thus, point estimates of the coefficient on cumulative output obtained from OLS regressions of a log-linearized version of equation (1) might be expected to correspond fairly precisely to the elasticity of output with respect to capital. Yet one might object that some or even all of the incremental investment could have been the direct result of production experience enabling managers to identity capital constraints. That is, the effects of learning by doing might just be embodied in capital. Indeed, Vice Admiral Vickery testified to the Truman Committee that additional capital expenditures were often a result of "everybody thinking of something new they wanted . . . like the youngster with candy who wants more" (Senate 1943, p. 912). Lane (1951, p. 473), noting possible inter-yard spillovers of investment decisions, also pointed out that additional capital expenditures were often suggested by Vickery himself as he "went from yard to yard, telling each of them what was being done better elsewhere."

However, closer analysis of the data clearly shows that all major incremental investments were direct and immediate responses to increases in the scope of the Emergency Program mandated by Congress. Lane (1951, pp. 40–71) documents the series of expansions in the scheduled production of Liberty ships that took place in 1941 and 1942. Calship's experience is representative. On January 3, 1941, the U.S. Government announced plans to supply 200 ships to the British under a lend-lease arrangement. Calship won its first contract for 31 ships several weeks later. On March 27, 1941, Congress approved the Defense Aid Supplemental Appropriation Act, which provided funds to construct an additional 200 ships for the British. A new contract with Calship, dated April 17, 1941, called for an additional 24 ships. The Japanese attack on Pearl Harbor on December 7, 1941 immediately generated another wave of expansion as the United States entered the war. On January 16, 1942, Calship won a new contract for an additional 109 ships. Finally, unexpectedly heavy losses to torpedo attacks in the Atlantic during the spring of 1942 generated a new round of contracts in June of that year, with Calship contracting for 60 more ships on June 16, 1942. These new contracts for ships uniformly coincide with authorizations for the major capital expansions of April 10, 1941, January 16, 1942

---

[4] The information is contained in attachments to Allen (1942), who commented in a letter to Vickery that "we are preassembling our material in sections as much as is possible. However, due to the fact that much of our preassembly area is either unserviced by cranes or is unavailable due to incomplete facilities, we are limited to a great extent in performing this work."

and June 16, 1942. Moreover, there is documentary evidence that the former motivated the latter. For example, J. E. Schmeltzer, a senior member of the USMC Technical Division, observed that the January 1942 incremental investment in Calship was necessary "to accelerate the ship construction schedule . . . to cover the increased scope of the plant and facilities for the purpose of facilitating the assembly of hulls; all in relation to the augmented and accelerated shipbuilding program." In June 1942, C. W. Flesher, West Coast regional director for construction, commented that the June 1942 expansions at Calship were necessary "in order to increase the deliveries of ships to the largest number possible within the physical limitations of [Calship]."[5]

## IV  SOURCES OF GROWTH: CAPITAL VS. EXPERIENCE

This section reports attempts to allocate productivity growth between the two main sources of learning by doing and capital investment. I take the familiar approach of estimating a temporal production function, which I assume takes the form

$$\ln y_{it} = A_i + a\ln K_{it} + \beta\ln L_{it} + \gamma\ln E_{it} + \varepsilon_{it}. \tag{2}$$

in which $y_{it}$ is monthly deliveries of yard $i$, $K_{it}$ is the stock of physical capital, $L_{it}$ is the monthly rate of physical labor inputs, and $E_{it}$ is a measure of experience to be discussed below. The important distinction between (1) and (2) is that the latter specification incorporates a measure of all physical capital – structures and non-structures – while the former incorporates only a subset of structures. The specification of (2) allows for yard fixed effects. As in Argote et al. (1990), the disturbance term is assumed to exhibit up to third-order yard-specific serial correlation. The monthly output data are constructed by aggregating individual ship data, as explained in the appendix.

### Measurement issues

#### Labor

For a substantial part of the war, many of the Emergency yards were producing ships other than Libertys. For example, beginning in November 1943, over half of the yards began to build Victory ships, and the available employment data do not distinguish employment on the production of Libertys from employment on the production of Victorys. To avoid this mismeasurement problem, it will be necessary to limit the sample period to months in which yards were not actively engaged in the production of Victorys.

---

[5] Both quotes from untitled typescripts containing summaries of USMC minutes, Schmeltzer's dated January 18, 1942 and Flesher's dated June 11, 1942. Located in the Records of the Historian's Office, Box 32, Records of the US Maritime Commission (National Archives, RG178). Almost identical justifications accompany requests for, and approvals of, additional facilities at Todd-Houston (Vickery 1943a), Jones-Brunswick (Vickery 1943b), and Oregon (Oregon Shipbuilding Corporation 1942, p. 1).

Over the course of the war the distribution of employees over shifts varied significantly. According to Bureau of Labor Statistics tabulations, most yards began production in 1941 with two construction shifts per day, and a six-day week. During 1942, a 21-shift week gradually became the norm. Then, in December 1944, overcapacity at the yards persuaded the USMC to immediately abolish Sunday employment,[6] and to discourage the employment of construction labor on the graveyard shift (in which labor was generally held to be less productive). By July 1944, only a skeleton crew remained at night. These changes in the distribution of labor inputs across shifts obviously induce corresponding changes in capacity utilization that affect the correct measure of the flow of capital services per month.

Capital and labor will both be treated as exogenous. A case has already been made for the exogeneity of capital, which was ultimately chosen by the USMC. But the yards themselves were allowed to hire and dismiss labor, and in this setting the usual inference is that profit-maximizing firms will hire more workers when productivity shocks are positive and will dismiss workers in the face of negative productivity shocks. The extent to which the joint determination of output and employment causes estimation problems depends, of course, on the sensitivity of labor demand to productivity shocks. The standard solution is to instrument for labor hours with wage rates. However, the yards were regional monopsonists in the labor market, so wage rates are not valid instruments. Fortunately, I think a strong case can be made for the view that labor demand was in fact largely unresponsive to productivity shocks.

Consider first the limited incentives that firms had to adjust labor inputs. In negotiations over a ship delivery contract, each yard and the USMC settled on an average production speed and an average labor requirement (called the "bogie hours") for all ships to be delivered under the contract. If the yard met these agreed targets, all production costs were paid, plus a fixed base fee for profits. To encourage rapid production, a bonus of $400 was paid for each day's increase in production speed, while the base fee was reduced by $400 for each day taken beyond the agreed production speed. To encourage labor efficiency, the yard was paid fifty cents for each labor hour saved in production while its fees were reduced by 33 cents for each labor hour in excess of the bogie. However, these incentives were muted by bounds placed on the fees that could be earned. At the beginning of the war, no yard was permitted to earn a fee in excess of $120,000 per ship, and no yard could earn less than $60,000. These bounds, which were lowered and narrowed several times during the war, effectively converted many cost plus variable fee contracts into simple cost plus fixed fee contracts under which there are no incentives to lay off employees during periods of low productivity. Figure 12.4 shows the maximum, minimum and actual fees paid for 36 contracts awarded by the USMC. While the caps were not always binding, particularly at the earliest stages of production, in two-thirds of the contracts signed (accounting for 68 percent of the 1,987 ships included in the 36 contracts), either

---

[6] The North Carolina yard was granted a permanent exemption and continued to employ construction workers on Sundays. Other yards were given temporary exemptions on occasions.

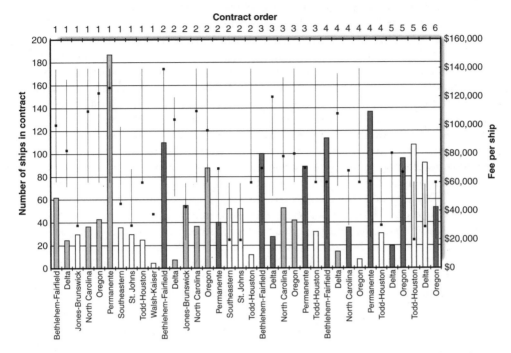

**Figure 12.4** Per ship fees on bogie hour contracts, ten yards. The vertical bars show the number of ships ordered in each contract, after amendments (left-hand scale). The vertical lines span the range of allowed fees (right-hand scale), while the marker on each line indicates the actual fees paid. The bars are shaded dark when at least 90% of the maximum fee was paid, light when the minimum fee was paid, and have intermediate shading otherwise. The lower horizontal axis indicates the yard with which the contract was signed. The upper horizontal axis indicates whether the contract was the first, second, etc., to be signed with the yard. Because certain expenses were invariably disallowed by the USMC, fees paid in excess of 90% of the maximum generally could not be raised by increased productivity or production speed. After April 1942, when the Renegotiation Act was passed, yards also knew that any fees earned could be further reduced. Between November 1943 and May 1947, the fees shown in the figure were reduced by an average of 40%. "Excess" fees were taxed at a marginal rate of 80%. The average tax rate on fees was approximately 65%. Source: author's calculations, based on testimony given in House (1946).

the minimum or maximum fees were earned, and the bogie formula provided no incentive for efficiency.

Bogie contracts provided little incentive to lay off workers.[7] There were also substantial incentives to hoard labor. For much of the war, labor movements were controlled by the War Manpower Commission (WMC). If a shipyard worker wanted

---

[7] In a May 1944 letter to President Roosevelt, Henry J. Kaiser (whose companies ran six USMC yards) pressed the government to substitute competitive bidding for the bogie contracts, a policy which Kaiser argued would put an end to labor hoarding. The transcript of the letter is an exhibit in House (1946).

assistance to relocate, a certificate of availability had to be obtained from the WMC. As one of the easiest ways to get the certificate was for a worker to show the WMC that he or she was not currently employed full time, a yard could limit the loss of skilled employees who wanted to move simply by keeping them employed full time. On the other side of the coin, a yard that wanted to hire more workers was often required to obtain approval from the WMC, which classified vacancies by degree of urgency. It was, naturally, rather difficult for a yard that had recently let workers go to claim a high degree of urgency for new recruits. Hiring restrictions presented a real danger to the yards: if a yard could not demonstrate that it had an adequate labor force, winning new contracts became more difficult. Inevitably, labor hoarding was a common phenomenon. Evidence of hoarding can be found during 1942 when steel and engine shortages slowed down production at many yards. In Spring 1942, Admiral Land, chairman of the USMC, began a public campaign against loafing which quickly led to an acrimonious exchange, largely through the media, between Land and labor leaders. In an attempt to end the dispute Roosevelt publicly commented that he believed shortage of steel plates to be the chief cause of idle labor (*New York Times*, April 25, 1942, p. 1). Following up his public defense of labor with a personal letter to Admiral Land dated May 2, 1942, Roosevelt said that "many of the so-called slow-downs in shipbuilding plants are due not to organized labor but to strict orders or suggestions from the foreman or their management that a slow-down would be advantageous because the non-delivery of shapes and plates will cause a lay-off if there is not a slow-down." Land agreed. On May 20 he responded that "inefficiency is one cause [of the slow-down]; lack of material is another cause; and fear of losing some of their good personnel is a third cause" (Admiral Land's correspondence files, RG178, National Archives).

## Experience

The most common measure of experience, cumulative output, is the measure used by Rapping and by Argote, Beckman and Epple. It will also be the primary measure used in this paper. However, its use in estimation of the production function may induce finite sample bias. The term $\ln(Y_{it})$ can be written as $\ln(Y_{it-1} + y_{it-1})$ and $\ln(Y_{it-1})$ is correlated with the disturbance term in the presence of serial correlation. Note, however, that $\lim_{Y \to \infty} d(\ln Y + y)/d(\ln y) = 0$, so the correlation vanishes asymptotically. Another measure of experience, cumulative labor hours, avoids this potential problem and estimates using it in place of cumulative output will also be reported. The distinction between the two measures is that cumulative output measures the number of times a task has been done, while cumulative employment measures the amount of time spent trying to accomplish the same set of tasks. I do not know of any compelling reason to prefer one measure to the other.

## Capital

I do not have capital stock data. The capital authorization data described earlier represent only the *desired* capital stock, in the sense that they document requests for capital, and time-to-build delays were substantial. To capture time-to-build delays,

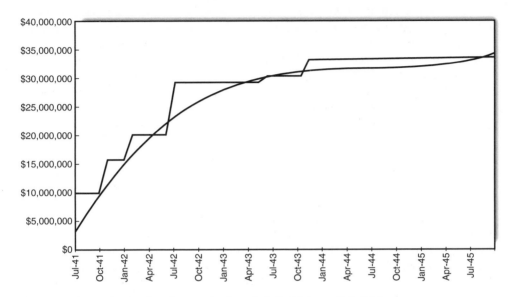

**Figure 12.5**   Authorized and smoothed capital, Bethlehem–Fairfield.

I create a proxy for the installed capital by smoothing the authorization data. This was carried out by fitting polynomial functions of time to the data points on capital authorizations that correspond to the right-most point of each horizontal segment in the capital data shown in figure 12.3. Figure 12.5 plots a typical series for smoothed capital.

A final difficulty, which affects capital in all estimating equations, is that there are no yard-specific price indices, yet the cost of capital undoubtedly varied across yards. Thus, although the discussion of section III supports the assumption that desired capital is exogenous, it is measured with error. Two approaches present themselves. First, one could attempt to instrument for capital. However, problems of selecting useful instruments lead to the second approach of ignoring the measurement error. This will, of course, attenuate the role of capital. However, there are reasons to suppose that biases induced by potential measurement error will be small. For example, at least part of the measurement error will be due to systematic proportional differences across yards in the cost of installed capital (due, for example, to persistent regional differences in nominal wages). The log-linear functional forms employed conveniently separate out these differences and allow them to be captured by yard fixed effects.

## Estimation

Columns 3 through 6 of table 12.2 report estimates of (2) using cumulative output as a proxy for experience. SURE estimation is conducted to allow for contemporaneous correlation in the disturbances across yards. For comparison, the results for similar specifications estimated by Rapping (1965) and by Argote et al. (1990) are also reported. In my reduced sample of six yards, there is no variation over time in the number of authorized ways, which are consequently confounded with the yard fixed effects. Column 3, which omits any proxy for capital, therefore reports my attempt to replicate the earlier results. As noted earlier, the two previous studies produced rather different estimates of the importance of cumulative output. In particular, Rapping produced consistently smaller coefficients on experience than did Argote et al. On can readily shown that this difference is at least in part because Rapping used annual data while Argote et al. used monthly data.[8] My estimate of the coefficient on experience in column 3 is very close to the Argote et al. estimate.

Column 4 uses a proxy for capital constructed from the number of ways in use, rather than the number of ways that had been authorized. This proxy is. I think, what previous researchers intended to measure with their way data. However, even though the number of ways in use does rise over time, its inclusion in the regression proxy has no effect on the estimated importance of experience. Note also that Argote et al. obtained a very large value for the coefficient on ways, and a very small coefficient on labor inputs, neither of which I can replicate. The reason for this seems to be that their monthly output series was constructed from Fischer's data on average production speed per way and multiplying these data by the number of authorized ways. The use of the same data on the left and right hand sides of (2) have obvious implications for the coefficient on ways.

Column 5 introduces the capital series obtained from smoothing the capital authorization data. The main result of interest is that the coefficient on experience declines, from almost 0.50 in the previous columns, to 0.29. Wald tests confirm that this decline is statistically significant. Finally, column 6 attempts to account partially for variations in capacity utilization by exploiting data on shift employment. Each month's capital data is given a weight of $w_{it} = (6 + S_{it})/7$, where $S_{it}$ is Sunday employment as a fraction of weekday employment. Because of the log-linear specification, the weights and the capital data are additively separable. One can therefore estimate by restricted least squares and test the linear restriction that the coefficients on unweighted capital and the weights are equal. Column 6 reports the restricted estimate.[9] While the coefficient on labor is now substantially smaller, the main result is much the same as in column 5: the introduction of capital reduces the coefficient on experience, and Wald tests again confirm that the decline is significant.

---

[8] Recall that cumulative output can be written as $\ln(Y_{it-1} + y_{it-1})$, so that this variable is a nonlinear function of the lagged dependent variable. Temporal aggregation has serious consequences for parameter estimates in this context. The point can best be made by considering the deterministic linear model $y_t = \rho y_{t-1} + \beta x_t$, where the subscript indexes monthly observations. Imagine that data are only available bimonthly, so that the econometrician is forced to regress $y_{t+1} + y_t$ on $y_{t-1} + y_{t-2}$ and $x_{t+1} + x_t$. Some straightforward manipulations yield $y_{t+1} + y_t = \rho^2(y_{t-1} + y_{t-2}) + \beta(x_{t+1} + x_t) + \rho\beta(x_{t-1} + x_{t-2})$. The coefficient on the lagged dependent variable is biased downward for $\rho < 1$, as it must be in the present application. Note that when $\rho = 0$, no bias is induced by temporal aggregation.

[9] Some observations are lost because of missing data. The restriction is not rejected by a Wald test ($p$ value 0.504). The unrestricted coefficient estimates (standard errors in parentheses) are 0.84 (0.18) on unweighted capital and 0.54 (0.39) on the capacity utilization weights.

**Table 12.2**   SURE production function estimates: experience proxy (cumulative output)

| | Rapping | Argote et al. | (3) | (4) | (5) | (6) |
|---|---|---|---|---|---|---|
| | | | *Dependent variable: log monthly output in ship equivalents* | | | |
| Log experience | 0.110 | 0.44 | 0.493 | 0.481 | 0.291 | 0.263 |
| (Cum. output) | (0.013) | (0.03) | (0.025) | (0.027) | (0.045) | (0.037) |
| Log authorized ways | 0.293 | 1.15 | . . . | . . . | . . . | . . . |
| | (0.096) | (0.05) | | | | |
| Log operating ways | . . . | . . . | . . . | 0.274 | . . . | . . . |
| | | | | (0.236) | | |
| Log capital, $K_{it}$ | . . . | . . . | . . . | . . . | 0.743 | 0.780 |
| | | | | | (0.180) | (0.154) |
| Capacity utilization weight, $w_{it} = (6 + S_{it})/7$ | . . . | . . . | . . . | . . . | . . . | 0.780 |
| | | | | | | (0.154) |
| Log labor hours | 1.11 | 0.18 | 0.414 | 0.422 | 0.414 | 0.253 |
| | (0.032) | (0.04) | (0.061) | (0.061) | (0.057) | (0.088) |
| Wald tests (ρ values) | | | | | | |
| (3) | . . . | . . . | . . . | 0.656 | 0.000 | 0.000 |
| (4) | . . . | . . . | . . . | . . . | 0.000 | 0.000 |
| Adjusted $R^2$ | 0.967 | 0.990 | 0.925 | 0.922 | 0.919 | 0.711 |
| Observations | 48 | 337 | 182 | 182 | 182 | 149 |

Standard errors in parentheses. The Rapping column reports coefficients from regression (6) in Rapping (1965, table 1). Rapping's regression (6) produced his lowest point estimate for the coefficient on experience, but the specification is closest to that used in the remaining columns of the table. The Argote et al. column reports coefficients from column (2) of Argote, Beckman and Epple (1990, table 1). Regressions in columns (3) through (6) include yard fixed effects and yard-specific AR(3) errors. Wald Test (3) [(4)] is a test that the coefficient on experience is the same as the point estimate in column (3) [(4)]. In column (6) the coefficients on capital and the capacity utilization weights are restricted to be equal. Because total sample $R^2$ measures can mislead in pooled data, the adjusted $R^2$ in columns (3) through (6) are the *lowest* of six yard-specific coefficients of determination. Total-sample coefficients of determination were all in excess of 0.92.

Introducing the capital data to the regressions uniformly induces a significant reduction in the estimated impact of experience on productivity. Compare, for example, my attempt to replicate previous findings in column 3 of table 12.2, with the estimates in column 5. The estimates in column 3 indicate that a *ceteris paribus* doubling of experience would raise monthly output by 41 percent, while the estimates in column 5 reduce that figure to 22 percent. At the same time, a doubling of the amount of capital in the yard is estimated in column 5 to raise monthly output by 67 percent. These numbers are somewhat sensitive to model specification. The

**Table 12.3** SURE production function estimates: experience proxy (cumulative employment)

| | Dependent variable: log monthly output in ship equivalents | | | |
| --- | --- | --- | --- | --- |
| | (3) | (4) | (5) | (6) |
| Log experience | 0.359 | 0.355 | 0.228 | 0.208 |
| (Cum. labor hours) | (0.040) | (0.038) | (0.038) | (0.050) |
| Log operating ways | . . . | −0.278 | . . . | . . . |
| | | (0.299) | | |
| Log capital, $K_{it}$ | . . . | . . . | 1.040 | 1.117 |
| | | | (0.127) | (0.165) |
| Capacity utilization weight, | | . . . | | |
| $w_{it} = (6 + S_{it})/7$ | . . . | | . . . | 1.117 |
| | | | | (0.165) |
| Log labor hours | 0.542 | 0.566 | 0.462 | 0.343 |
| | (0.074) | (0.072) | (0.065) | (0.086) |
| Wald Tests (ρ values) | | | | |
| (3) | | 0.902 | 0.001 | 0.003 |
| (4) | . . . | . . . | 0.001 | 0.004 |
| Lowest adjusted R² | 0.905 | 0.901 | 0.98 | 0.716 |
| Observations | 177 | 177 | 177 | 149 |

See notes to table 12.2.

importance of capital *rises* when adjustment is made for capacity utilization, so that a doubling of capital is estimated in column 6 to induce a 72 percent increase in monthly output; the importance of experience is correspondingly lower, and a doubling of cumulative output is associated in column 6 with a 20 percent increase in monthly output.

Finally, table 12.3 reports results of the same analysis conducted using cumulative labor hours as the proxy for experience. Although the point estimates on capital appear less plausible than when cumulative output was the proxy for experience, the results are generally consistent: the addition of capital to the regression reduces the point estimate on experience by more than a third, and Wald tests again show that the decline is significant.

## V   WERE ALL LIBERTY SHIPS CREATED EQUAL?

Unobserved variations in quality inevitably introduce measurement error into growth accounting exercises. Random variations in quality that are not affected by production decisions do not need to be measured. In contrast, productivity increases secured at the expense of quality need to be discounted from measured growth rates. Adjusting for the systematic component of quality change is usually a challenging task. First, one must be able to measure quality. Second, one must be able to show that at least part of any quality variations can be predicted by productivity levels. Finally, one needs to be able to value the predictable changes in quality. In this section, I use new data on the eventual fate of each Liberty ship to show that part of the measured productivity growth was secured by allowing quality to decline. It will turn out that the indicated quality adjustments to measured output per worker are modest in relation to the high measured rates of productivity growth rates. However, because it has long been argued that homogeneity of output is one of the most attractive features of the Liberty ship experiment, this section should be of independent interest.

## Fractures in Liberty ships

Just as the peak productivity levels were being recorded in the winter of 1942–43, some remarkable hull failures occurred. On January 16, 1943, a tanker, *Schenectady*, split in two while moored in calm water at the outfitting dock at Swan Island, Oregon. A U.S. Coast Guard (1944) report described the incident:

> Without warning and with a report which was heard for at least a mile, the deck and sides of the vessel fractured just aft of the bridge superstructure. The fracture extended almost instantaneously to the turn of the bilge port and starboard. The deck side shell, longitudinal bulkhead and bottom girders fractured. Only the bottom plating held. The vessel jack-knifed and the center portion rose so that no water entered. The bow and stern settled into the silt of the river bottom.

The ship was twenty-four hours old.

The *Schenectady* was not the first merchant ship to fracture, although it was certainly one of the more dramatic cases. In fact ten USMC ships, eight of them standard Libertys, had already suffered a serious fracture by the time of the *Schenectady* incident. But the *Schenectady* fracture was the first to happen in full view of the population of a major city, and hence the first to attract widespread attention. Portland newspapers of January 17, 1943 reported the story, and publicity about several more serious casualties in the months following could not be suppressed.[10] On February 2, 1943, an editorial in the *New York Journal of Commerce* observed that

> For the last year the Maritime Commission has used the construction records of the Kaiser yards as a sort of whip with which to goad other of the nation's yards into speedier construction. No one will deny that speed is needed in the construction and delivery of ships. However, no matter how speedily a ship is delivered its worth is

---

[10] Several of these casualties also occurred in calm water. On February 12, 1943, *Belle Isle*, an ore ship, was traveling partly loaded in calm seas. She split across the deck and part way down the sides. A complete rupture was only prevented by rivets on the side seams. Four days later, the new Liberty ship *Henry Wynkoop* fractured her deck while being loaded in New York, and on March 29 the tanker *Esso Manhattan* broke in two just after leaving the entrance to New York Harbor.

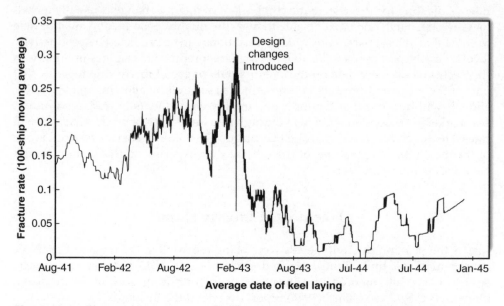

**Figure 12.6**   Observed fracture rates. The figure was constructed by ordering all ships, irrespective of yard, by date of keel laying. The fracture rate is a moving 100-ship window measuring the fraction of all the ships within the window that eventually produced fractures.

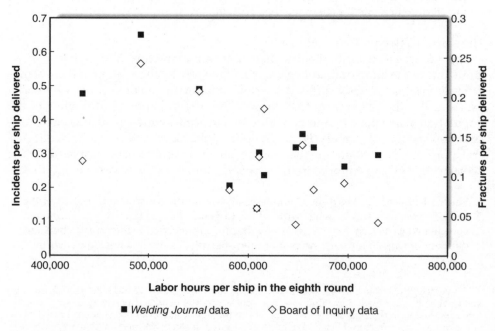

**Figure 12.7**   Fracture rates and productivity.

**Table 12.4**  Fracture incidents by yard

| | | Fracture incidents | | Ships fractured | |
|---|---|---|---|---|---|
| | Number built | Number of incidents | Incidents per ship delivered (%) | Number fractured | Fractures per ship delivered (%) |
| Bethlehem-Fairfield | 384 | 90 | 23.4 | 71 | 18.5 |
| Jones-Brunswick | 85 | 27 | 23.7 | 7 | 8.2 |
| Calship | 336 | 164 | 48.8 | 70 | 20.8 |
| North Carolina | 126 | 60 | 47.6 | 15 | 11.9 |
| Delta | 188 | 57 | 30.3 | 23 | 12.2 |
| New England | 244 | 72 | 29.5 | 10 | 4.1 |
| Todd-Houston | 208 | 74 | 35.5 | 29 | 13.9 |
| Oregon | 330 | 215 | 65.2 | 80 | 24.2 |
| Jones-Panama | 102 | 14 | 13.7 | 6 | 5.9 |
| Permanente #1 & #2 | 489 | 100 | 20.4 | 40 | 8.2 |
| Southeastern | 88 | 23 | 26.1 | 8 | 9.1 |
| St. Johns | 82 | 26 | 31.7 | 3 | 3.7 |
| **Total** | **2,692** | **922** | **34.6** | **362** | **13.6** |

The table excludes yards producing 20 Liberty ships or fewer.

*Source*: Fracture incidents from *Welding Journal* (1947, p. 588). Number of ships fractured from Bates (1946) and Board of Investigation (1945).

practically nil if its plates crack, or if for any other reason that vessel must spend thirty to sixty days in a repair yard after one or two trips.

Lane (1951, p. 545) reports that there were "other less sensational fractures during the opening months of 1943." In fact there were many more, and they were to continue throughout the war. By February 1946, 362 ships, over 13 percent of the Liberty fleet, had suffered at least one major fracture. Of these, 103 ships suffered class I fractures that threatened the structural integrity of the ship.[11]

Following the *Schenectady* incident, the Maritime Commission established a Board of Investigation to study the causes of, and provide solutions to, the problem of fracturing. The Board immediately funded over thirty distinct research projects at laboratories and universities throughout the country. Interim reports of the Board of Investigation (1944, 1945) have extensive discussions of "locked in stresses" in certain areas of the ship, exacerbated by shifting loads in rough weather and sudden drops in air or water temperature. These stresses were believed to be "relieved"

[11] Some vessels fractured as many as five times, and there were in fact over one thousand fracture incidents, often involving multiple fractures, on the 362 ships. The *Welding Journal* (1947) documents a total of 2,504 fractures in 964 separate incidents.

by the crackings. But, as Lane (1951, p. 572) notes, such phrases were "figures of speech used to describe the unknown, just as psychiatrists describe the mysteries of human personality by talking about the need of relieving inhibitions." Despite the uncertainty about the causes of the fractures, the major research effort funded by the Board generated numerous important design changes between February and May 1943. These, along with additional modifications mandated in January and February 1944, are described in some detail by Lane (1951, pp. 548–50). The effect of the design changes was a decline in the fracture rate from 30 percent for ships with keels laid in February 1943 to about 5 percent only four months later. Figure 12.6 shows this dramatic decline.

Locked in stresses won't lead to fractures if materials are strong enough and workmanship good enough to withstand them. Moreover, stresses resulting from design flaws cannot fully explain several features of the data. Fracture rates varied significantly across yards (see table 12.4). This variation could be accounted for by systematic variations in steel quality in the mills supplying the yards, an issue that received much attention in 1943 and 1944. However, steel quality cannot be all the explanation, because yard differences in fracture rates were clearly related to productivity differences. Figure 12.7 plots the two measures of fracture rates from table 12.5 against labor requirements for the first ship built in the eighth round of the ways. The correlation between productivity and fracture rates is clearly visible, and is statistically significant at conventional levels. Moreover, fracture rates exhibited a marked tendency to rise during the first two years of the program. In fact, figure 12.6, which pools data across yards, understates the extent to which fracture rates increased over time within some of the larger yards. These features of the data strongly suggest that, even though design and steel quality were contributing factors, production practices were related to the fracture problems.[12]

## Trading quantity for quality

While experts were talking about locked in stresses, they were also paying attention to the quality of welding. In fact, the official Coast Guard report on the *Schenectady* incident attributed the fracture to welds in critical seams that "were found to be defective." By the time Tyler (1947) surveyed the fracture problem, the quality of welding had become the central theme,[13] while the *Welding Journal* (1947, p. 591) concluded in the same year that defective workmanship was an identifiable contributing factor in half of the fracture incidents:

---

[12] Whether or not a defect in a weld leads to a fracture depends on the size of the defect, the stress, and the toughness of the material. For a given stress, tougher steel can withstand larger defects without fracturing. Modern methods of fracture mechanics can use these parameters to calculate the critical defect size above which a fracture is expected to occur. Most descriptions of Liberty fractures indicate that the cracks were accompanied by loud bangs which is characteristic of brittle fractures (i.e. failures because of insufficiently tough steel).

[13] Half of Tyler's report is devoted to the topics of welder training, supervision, and welding practices. Senate (1944, pp. 9943–8) contains fascinating testimony from a Robert P. Day, a ship inspector who had worked at several Kaiser yards, about failures to correct welding problems that he reported.

The fractures occurring on the EC2-S-C1 design have been grouped to determine the proportionate contribution of design and workmanship to the number of fractures which occurred. It is impossible to make a breakdown with a clear line of demarcation between the groups because in many cases, poor design details and poor workmanship went hand in hand in their contribution to the fracture. In other cases, awkward design resulted in defective welds because of the difficulty in performing the welding ... It has been possible to make a reasonably reliable judgment regarding the part played by workmanship in 1,800 of the 2,504 fractures reported occurring on the EC2-S-C1 vessels before August 1945. It was found that in 25% of these cases, no fracture would have resulted had good workmanship been used. In 20% of the cases, there was some question but it was believed that the failure might have been avoided had the workmanship been good.

Defective welds were associated with increased use of automatic welding machines beginning in late 1942. While automatic welding greatly increased labor productivity,[14] over 50 percent of the fractures are known to have originated in the loading hatches and, as the *Welding Journal* (p. 588) reported.

> it was common practice in some shipyards to weld with a Unionmelt machine to within a few inches of the hatch coaming where the automatic equipment had to be stopped. The remainder of the seam was completed by hand welding without further preparation and a saddle weld resulted because of the failure of the welding to penetrate the square-edged butt.

Automatic welding in the neighborhood of critical joints was prohibited after February 1943.

However, C. E. Wilson, Production Vice-Chairman of the War Production Board, clearly believed that poor welding was due to more factors than just automation. He visited most of the yards in the weeks following the *Schenectady* incident, and documented numerous cases of poor supervision of welders, poor craftsmanship, and even fraud (Lane 1951, pp. 544–73; Tyler 1947). Bonus wage payments for fast work led in some instances to intentionally defective welding and fraudulent actions. In April 1943, Wilson appeared in Baltimore as an expert witness in the civil trial of one of nine welders accused of placing unfused electrodes and slugs of iron in plate grooves and then covering them with superficial welds. The process, known in welding circles as slugging, greatly increases the speed of welding but seriously weakens the joint. The defendant was convicted of "making war material in a defective manner with the intent that his act would hinder, obstruct and interfere with the United States Government in preparing for and carrying on the war" (Wilson, quoted in Tyler 1947, p. 72), and, being a minor, was sentenced to eighteen months in a reformatory school. Wilson found that some welders at the Bethlehem-Fairfield yard in Baltimore had tried to use two electrodes with machines designed for only one. At Calship, poorly skilled welders were found to have been hired on

---

[14] *Marine Engineering and Shipping Review* (1942) reported that Liberty shipyards were introducing new automatic welding techniques which increased production by over 100 percent. Kaiser Co. (1943) reported that a good welder could turn out about 500 feet in eight hours on a machine weld, compared with 100 feet in the same time by manual weld.

the basis of test plates made by others, while some unskilled welders had skilled friends and relatives take qualifying tests for them.

Not all the blame can be laid on the yard employees. In fact, from the beginning of the program, top administrators in the construction program encouraged greater production speed with the full knowledge that reliability might suffer as a consequence. The American Bureau of Shipping (ABS) was the agency responsible for coordinating safety inspections at the yards. Yet, in early 1942, the ABS issued a statement that explicitly directed its inspectors and the shipyards to favor speed over safety:

> It must be recognized, not only by inspectors but also by the building yards, to whom copies of this letter are being furnished, that under the present circumstances early completion of serviceable ships is of greater national importance than the high measure of perfection required for full durability.[15]

Workers, managers and even safety inspectors were willing to trade quality for quantity. To assess the magnitude of this tradeoff, I have matched data on dates of fractures and losses by enemy action to productivity data for 2,662 Liberty ships. Probit and duration models are estimated to measure the effect of labor productivity and production speed on ship fracture rates.

The probit model is

$$y_{ij}^* = \mathbf{x}_{ij}\beta + u_{ij} \tag{3}$$

$$y_{ij} = \begin{cases} 0, & \text{if } y_{ij}^* < 0 \\ 1, & \text{if } y_{ij}^* \geq 0, \end{cases}$$

where $y_{ij} = 1$ if ship $j$ at yard $i$ developed at least one fracture by February 2, 1946, and $y_{ij} = 0$ otherwise. The regressors include labor hours expended on ship $ij$ or production speed in days: the length of war service, which controls for the fact that the observation for each ship is truncated either by the sampling date of February 2, 1946 or because the ship was lost at an earlier date due to enemy action; a dummy variable equal to one if the ship's keel was laid after the design changes of March–May 1943 were instituted; and the date and order of keel laying, to control for possible spurious results arising from the trend in productivity. Yard dummies are included to control for systematic variations in steel quality, and for differences in yard practices that were not associated with productivity.

The duration model estimates the hazard rate from a Weibul distribution,

$$\lambda_{ij}(t) = e^{\mathbf{x}_{ij}\beta} \, v(e^{\mathbf{x}_{ij}}t)^{v-1} \tag{4}$$

---

[15] Quoted in Tyler (1947, p. 17). Tyler (1947, p. 18) notes that the letter was discussed without adverse comment in a meeting of the Production Division of the USMC. John Wilson, Assistant Chief Surveyor of the ABS testified before the Truman Committee (Senate 1944, pp. 9955–82), where ABS safety procedures came under considerable fire.

**Table 12.5** Determinants of fracture probabilities and hazard rates in Liberty ships

| | Probit y = 1 if fracture reported before February 2, 1946, 0 otherwise | | | Weibull duration model | |
| | (1) | (2) | (3) | (4) |
|---|---|---|---|---|
| Constant | −0.70 | −0.78 | −2.07 | −2.95 |
| | (0.37) | (0.27) | (0.96) | (0.62) |
| Labor hours per ship (millions) | −0.63 | . . . | −1.83 | . . . |
| | (0.29) | | (0.77) | |
| Production speed (hundreds of days) | . . . | −1.28 | . . . | −2.43 |
| | | (0.41) | | (0.97) |
| War service (years) | 0.06 | 0.05 | . . . | . . . |
| | (0.02) | (0.02) | | |
| Design changes | −0.62 | −0.55 | −1.48 | −1.38 |
| | (0.12) | (0.12) | (0.27) | (0.28) |
| Date of keel laying (years since first keel laid) | −0.21 | −0.27 | −0.43 | 0.35 |
| | (0.15) | (0.14) | (0.42) | (0.36) |
| Order of keel laying | −0.00 | −0.00 | −0.00 | −0.00 |
| | (0.00) | (0.00) | (0.00) | (0.00) |
| $v$ | . . . | . . . | 0.82 | 0.81 |
| | | | (0.06) | (0.06) |
| No. of observations | 2,662 | 2,654 | 2,662 | 2,654 |
| Log likelihood | −819.2 | −816.4 | −1.174.2 | −1,174.4 |

All regression include yard dummies. Standard errors in parentheses. War service is years to delivery to end of sampling period or February 2, 1946, whichever comes first. Design changes equals zero if keel was laid before May 1943, 1 otherwise. Eight ships delivered by Oregon had been partially built by Kaiser-Vancouver; data on production speed are not available for these ships.

where $t$ is the time that has elapsed since delivery and $v$ is a parameter to be estimated. The log-likelihood function is:

$$\ln L = \sum_i \sum_j [\delta_{ij}(v(\ln s_{ij} + x_{ij}\beta) + \ln v) - \exp(v(\ln s_{ij} + x_{ij}\beta))] \tag{5}$$

where $\delta_{ij} = 1$ if the ship developed fractures and $\delta_{ij} = 0$ otherwise; $s_{ij}$ is the time between delivery and whichever came first among fracture date, war loss and the end of the sampling period. The list of regressors is the same as for the probit model, with the exception of length of war service.

Table 12.5 reports the estimates of equations (3) and (4). The coefficients on labor hours, production speed, war service, and design changes are all significant and have the expected sign. In particular, a reduction in labor hours or time expended on the production of a ship is strongly associated with an increase in the likelihood that the ship subsequently developed fractures. This link is particularly strong for ships built prior to the design changes of early 1943. For example, holding other variables at the sample means, a reduction in labor hours per ship from 1.25 million hours to 350,000 is associated with an increase in the fracture rate from 6 percent to 20 percent. The design changes mandated in the spring of 1943 significantly reduced the predicted risk of fractures. Holding constant war service and total labor requirements at the sample mean, the design changes reduced the probability of fracturing from 18 percent to just 4 percent.

Coefficients on yard dummies (not reported) exhibit large fixed effects, and the hypothesis of no yard effects is strongly rejected. Moreover, the relationship between productivity and fracturing is robust to the inclusion of calendar time and production order. Results are almost identical (in regressions not reported) when data enter in logarithms, when direct labor hours are used instead of total labor hours, when time to launching is used instead of time to delivery, and when the binary model is estimated by logit. Note also that the parameter $v$ in the duration model is significantly less than one, indicating that hazard rates declined with time in service. Declining hazard rates point to defects, rather than stress in service, as a significant cause of fractures.

## Adjusting productivity growth estimates for quality

To estimate the extent to which the official statistics overstate productivity growth, the probability of a fracture for each ship is predicted from the duration model in column 3 of table 12.5. Ships within each yard are standardized by predicting the probability of a fracture occurring within 2.2 years. Productivity data can then be adjusted for quality by combining these predictions with estimated costs of fractures, in labor hour equivalents. The following assumptions are then used to transform fracture probabilities into labor hour equivalents. Data from Economics and Statistics Division (1946) indicate that the majority of ships were repaired between two and four months after the date of fracture. I therefore assume that one cost of a fracture, irrespective of the class of fracture, is the loss of three months (out of an average of 2.2 years) of ship service time. The labor cost of lost service for a fractured ship is calculated using each yard's mean labor requirement. Adding these imputed costs to the direct labor cost of repairs, one could then adjust measured labor productivity for quality by weighing the labor cost of each type of fracture according to the shares of class I and II fractures in all fracture incidents reported, and multiplying the weighted sum by the yard-specific predicted probability of a fracture appropriate for a vessel with the indicated labor requirement.

The weak link in this chain of adjustment is that I have no data on hours required to effect fracture repairs. I think it is reasonable to assume that direct repairs did not exceed 150,000 labor hours for a class I repair or 50,000 hours for a class II repair. These are, after all, as much as 50 percent and 17 percent respectively of the cost of constructing an entire ship. Even with these upper limits, the effects of quality adjustment on the productivity numbers are modest. For example, a ship produced in 1941 with one million hours of labor has a predicted fracture probability of 7 percent, while one produced in March 1943 using 450,000 hours of labor has a fracture probability of twenty percent. The unadjusted productivity increase is 122 percent while the adjusted productivity increase is no less than 113 percent; thus, the raw data contain a measurement error equivalent to no more than six percent of measured productivity growth. Moreover, the gap between measured and quality-adjusted productivity growth obviously diminished markedly after the design changes of early 1943. However, the implied increase in quality-adjusted productivity after March 1943 should be attributed to the research program authorized by the Board of Investigation.

## VI   CONCLUSIONS

Growth accounting in the presence of learning by doing is fraught with danger. Omitting factors which may be correlated with time or with cumulative production would cause a researcher to mistakenly attribute their effects to learning. This paper exploits new evidence on the Emergency Shipbuilding Program of World War II to show that this classic case study of learning suffers from omitted variable bias. Conventional wisdom, which attributes virtually all productivity growth in the Liberty ship program to learning, derives from studies that did not incorporate the extensive capital investments that took place during the war. The inclusion of capital in estimates of production and labor requirements functions reduces the estimated size of the learning effect by about 50 percent. I also show that the quality of Liberty ships, as measured by the fracture rate, declined systematically with labor productivity and production speed. Contrary to conventional wisdom, then, all Liberty ships were not alike. However, the extent of mismeasurement induced by omitting quality changes appears to be small.

My estimates of the size of the learning effect should continue to be treated with caution. First, cumulative capital investment and experience are highly correlated, so that separating their effects reliably is difficult. More important, however, is that this study continues to omit variables that may further reduce the residual productivity growth attributed to learning. Lane (1951) documents how the USMC introduced and then expanded training programs, maintained an active and sizable research department, contracted research out to numerous engineering companies and universities, and instituted numerous minor design changes. Shipyards also had active research programs and often instituted their own process innovations. Senate (1945) describes 48 new products and processes developed and implemented during 1942 and 1943, specific to shipbuilding, and that were sufficiently important to merit media attention. Some of these appeared to have been suggested by shipyard workers, and might well be attributed to on the job learning; other innovations were developed by outside suppliers of equipment and materials; in several other cases new tools were first suggested by yard workers, adopted in rudimentary form, and subsequently developed and marketed by an independent tool company. The same Senate report also documents media reports on 35 innovations in automatic welding products and techniques during the same period. Again, some were techniques developed by yard workers that one might attribute to learning. However, the most important innovations, several of which were claimed to increase welder productivity by more than 100 percent, were new machines developed entirely outside the shipbuilding industry.

It is unlikely that sufficient data will ever be available to measure the effects of these omitted variables. Even then, no doubt some of the effects should ultimately be traced to ideas developed as a result of production experience, although how much is probably an insoluble matter of semantics. One must also be careful in making general inferences from a single case study. But it does seem reasonable to draw one conclusion from the Liberty ship program that is likely to resonate elsewhere: in a case study that is widely viewed as one of the cleanest examples of learning by doing on record, the real causes of productivity growth have turned out to be more complex and more diverse than economists have long believed to be the case.

## APPENDIX: DATA SOURCES

Unless otherwise stated, box numbers refer to boxes in the Records of the Office of the Historian, U.S. Maritime Commission, Record Group RG178, National Archives, Washington D.C.

### Ship identifiers

Hull names and Maritime Commission identifying numbers (MCE numbers) were taken from Bunker (1972, pp. 207–58). Supplementary information, particularly to track numerous name changes during the war, was taken from Sawyer and Mitchell (1985). Builders' hull numbers are contained in handwritten tabulations located in Records of the Production Division. USMC, various boxes, RG178. National Archives.

### Production dates

Production times, decomposed into days between keel-laying and launching, and days between launching and delivery, were taken from handwritten tabulations by G. J. Fischer, Chief Statistician, USMC; located in Boxes 30 and 31. For each ship, either a date of keel-laying or a date of delivery was taken from unattributed type-script tabulations (presumably written under the direction of G. J. Fischer, as several copies have annotations in Fischer's handwriting), located in Boxes 35 and 37. Records indicate that delivery to the USMC was always made the same day that the ship was made ready for delivery. Missing dates were therefore obtained by combining production times with the known dates of delivery or keel laying.

## Monthly output

The rate of output was constructed from the dates of keel laying and delivery. For each ship, a linear rate of production was assumed, so that the allocation of production of a ship to any given month is proportional to the fraction of total production time which fell in that month.

## Productivity

Direct, indirect, and total labor hours per ship were obtained from unattributed typescript tabulations located in Boxes 35 and 37. These data should be uncommonly accurate. The USMC stationed auditors at each yard to calculate direct labor hours expended on each ship on a daily basis. Indirect labor was allocated to ships from weekly payroll data. No information is available on how indirect labor hours were allocated to each ship, although the methodology appears to approximate a weighted combination of production time and labor hours expended on each ship. Every two weeks, the data were compiled and submitted to the Finance Division of the USMC for reimbursement.

## Ship quality

Dates and severity of fractures are from James L. Bates, *Report on Crack-Up of Ships, Either in the Shipyard, at the Docks or at Sea*, Technical Division, USMC, February 12, 1946, attachments A and B; located in Box 47; and from *Second Interim Report of a Board of Investigation to Inquire into the Design and Methods of Construction of Welded Steel Merchant Ships*, U.S. Coast Guard, March 1945, located in Records of the U.S. Coast Guard, Reports of the Board, Box 3, RG26 National Archives. Fracture severity is indicated by class. A class I fracture is one which results in either the actual loss of a vessel, or which has progressed to such an extent into the strength deck or shell as to endanger the safety of the vessel. A class II fracture is one which does not immediately place the vessel in danger, but which has the potential to develop into a class I fracture. Descriptions of fracture types are given in Board of Investigation (1945). Dates of war losses (by cause) or from *United States-Flag Merchant Ships Sunk from War Causes*, typescript, Economics and Statistics Division, USMC (undated response to Congressional request for information dated July 17, 1946), located in Box 57. War loss data were supplemented by information in Sawyer and Mitchell (1985).

## Employment

Monthly employment data are constructed from the number of direct and indirect workers, and average hours worked, contained in Bureau of Labor Statistics forms

BLS 1761, *Plant Operations*, Box 36. The data refer to employment on the fifteenth of the month. These data differ slightly from employment data tabulated in Fischer (1949). Fischer's data combine two sources, some of which report end of month employment and some of which report employment mid-month. Sunday shift employment data were also taken from BLS 1761.

## Capital authorizations

The dates, amounts, and purpose of each authorization for shipyard facilities were taken from *Statement of Facilities Contracts, Vouchers Passed for Payment, as of March 31, 1946*, Box 56; Facilities Allotments from Minutes Cards, handwritten tabulations, Box 32; and *Major, Minor and Military Types of Vessels Constructed in 1936–1945*, undated typescript, Box 42. The source for these data was found damaged in the National Archives and sheets for several large yards are missing. Detailed capital authorizations by date are available for (number of Liberty ships delivered in parethenses): Bethlehem-Fairfield (384), Calship (336), Delta (188), North Carolina (126), Oregon (330), and Todd-Houston (208). These six yards account for a little over 50 percent of all Liberty ship production.

## REFERENCES

Allen, T. R. "Report on Construction Progress at South Portland." Form OPM-251, Records of the Office of the Historian, Box 17, Records of the USMC, National Archives RG178, January 7, 1942.

Argote, Linda, Beckman, Sara L., and Epple, Dennis, "The Persistence and Transfer of Learning in Industrial Settings," *Management Science* 36 (February 1990), pp. 140–54.

Bates, James L., "Report on Crack-Up of Ships, Either in the Shipyard, at the Docks, or at Sea," Technical Division, USMC, Attachments A and B, Records of the Office of the Historian, Box 47, Records of the USMC, National Archives RG178, February 12, 1946.

Bell, R. M., and Scott-Kemmis, D., "The Mythology of Learning-by-Doing in World War II Airframe and Ship Production," Manuscript (1990).

Board of Investigation, "Interim Report of a Board of Investigation to Inquire into the Design and Methods of Construction of Welded Steel Merchant Ships," Typescript, Records of the U.S. Coast Guard, Boxes 1–3, National Archives RG26, 1944.

Board of Investigation, "2nd Interim Report of a Board of Investigation to Inquire into the Design and Methods of Construction of Welded Steel Merchant Ships," Typescript, Records of the U.S. Coast Guard, Boxes 1–3, National Archives RG26, 1945.

Bunker, J. G., *Liberty Ships: The Ugly Ducklings of World War II* (Annapolis, Md.: Naval Institute Press, 1972).

David, P. A., "The 'Horndal Effect' in Lowell, 1834–56: A Short-Run Learning Curve for Integrated Cotton Mills," *Explorations in Economic History* 10 (winter 1973), pp. 131–50.

Dutton, J., and Thomas, A., "The History of Progress Functions as a Managerial Technology," *Business History Review* 58 (Summer 1984), pp. 204–33.

Economics and Statistics Division, "United States-Flag Merchant Ships Sunk from War Causes." Typescript (undated response to a Congressional request for information dated July 17, 1946), Records of the Office of the Historian, Box 57, Records of the USMC, National Archives RG178, 1946.

Fischer, Gerald J., "Labor Productivity in Shipbuilding under the U.S. Maritime Commission During WWII," Typescript, Records of the Office of the Historian, Box 55, Records of the USMC, National Archives RG178, May 20, 1948.

Fischer, Gerald J., *A Statistical Summary of Shipbuilding Under the U.S. Maritime Commission During World War II* (Washington, D.C.: Historical Reports of the War Administration, United States Maritime Commission, 1949).

House of Representatives, *Investigation of Shipyard Profits* (Washington, D.C.: Government Printing Office, 1946).

Jovanovic, Boyan, and Nyarko, Yaw, "A Bayesian Learning Model Fitted to a Variety of Empirical Learning Curves," *Brookings Papers on Economic Activity, Microeconomics 1995* (1995); pp. 247–99.

Kaiser Co., *Richmond Shipyard Number Three* (Richmond, Calif., public relations pamphlet, 1943).

Lane, Frederic C., *Ships for Victory* (Baltimore, Md.: Johns Hopkins Press, 1951).

Lazonick, W., and Brush, T., "The 'Horndal Effect' in Early U.S. Manufacturing," *Explorations in Economic History* 22 (January 1985); pp. 53–96.

Marine Engineering and Shipping Review, "New Welding Technique Increases Production," *Marine Engineering and Shipping Review* 48 (August 1942), pp. 112–14.

Mishina, Kazuhiro, "Learning by New Experiences: Revisiting the Flying Fortress Learning Curve," in *Learning By Doing in Markets, Firms, and Countries*, edited by Naomi Lamoreaux et al. (Chicago: University of Chicago Press, 1999).

New York Times, "President Calls War Output So Big Goal Can Be Raised," *New York Times* April 25, 1942, pp. 1, 6.

Oregon Shipbuilding Corporation, "Estimate of Additional Facilities Required to Maintain a Production Schedule of Two Ships per Week," Typescript, Shipyards Facilities File, Oregon Shipbuilding Corporation Box 440. Records of the USMC, National Archives RG178, April 21, 1942.

Rapping, Leonard, "Learning and World War II Production Functions," *Review of Economic Statistics* 47 (February 1965), pp. 81–6.

Rosenberg, Nathan, *Perspectives on Technology* (Cambridge: Cambridge University Press, 1976).

Sawyer, L. A. and Mitchell, W. H., *The Liberty Ship*, 2nd edn (London: Lloyds of London Press, 2nd edn, 1985).

Searle, Allen D., "Productivity Changes in Selected Wartime Shipbuilding Programs," *Monthly Labor Review* (December 1945), pp. 1132–47.

Senate, *Cancellation of Higgins Contract, Hearings* (Washington, D.C.: Government Printing Office, 1942).

Senate, *Hearings Before a Special Committee Investigating the National Defense Program. Part 3: Production in Shipbuilding Plants, Hearings* (Washington, D.C.: Government Printing Office, 1943).

Senate, *Hearings Before a Special Committee Investigating the National Defense Program. Part 23: Merchant Shipping* (Washington, D.C.: Government Printing Office, 1944).

Senate, *Wartime Technological Development. A Study Made for the Subcommittee on War Mobilization* (Washington, D.C.: Government Printing Office, 1945).

Sinclair, Gavin, Klepper, Steven, and Cohen, Wesley, "What's Experience Got to Do With It? Souces of Cost Reduction in a large Specialty Chemical Producer," Manuscript. Carnegie-Mellon University, Department of Social and Decision Sciences, 1999.

Statistics and Reports Unit, "Cost Distributions for Various Vessel Designs," Typescript. Records of the Office of the Historian, Box 36, Records of the USMC, National Archives RG178, 1944.

Tyler, David B., "A Study of the Commission's Experience with Welding during World

War II," Typescript, U.S. Maritime Commission, April 1947.

U.S. Coast Guard, "Report of Structural Failure of Inspected Vessel Schenectady." Form CG796, April 1, 1944. Reproduced in H. C. Campbell, "Brittle Fracture and Structural Failure of the Liberty Ships During WW-II (A)," Manuscript. Engineering Case Library, Leland Stanford Junior University, 1967.

U.S. Maritime Commission, *Report to Congress for Period Ending June 30, 1944* (Washington, D.C.: Government Printing Office, 1945).

Vickery, H. L., "Letter from Vickery to J. N. Franklin," Commissioner Vickery's Reading File Box 2, Records of the USMC. National Archives RG178, January 13, 1943a.

Vickery, H. L., "Untitled Memorandum," Commissioner Vickery's Reading File Box 2, Records of the USMC, National Archives RG178, March 11, 1943b.

Welding Journal, "Welded Steel Merchant Ships," *Welding Journal* (July 1947), p. 588.

# 13

# Financial Legends

## The Economist

**The copper price dives and zillionaire George Soros is said to be laughing all the way to the bank. Another financial myth in the making?**

Legends are the stuff of money markets. They thrive because of the particular nature of stock, bond and currency trading, which is driven by rumour and by the visceral emotions of greed and fear. Some legends are parables about gullibility, dishonesty and wildly inflated market valuations. Others are linked to changes in the financial markets. Most are satirical and provide admonition against future folly.

Among the earliest financial legends are those about the tulip mania of 1635–6. During this period the bulbs of rare and exotic tulips sold for the price of a fine town house in Amsterdam. One story tells of a merchant giving a herring to a sailor who had brought him some goods from abroad.

> The sailor, seeing some valuable tulip-roots lying about, which he considered as of little consequence, thinking them to be onions, took some of them unperceived and ate them with his herring. Through this mistake the sailor's breakfast cost the merchant a much greater sum than if he had treated the Prince of Orange.

The most famous legend of the mania is the story which inspired Alexandre Dumas's novel *The Black Tulip*:

> A syndicate of Haarlem florists, hearing that a cobbler at The Hague had succeeded in growing a black tulip, visited him and after some haggling purchased the bulb for fifteen hundred florins. No sooner was it in their possession than they threw it on the ground and trampled it underfoot. "Idiot!" cried one of them when the astonished cobbler began to protest; "we have a black tulip, too, and chance will never favour you again. We would have given you ten thousand florins if you had asked for it." The wretched cobbler, inconsolable at the thought of the wealth which might have been his, took to his bed and promptly expired.

Although the black tulip never existed, the tale survived – not least because it was reinforced by lots of contemporary satirical prints designed to remind the Dutch people of the folly of the speculation and the disruptive dishonesty which it generated.

Credulity of investors is a theme in the legends of the South Sea Bubble, a financial crisis that ruined thousands in England in 1720. Although speculation centred on the shares of the South Sea Company, which had a monopoly of trade with South America, several smaller projects, or "bubble companies", were also inspired by the feverish speculation. Some, such as the future Sun Insurance Company, were bona fide enterprises; others were fraudulent, but the bubble companies best remembered today never, in fact, came to the market. They include the projects "For better curing Venereal Disease", "For a Wheel of Perpetual Motion" and, most famously, "A Company for carrying on an undertaking of great advantage, but nobody to know what it is."

Alongside credulity and dishonesty there has always been a suspicion that speculation in the financial markets distracts people from honest labour. This is exemplified by a story thrown up by the Mississippi Bubble, also of 1720:

> M. Chirac, principal physician to the Regent, on his way to visit a female patient, having been informed that the price of actions was falling, was so affected by that piece of news that he could think of nothing else; and accordingly, while holding the lady's pulse, kept exclaiming, O good God, it falls, it falls. The invalid, naturally alarmed, began to ring the bell with all her force, crying out that she was a dead woman, and had almost expired with apprehension, till the doctor assured her that her pulse was in a very good state, but that his mind ran so much upon the actions, that he came to utter the expressions that terrified her, in reference to the fall of their value.

Greed, panic and fear of financial loss are the source of the legends of suicide during the Great Crash of October 1929 on Wall Street. Wild rumours swept unchecked through the stockmarkets after a storm in the mid-west brought down many of the telephone lines connecting New York to the rest of the country on Wednesday, October 23. As shares fell the following day, "Black Thursday", the ticker tape, reporting the latest share prices, ran late and telephone lines were jammed with inquiries.

Eleven speculators were said to have committed suicide and troops were reported to be guarding the New York Stock Exchange from an angry mob. Later it was said that the top hats of drowned speculators could be seen floating down the East river. Two speculators had jumped holding hands from a high window in the Ritz because they shared a joint account. Those checking into downtown hotels were asked whether they intended to sleep or jump.

In fact, as John Kenneth Galbraith, the great authority on the episode, has shown, although there were two authenticated cases of suicide (that of J. J. Riordan, the president of the County Trust Company, and, three years later, that of the Swedish match king, Ivar Kreuger), the number of suicides during and immediately after the Great Crash was within the average for New York at that time.

The propensity of stockbrokers to gull their clients is part of a legend about the crash on the world's stockmarkets on October 19, 1987. An elderly gentleman has come to his broker's office to sign a "hold harmless" letter taking responsibility for losses on his own account. For weeks he has said he wants to take his profits, but his broker has dissuaded him. Now, in the midst of the crash, he sits opposite his broker who has turned away the Quotron screen on his desk. As Tim Metz retells the story in *Black Monday* (1988):

> The customer has said little during the brief, post-lunch huddle. But now he asks the killer question: "How are the markets doing today?" The broker doesn't reply, but he slowly turns the Quotron machine until his customer is looking straight at the screen. The customer says nothing, either. He bolts to his feet, a gurgling noise rising from deep in his throat, then falls to the floor, unconscious.

It isn't a heart attack. The customer has simply fainted, and he will recover quickly once the ambulance gets him to the emergency room of a nearby hospital. However, nobody yet knows that there will be a happy ending. As the stricken investor is carried away on a stretcher, the sales manager approaches his broker and fixes him with a panicky stare. "Don't worry", the broker tells him. "He's signed already."

The Roaring Eighties – the decade when Ivan Boesky, a spiv bound for jail, announced to the students of Berkeley's business school: "Greed is all right, by the way . . . You can be greedy and still feel good about yourself" – have spawned a crop of financial legends. As exchange rates floated and capital markets were deregulated, the role of the trader was mythologised, because he took risks with great nerve and was fabulously rewarded.

Perhaps the best known trader's tale is related by Michael Lewis in *Liar's Poker* (1989). He claims that in early 1986 John Gutfreund, then chief executive of Salomon Brothers, challenged that New York investment bank's chief trader, John Merriwether, to a game of liar's poker (a game of bluff played over the serial numbers of dollar bills): "One hand, one million dollars, no tears." Merriwether is said to have replied, "No John . . . if we're going to play for those kind of numbers, I'd rather play for real money. Ten million dollars. No tears." The trouble with this story is that it seems to be apocryphal: both principal participants adamantly deny it and Mr Lewis himself attributes it to an eavesdropping trader.

Another feature of the 1980s was the rise of Japan, with its vast trade surpluses and high domestic savings. Japanese investors financed America's federal budget deficits during the decade, while their companies started buying American firms. As Tokyo property prices soared it was calculated that the value of the Imperial Palace exceeded the real-estate value of the entire state of California.

Books such as Daniel Burstein's *Yen! Japan's New Financial Empire and its Threat to America* (1989) and later Michael Crichton's *Rising Sun* (1992), expressed fears that America's economic supremacy was being eclipsed. At the end of the decade, when Mitsubishi Estate bought the Rockefeller Center, the fears grew and inspired legends with an alarmist story line: Japan is taking over America. The most far-fetched concerns the sale in 1986 of the Exxon Building in New York to Mitsui Real Estate. Though the purchaser paid $610 million for the building, Exxon's asking price was said to be only $375 million. When asked why the Japanese property company was prepared to pay such a large premium, an officer for Mitsui is purported to have replied: "Our president has read that the current record price for a single building, as listed in the Guinness Book of World Records, is $600 million. He wants to beat the record." If you cannot imagine anybody believing such a tall story, you don't know anything about the financial markets.

## REFERENCES

Burstein, Daniel (1989) *Yen! Japan's New Financial Empire and Its Threat to America* (New York: Simon and Schuster).

Crichton, Michael (1992) *Rising Sun* (New York: Ballantine Books).

Galbraith, John, Kenneth (1979) *The Great Crash, 1929,* 50th Anniversary edn (Boston, Mass.: Houghton Mifflin).

Lewis, Michael M. (1989) *Liar's Poker: Rising through the Wreckage on Wall Street* (New York: W. W. Norton).

Metz, Tim (1988) *Black Monday: The Catastrophe of October 19, 1987, and Beyond* (New York: W. Morrow).

# Index

1 All references are to *United States*, unless otherwise indicated.

2 **Emboldened** page numbers indicate chapters or major treatment of topics.

3 Footnote references are indicated by n; *passim* indicates separate mentions on several contiguous pages